Essentials of
Rorschach Assessment

Essentials of **Psychological Assessment** Series

Everything you need to know to administer, score, and interpret the major psychological tests

I'd like to order the following *Essentials of Psychological Assessment:*

❑ WAIS®-IV Assessment, Second Edition (w/CD-ROM)
978-1-118-27188-9 • $50.00

❑ WJ® IV Tests of Achievement
978-1-118-79915-4 • $40.00

❑ Cross-Battery Assessment, Third Edition (w/CD-ROM)
978-0-470-62195-0 • $50.00

❑ Executive Functions Assessment (w/CD-ROM)
978-0-470-42202-1 • $50.00

❑ WPPSI™-IV Assessment (w/CD-ROM)
978-1-11838062-8 • $50.00

❑ Specific Learning Disability Identification
978-0-470-58760-7 • $40.00

❑ IDEA for Assessment Professionals (w/CD-ROM)
978-0-470-87392-2 • $50.00

❑ Dyslexia Assessment and Intervention
978-0-470-92760-1 • $40.00

❑ Autism Spectrum Disorders Evaluation and Assessment
978-0-470-62194-3 • $40.00

❑ Planning, Selecting, and Tailoring Interventions for Unique Learners (w/CD-ROM)
978-1-118-36821-3 • $50.00

❑ Processing Assessment, Second Edition (w/CD-ROM)
978-1-118-36820-6 • $50.00

❑ School Neuropsychological Assessment, Second Edition (w/CD-ROM)
978-1-118-17584-2 • $50.00

❑ Gifted Assessment
978-1-118-58920-5 • $40.00

❑ Working Memory Assessment and Intervention
978-1-118-63813-2 • $50.00

❑ Assessing, Preventing, and Overcoming Reading Difficulties
978-1-118-84524-0 • $50.00

❑ Evidence-Based Academic Interventions
978-0-470-20632-4 • $40.00

❑ Nonverbal Assessment
978-0-471-38318-5 • $40.00

❑ PAI® Assessment
978-0-471-08463-1 • $40.00

❑ CAS Assessment
978-0-471-29015-5 • $40.00

❑ MMPI®-2 Assessment, Second Edition
978-0-470-92323-8 • $40.00

❑ Myers-Briggs Type Indicator® Assessment, Second Edition
978-0-470-34390-6 • $40.00

❑ Rorschach® Assessment
978-0-471-33146-9 • $40.00

❑ Millon™ Inventories Assessment, Third Edition
978-0-470-16862-2 • $40.00

❑ TAT and Other Storytelling Assessments, Second Edition
978-0-470-28192-5 • $40.00

❑ MMPI-A™ Assessment
978-0-471-39815-8 • $40.00

❑ NEPSY®-II Assessment
978-0-470-43691-2 • $40.00

❑ Neuropsychological Assessment, Second Edition
978-0-470-43747-6 • $40.00

❑ Essentials of WJ IV® Cognitive Abilities Assessment
978-1-119-16336-7 • $50.00

❑ WRAML2 and TOMAL-2 Assessment
978-0-470-17911-6 • $40.00

❑ WMS®-IV Assessment
978-0-470-62196-7 • $40.00

❑ Behavioral Assessment
978-0-471-35367-6 • $40.00

❑ Forensic Psychological Assessment, Second Edition
978-0-470-55168-4 • $40.00

❑ Intellectual Disability Assessment and Identification
978-1-118-87509-4 • $40.00

❑ Bayley Scales of Infant Development II Assessment
978-0-471-32651-9 • $40.00

❑ Career Interest Assessment
978-0-471-35365-2 • $40.00

❑ 16PF® Assessment
978-0-471-23424-1 • $40.00

❑ Assessment Report Writing
978-0-471-39487-7 • $40.00

❑ Stanford-Binet Intelligence Scales (SB5) Assessment
978-0-471-22404-4 • $40.00

❑ WISC®-IV Assessment, Second Edition (w/CD-ROM)
978-0-470-18915-3 • $50.00

❑ KABC-II Assessment
978-0-471-66733-9 • $40.00

❑ WIAT®-III and KTEA-II Assessment (w/CD-ROM)
978-0-470-55169-1 • $50.00

❑ Cognitive Assessment with KAIT & Other Kaufman Measures
978-0-471-38317-8 • $40.00

❑ Assessment with Brief Intelligence Tests
978-0-471-26412-5 • $40.00

❑ Creativity Assessment
978-0-470-13742-0 • $40.00

❑ WNV™ Assessment
978-0-470-28467-4 • $40.00

❑ DAS-II® Assessment (w/CD-ROM)
978-0-470-22520-2 • $50.00

❑ Conners Behavior Assessments™
978-0-470-34633-4 • $40.00

❑ Temperament Assessment
978-0-470-44447-4 • $40.00

❑ Response to Intervention
978-0-470-56663-3 • $40.00

❑ ADHD Assessment for Children and Adolescents
978-1-118-11270-0 • $40.00

Please complete the order form on the back. • To order by phone, call toll free 1-877-762-2974
To order online: www.wiley.com/essentials • To order by mail: refer to order form on next page

Essentials
of **Psychological Assessment** Series

ORDER FORM

Please send this order form with your payment (credit card or check) to:
Wiley, Attn: Customer Care, 10475 Crosspoint Blvd., Indianapolis, IN 46256

QUANTITY	TITLE	ISBN	PRICE

Shipping Charges:	Surface	2-Day	1-Day
First item	$5.00	$10.50	$17.50
Each additional item	$3.00	$3.00	$4.00

For orders greater than 15 items,
please contact Customer Care at 1-877-762-2974.

ORDER AMOUNT _____

SHIPPING CHARGES _____

SALES TAX _____

TOTAL ENCLOSED _____

NAME_____

AFFILIATION_____

ADDRESS_____

CITY/STATE/ZIP _____

TELEPHONE _____

EMAIL_____

❑ Please add me to your e-mailing list

PAYMENT METHOD:

❑ Check/Money Order   ❑ Visa   ❑ Mastercard   ❑ AmEx

Card Number _____ Exp. Date _____

Cardholder Name (Please print) _____

Signature _____

Make checks payable to **John Wiley & Sons.** Credit card orders invalid if not signed.
All orders subject to credit approval. • Prices subject to change.

To order by phone, call toll free 1-877-762-2974
To order online: www.wiley.com/essentials

Essentials of Psychological Assessment Series
Series Editors, Alan S. Kaufman and Nadeen L. Kaufman

Essentials

of Rorschach Assessment

Comprehensive System and R-PAS

Jessica R. Gurley

WILEY

Copyright © 2017 by John Wiley & Sons, Inc. All rights reserved.

Published by John Wiley & Sons, Inc., Hoboken, New Jersey.

Published simultaneously in Canada.

No part of this publication may be reproduced, stored in a retrieval system, or transmitted in any form or by any means, electronic, mechanical, photocopying, recording, scanning, or otherwise, except as permitted under Section 107 or 108 of the 1976 United States Copyright Act, without either the prior written permission of the publisher, or authorization through payment of the appropriate per-copy fee to the Copyright Clearance Center, Inc., 222 Rosewood Drive, Danvers, MA 01923, 978-750-8400, fax 978-646-8600, or on the Web at www.copyright.com. Requests to the publisher for permission should be addressed to the Permissions Department, John Wiley & Sons, Inc., 111 River Street, Hoboken, NJ 07030, 201-748-6011, fax 201-748-6008, or online at www.wiley.com/go/permissions.

Limit of Liability/Disclaimer of Warranty: While the publisher and author have used their best efforts in preparing this book, they make no representations or warranties with respect to the accuracy or completeness of the contents of this book and specifically disclaim any implied warranties of merchantability or fitness for a particular purpose. No warranty may be created or extended by sales representatives or written sales materials. The advice and strategies contained herein may not be suitable for your situation. You should consult with a professional where appropriate. Neither the publisher nor author shall be liable for any loss of profit or any other commercial damages, including but not limited to special, incidental, consequential, or other damages. Readers should be aware that Internet Web sites offered as citations and/or sources for further information may have changed or disappeared between the time this was written and when it is read.

This publication is designed to provide accurate and authoritative information in regard to the subject matter covered. It is sold with the understanding that the publisher is not engaged in rendering professional services. If legal, accounting, medical, psychological or any other expert assistance is required, the services of a competent professional should be sought.

For general information on our other products and services, please contact our Customer Care Department within the U.S. at 800-956-7739, outside the U.S. at 317-572-3986, or fax 317-572-4002.

Wiley publishes in a variety of print and electronic formats and by print-on-demand. Some material included with standard print versions of this book may not be included in e-books or in print-on-demand. If this book refers to media such as a CD or DVD that is not included in the version you purchased, you may download this material at http://booksupport.wiley.com. For more information about Wiley products, visit www.wiley.com.

Library of Congress Cataloging-in-Publication Data

Library of Congress Cataloging-in-Publication Data
Names: Gurley, Jessica R., author.
Title: Essentials of Rorschach assessment : comprehensive system and R-PAS / Jessica R. Gurley, PhD, Associate Professor, American School of Professional Psychology at Argosy University, Washington, DC.
Description: Hoboken : Wiley, 2016. | Series: Essentials of psychological assessment | Includes index.
Identifiers: LCCN 2016021298 (print) | LCCN 2016034177 (ebook) | ISBN 9781119060758 (paperback) | ISBN 9781119060765 (pdf) | ISBN 9781119060789 (epub)
Subjects: LCSH: Rorschach Test. | BISAC: PSYCHOLOGY / Assessment, Testing & Measurement.
Classification: LCC BF698.8.R5 G87 2016 (print) | LCC BF698.8.R5 (ebook) | DDC 155.2/842--dc23
LC record available at https://lccn.loc.gov/2016021298

Cover design by Wiley

Cover image: © Greg Kuchik/Getty Images

Printed in the United States of America

FIRST EDITION

PB Printing   10 9 8 7 6 5 4 3 2 1

CONTENTS

SERIES PREFACE

In the *Essentials of Psychological Assessment* series, we have endeavored to provide the reader with books that deliver key practical information in the most efficient and accessible style. Many books in the series focus on a specific type of instrument, and these instruments address a variety of domains, such as cognition, personality, education, and neuropsychology. Other books focus on crucial topics for professionals who are involved in any way with assessment—topics such as specific reading disabilities, evidence-based interventions, or ADHD assessment. For the experienced professional, each book in the series offers a concise yet thorough review of a test instrument or a specific area of expertise, including numerous tips for best practices. Students can turn to series books for clear and concise overviews of the important assessment tools, and key topics, in which they must become proficient to practice skillfully, efficiently, and ethically in their chosen fields.

Wherever feasible, visual cues highlighting key points are displayed alongside systematic, step-by-step guidelines. Chapters are focused and succinct. Topics are organized for an easy understanding of the essential material related to a particular test or topic. Theory and research are continually woven into the fabric of each book, but always in ways that enhance the practical application of the material and that avoid sidetracking or overwhelming readers. With this series, we aim to challenge and assist readers interested in psychological assessment to aspire to the highest level of competency by arming them with the tools they need for knowledgeable, informed practice. We have long been advocates of *intelligent testing*—the notion that numbers are meaningless unless they are brought to life by the clinical acumen and expertise of examiners. Assessment must be used to make a difference in the child's or adult's life, or why bother to test? All books in this series—whether devoted to specific tests or general topics—are consistent with this credo. We want this series to help our readers, novice and veteran alike, to benefit from the intelligent assessment approaches of the authors of each book.

The *Essentials of Rorschach Assessment: CS and R-PAS* organizes the material from the two most commonly used Rorschach systems, the Comprehensive System (CS) and Rorschach Performance Assessment System (R-PAS), into an easy-to-use book designed to supplement both systems. This book provides information on how to administer, score, and interpret both systems, and also discusses the strengths and weaknesses of both systems. In order to assist students first learning the Rorschach and also clinicians switching between the two systems, this book contains case samples, reports, and coding samples. Additional information, including materials to improve administration, coding, and interpretation, is provided online in the Book Companion Website Materials.

Alan S. Kaufman, PhD, and Nadeen L. Kaufman, EdD, Series Editors
Yale Child Study Center, Yale University School of Medicine

One

OVERVIEW AND HISTORY OF THE RORSCHACH TECHNIQUE

Personality can be defined as a person's individual patterns of thinking, behaving, emoting, and interacting with his or her environment in both the short term and the long term. People are often surprised to find out that personality assessment does not focus solely on the assessment of personality traits, such as extraversion or introversion. Instead, personality assessment assesses both personality traits, which are considered to be stable characteristics (e.g., extraversion), and personality states, which are more short lived (e.g., depression, anxiety). In other words, personality assessment encompasses both personality (personality traits) and emotional functioning (personality states).

Many mental health professionals use personality assessment instruments as part of an evaluation of a client's personality and emotional functioning. There are multiple personality assessment instruments that are commercially available from a variety of publishers. Until relatively recently, these instruments were divided into objective measures and projective measures. *Objective* measures, on the one hand, were considered to be measures such as the Minnesota Multiphasic Personality Inventory, Second Edition (MMPI-2) (Butcher, Graham, Ben-Porath, Tellegen, & Dahlstrom, 2001) and the Millon Clinical Multiaxial Inventory, Fourth Edition (MCMI-IV) (Millon, Grossman, & Millon, 2015). These measures all use forced choice questions and rely on the ability of the clients to self-report their distress. *Projective* measures, on the other hand, were considered to be measures that presented clients with an ambiguous stimulus and asked them to use the stimulus to engage in a specific task (e.g., to tell a story about a picture). This category included measures such as the Rorschach (Rorschach, 1921, 1942) and the Thematic Apperception Test (TAT) (Murray, 1943). In theory, individuals would project their unconscious wishes, desires, and so forth onto the ambiguous stimulus and thus their needs would present themselves in their responses.

However, it became clear that this distinction was leading some mental health professionals to believe that the objective measures were superior, as the term *objective* implied that the objective measures did not rely on subjective factors, such as clinical judgment and client introspection. In reality, however, clients can misrepresent themselves on the objective personality instruments, thereby affecting the interpretive value of the instruments. There is also the issue that clients can interpret questions differently, so the same question may mean different things to different people. As an example, the item "I often feel sad" requires the examinee to determine what *sad* is for them and what *often* means. For some, often may be multiple times per week and for others, often could mean once every two weeks. In other words, you could have two people responding to the item in the affirmative, one who feels sad multiple times per week and one who feels sad twice per month. Finally, it is important to note that *all* personality measures require clinical judgment and skill for interpretation. For these reasons, Meyer and Kurtz (2006) recommended that the mental health fields retire the term *objective* and start using a more appropriate term, such as *self-report*, to describe measures where clients report on their own behaviors, thoughts, and emotions. It is now common practice to refer to the objective measures as self-report measures.

The use of the terms *projective* and *objective* also negatively affected the measures that were classified as projective, as they were seen as being more subjective (Meyer & Kurtz, 2006). Additionally, there was another issue with the terminology, as some of the measures classified as projective did not rely purely on projection. The Rorschach is an excellent example of this. As will be discussed later in this chapter, the Rorschach, when administered using either the Comprehensive System (CS) (Exner, 2003) or the Rorschach Performance Assessment System (R-PAS) (Meyer, Viglione, Mihura, Erard, & Erdberg, 2011), is actually a problem-solving task. That is not to say that the Rorschach cannot be used as a projective measure; some clinicians do use it as a purely projective measure and do not use an administration, scoring, and interpretation system. It is also important to note that the stimuli used during the administration of the Rorschach are not actually ambiguous. As will be discussed in Chapters 3 and 6, there are common responses for nine of the ten cards, responses that occur in at least one third of protocols. In other words, the cards *pull* for some responses. This same pull for certain types of responses can be seen on other projective tests, such as the TAT. For example, one of the TAT cards that an examiner can choose to present is a picture of a man in a graveyard. There is a clear pull for death on this card. Some interpretive guides for the TAT provide a list of common themes that cards may pull for, again indicating that the test is not completely projective (Bellak & Abrams, 1996).

Meyer and Kurtz (2006) suggested a variety of other names for projective tests, including *free response* measures and *performance-based* measures. It is my

≡ Rapid Reference 1.1

Self-Report Versus Performance-Based Measures

Self-Report Measures	Performance-Based Measures
• Forced choice.	• Free response.
• Can be administered by computer.	• Need an examiner to administer.
• Can be scored using software or cloud-based scoring.	• Require the examiner to score before using software or cloud-based system.
• Examinee must be able to read at a certain level to take the test.	• Can be used with examinees who cannot read.
• Interpretation requires clinical judgment.	• Interpretation requires clinical judgment.

experience that many in the field have adopted the term *performance-based* to describe tests where the examinee is not constrained by having to provide only one or two of a variety of circumscribed responses, such as is the case with self-report measures (e.g., the MMPI-2). Instead, *performance-based* measures permit examinees to provide any response they wish, allowing for more individualism in the response. Consistent with the recommendation of Meyer and Kurtz (2006), this book will use the term *self-report measures* to refer to tests where examinees are directly reporting on their own experiences in a forced choice format (e.g., multiple choice), and the term *performance-based measures* to refer to tests where the examinee is not constrained by having to select one of only a few choices and is assessed based on his or her individual performance. Rapid Reference 1.1 outlines the differences between self-report and performance-based measures.

THE RORSCHACH

There is no "one size fits all" personality assessment instrument. There are a variety of personality assessments commercially available, including highly structured interviews (e.g., the Structured Clinical Interview for DSM-5 Personality Disorders [SCID-5-PD]), self-report measures (e.g., the MMPI-2), and performance-based measures (e.g., CS, R-PAS). Each instrument has its own strengths and weaknesses. It is important for clinicians using personality instruments to know the strengths, weaknesses, and psychometric information of the instruments they use. This will help the clinician to determine whether the instrument in question is appropriate for the examinee being assessed, given the referral question and the examinee's unique characteristics.

This book focuses on one of the oldest psychological assessment measures still commercially available: the Rorschach. Although many Rorschach systems are available, this book focuses on two administration, scoring, and interpretative systems: the Comprehensive System (CS) (Exner, 2003) and the Rorschach Performance Assessment System (R-PAS) (Meyer et al., 2011). These systems were chosen because they appeared to be the most commonly used systems in the United States at the time this book was being written. Although this book describes both systems, it is not designed to replace John Exner's three-volume set on the CS (Exner, 2003; Exner & Erdberg, 2005; Exner & Weiner, 1994) nor the R-PAS manual (Meyer et al., 2011). Instead, it is designed to provide an overview of both systems, to explain some of the technical language from both systems in simpler terms, and to serve as a resource on both systems. To this end, this book has chapters dedicated to the CS and to R-PAS, discussing administration, coding (scoring), and interpretation, and presenting a case sample for each system. Another goal of this book is to help clinicians bridge the gap between the CS and R-PAS. To achieve this goal, an additional chapter focuses on the similarities and differences of the two systems and also their strengths and weaknesses. Finally, this book uses the same sample case for both the CS and R-PAS, which will also allow the reader to see the similarities and differences between the systems in administration, scoring, and interpretation.

This chapter begins by discussing when the Rorschach can be useful in psychological assessment, including how often it is used. It also discusses referral questions for which the Rorschach may not be an appropriate part of the battery. The remainder of the chapter focuses on the history behind the Rorschach test, beginning with its inception by Hermann Rorschach and progressing through the development of the Comprehensive System and R-PAS. It also discusses significant factors in the creation of R-PAS, including the common belief that Exner's estate had decided to halt work on the Comprehensive System.

Frequency of Use

In recent years, survey research has attempted to ascertain the instruments mental health professionals rely on the most in their practice. Much of this research has focused on discrete subgroups of professionals rather than the mental health profession as a whole. For example, among clinical neuropsychologists, the MMPI-2 is the most commonly used personality assessment measure. Still, approximately one third (32.7%) of the clinical neuropsychologists surveyed reported using the Rorschach. However, it is unclear which system, if any, they were using (Smith, Gorske, Wiggins, & Little, 2010). Surveys of forensic psychologists have yielded similar results; while the Rorschach is used by forensic psychologists, it is used less often than self-report measures (Archer, Buffington-Vollum, Stredny, & Handel, 2006). The less frequent use among forensic psychologists appears to be related to concerns about the instrument's admissibility in court (Grove, Barden, Garb, & Lilienfeld, 2002; Gurley, Sheehan, Piechowski, & Gray, 2014; Kivisto, Gacono, & Medoff, 2013; Lally, 2003). Still, it is important to point out that while forensic psychologists have expressed concern regarding the Rorschach's admissibility in court, reviews of appellate cases have indicated that there have been few challenges to testimony that relies on the Rorschach (Gurley et al., 2011; Meloy, Hansen, & Weiner, 1997; Weiner, Exner, & Sciara, 1966).

A survey of members of the American Psychological Association (APA) and the Society for Personality Assessment (SPA) has shown that while self-report measures are used more often than performance-based personality measures by clinical psychologists, there is a difference in the field in that members of SPA are more likely to use performance-based personality measurement than are non-members (Musewica, Marczyk, Knauss, & York, 2009). Nonetheless, what all these studies have found is that while it is not the most common personality instrument used, the Rorschach is used by a significant number of psychologists in a variety of specialty areas.

Given the results of some recent surveys, it is apparent that not all professionals are using the same version of the Rorschach. For example, Corum and Gurley (2015) found that in a survey of predoctoral internship sites, 63 percent used the Rorschach and the majority of these sites (97%) used the CS. Approximately one third (29%) of sites reported using R-PAS as well. However, it does seem that a shift may be occurring in the predominant system in the United States, as 51 percent of sites that used the Rorschach indicated that competitive predoctoral internship applicants should have some experience with R-PAS. Still, a handful of other sites were using other Rorschach systems, including the Beck system. Although the CS was still the predominant system at the time this book was written, it appears that R-PAS is becoming more and more commonly used.

When to Use the Rorschach

There is no assessment measure currently available that can provide useful information in every single type of evaluation, as the usefulness of the measure depends on the referral question and the client's individual characteristics. For example, a

Rorschach would likely have little clinical utility when determining whether an examinee meets criteria for a diagnosis of intellectual disability, as the Rorschach cannot provide an IQ score. Although it can provide some information regarding current functioning, there are instruments available that can more directly assess specific areas of adaptive functioning, such as the Adaptive Behavior Assessment System, Third Edition (ABAS-III) (Harrison & Oakland, 2015). However, when the referral question is whether the examinee may have some underlying psychosis, the Rorschach can be extremely useful, as both the CS and R-PAS contain variables that directly assess the examinee's thought processes.

CAUTION

The Rorschach is not appropriate for all referral questions. Be sure to consider the examinee and the referral question(s) when deciding whether the Rorschach would be appropriate.

The Rorschach is considered to be useful for a variety of purposes. Exner (2003) stated that the Rorschach can be extremely useful when a complete understanding of the person, including why he or she is engaging in the patterns of behavior at issue, is desired. Additionally, the CS and R-PAS both require decision making and can provide information regarding the way the examinee makes decisions. These systems can also provide information about a person's functioning on a day-to-day basis and can inform treatment. Exner (2003) and others (e.g., Ganellen, 1996; Viglione, 1999) have shown the test is useful with psychosis and thought disorders. Some have suggested that the Rorschach could be useful in other settings as well, including for personnel selection and for understanding personality disorders and risk of completed suicide (Del Giudice, 2010; Huprich & Ganellen, 2006).

The CS and R-PAS have a number of unique qualities that other personality instruments do not have. First, because neither requires the examinee to read, they can be used with individuals whose reading abilities are not at the level required by self-report measures. Additionally, because they are not self-report measures and lack face validity, they are not so susceptible to inaccurate self-presentation as other measures may be (Del Giudice, 2010). As described above, because the Rorschach is a problem-solving task, it provides more information about the inner-workings of the individual than other product-based (e.g., behavior-based) tests are able to offer.

Still, there are some weaknesses to the Rorschach. First, administration, scoring, and interpretation are time consuming; Ball, Archer, and Imhof's (1994) survey of licensed professionals indicated that psychologists spend an average of almost two and a half hours administering, scoring, and interpreting the Rorschach. To put this in perspective, according to their research, the average time to administer, score, and interpret the MMPI was just under two hours. Still, it is important to note that unlike a clinician administering the Rorschach, a clinician is not typically active during the administration of the MMPI; during administration of the MMPI the client is reading and responding to written questions. Depending on the referral question, the examiner may be able to get the necessary information more quickly with another instrument than with the Rorschach.

Also, because the various Rorschach systems require the examinee to provide relatively complex oral responses (e.g., why they saw what they saw), examinees with expressive language difficulties, due to being tested in a non-native language, having a language disorder, or having limited cognitive abilities, may be at a disadvantage with the instrument. For example, clients may not be able to explain why the blot looks like a flower to them because they do not have the words to describe it. Thus, an examinee may be more likely to provide a simple explanation ("the shape") rather than a more complex explanation ("the different variations in colors remind me of petals; the green looks like a stem because of the color and the shape") because of difficulties with expressive language. Unless such difficulties are taken into account, a clinician could incorrectly attribute the simplicity of the explanations to defensiveness or avoidance rather than to a disadvantage.

HISTORY OF THE RORSCHACH

Hermann Rorschach, the creator of the ten inkblots used in the administration of the CS and R-PAS, was not the first to research the use of inkblots in psychological testing. For example, prior to Rorschach's use of inkblots, Alfred Binet and Victor Henri had researched the possibility of using inkblots as part of an intelligence test. However, there were difficulties with group administration, so they ceased their attempts (Exner, 2003).

Rorschach, like many others of his generation in Switzerland, likely grew up playing the game *Klecksographie*, where individuals would make inkblots then respond to them (Exner, 2003). During his work with psychiatric patients, Rorschach, a medical doctor, noted that patients who had been diagnosed with schizophrenia responded to the blots differently from patients with other diagnoses. However, it is unlikely that this observation was the impetus for Rorschach to study the game more systematically. The inspiration to study the inkblots more systematically may have come from one of Rorschach's friends, Konrad Gehring, who was a teacher at a school near where Rorschach was completing his residency. Gehring used the game as an incentive and noticed fewer management issues with the use of the incentive (Exner, 2003).

Rorschach's eventual decision to study the inkblots more systematically resulted in the publication of *Psychodiagnostik* (*Psychodiagnostics*) (Rorschach, 1921, 1942), a monograph designed as a "Form Interpretation Test" (Exner, 2003). In addition to publishing the ten inkblots we still use today, *Psychodiagnostik* provided information regarding Rorschach's empirical study of the blots. Specifically, he examined the responses of 400 individuals, including nonpatients and inpatients, documenting some of the differences he saw between the nonpatients and the individuals with schizophrenia. In his monograph, he also formulated a standard question regarding the blots ("What might this be?") and discussed various scoring categories, such as location, contents, and movement. Furthermore, Rorschach did not consider his work to be complete and stressed the importance of further research with the inkblots. Unfortunately, Rorschach was unable to continue his work as he passed away in 1922, soon after his monograph was published.

Rorschach's colleagues continued to use his test after his death, but rather than focus on systematic data collection, as Rorschach had, they began to focus more on the clinical applicability of the test (Exner, 2003). They also started to attempt to apply the test to psychoanalytic theory and would conduct content analyses of responses. This differs from Rorschach's initial intention, as he minimized the use of content analysis.

Three of Rorschach's colleagues became advocates for the test (Exner, 2003). David Levy, an American psychiatrist, studied with one of these individuals, Emil Oberholzer, in Switzerland. When Levy returned to the United States, he brought copies of the blots with him. A student who was studying at the institute where Levy was a staff member, Samuel Beck, was looking for a dissertation topic and Levy mentioned that he had copies of the Rorschach blots. Beck went on to conduct the first systematic study of the Rorschach in the United States for his dissertation. At around this same time in the 1930s, a colleague of Beck's, Marguerite Hertz, also used the Rorschach as the basis of her dissertation (Hertz, 1986). Beck and Hertz continued to systematically study the Rorschach and developed their own separate systems of administering, scoring, and interpreting the instrument.

Around the same time, Bruno Klopfer, a psychologist, was training to be a psychoanalyst in Germany. However, due to the rise of the Nazis in Germany, Klopfer and his family left that country for Switzerland, where they remained for

≡ *Rapid Reference 1.2*
....

Some Important Individuals in Rorschach History

Hermann Rorschach: Developed the ten inkblots still in use today. His work became the framework for multiple Rorschach systems.

David Levy: Studied with Emil Oberholzer in Switzerland and brought the Rorschach to the United States.

Samuel Beck: Conducted the first systematic study of the Rorschach in the United States; developed the Beck system of administration and scoring for the Rorschach.

Marguerite Hertz: Conducted a systematic study of the Rorschach in the United States; developed the Hertz system of administration and scoring for the Rorschach.

Bruno Klopfer: Started the *Rorschach Research Exchange*; developed the Klopfer system of administration and scoring for the Rorschach.

John Exner: Developed the CS.

Gregory Meyer, Joni Mihura, Philip Erdberg, Donald Viglione, and Robert Erard: Developed the R-PAS.

Source: Based on Information from Exner, 2003; Hertz, 1986; Meyer et al., 2011; Skadeland, 1986.

a year (Skadeland, 1986). There, Klopfer studied with Carl Jung and was introduced to the Rorschach. The following year, he and his family immigrated to the United States, where he worked at Columbia University in the anthropology department (Exner, 2003; Skadeland, 1986).

Shortly after he began working at Columbia University, graduate students in the department of psychology asked that Klopfer conduct a seminar on the Rorschach. However, Robert Woodworth, who was chair of the psychology department at the time, suggested that Beck run the seminar (Exner, 2003; Skadeland, 1986). Beck was not immediately available, however, and the students and Klopfer opted instead to do an informal seminar in his apartment twice per week for six weeks.

Klopfer's seminars proved to be extremely popular, and within a year, much of Klopfer's work was focused on the Rorschach (Skadeland, 1986). In the course of these seminars, Klopfer and his students added several new scores, most of which were intuitive and not based on systematic research, unlike the work of Rorschach, Beck, and Hertz. Klopfer went on to start a newsletter called the *Rorschach Research Exchange*, which eventually became the *Journal of Personality Assessment*

(Exner, 2003). (Rapid Reference 1.2 lists the key individuals in the development of the Rorschach.)

By 1957, there were five distinct Rorschach systems in use in the United States, with different administration, scoring, and interpretation principles (Exner, 2003). Exner began his comparison of these five systems with the intention of writing an article about his findings. However, because of the amount of information, the article became a book.

In this book, originally published in 1974, Exner noted many differences among the five systems. Only two of the five used the same seating, none used the same set of instructions, each system collected data differently, they had different formats for coding, and some used different coding criteria for certain codes. Exner came to the conclusion that there were five separate tests. In 1968, the Rorschach Research Foundation was established by Exner to determine which system was most empirically supported and had the greatest clinical utility (Exner, 2003).

As part of his research, Exner conducted a series of surveys on the use of the Rorschach in clinical practice. He found that although many psychologists had formal training in at least one system, the majority of psychologists mixed systems, and some did not use a set administration, coding, and interpretation system. In fact, according to Exner's research, only about 20 percent of psychologists relied on only one system at a time. Further, the predominant systems were Klopfer's and Beck's (Exner, 2003).

Exner's research led him to create a data pool to compare the five systems (Exner, 2003). By the early 1970s he had compared 835 protocols, administered by 153 different psychologists, and each administered and scored using one of the five systems. In his examination of the data, he noticed differences in the systems, including that each system produced different kinds of records, each system had scores that were empirically supported, and each system had scores that were not empirically supported. At this point, the Rorschach Research Foundation started to focus its attention on the development of a system that contained empirically defensible data and features that were not yet empirically supported but that could be researched.

The Rorschach Comprehensive System was first published in 1974 (Exner, 1974). Although the initial prognosis for wide use of the system was poor, due to the timing (Stricker, 1976), the system was well received and became the most commonly used Rorschach system in the United States. The system was designed to be atheoretical, so it could be used with a variety of theories (Exner, 1997). It also was periodically revised, up to the time of Exner's death in 2006 (Exner, 2003; Sciara & Ritzler, 2009).

After Exner died, the legal rights to Rorschach Workshops (the primary organization for training on the CS), his writings, and his files reverted to his family (Sciara & Ritzler, 2009). He also never appointed a successor; so among CS researchers and trainers, there was a leadership void. After his death, a family member of Exner's had announced that there would be no further changes to the CS. This announcement had the potential to have a negative impact on the CS, as any psychological test needs to be periodically revised to account for normative changes and updated research. However, the family has recently announced that the announcement that the CS could not be changed was in error; the family is supporting continued research and the evolution of the CS (Sciara & Ritzler, 2015).

Multiple researchers wanted to make changes to the CS (Sciara & Ritzler, 2009). Five researchers—Gregory Meyer, Joni Mihura, Philip Erdberg, Donald Viglione, and Robert Erard—four of whom had been members of Exner's Rorschach Research Council, expressed a number of concerns about the current status of the CS. Specifically, through their research as part of the Rorschach Research Council, their own research, and their own experiences, they identified a number of concerns with the CS. These included variations in administration and coding, possible error variance due to the number of responses an examinee provided, interpretations of scores that were not always consistent with the empirical evidence, inaccurate normative data, and an overreliance on negative interpretations

≡ *Rapid Reference 1.3*

Goals of the R-PAS

1. Focus on using variables with the most empirical, clinical, and response/behavioral support.
2. Use an international comparison group with standard scores and percentiles.
3. Reduce redundancy and make the system simpler.
4. Describe the empirical and theoretical basis of each variable that is included.
5. Be able to adjust for the complexity of the protocol.
6. Optimize the number of responses in order to reduce the incidence of high and low numbers of protocol responses.
7. Develop new indices, and revise indices.
8. Offer scoring on a secure, web-based platform.

Source: Meyer et al., 2011, p. 3.

of Rorschach scores. At that point, Meyer and colleagues opted to develop a new system, the Rorschach Performance Assessment System. R-PAS was developed to reduce examiner variability, to make the system more consistent with the empirical literature, and to simplify the system. The development of R-PAS was focused on meeting eight goals; these goals are displayed in Rapid Reference 1.3.

Still, some questioned whether a new system was actually needed (e.g., Sciara & Ritzler, 2009). Furthermore, Sciara and Ritzler predicted that there would be some who would be comfortable with the CS and would not want to learn a new system. From the current literature, it appears that the field is at least examining R-PAS (Gurley et al., 2014). Time will tell whether R-PAS will become the predominant system in the United States, the CS will remain the predominant system, or whether there will be another outcome, such as individuals mixing systems, as occurred prior to the creation of the CS.

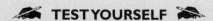

🐿️ TEST YOURSELF 🐿️

1. **Which of the following is a strength of performance-based personality measures?**
   a. Performance-based personality measures can be used with examinees who cannot read.
   b. All performance-based measures can provide an IQ score.
   c. Performance-based measures can be used with all referral questions.
   d. All of the above are strengths of performance-based personality measures.

2. **True or False: The CS and R-PAS may be difficult for examinees with expressive language difficulties.**
   a. True
   b. False

3. **True or False: Rorschach was the first to consider using inkblots as part of psychological testing.**
   a. True
   b. False

4. **Which of the following was a purpose of the CS?**
   a. To develop a system that derived from psychodynamic principles.
   b. To develop a system that had empirically defined data and features that could be defined.
   c. To develop a system that could be used to directly assess DSM-III disorders.
   d. None of these were purposes of the CS.

5. **What were the concerns about the CS identified by Meyer and colleagues that resulted in the development of R-PAS (select all that apply)?**

a. Variations in administration and coding.

b. The impact of the color present in blots VIII and IX.

c. Possible error variance due to the number of responses the examinee provided.

d. Interpretation of a score was not always consistent with the empirical evidence.

e. Inaccurate normative data.

f. Recent changes to the CS.

g. Overreliance on negative interpretations of Rorschach scores.

Answers: 1. a; 2. a; 3. b; 4. b; 5. a, c, d, e, g.

Two

COMPREHENSIVE SYSTEM ADMINISTRATION

Proper administration of a standardized test instrument is vital. The interpretation of standardized instruments assumes that the test was administered and scored correctly. Without proper test administration, the scores will have little meaning. However, administering the test correctly is only one part of proper testing. In addition to administering the test correctly, in order for an examiner to get accurate results, that examiner must have developed rapport with the examinee. The examiner also has to attend to the examinee's mood, experience, and the testing situation, because if the examinee is tired, feels hungry, or needs to use the restroom, this can affect administration. For instance, if examinees need to use the restroom, they may rush through a test in order to have a break. Conversely, if they are tired, they may not be attending to the test materials, which can influence how they respond to the test. In other words, administration is a multifaceted process that is not limited just to an accurate administration of the test itself; other factors also need to be taken into consideration.

Prior to administering the Rorschach Comprehensive System, the examiner should determine whether the CS is an appropriate instrument to administer, given the referral question and the desired type of information. No test is capable of providing information for every referral question. The CS, for example, can provide information on personality and emotional functioning, thinking patterns, and emotional reactivity, to name a few things, but it is unable to provide information such as an IQ or documentation of academic achievement. Thus, when the CS is used, it is often used as part of a multimethod battery that incorporates multiple assessment techniques. Of course, that does not prohibit its use as a solitary assessment measure, and it can also be used to monitor change during treatment or to help inform therapy.

In addition to determining whether the CS can assist with answering the referral question, an examiner must determine whether the CS is an appropriate instrument to use with the particular examinee, given the examinee's characteristics, background, and abilities. For example, the CS is a highly verbal test, making it inappropriate for individuals who are nonverbal. Additionally, I recommend against using the test with individuals with expressive language disorders, as the test requires a high degree of verbal ability from the examinee. Individuals with expressive language disorders have difficulty expressing themselves; as a result, they may provide relatively simplistic explanations for their responses because of their language deficits. Because frequent simplistic explanations for responses (e.g., it's a bat because of the shape) can be interpreted as disengagement or defensiveness, individuals with expressive language disorders may be erroneously seen as not engaging in the test or as being defensive, when simplistic responses may, in reality, be due to their disability. If the CS is going to be administered to someone with expressive language disability, the nature of the disability needs to be taken into account during interpretation.

I also caution against using the test with individuals with uncorrected visual impairments or with individuals who have intellectual disabilities. Given that the test is made up of complex visual stimuli, it should not be used with individuals with severe visual impairment. It should also be used with caution with people who are color-blind. There have been a few studies examining use of the Rorschach with individuals who are color-blind; however, these studies only examined the impact on color-based responses (e.g., Corsino, 1985). As individuals with color blindness can have difficulty seeing different hues, it is very possible that there may be an impact on shading-based responses as well, but this still needs to be examined. Individuals with cognitive disabilities (e.g., those who meet criteria for intellectual disability) may find the test too challenging and not engage or may not be able to engage due to cognitive limitations. Exner (2003) also noted that the CS was not appropriate for those with significant neurological impairment, but research has shown it is used by some neuropsychologists as part of their evaluations (Smith et al., 2010). Later in this chapter, I discuss ways to adapt the test for use with other populations, such as individuals who are deaf and those with limited attention spans.

Examiners should also determine where in the battery the CS should be administered. When determining the order of a battery of tests, it is important to consider that psychological testing is anxiety provoking for many examinees and anxiety can interfere with testing. To minimize the effects of anxiety, I suggest adopting a flexible order that can be tailored to the examinee. If unstructured tasks appear to cause anxiety for the examinee, then a test like the Rorschach should be used later in the battery. Conversely, if the examinee appears anxious around academic and school-related tasks, then it would be appropriate to start with an instrument such as the Rorschach because it does not mimic an academic test.

Examiners should also be aware of the impact of fatigue on assessment; an examinee's (and examiner's) attention and effort can wane over time. When examiners notice signs of fatigue, in either themselves or their examinee, they should takes steps to reduce the fatigue in order to ensure that both they and the examinee have the energy to engage appropriately with the test. This could include taking a break, switching tasks, or completing testing at a later date.

PREPARING TO ADMINISTER THE RORSCHACH CS

There are only a few required materials for a CS administration. The examiner needs a copy of the Rorschach blots, pens or pencils, paper, a few location sheets, and something to write on, such as a clipboard. Location sheets can be purchased from a variety of psychological testing companies and via the R-PAS online store. The blots should not have any marks on them.

The Rorschach, unlike many other performance-based psychological tests, such as the Wechsler Adult Intelligence Scale, Fourth Edition (WAIS-IV), does not have a specific protocol that examiners need to use when recording the examinee's responses. Examiners are able to create and use their own forms. Some examiners choose to use lined paper that is divided into two small columns on the left and two larger columns on the right (see Figure 2.1). Other examiners have developed their own forms to use; a form that can be used is available in the Book Companion Website Materials.

Card	Resp#	Response	Inquiry

Figure 2.1 Example of a Protocol to Use for a CS Administration

Examiners should bring multiple copies of the recording form they plan to use, or a lot of blank paper, in order to record the examinee's responses. The record for each card should start on a new page; responses from two different cards should never be placed on the same page. This is done to keep the responses accurately organized. Additionally, I recommend putting no more than two responses per page and organizing the form in such a way that the two phases of administration (Response and Inquiry) are aligned for each response. The easiest way to do this is to divide the form into columns, with the two widest columns used to report responses and inquiries, as shown in Figure 2.1.

It is also important that the examiner number everything correctly. Cards are identified by Roman numerals (e.g., I, II, III) whereas the responses are given Arabic numerals (e.g., 1, 2, 3). Responses are numbered consecutively across the cards. This allows the examiner to easily determine whether the examinee has provided enough responses for the administration to be valid (fourteen responses). Do not restart the numbering with each card. Thus, if a person gives two responses for Card I, Card II should start with Response 3.

As the CS measures both personality states and traits, it needs to be administered in one sitting. A typical CS administration takes between forty and sixty minutes; however, the time necessary relies both on the skill of the examiner and on the ability of the examinee. I recommend reserving ninety minutes for the administration, just to ensure adequate time to complete the testing. The room being used for the testing session should be quiet and free from distractions. The room should have a table for the examiner to keep the cards on. Some examiners prefer to have a table in front of them, while others prefer to have the table to the side; either way, it is important that the cards be kept out of the reach of the examinee. The room should also have two chairs that can be placed so the examiner and the examinee are sitting next to each other. This setup allows the examiner to easily see where the examinee is pointing on the blots and also makes it difficult for the examinee to see the examiner's nonverbal reactions to the examinee's responses. This is important; if the examinee sees the examiner respond negatively to a response, such as by raising an eyebrow, rolling his or her eyes, or seeming surprised, it can cause the examinee to censor subsequent responses so as to not elicit a further negative reaction from the examiner (Magnussen, 1960; Masling, 1965). Some examiners prefer to sit slightly behind the examinee, as it facilitates being able to see where the examinee points to on the blot. Also, right-handed examiners tend to sit on the examinee's right side and left-handed examiners tend to sit on the examinee's left side; this reduces the chance that the examiner will bump the examinee when writing. Figure 2.2 displays possible room setups.

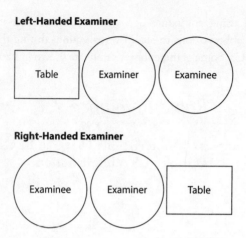

Figure 2.2 Examples of Ways to Set Up a Room for a CS Administration

CS administration requires that the examiner record all of the examinee's responses verbatim. This is done to facilitate coding (scoring). The examiner should also record the examinee's gestures, such as pointing to or touching the card, as these gestures can also inform coding. The examiner also records his or her own verbalizations verbatim. This allows the examiner to determine whether anything he or she said might have induced a pattern of responding by the examinee.

Transcribing everything verbatim can seem like a daunting task, especially for a beginning administrator. However, there are techniques and tricks an examiner can use to keep up with the examinee. These include the use of abbreviations. Exner outlined a set of standard abbreviations that can be used; however, some of these abbreviations are not necessarily intuitive. I have found that students often have difficulty remembering the standard abbreviations and actually take longer to administer a Rorschach using the abbreviations than if they would if they were recording the actual words, because of the time they take trying to remember the abbreviations for specific words. Additionally, some of the standard abbreviations differ from today's common texting abbreviations, which can result in confusion when going back to score the protocol. As an example, Exner recommended using BF for "butterfly" but BF is a common texting abbreviation for "boyfriend" and "best friend." This could be problematic, as the examiner may not remember whether the abbreviation was intended to mean butterfly, boyfriend, or best friend. I tend to abbreviate butterfly as "butfly," boyfriend as "boyf," and best friend as "bstfrd" to differentiate. I also strongly advise examiners to type out the responses and inquiries immediately after administration in order to facilitate coding, as it is much easier to code when you are not struggling after a lapse of some time to decipher your own handwriting.

I recommend using a mixture of Exner's recommended abbreviations and common texting abbreviations to record verbalizations during the administration of the Rorschach CS. Some of these abbreviations are shown in Rapid Reference 2.1.

≡ Rapid Reference 2.1

Examples of Abbreviations That Can Be Used During a CS Administration

Be	b
See	c
Are	r
You	u
Your/you're	ur
About	abt, @
Around	ard
Anything	at
Because	bec; b/c
Don't know	DK
Everything	et
Whole	W
Looks like	ll
Maybe	mb
Some sort	ss
-ing	-g
Human	H
Animal	A
Blood	Bl
Clothing	Cg
Cloud	Cl
What makes it look like	WMILL
To	2
In my opinion	IMO
On the other hand	OTOH
Extraterrestrial	ET
Help me see it	HMSI
You said	U sed

Source: Based on information from Exner, 2003; Meyer et al., 2011.

It is permissible for an examiner to slow down an examinee in order to ensure accurate transcription. Exner (2003, p. 57) wrote that prompts to slow down an examinee could include "Wait, I'm having trouble keeping up with you. Go a little slower please," and, "I'm sorry I didn't get all of that. You said. . ." I have also had success with saying, "Wait a second, you said. . ." However, continually slowing down an examinee could affect rapport as well as significantly slow the pace of testing, so examiners should do their best to keep up with their examinees, if possible.

There is some debate on whether computers should be used during the administration of the CS. The normative data for the CS were derived from paper-and-pencil administrations; now, however, many people type much faster than they can write. Additionally, computers and other technology have become commonplace in many facets of society. Still, as of this writing, there is no published, peer-reviewed research that shows a computer-administered CS Rorschach test (e.g., one where the examiner types) is equivalent to a paper-and-pencil one. Some research has been presented at conferences indicating that computer-based administrations and paper-and-pencil administrations are equivalent in many respects (Gavela, Gil, & Sciara, 2014). However, this study by Gavela and colleagues (2014) used a very small sample size and examined the differences between the two modalities of administrations on only nine variables. Additionally, there was a significant difference between the computer and the paper-and-pencil administrations in the complexity of the protocols, and there was a trend toward the different administration types producing a different number of responses. More research is clearly needed at this point to demonstrate equivalency between a computer-assisted CS administration and a paper-and-pencil-administered one.

In addition to asking about using their computers to administer the CS, students often ask if they can audiotape the administration so they can be sure they have a record of everything that is said. Although taping is often used as part of research studies on the CS, it is ill-advised for clinical purposes, for many reasons. First, as part of informed consent procedures, examiners would have to inform examinees that they are recording the session. Second, there is research indicating that individuals react differently when they know they are being recorded, so it is possible that examinees' recorded responses will be different from what they would have been had they not been recorded (Constantinou, Ashendorf, & McCaffrey, 2005). Third, examiners who record could over-rely on the recording and not attend so closely as they otherwise would to what the examinee is saying during the administration, instead assuming they can rely on the recording for the information. However, in order to properly complete a CS administration, examiners must be able to recite an examinee's initial responses verbatim and question important details. This cannot be done if examiners do not have the verbatim record in front of them while making inquiries. An audio recording also cannot provide information on relevant gestures, such as the examinee touching the card. There is also the issue that technology can fail, and consequently, may not be available to fill in any information that an examiner missed.

WHAT IS NEEDED FOR A VALID ADMINISTRATION

In order for an administration to be valid, an examinee must provide at least fourteen responses, with at least one response to each card. As there are ten cards, in order to reach the minimum fourteen responses, examinees will have to provide multiple responses to at least one card. Although fourteen is the absolute minimum number of responses for a valid CS protocol, the amount of data that can be obtained from such a short protocol is minimal, so a fourteen-response protocol is not ideal. At no time should the examiner tell the examinee how many responses are needed; however, there are instances where an examiner can intervene to increase the chances of achieving a valid protocol. These are described in the "Troubleshooting the Response Phase" and "Troubleshooting the Inquiry Phase" sections of this chapter.

ADMINISTERING THE CS

Prior to administering the CS, the examiner should ensure that the examinee is properly prepared for testing. This includes obtaining informed consent—or assent if the examinee cannot legally provide consent or does not have to provide consent—and developing a working rapport. The examiner should also have all required materials readily available, and the room should be set up appropriately.

The CS has two parts: the Response Phase and the Inquiry Phase. Generally, the complete administration takes no more than sixty minutes, with the Response Phase taking less time than the Inquiry Phase. During the Response Phase, the job of examinees is to tell the examiner *what* the blots look like to them. In the Inquiry Phase, the job of examinees is to explain *why* the blots look like that to them and *where* in the blots they saw what they saw. In other words, they need to help the examiner see it how they see it.

Response Phase

For this part of the administration, the examiner will need paper and pens or pencils to write the examinee's responses and the ten cards. (The location sheets that will be used in the next phase should be placed out of view of the examinee; generally, they are kept under the paper the examiner will be writing on.)

Prior to starting the test, the examiner should introduce the procedures. This helps to reduce the examinee's anxiety as it informs the examinee what he or she is about to do. The examiner should start by asking if the examinee has heard of the Rorschach. The examiner could make a statement such as, "And one of the tests we will be doing is the inkblot test, the Rorschach. Have you ever heard of it, or have you taken it?" (Exner, 2003, p. 50). This is important because it lets the examinee know what the next test is and provides the examiner with information about the examinee's previous exposure to the test. When examinees state that they are familiar with the test, the examiner should query further about what an examinee knows, and take steps to correct any misconceptions. When examinees say they have already taken the test, the examiner may still need to correct some misconceptions; the fact that an examinee has already taken the test does not mean that the test was administered according to the CS. When examinees say they are not familiar with the test, the examiner should provide a brief summary by saying something like, "It's just a series of inkblots that I will be showing you and ask what they look like to you" (Exner, 2003, p. 50). The examiner should also ask if the examinee has any questions, and should answer those questions as honestly as possible, without providing specific details about interpretation. Rapid Reference 2.2 offers a sampling of examinee questions and potential ways for the examiner to respond. After these introductory tasks are completed, the examiner then moves on to the actual CS administration.

Administration of the Response Phase

To administer the Response Phase of the CS, the examiner hands the examinee Card I, upright, and says, "What might this be?" The examinee should hold the card, but if the examinee puts it down on the table, the examiner should not correct the examinee. The examiner then records the examinee's responses verbatim. Throughout this task, the examiner does his or her best to remain as silent as possible and makes comments only when absolutely necessary. Except under exceptional circumstances (see the troubleshooting section later), the examiner does not take the card from the examinee. Instead, the examiner waits until the examinee hands the card back. The examiner then hands the next card to the examinee, and this process is repeated until all ten cards have been presented.

CAUTION

It is important to introduce the cards with the question, "What might this be?" Changing this phrase changes the nature of the test. For example, if you asked, "What is this?," it would imply that there is a correct answer. "What might this be?" indicates there is some ambiguity in the test and that there is no correct or incorrect answer.

≡ *Rapid Reference 2.2*

Sample Examinee Questions and Examiner Responses

Examinee Question	Examiner Response
This is the test that tells if I am crazy, right?	That's not quite right. There's no test that tells if a person is crazy. This test will help to determine (insert referral question here).
Oh I saw this on TV. I'm just supposed to say the first thing that comes to my mind, right?	I want you to tell me what they look like to you.
Should I use my imagination?	Just tell me what it looks like to you.
Is that what you're looking for?	Yes, just whatever it looks like to you
Is there a right answer?/Is that the right answer?	People see many different things.
Does it look like that to you?	I can see lots of things.
How can you make anything out of what I see?	Let's talk about that after the test.
Do you buy these or make them?	I buy them.
How many of these are there?	Ten.
How long with this take?	Usually not very long.
How many things should I find?	Take your time. I'm sure you will find more than one./It's up to you.

Source: Adapted from Exner, 2003, p. 52.

The examinee is allowed to rotate the card, but the examiner should not volunteer this information. If the examinee rotates the card, the examiner should record it, as this information is necessary for the Inquiry Phase and for coding. Usually examiners record a card rotation by using a caret-shaped mark next to the response number to identify which way the top of the card was pointing when the examinee provided a response. For example, if the top of the card is facing to the right when the examinee provides a response, the > symbol should be recorded; if the top of the card is facing down, then the v symbol should be recorded, and if the top of the card is facing to the left, the < symbol is used. No notation is necessary if the top of the card is facing up when the examinee provides a response.

Troubleshooting the Response Phase

There are some points when the examinee is responding to the first card where the examiner needs to intervene. First, the examinee may respond to the blot by saying it is an inkblot. If this occurs, then the examiner should say, "That's right, that's what it is, but I want you to tell me what might it be, what else does it look like?" (Exner, 2003, p. 51). If the examinee persists in saying that it is an inkblot, then the examiner may need to stop testing, reacclimate the examinee to testing, then start testing again.

The examiner also needs to intervene on the first card if the examinee provides only one response or provides five responses. If the examinee provides only one response, the examiner should not take the card back and should prompt for additional responses in order to decrease the risk of an invalid protocol. Exner (2001, p. 6; 2003, p. 52) recommends saying, "If you take your time and look some more I think that you will find something else too," or, "Take your time and look some more, I'm sure you'll see something else too." After this prompt, most examinees will provide a second response; however, there are some who will not. If the examinee does not provide a second response, the examiner should not press for more responses and should move on to the second card.

The examiner has the option of prompting again on Card IV in certain circumstances. If the examiner prompted on Card I, and even after the prompt the examinee provided only one response on Card II, one response on Card III, and attempts to return Card IV after providing only one response, then the examiner can prompt for an additional response. The examiner can use a prompt like, "Wait, don't hurry through these. We are in no hurry, take your time" (Exner, 2003, p. 53).

Conversely, if the examinee provides five responses to the first card and does not return the card, the examiner needs to intervene in order to reduce the chance of an extremely lengthy protocol. In this case, the examiner should take the card back from the examinee and say, "Alright, let's do the next one" (Exner, 2003, p. 55). The examiner will continue to give this prompt on subsequent cards, as long as the examinee provides five responses to each card. However, once the examinee provides fewer than five responses to a card, the examiner can no longer provide this prompt. Thus, if an examinee provides four responses to Card II, the examiner can no longer take the card from the examinee, even if the examinee provides six or more responses to later cards. Rapid Reference 2.3 presents examples of troubleshooting the Response Phase.

In some cases, an examinee will provide only a few responses to the first few cards but then provide more than five responses to the later cards, such as the

≡ Rapid Reference 2.3

Troubleshooting the Response Phase

Issue	What to Do
Examinee provides only one response on Card I.	Request a second response: e.g., by saying, "Take your time and look some more. I'm sure you'll see something else too."
Examinee provides 5 responses to Card I and looks ready to provide more.	Take the card from the examinee, and say something like, "Thank you, let's do the next one."
Examinee refuses to provide a response to one of the first few cards (Cards I, II, or III).	Reacclimate the examinee to the test and start again.
Examinee refuses to provide a response to a later card.	Encourage a response, and say something like, "We're in no hurry. Take your time."
Examinee does not provide a total of 14 responses to the 10 blots.	Evaluate whether you are likely to get a valid Rorschach if you readminister. If you believe you can, provide instructions stating that the examinee provided too few responses.

Source: Based on information from Exner, 2001, 2003.

ones that contain color (blots VIII–X). At this point, the examiner should not take the card from the examinee, as standard CS procedures state that this *pull* procedure needs to start on Card I. Still, this situation has the potential to result in a high-response protocol that can affect interpretation, so examiners should use their best judgment when deciding whether or not to intervene. If examiners opt to use a nonstandard intervention, they should note on the report that the CS was not administered according to standard procedures.

The examiner also needs to intervene when the examinee attempts to reject a card. In order for the administration to be valid, the examinee needs to provide at least one response to every card. If the examinee rejects a card and does not provide any response to it, the administration is not valid. If the examinee attempts to reject one of the first few cards, the examiner should stop testing, review the purpose of testing, and ensure that there is a good working rapport. Once these issues are corrected, testing should restart. If the examinee attempts to reject a later card, generally Card IX, the examiner should not accept the card and should encourage the examinee to provide a response. The examiner could say something like, "Take your time. We're in no hurry." Generally, after receiving this encouragement, examinees will provide a response.

The final time an examiner may need to intervene during the Response Phase occurs when the examinee finishes the Response Phase but provides fewer than fourteen responses. In this case, the protocol is not valid. The examiner needs to make a decision either to discard the testing and rely on other assessment data or to conduct an immediate retest. The decision should be based on a number of factors including the examiner's judgment about the likelihood of obtaining a valid CS protocol and the importance of the data from the CS. If the examiner determines that it is highly unlikely that the examinee will provide at least fourteen responses on a retest, due either to severe impairment or to a high degree of resistance that is unlikely to be resolved in a reasonable amount of time, then the examiner should stop testing. However, if the examiner believes that a valid protocol can be obtained, then he or she should immediately retest the examinee. If the examiner is unsure, then he or she should retest the examinee. To start the retest, the examiner should state:

> Now you know how it's done. But there's a problem. You didn't give enough answers for us to get anything out of the test. So we will go through them again and this time I want you to make sure to give me more answers. You can include the same ones you've already given if you like but be sure to give me more answers this time [Exner, 2001, p. 54].

This starts the new testing session. The verbatim responses from the previous testing session should be discarded; they are not to be considered during the retest. Generally, examinees provide the same responses they provided before with some additional responses, but there will be times when an examinee provides a completely different set of responses. Only the responses the examinee provides during the retest are used in the second phase of the administration, the Inquiry Phase, and are coded and interpreted.

Inquiry Phase

The Inquiry Phase is arguably the more important of the two phases of the CS. During this phase, the examiner's job is to obtain the necessary information to properly code the administration. For each response received in the Response Phase, the examiner needs to know *what* the examinee saw, *where* they saw it, and *why* it looked like that to them. If any part of the Inquiry Phase is not done correctly and there is missing information, it will affect coding and therefore interpretation (Lis, Parolin, Zennaro, & Meyer, 2007).

The purpose of the Inquiry Phase is to help the examiner code the existing protocol correctly. As a result, a proper inquiry requires the examiner to have a good understanding of coding. CS coding is discussed in the next chapter. Briefly, during coding the examiner will be scoring the contents (*what* the examinee saw in the blot), location (*where* on the blot the examinee saw it), and determinants (*why* it looked like that to the examinee). Generally, the examinee will have provided most, if not all, of the information necessary to code the contents (the *what*) during the Response Phase. Consequently, much of the Inquiry Phase is focused on obtaining the information necessary to code the location (the *where*) and determinants (the *why*). The inquiry is not a time for examinees to provide new responses; the focus needs to be on the responses they already provided during the Response Phase.

DON'T FORGET

The purpose of the inquiry is to help the examiner code. You need *what* the examinee saw, *where* the examinee saw it, and *why* it looks like that to the examinee.

Administration of the Inquiry Phase

For this part of the administration, the examiner will need the examinee's responses from the Response Phase, the ten cards in order, and location sheets. As mentioned earlier, the location sheets should remain hidden from view until the examiner needs to use them to write on. Usually examiners keep the location sheets under the paper they are writing on until they need them.

To introduce the Inquiry Phase, the examiner should say:

> Now we are going to go back through the cards again. It won't take very long. I want to see the things that you said you saw and make sure that I see them like you do. We'll do them one at a time. I'll read what you said and then I want you to show me where it is in the blot and then tell me what there is there that makes it look like that to you, so that I can see it too, just like you did. Is that clear? [Exner, 2003, p. 59].

Once the client understands the purpose of the Inquiry Phase, the examiner begins by handing the examinee the first card and saying, "Here you said (repeats examinee's response verbatim)." Ideally, examinees will point to where on the blot they saw the response and describe why it looked like that to them, but this does not always happen. Usually the examiner has to intervene with some questions to ensure he or she gets the necessary information to code the *what, where,* and *why.* Once the examiner has this information, it is time to move on to the next response. As in the Response Phase, it is very important that the examiner record everything *verbatim* in order to facilitate coding.

Querying for Additional Information

Beginning Rorschach examiners have a tendency to over-query. Believing that they need to see the response exactly as the examinee saw it, they continue to query until they can see the response the same way or until the examinee is unable to provide additional information. However, examiners are not going to be able to see all of the responses the way the examinee does; experienced Rorschach examiners can all recall times where they were completely unable to see what the examinee saw, no matter how hard they tried. However, even without being able to see a response as the examinee saw it, examiners can still code it, as long as they have the *what, where,* and *why.* In addition, repeated querying can frustrate the examinee, because it reveals that the examiner cannot see what the examinee saw, implying that the answer may have been "incorrect." Also, from a practical standpoint, the more the examiner queries, the more he or she has to write, so unwarranted querying can result in excessively long protocols that are difficult to code due to the large amount of information. Before asking a question, examiners looking to avoid over-querying should ask themselves, "Will this question help me code?" If the answer is no, then the examiner should not ask the question.

CAUTION

Before asking a question during the Inquiry Phase, ask yourself, "Will this question help me code?" If the answer is no, do not ask the question.

During an inquiry, the examiner's questions and prompts should be as nondirective as possible. Consequently, the primary queries and prompts the examiner uses in the CS are very general and include such formulations as "I'm not sure I see it as you do, help me," "I'm not sure what there is that makes it look like that," and "I know it looks like that to you but remember I have to see it too. So help me understand why it looks like that to you" (Exner, 2001, 2003). The following is an example of an appropriate use of these general queries.

Response: A bat.

Examiner repeats response.

Inquiry-1: Yup (points). Don't you see it?

I know it looks like that to you, but remember, I have to see it too. So help me understand why it looks like that to you.

Inquiry-2: Oh well it's here (points) and it has wings, a head, and a body. It looks bat-like to me.

At this point, the examiner can move onto the next response. The examinee has provided the *what* (a bat), the *where* (pointed to location), and the *why* (wings, head, body, looks bat-like). No further questioning is needed to get what the examiner needs to code. Additionally, there is no indication that any other aspects of the blot, such as color, caused the examinee to perceive the blot as a bat. The inquiry for this response is complete.

Key Words

There are times where examinees imply, either through their words or through their gestures, that they are either seeing something else (more *what*) or that something else in the blot caused them to see what they saw (more *why*). These extra *what* and *why* responses are called *key words*. Key words in a response or *spontaneously* offered by an examinee early during the inquiry about a response should be queried. Some key words, like "pretty" or "night," imply that examinees may have seen what they saw because of the color of the blot. Others imply that examinees may have seen a texture (e.g., "soft"), dimensionality ("behind"), or shading ("dark"). A list of some key words can be found in Rapid Reference 2.4.

≡ Rapid Reference 2.4

Examples of Key Words

Color	Pretty, bright, happy, party, blood, sad, dreary, paint
Achromatic color	Night, evil, dark, tuxedo, dreary, depressing, snow, bright, lighter, darker
Dimensionality	Hole, deeper, behind, looking up, mountain, valley, carved, bumpy
Texture	Soft, fluffy, hairy, hot, cold, smooth, rough, bumpy
Shading	Smoky, darker, lighter

Querying based on key words is often more directive. Rather than using the more general "Help me see it like you do," key word querying often takes this form: "You said it was (insert key word)," or, "What made it look (insert key word)?" Here is an example of an appropriate use of a key word query:

Response: It is a pretty flower.
Examiner repeats response.
Inquiry-1: Yes, here (points). It's the whole thing. Here are the petals, the leaves, and the, oh what do they call it, um, the stamen, yes that's it.
You said it was pretty?
Inquiry-2: Yeah, because of all of the colors.

After the initial part of the inquiry (Inquiry-1), the examinee had provided the *what* (a flower), the *where* (a location, by pointing), and the *why* (petals, leaves, stamen). However, the examinee used a key word in the Response Phase ("pretty"), which indicated the color of the blot might be an additional reason why it looks like a flower to the examinee. The examiner correctly queried this word to see if the examinee was using color as part of the original response, and the response to the query (Inquiry-2) showed that the examinee was. If the examiner had not queried, he or she would not know the examinee was using color in the response and would have been unable to code it. The examiner would have been missing an important piece of information.

Of course, inquiring about a key word does not always lead to additional information to code. Here is the same inquiry with a different outcome:

Response: It is a pretty flower.
Examiner repeats examinee's response.
Inquiry-1: Yes, here (points). It's the whole thing. Here are the petals, the leaves, and the, oh what do they call it, um, the stamen, yes that's it.
You said it was pretty?
Inquiry-2: Yeah, because it's a flower.

Here, the examiner correctly queried the word "pretty" because it is a key word that indicates the examinee may have been using color. However, given the examinee's response to the question, the examinee was not using color as part of the response. Instead, the flower was said to be pretty because it was a flower, not because of the color (Inquiry-2).

It is also important to understand that there are some cases where key words do not need to be queried. For example, if the examinee has already explained why he or she used the key word, there is no need to query, as the additional querying will not provide any additional information. For example:

Response: It is a pretty flower.
Examiner repeats examinee's response.
Inquiry-1: Yes, here (points). It's the whole thing. The colors are beautiful and remind me of the flowers in my garden. Here are the petals, the leaves, and the, oh what do they call it, um, the stamen, yes that's it.

Here the examinee has already commented on the reason for using the word "pretty": the color. There is no need to inquire further about the key word because the examinee has already explained it.

In general, key words that appear in the Response Phase and in the examinee's first spontaneous response during the inquiry should be queried. Key words may appear later in the inquiry, but many of these do not need to be queried, as it would cause the examiner—and the examinee—to chase leads that are not there. For example, here is a response and an inquiry for Card III:

Response: Two women cooking.
Examiner repeats examinee's response.
Inquiry-1: Yeah.
Remember, I need to see it like you do.
Inquiry-2: Oh sorry, I thought it was obvious. Here's one here and the other here. Heads, breasts, backs, legs, feet, looks like they are wearing high heels.
You said they were cooking?
Inquiry-3: Yeah. I don't know why I said that. This looks like a pot. Maybe this is fire.
It looks like fire?
Inquiry-4: I guess so, it's red. Maybe this is a decoration of some sort. . .

The examiner's query of cooking leads to the examinee saying that something "maybe" fire. The examinee is not certain of it, yet the examiner continues to query, and the examinee finally says that it is fire because it is red. Here, the examiner has induced a determinant (a *why*) that the examinee did not appear to initially be using. The query about fire was incorrect because the examinee was not certain that part of the blot was fire. However, had the examinee been certain of it, a query for fire would have been appropriate because it relates back to the women cooking.

There are some queries that are always inappropriate. These are leading questions, such as "Did you use color?" "Are they doing anything?" and "Do you see the bat too?" Some other questions are always inappropriate because they will not yield additional information for coding: for example, "Why is the dog feeling sad?" and "Are they boys or girls?"

Recording Location and Location Queries

Usually, the examinee will provide the location by pointing to it during the inquiry. This is one of the reasons why it is so important for examiners to attend to examinees' gestures as well as their verbalizations. However, there are times when the examinee does not indicate location during either the Response or the Inquiry Phase. In order to get this information (the *where*), the examiner then needs to query. The examiner could say something like "Where do you see that?" or "Show me the (insert response here)." In some cases, examiners may need to get more specific and ask examinees to trace the part of the blot they are using or to put their finger on it, but these types of queries should be avoided, if possible.

For each response, the examiner needs to record on the location sheet the location the examinee indicated. This is done by circling the area of the blot used, identifying by number the response the location is associated with, and identifying a few parts of the response to aid with coding. If the examinee is using the whole blot (coded as W) in a response, rather than circle the whole blot, the examiner simply needs to write that this response equals W (e.g., for Response 3, the coding would be 3 = W). I recommend recording no more than two or three responses per blot, because the blots on the location sheets are small and can get crowded with codes; this makes it difficult to determine which areas are associated with which response. An example of recorded locations on a simulated blot is shown in Figure 2.3.

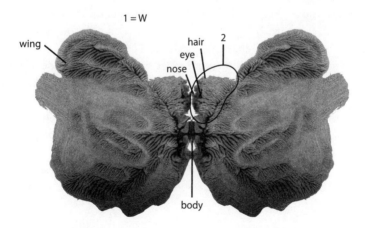

Figure 2.3 Example of Locations Recorded on a Simulated Blot
Note: Blot created by Zachary Hasson

NOTE

In Figure 2.3, Response 1 uses the whole blot (1 =W), and the examiner has recorded a few features of the response in order to aid with coding ("wing" and "body"). The location used by Response 2 is circled and is in the center part of the blot, to the right. The examiner has also recorded some features of this response to aid with coding ("hair," "eye," and "nose").

Troubleshooting the Inquiry Phase

Usually, the problems that arise in the Inquiry Phase are due to the examiner having difficulty knowing which questions to ask and when. However, there are times where the difficulty lies with the examinee and not the examiner. For instance, if the examinee is having difficulty understanding the directions and is not providing the *what*, *where*, and *why*, then the examiner should reexplain the purpose of the inquiry and answer the examinee's questions, then restart the Inquiry Phase. Sometimes, examinees say they can no longer see a response they provided in the Response Phase. When this happens, the examiner should encourage the examinee to take another look, and usually, the examinee is able to see the response again and explain it. In cases where examinees are unable to locate what they saw in the Response Phase, the examiner should code based on the information provided in the Response Phase. If there is not enough information to code location (*where*), then Dd99 should be entered as the location code. If there is not enough information to code the determinants (*why*), then a code of F should be used. CS coding is described in more detail in the next chapter.

At other times, examinees may state that they did not provide a particular answer. When this occurs, the examiner should be tactful, yet firm. If an examinee continues to insist that he or she did not provide that response, the response should be coded based on the information provided in the Response Phase, if possible. If location cannot be coded based on the information provided, it should be coded as Dd99. If the determinants cannot be coded based on the information provided, then a code of F should be entered. Please see Rapid Reference 2.5 for possible ways to respond to statements your examinee may make during the Inquiry Phase.

≋ Rapid Reference 2.5

Samples of Examinee Statements and Examiner Responses

Examinee Statement	Possible Examiner Response
Yes, that's right.	Remember, I need to see it like you do.
I don't know why it just looks like that to me.	I know it looks like that to you, but remember, I need to see it too. So help me. Tell me what in the blot makes it look like (insert response) to you.
Should I find other things too?	No, I'm only interested in what you saw before.
You see it too, right?	Remember, I need to see it how you see it.
I don't see it any more.	Try your best to find it again.
It doesn't look like that now.	Try to remember what about the blot made it look like (insert response).
I didn't say that. You recorded it wrong.	I wrote down everything you said. Let's find it again so you can show me.

Source: Adapted from Exner, 2003, pp. 59–63.

ACCOMMODATING INDIVIDUALS WITH DISABILITIES AND USING INTERPRETERS

Although examiners strive to follow standard procedure whenever possible, there are times when standard procedure needs to be altered to accommodate the examinee. Any alterations to standard procedure should be documented in progress notes and in the report produced based on the test results. The examiner also needs to keep in mind that interpretations that result from administrations based on altered procedures may not be accurate, as they are not based on standard procedures. This is true for any standardized test.

Like any other psychological test administration, the CS administration can be altered in order to accommodate testing for individuals with disabilities. For example, if the person being tested has severe attentional or memory deficits, and thus after a delay may not remember where he or she saw the response, the examiner may want to conduct the inquiry on a response right after the examinee provides that response. In other words, there would be a mini-inquiry after each response, rather than going through the entire Response Phase then the entire Inquiry Phase. This tactic can also be used with young children.

Although this situation is not ideal, the CS can be used with an interpreter. It is preferable to have the CS administered in the examinee's native language by a practitioner who speaks that language. However, this is not always an option, and an interpreter is used instead. If an interpreter is going to be used, the examiner should make sure that the interpreter is aware that everything needs to be translated as close to verbatim as possible. In most cases, the interpreter should be placed behind the examinee to reduce the chance that the interpreter's nonverbal reactions could influence testing. However, in the case of a sign language interpreter, the interpreter needs to sit across from the examinee, so the examinee can see the interpreter. If a sign language interpreter is not available, some research suggests that having the examinee write out his or her responses is a viable option (Schwartz, Mebane, & Malony, 1990).

CONCLUSION

CS administration can seem daunting, especially for a beginning examiner. With practice, administration will become more automatic and fluid. Administration also improves when the examiner has a thorough understanding of scoring, known as *coding* in the Rorschach. Coding is discussed in the following chapter.

🐟 TEST YOURSELF 🐟

. . . .

I. How many responses are needed for a valid CS Rorschach administration?

   a. 10

   b. 12

   c. 14

   d. 16

2. What do you need to administer a CS Rorschach test?

   a. Location sheets, paper, writing utensil, the ink blots.

   b. The ink blots, paper, pencil.

   c. Computer, the ink blots, paper.

   d. Location sheets, paper, writing utensil.

3. **What should you do if the examinee provides only one response to the first card?**

   a. Stop testing and use another test.

   b. Stop testing and go over the instructions again.

   c. Prompt for a second response.

   d. Go on to Card II.

4. **What things are you looking for in the Inquiry Phase?**

   a. Person, place, and location.

   b. What they saw, where they saw it, and why it looks like that to them.

   c. What they saw and why they saw it.

   d. Any additional responses they can provide.

5. **Which of the following is not an appropriate query to use during the Inquiry Phase?**

   a. I'm not sure I see it yet.

   b. You said it was evil?

   c. Show me the dog.

   d. Why is the person sad?

6. **True or False: You have to record everything the examinee says verbatim during the administration of the CS.**

   a. True

   b. False

Answers: 1. c; 2. a; 3. c; 4. b; 5. d; 6. a.

Three

COMPREHENSIVE SYSTEM SCORING

L earning scoring, known in Rorschach circles as *coding*, is much like learning a new language. There are multiple categories to code, such as location and determinants, each with its own set of variables. In fact, there are over 100 variables on the Comprehensive System to code, and they are used to calculate over 50 interpreted variables or ratios. Clearly, there is a great deal of room for error. This, combined with the fact that applying many of the scoring criteria does rely, at least somewhat, on the clinical judgment of the examiner, can make scoring seem overwhelming, especially for the beginning Rorschach examiner.

In this chapter, the reader will find a description of each of the coding categories with its respective variables. There are also hints throughout this chapter to help the reader code as accurately as possible, along with resources to increase the likelihood of accurate coding. Some of these resources are in the Book Companion Website Materials. Additionally, this chapter contains a variety of examples of responses with their codings.

The different variables are coded on a coding form. These forms are commercially available; however, many individuals have created their own. An example of a coding form is displayed in Figure 3.1; this form is also available as part of the Book Companion Website Materials.

Card	Resp#	Loc	DQ	Loc#	Determinants	FQ	(2)	Contents	Pop	Z Score	Cognitive Special Scores	Content Special Scores

Figure 3.1 Example of a Coding Sheet for Coding the CS

LOCATION

In the Inquiry Phase, examiners request that examinees tell them *what* they saw, *where* they saw it, and *why* it looks like that. The location codes represent the *where*. These codes are listed in Rapid Reference 3.1.

The D and Dd areas for each blot can be found in a variety of resources, including Exner (2001, 2003) and Viglione (2010). Thus there is no need for an examiner to memorize the D and Dd areas for each blot, although examiners who frequently code Rorschachs will likely find that they start memorizing frequently used D and Dd areas.

Each location code also has a number associated with it. W location codes always have the number 1; D location codes have numbers ranging from 1 to 15; and Dd location codes are assigned numbers of 21 and higher. Again, there is no need to memorize these numbers. Although not included in this book, they can be readily found in a variety of sources, including Exner (2001, 2003).

W: Whole Blot

A W is coded whenever the examinee uses the whole inked part of the blot in a response. The response does not have to use any of the white space to receive

≡ Rapid Reference 3.1

Location Codes

Code	Name	Description
W	Whole	Examinee uses entire blot in response.
D	Common Detail	Examinee uses a common detail area for the response (i.e., an area that tends to be used with some frequency).
Dd	Uncommon Detail	Examinee uses an uncommon detail area for the response (i.e., an area that is not frequently used in responses).
S	Space Response	Examinee uses white space in the response. This code does not stand alone and must be attached to a W, D, or Dd (e.g., WS).

Source: Based on information from Exner, 2001, 2003.

a code of W; however, the response does need to use the entire blot. If the examinee excludes any part of the blot, no matter how small, then the response is no longer a W and will instead be coded D or Dd, depending on the areas being used.

Sometimes examinees will state that they are using the entire blot ("It's the whole thing") but not always. Consider the following examples of responses to Card I:

Example 1

Response: It's a bat.

Examiner repeats examinee's response.

Inquiry-1: Yes, it's the whole thing. Head here, wings, body (points).

Coding: Wo1 Fo A P ZW

Example 2

Response: It's a bat.

Examiner repeats examinee's response.

Inquiry-1: Head here, wing, body (points).

Coding: Wo1 Fo A P ZW

In the first example, the examinee clearly states that he or she is using the entire blot, making coding the location easy for the examiner. However, in the second response, the examinee does not specifically state which parts of the blot are used in the response. Instead, the examiner needs to determine, based on where the examinee was pointing, what the code is. In this case, based on the examinee's gestures during the inquiry phase, the examinee was most likely using the entire blot, so W is the appropriate code.

There are times when it initially seems that an examinee is using the entire blot, but then during the inquiry, the examinee specifically excludes parts of the blot. If an examinee clearly excludes any part of the blot, no matter how small, the response should not be coded W. Here is an example:

Response (Card I): It's a bat.

Examiner repeats examinee's response.

Inquiry-1: Head, wings, body. It's everything but this part (points to Dd23).

Coding: Ddo99 Fo A

Here the examinee specifically describes not using the entire blot. Even though the excluded part of the blot is very small (Dd23; see Exner, 2003, for this location), because the examinee is not using the entire blot, the response no longer meets the criteria for a W. In this case, the correct coding is Dd.

D: Common Detail

If the response does not meet criteria for a W location code, it will be coded either a D or a Dd. The D codes, or common details, are areas of a blot that were used in at least 5 percent of the responses of a sample of 3,000 protocols (Exner, 2003). These areas tend to be large, but are not always so. Do not make an assumption that a large area is a D area; some large areas are Dd areas while others are D. It is important that examiners check the location areas in Exner (2003) or another source to determine whether an area is a D or a Dd area.

Dd: Uncommon Detail

Uncommon details, in contrast, are areas of a blot that were used in fewer than 5 percent of the responses in the sample of 3,000 protocols. These areas, with their associated numbers, can be found in a variety of sources, as mentioned earlier in this chapter.

S: Space Response

The fourth code—S, or space response—is not a stand-alone code. This code is added to a W, D, or Dd code whenever the examinee uses white space in a response. For example, if the examinee uses the entire inked part of the blot and also white space in the blot, the response is coded WS. If the examinee uses a D area with white space, the response is coded DS, and so forth.

Examinees do not need to use any inked space in their responses. It is possible for an examinee to provide a response that is located entirely in white space. Consequently, there are some D and Dd areas that are only white space. As an example, there is a large, noninked area in the middle of Card VII. According to the location tables available in Exner (2003), this area is DS7. The fact that it is a D area indicates that a significant number of people (at least 5%) in the large sample of protocols analyzed by Exner (2003) used this area as a response.

Difficulty in Determining Location Codes

Generally, location is relatively easy to code. Each response will have one, and only one, location code. However, in some cases determining a location code can become difficult. A few of these scenarios are described here. For additional assistance in coding locations, Viglione (2010) is an excellent resource.

One difficulty beginning Rorschach examiners often face is determining a location code when the examinee's response location does not match any of the ones in Exner (2003). This means that so few people used that area in their response that it did not even make it onto the location charts. When an area is very rarely used, it will be assigned a Dd location, and it will be given the number 99, to designate that the examinee used a part of the blot not located in the location tables. So the location code will be Dd99.

Another difficulty often faced is that the individual's response encompasses multiple objects, each with its own discrete area. If the examinee uses the entire blot, as in the case of the following example, the response is coded as a W.

> Response (Card X): It's an underwater scene. Here's some fish, sharks, seahorses, and coral. It's the whole thing.
>
> *Examiner repeats examinee's response.*
>
> Inquiry-1: Yeah, see here are the crabs holding some seaweed, the fish, the seahorses, sharks, and the rest is coral (waves hand over card). The shapes remind me of those sea creatures and of seaweed.
>
> *Coding: W + 1 FMpo 2 A, Bt P ZW*

In this case, although the examinee reported a number of objects, they were all organized into one response that used the entire blot. The appropriate location coding for this response is W.

However, there are also times when the individual's response contains multiple objects, but the response does not include the entire area. In this case, the response will be coded D or Dd. In order to decide which coding is appropriate, the examiner should look at each of the location codes for the individual objects in the response. For example:

> Response (Card II): It looks like a spaceship taking off.
>
> *Examiner repeats examinee's response.*
>
> Inquiry-1: Here (points to DS5 and D3). This is the spaceship, here, it's white like shuttles are, and this part here is the fire from the launch. The red reminded me of fire.
>
> *Coding: DS + 5 ma.CF.C'Fo Sc, Fi ZS*

The location being used is a Dd area, a combination of the white and the red parts of the blot. However, in the response, the examinee identified two separate objects: the spaceship/shuttle and the fire. The spaceship is in area DS5 and the fire is in area D3. As these are two discrete objects in two different D areas, the examiner should credit the examinee with using a D area. The correct coding for this response is DS5 or DS3; either location number would be correct.

In general, the rule is that if the objects the examinee describes in the response are all in separate D areas, the response is coded D. If the objects the examinee describes in the response are all in separate Dd areas, the response is coded Dd. The difficulty arises when the examinee reports seeing separate objects located in both D and Dd areas. In general, such a response is coded Dd (Viglione, 2010).

DQ: DEVELOPMENTAL QUALITY

Developmental quality (DQ) is the quality of the cognitive organization of the objects in the response. It is not about whether the examinee's verbalizations are organized; the DQ code applies to the level of organization and sophistication in the objects that the examinee reports in the response. Responses can range from very vague, such as seeing "dirt," to a high level of organization and sophistication, such as "two people playing baseball." In the first example, "dirt," the response does not take on any specific shape and there are no specific features. In other words, the response object is not well formed. In contrast, the second response contains multiple well-formed objects—the people and the baseball—in a relationship. This response shows a high level of cognitive organization and sophistication.

Each response will have only one DQ code, which is recorded in the DQ column of the coding sheet. There are four DQ codes; they are presented in order of decreasing cognitive organization in Rapid Reference 3.2.

≡ *Rapid Reference 3.2*

Developmental Quality Codes

Code	Name	Description	Example
+	Synthesized	Examinee sees at least two objects in a relationship and at least one has form demand.	Two people playing baseball.
o	Ordinary	Examinee sees one object with form demand.	A person.
v/+	Vague/ Synthesized	Examinee sees at least two objects in a relationship, but none of the objects have form demand.	Water hitting the shore.
v	Vague	Examinee sees one object without form demand.	Blood.

Source: Based on information from Exner, 2001, 2003.

≋ Rapid Reference 3.3

DQ Codes: Form Demand and Relationship Presence or Absence

	Relationship Present	Relationship Absent
Form Demand Present	Synthesized (+)	Ordinary (o)
Form Demand Absent	Vague/Synthesized (v/+)	Vague (v)

Source: Based on information from Exner, 2001, 2003.

DQ codes can be described as assessing two parts of a response: the presence or absence of specific features (form demand) and the presence or absence of a relationship. The chart in Rapid Reference 3.3 shows each code in relation to these two parts.

Form Demand

The primary characteristic that distinguishes the vague codes (v, v/+) from the organized codes (o, +) is the presence of form demand. An item has form demand if an outline of it is easily recognizable: if it has a set structure. One way to determine whether something has form demand is to visualize the object but take away any color or texture associated with it, focusing just on the outline of the object. If you can identify the object by just its outline, then it probably has form demand. However, if you are unable to identify the object by seeing just an outline of it, then the object probably does not have form demand.

For example, a bird has form demand and would be classified as an organized response. In general, all birds have a similar set of organizing features; specifically, birds have heads, beaks, wings, and so forth. However, not all birds look alike. An ostrich, for example, looks very different from a robin. Still, an outline of either a robin or an ostrich is easily recognizable as a bird. As there is a set structure for a bird that contains a specific set of features, a response naming a bird is classified as having an organized level of DQ and generally would be coded as having an ordinary (o) or a synthesized (+) DQ. The organized codes (o, +) have form demand.

Vague (v, v/+) codes, in contrast, are assigned to responses that contain objects that have no specific features. There is no set structure for these responses. When you picture one of these objects in your mind, they generally do not take a specific shape; instead the focus tends to be on the color or the texture of the object. Some examples of objects usually given vague DQ codes are dirt, blood, and water. Although these objects have defining characteristics—dirt is usually brown, blood is red, and so forth—none have a specific set shape. It would be virtually impossible to recognize an outline of these objects as the object in question. The structure of the object is not sufficient to identify the object; we need the other distinguishing characteristics (e.g., color) to identify the object. These types of objects are usually classified as vague (v) or vague/synthesized (v/+).

DON'T FORGET

An object has form demand if you can identify the object by its structure; if you remove color, texture, and so forth, you can still identify the object. If you need other factors, like color, to identify the object, then the object probably does not have form demand.

Examinees can interject form demand into a vague object. For example, if the response is that the blot looks like "a ball of dirt," that response should be coded as being ordinary, an organized code. By interjecting a specific form ("a ball"), the examinee has provided an increased level of organization and the coding should reflect that.

Relationship

The primary difference between the synthesized codes (+, v/+) and the nonsynthesized codes (o, v) is the presence of a relationship. The bar for a relationship on the CS is relatively low; the objects need only be interacting in a relatively minor way for there to be a relationship. Additionally, an object on the CS is anything that is visualized on the blot. Thus, if the examinee sees "magic" on the blot and gives it a location, it can count as an object. Examples of responses that should receive a DQ synthesized code follow:

It is two people singing together (DQ = +).
It is water hitting the shore (DQ = v/+).
It looks like two girls hanging on monkey bars (DQ = +).
It looks like a shuttle taking off. Here is the exhaust (DQ = +).

Just having more than one object in the response is not sufficient for a synthesized coding. In order to receive a synthesized code, the objects need to be in some sort of relationship. So if the examinee states the blot looks like "two people," that is not sufficient for a synthesized DQ coding because the objects ("two people") are not in any sort of relationship. However, "two people talking to each other" is a synthesized response (DQ = +).

Summary of DQ Codes

Each response will have one DQ code. Vague (v) codes are assigned to responses where none of the objects has a form demand and there is no relationship between objects. An example of this is "clouds" or "dirt." Vague/synthesized (v/+) codes are assigned to responses where none of the objects have form demand but there is a relationship between objects. An example of this is "water hitting the shore." Neither water nor shore has a form demand, but they are in a relationship, which is why the v/+ code is appropriate. Ordinary (o) codes are assigned when the object in the response has a form demand but there is no relationship between objects. An example of this type of response is "dog" or "chair." Finally, the synthesized (+) code is assigned when there are at least two objects in a response that are in a relationship and at least one of these objects has a form demand. An example of this type of response is "a shuttle taking off. Here is the exhaust." The shuttle, which has a form demand, is in a relationship with the exhaust, which does not. Because at least one object has a form demand, a synthesized (+) code is appropriate. Only one object in the relationship needs to have a form demand for the response to be coded as synthesized.

In the Book Companion Website Materials, there is a flowchart that can be used to help examiners decide which DQ to assign. It is important to remember that only one DQ is assigned per response.

DETERMINANTS

The determinants represent the *why* of the Inquiry Phase. These codes represent why the object the examinee saw looked like it to them. There are multiple determinants, and they are divided into seven categories: form, movement, color, achromatic color, shading, form-based dimensionality, and symmetry. Unlike location and DQ codes, multiple determinants can be coded in the same response. A response with two or more determinants is referred to as a *blend*, and in a coding list, the different determinant codes are separated by periods (e.g., *ma.CF.CF*).

An excellent understanding of determinants is necessary for a good inquiry, as the determinants represent the *why* of the inquiry. The key words referenced in Chapter 2 of this book can be useful here, because these words may indicate the presence of a determinant (e.g., "night" may indicate the use of achromatic color). Similarly, a good understanding of determinants will assist the examiner to better identify key words. A list of all the determinants, as well as key words that may be associated with them, is given in Rapid Reference 3.4.

≡ Rapid Reference 3.4

Determinants

Code	Name	Description	Examples of Possible Key Words
F	Form	Examinee uses shape of the blot.	Words used in pointing out different parts.
Ma Mp Ma-p	Human Movement	Examinee sees human movement in the response.	Any movement word.
FMa FMp FMa-p	Animal Movement	Examinee sees animal movement in the response.	Any movement word.
ma mp ma-p	Inanimate Object Movement	Examinee sees inanimate object movement in the response.	Any movement word.
C CF FC	Color	Examinee uses chromatic color to explain why it looks like that to them.	Pretty. Blood. Grassy.
Cn	Color Naming	Examinee simply names the color(s) on the card.	Names of colors.
C'	Achromatic Color	Examinee uses achromatic color (black, white, or gray) to explain why it looks like that to them.	Darker. Night. Evil. Bright.
T TF FT	Texture	Examinee uses shading in the blot to indicate a tactile sensation.	Bumpy. Soft. Cold.
V VF FV	Vista (shading-based dimensionality)	Examinee uses shading in the blot to indicate dimensionality.	Deeper. Farther away. Looking down.
Y YF FY	Diffuse Shading	Examinee uses shading in the blot, but no dimensionality or texture.	Smoky. Bright. Dark.
FD	Form Dimension	Examinee uses dimensionality in the blot, but due to the structure of the blot rather than shading.	Deeper. Farther Away. Looking down.
rF Fr	Reflection	Examinee uses reflection or a mirror image, based on the symmetry of the blot.	Mirror image. Reflection. Water.

Source: Based on information from Exner, 2001, 2003.

F: Form

When examinees are relying on the shape of the blot to explain why the blot looks that way to them, they are using Form (F). Occasionally, examinees will state that the response looks that way to them because of the shape, but more often, they point out parts of the blot that look like parts of their response. Consider the following response:

Response (Card IX): It looks like a flower.
Examiner repeats examinee's response.
Inquiry-1: Petals, stem, leaves (points to whole card).
Coding: Wo1 Fo Bt ZW

Although the examinee never mentions using the shape, the fact that the examinee points out different aspects of the response—in this case, the petals, stem, and leaves—indicates that form is being used.

Form is rarely involved in a blend. Instead, form is usually subsumed in another determinant. These instances are described throughout this chapter.

CAUTION

Form is rarely in a blend. It is usually a stand-alone determinant or subsumed in another determinant (such as color-form).

Movement

Examinees sometimes report seeing movement in the blot. This does not mean that they see the inked areas physically moving; rather, it means that something about the blot causes them to perceive movement. This can include human movement (M), animal movement (FM), and inanimate object movement (m). A list of the movement codes, along with a brief description and some examples, can be found in Rapid Reference 3.5.

All movement is also classified as either being active (a) or passive (p), which has traditionally been coded as a superscript next to the movement determinant (e.g., M^a). However, it has now become common to write a movement code without the superscript (e.g., Ma), which is the practice followed in this book. The distinction between active and passive is discussed later in this section.

It is important to remember that form is assumed with movement. Consequently, there is no need to code form when you code human movement; in fact, it would be a mistake to do so.

≡ Rapid Reference 3.5

Movement Codes

Code	Name	When Used	Examples
M	Human Movement	Examinee sees human movement. Sees disembodied emotions. Sees an animal engaging in movement not consistent with its species. Sees an inanimate object engaging in movement not typical for the object.	A man standing. Two people fighting. Depression. A dog buying groceries. A flying paper clip. A tree dancing around some children. A snake flying through the air.
FM	Animal Movement	Examinee sees an animal engaging in movement that is consistent with its species.	A dog barking. A slithering snake. That bat is flying.
m	Inanimate Object Movement	Examinee sees an inanimate object moving in a way that is consistent with the object.	A flag flying. A bleeding heart. A launching shuttle.

Source: Based on information from Exner, 2001, 2003.

Human Movement (M) is coded whenever the examinee reports seeing human movement, such as a person walking, in a response. However, the human movement code is used in other cases as well. Emotions, such as depression, are coded as human movement. Animals engaging in movement that is not typical of their species, such as a snake that is flying, are also coded as human movement. This is done to reflect the human fantasy that went into the response. Finally, an inanimate object that is engaging in movement inconsistent with that object, such as a tree that is dancing, is also coded as human movement. Refer to Rapid Reference 3.5 for examples of responses that should be coded as having human movement.

Animal Movement (FM) is coded when an animal that is moving is identified in the response. However, in order to be coded as animal movement on the CS, the animal needs to be engaging in a movement that is consistent with the abilities of its species. So, "a snake slithering on the ground" is coded FMa whereas "a snake flying through the air" is coded Ma. Viglione (2010) has suggested that animals experiencing emotions that are consistent with their species should be coded as animal movement. Using this approach, "A happy dog wagging its tail" would be coded FMa. This covers both the emotion and the movement of the dog wagging its tail. However, "a happy dog toasting the bride and groom" would be coded Ma, as "toasting the bride and groom" is not consistent with what a dog would normally do when happy.

Inanimate Object Movement (m) is coded whenever an inanimate object is moving in the response. Inanimate objects are anything that is not either human or an animal and thus include a variety of things, such as staplers, plants, and weapons. So a "gun firing" is coded ma. However, if the animate object is engaging in an activity that is not consistent with the object, such as "a flower dancing," the response is coded as a human movement response (Ma), to reflect the fantasy that went into the creation of the response.

CAUTION

If you are typing your coding, be aware that many word processing programs will automatically capitalize the letter "m" when it is inserted as a single letter. Be sure to check your coding to make sure your word processing software has not changed your inanimate object movement code (m) to a human movement code (M)!

Active Versus Passive Movement

Determining whether a movement is active or passive is one of the more difficult aspects of coding. The rule is that "talking" is the most active of the passive movements. Thus, "talking" is coded as passive and anything more active than talking, such as "yelling" is coded as active. Exner (2003, pp. 92–94) and others (e.g., Holaday, 1997) have conducted research on the determination of active and passive movement and have provided lists of movement responses and how their participants coded them. These lists can be beneficial in determining whether a movement is active or passive. Still, examiners need to keep in mind that they need to evaluate the whole response, and not just the movement word, in determining whether a movement is active or passive. As an example, "praying" is generally coded as passive, but a "person praying, look how excited they are! They are waving their arms in the air," would be coded as active because it has an active component to it ("waving their arms in the air").

Multiple Movements in the Same Response

There are times where an examinee reports seeing multiple movements in the response. In general, if they are different types of movement from different objects, such as an animal and a human, then both types of movement will be coded. For example:

> Response (Card I): A person with a dog.
> *Examiner repeats examinee's response.*
> Inquiry-1: It looks like a person (points to D4) running with her dog (points to D2). The dog is running with her. His tail is here (points to Dd33). This is his ear (points to Dd34).
> *Coding: D + 4 Ma.FMao H, A, ZA GHR*

In this response there are two separate types of movements coming from different objects: human movement ("a person running," Ma) and animal movement ("the dog is running," FMa). As a result, both human movement and animal movement are coded.

At times, people may see one object engaging in two different movements, such as "a person jumping rope and talking to these people." In this case, typically only one movement, the most active movement, is coded. So for the response "a person jumping rope and talking to these people," the correct determinant is Ma, as one of the movements (jumping) is active. The other movement, talking, is passive. We want to give credit for the active movement when it is present, so the correct determinant is Ma.

There is a set of rarely used movement codes: Ma-p, FMa-p, and ma-p. These codes are used when there are two objects of the same type, such as two humans, engaging in different movements in the same response. This code is rarely used, as it requires two separate objects in the same response engaging in different movements. Here is an example:

> Response (Card II): It looks like a mother bear and her cub. See here, the cub is sleeping.
> *Examiner repeats examinee's response.*
> Inquiry-1: Mother bear here (points to D1), cub here (points to D1, other side). The mother bear is protecting her cub, see, she's growling.
> *Coding: D + 1 FMapo A P ZA AG PHR*

In this case there are two separate objects, each engaging in its own movement (the mother and the cub), with one engaging in an active movement (the mother, growling) and the other engaging in a passive movement (the cub, sleeping). The correct code is FMa-p.

Color

The chromatic color codes are used when the examinee is relying on the chromatic parts of the blot to explain a response. These codes are used only when the examinee explicitly states that color was important to the nature of the response; simply seeing something that is typically colored, such as a flower, is not enough to code color. The examinee needs to state that the color was a factor in seeing the item. These codes are not used when the examinee is relying on the color white, black, or gray in the response; white, black, and gray are referred to as achromatic colors and are discussed later in this chapter.

There are four color determinants: Pure Color (C), Color-Form (CF), Form-Color (FC), and Color Naming (Cn). Of these determinants, Cn is the rarest. Color naming and pure color responses are generally readily identifiable; however, distinguishing between a color-form and a form-color response can be difficult. It is important to distinguish between these two codes, as there is an interpretive significance, which will be discussed in the next chapter.

C: Pure Color

When examinees are using the color of the blot only to explain why they saw what they saw, the appropriate determinant is Pure Color (C). Here are two examples of this type of response:

Example 1 (Card II)

Response: Blood. Here (points to D2).
Examiner repeats examinee's response.
Inquiry-1: It's red, so I thought blood.
Coding: Dv2 C Bl

Example 2 (Card X)

Response: Happiness.
Examiner repeats examinee's response.
Inquiry-1: All of the colors (waves hand over card). It looks like what happy would look like if I could visualize it.
Coding: Wv1 Mp.C Hx AB PHR

In the second example, Pure Color (C) is blended with human movement, because the person reported seeing a human emotion ("happiness"), which is coded Mp.

CF: Color-Form

The color-form determinant is used when examinees use both the chromatic color of the blot and the shape of the blot to explain why they saw what they saw. However, the color of the blot is more important to their response than the shape is. Occasionally an examinee will specifically state whether color or shape is more important, but more often than not, the examiner will need to decide which is more important, based on the examinee's verbalizations and gestures.

Response (Card IX): The whole thing is beautiful flower, a rose.

Examiner repeats examinee's response.

Inquiry-1: See the beautiful colors? All the pinks, oranges, and greens? They are lovely. The green is the leaves and the pink and orange are the petals.

Coding: Wo1 CFo Bt ZW

Here, in the response, the examinee provided a key word ("beautiful"). Had the examinee not gone on to explain why the flower was beautiful (e.g., "the beautiful colors"), we would have wanted to query the word, "beautiful," to see if the examinee was using color. The examinee does not mention shape until the very end ("leaves," "petals"). According to these verbalizations, color is more salient than shape, so the determinant should be a CF.

FC: Form-Color

Like the Color-Form (CF) code, the Form-Color (FC) code is used when examinees use both the chromatic color of the blot and the shape of the blot to explain why they saw what they saw. However, in this case, the shape of the blot is more important to their response than the color is.

Response (Card IX): It is a flower.

Examiner repeats examinee's response.

Inquiry-1: It's a rose. See, here are the petals, the leaves. I guess I thought leaves because they are green.

Coding: Wo1 FCo Bt ZW

There is no color key word in the response, and the examinee does not mention color until the end of the inquiry ("leaves because they are green"). In this case, the shape of the blot is more important to the nature of the response than color is, so the appropriate coding is FC.

Cn: Color-Naming

The Color Naming (Cn) determinant is the rarest of the color determinants. This determinant is used when examinees name only colors as their response. They do not see anything else; they name the color, or colors, then either return the card or move on to their next response. It is important that the examiner distinguish between causal comments and a true color naming response; consider these examples:

Example 1 (Card VIII)

Response: It's pink.

Examiner repeats examinee's response.

Inquiry-1: Yeah, it's pink. Here.

Coding: Dv1 Cn Art

Example 2 (Card VIII)

Response: It's pink! It's a lion. A pink lion.

Examiner repeats examinee's response.

Inquiry-1: Yeah, the lion is pink. Here (points). See here are the legs, head, and feet.

Coding: *Do1 FCo A P INCOM1*

In the first case, the examinee's entire response is that the card is pink. No other response or information is provided, so Cn is an appropriate code. However, in the second response, the examinee's initial comment about color is likely a reaction to the card ("It's pink."), and it is followed up immediately with a response. The inquiry also makes it very clear that the examinee does not intend "it's pink" to be a response, as that comment is integrated with the mention of the lion. In this case, a Cn determinant is not appropriate.

Step-Down Principle

There are some cases where a C determinant is coded as a CF rather than a C. This occurs owing to the *step-down principle*. Whenever an object that should have a C determinant touches something with form, the determinant is stepped down to a CF. For example:

Response (Card II): It's two bears fighting.

Examiner repeats examinee's response.

Inquiry-1: Here's one (points to D1) and here's the other (points to D1, other side). They're injured. This is blood here (points to D3).

You said it was blood?

Inquiry-2: Yeah, it's red.

Coding: *D + 1 FMa.CFo 2 A, Bl P ZA AG, MOR PHR*

In this case, the blood is blood because it is red, which would normally be coded as a C determinant. However, the blood is touching something with form (the bear), so the determinant is stepped down to a CF.

Color as a Locator

Color can also be used as a locator rather than as a determinant. For example, examinees may say, "this red could be a flower," but it could be unclear whether they are using color as a determinant to support their response of a flower or simply as a locator code (e.g., this spot, which happens to be red, looks like a flower). In the second case, the color does not matter; they are using color only to indicate which part of the blot they are using. In order to determine whether an examinee is using color as a determinant or a locator, the examiner needs to query. An appropriate query would be, "You said it was red?"

Color Convergence Principle

There are some cases where it is acceptable for an examiner to assume that color is being used as a determinant and not solely as a locator. This is owing to the *principle of color convergence*; if the color being used is consistent with the object being reported in that area, then the assumption is that color is a determinant. Some examples of this are

> This green could be grass.
> This red is blood.

CAUTION

. . . .

The color convergence principle can be applied only when the examinee names the color and the object in the area is prototypically that color. It cannot be used with objects that do not have a typical color, such as flowers. Flowers can have many colors, so being "red" or "purple" is not enough to code color using the color convergence principle.

In both cases, the color of the part of the blot the examinee is using is consistent with the expected color of the object (blood is red; grass is usually green). This principle can be used when there are colors that are strongly associated with an object and the examinee verbalizes the color. Thus, if the examinee does not verbalize the color ("This spot could be blood"), then there is no color convergence. There still may be a color determinant, but the examinee would have to provide additional information indicating the use of color. The color convergence principle cannot be used when an object does not have a specific color, so "this purple could be a flower" should still be queried to determine whether color is being used as a locator or a determinant.

Achromatic Color

The achromatic color codes—Pure Achromatic Color (C'), Achromatic Color-Form (C'F), and Form-Achromatic Color (FC')—are used when the examinees are relying on the achromatic parts of the blot to explain their response. Black, gray, and white are considered to be achromatic colors. These codes are used only when the examinee explicitly states that achromatic color is important to the nature of the response, so using white space is not sufficient to code an achromatic color code.

DON'T FORGET

Using white space is not sufficient to code an achromatic color code. Examinees must explicitly say (or strongly imply via the *determinant convergence principle*) that an achromatic color was a reason why they saw what they saw in the blot.

Unlike the color codes, where it is vital to distinguish between pure color, color-form, and form-color, differentiation among pure achromatic color, achromatic color-form, and form-achromatic color is less important. This is because all three codes are interpreted the same way in the CS.

C': Pure Achromatic Color
The Pure Achromatic Color (C') code is used when examinees are relying only on achromatic color to explain their response; they are not using form. Here are some examples:

Example 1 (Card V)
Response: It's night.
Examiner repeats examinee's response.
Inquiry-1: It's black. The whole thing.
Coding: Wv1 C' Na

Example 2 (Card II)
Response: This part reminds me of snow (points to DS5).
Examiner repeats examinee's response.
Inquiry-1: It's white. That's it.
Coding: DSv5 C' Na

In both cases, form is not used at all. The appropriate determinant for both is C'.

C'F and FC': Achromatic Color-Form and Form-Achromatic Color
The Achromatic Color-Form (C'F) and Form-Achromatic Color (FC') codes are used when examinees use both the achromatic color of the blot and the shape of the blot to explain why the blot looks like that to them. Unlike the CF and the FC codes, which are interpreted differently, the C'F and FC' codes are interpreted the same way. Consequently, it is not essential to distinguish between a C'F and a FC', although many clinicians continue to do so. Here are two examples of these codes:

Example 1 (Card I)

Response: It is an evil woman (points to D4).

Examiner repeats examinee's response.

Inquiry-1: Here are her hands, dress, legs.

You said she was evil?

Inquiry-2: Everything she's wearing is black. See, the black dress here (traces shape).

Coding: D + 4 FC'o H, Cg ZA GHR

Example 2 (Card V)

Response: A black bat.

Examiner repeats examinee's response.

Inquiry-1: It's black, so I thought bat. Wings here. Head here (points).

Coding: Wo1 C'Fo A P ZW

In the first case, the examiner queried a key word ("evil"). The word "evil" suggests possibly that the examinee is using achromatic color, as things that are evil are often seen as being dark or wearing dark clothes. The inquiry resulted in the examinee verbalizing her use of achromatic color ("Everything she's wearing is black") and the shape of the blot ("hands, dress, legs"). In this case, a code of either FC' or C'F is appropriate, as both are interpreted the same way.

In the second example, the examinee immediately verbalized that the bat was black and then reinforced it during the inquiry. In this case, a determinant of either C'F or FC' is appropriate because it is clear that the examinee is relying on both the achromatic color of the blot and the shape for her response.

Light and Dark

When using achromatic color, examinees do not always use the words "black," "gray," or "white." Instead, they sometimes use the terms "light" and "dark." However, these terms can also be used to indicate shading (discussed in the next section). If the examiner is confident that the use of the term light or dark is meant to indicate achromatic color, then the response should be coded as a C', C'F, or FC', as appropriate. However, if the examiner is not certain, then the response should be queried. If even after querying it is still not clear, then the response should be coded as diffuse shading (Y; discussed in next section). Here are two examples to demonstrate the difference:

Example 1 (Card I)

Response: It is a scary mask.

Examiner repeats examinee's response.

Inquiry-1: Here are the eye holes (points to DdS30), these are the cheeks (points to bottom half of D2), here is an ear (points to D7), another ear (points to D7 other side), the mouth hole (points to DdS29).
I'm not sure what makes it look scary.
Inquiry-2: It's dark.
Coding: WSo1 FC'o (Hd) GHR

Example 2 (Card VII)

Response: It looks like a sunrise.
Examiner repeats examinee's response.
Inquiry-1: The light and the dark colors make it look like the sun is rising. This is the sun (points to DS7).
I'm not sure I see it like you do.
Inquiry-2: I don't know how else to explain it. The light and dark remind me of a sunrise.
Coding: WSv1 ma.YF– Na

In the first example, the way the examinee explains the response indicates that "dark" is being used as a color. There is no indication of using shading. In the second example, it is still unclear whether the phrase "the light and the dark colors" refers to colors or shading. In this case, a code of diffuse shading is appropriate.

Achromatic Color as a Locator

Like chromatic color, achromatic color can be used as a locator rather than a determinant. For example, an examinee can say, "this white could be a ballerina." It is unclear whether achromatic color is being used as a determinant to support the response of a ballerina or whether achromatic color is simply a locator code (e.g., this spot, which happens to be white, looks like a ballerina). In order to determine whether an examinee was using achromatic color as a determinant or a locator, the examiner would need to query.

The principle of color convergence also applies here. If the achromatic color being used is consistent with the object being reported in that area, then the assumption is that achromatic color is a determinant. Some examples of this are

This white is snow.
This gray is a storm cloud.

In both cases, the achromatic color of the part of the blot the examinee is using is consistent with the expected color of the object.

Rapid Reference 3.6 lists the achromatic color and the shading codes.

≣ Rapid Reference 3.6

Achromatic Color and the Shading Codes

Code	Name	When Used	Examples
C'	Achromatic Color	Examinee is using black, white, or gray to explain why the response looks the way it does.	Black bat. This white is snow. Gray cloud. Evil witch wearing all black.
C'F			
F'C			
T	Texture	Examinee is using shading to indicate texture.	Fuzzy tail. Spikey hat. Hot lava.
TF			
FT			
V	Vista (shading-based dimensionality)	Examinee is using shading to indicate dimensionality.	Carvings. Deep cavern.
VF			
FV			
Y	Diffuse Shading	Examinee is using shading, but it is not related to texture or dimensionality.	Smoke. Bright eye.
YF			
FY			

Source: Based on information from Exner, 2001, 2003.

Shading

There are three types of shading determinants: Texture (T), Dimensionality (Vista, V), and Diffuse (Y). Although they are all interpreted differently, they do have a few things in common. First, all require the use of shading in order to code. For instance, examinees simply stating that they saw a texture is not sufficient to code T; the examinee needs to have seen texture in the blot due to the shading in the blot rather than for other reasons (e.g., the shape of the blot). Another thing all these codes have in common is that, as for achromatic codes, the presence of form does not affect the way the variable is interpreted. Thus, a T is interpreted the same way as a TF and an FT. Consequently, it is not essential to distinguish between a TF and FT, a YF and FY, or a VF and FV.

Shading as Texture

Texture is coded when the examinee is using the shading present in the blot to indicate a texture or tactile sensation (e.g., heat, cold). Examinees simply saying a texture key word (see Rapid Reference 3.7) is not sufficient to code texture. Examinees need either to verbalize that the shading in the blot is resulting in their seeing texture (e.g., "the different hues make it look furry") or to touch the card

Rapid Reference 3.7

Examples of Texture Key Words

Abrasive
Barbed
Bumpy
Cold
Cotton
Damp
Fluffy
Hairy
Hot
Itchy
Moist
Mushy
Padded
Rough
Sharp
Sticky
Wool

while saying the texture word (e.g., "it looks fuzzy" [pets card]). A nonverbal indication of a tactile sensation, such as petting a card in the case of something that the examinee says is fuzzy, is sufficient to code texture.

T: Pure Texture

This code is used when examinees are relying only on texture to explain their responses; they are not using form. Here are two examples of this type of response:

Example 1 (Card VI)

Response: It's fuzzy (touches card).
Examiner repeats examinee's response.
Inquiry-1: It just looks like it would be fuzzy to me.
Coding: Wv1 T Id

Example 2 (Card VII)

Response: It looks cold.
Examiner repeats examinee's response.

Inquiry-1: The shading. It makes it look like it would be cold if I touched it.
Coding: Wv1 T Id

In both cases, form is not used at all. The appropriate determinant for both examples is T.

TF and FT: Texture-Form and Form-Texture

The Texture-Form (TF) and Form-Texture (FT) codes are used when examinees are using both the shading of the blot to indicate texture and the shape of the blot to explain why the blot looks like that to them. Again, it is not necessary to distinguish between TF and FT, because they are interpreted in the same way. Here are a couple of examples of these codes:

Example 1 (Card II)

Response: It is a bunny.
Examiner repeats examinee's response.
Inquiry-1: Fuzzy tail here, ears, nose, body (points to D1).
Fuzzy?
Inquiry-2: Yeah, the tail looks fuzzy to me (touches card where tail is).
Coding: Do1 FTo A

Example 2 (Card VII)

Response: An ice sculpture (indicates whole blot).
Examiner repeats examinee's response.
Inquiry-1: The shading made me think it would be cold, like ice. Here is the base of the sculpture (points to D4), and the rest of the sculpture (points to D2). Not sure what it's supposed to be though.
Coding: Wv1 TFu Na, Art

In the first case, the examiner queries a key word ("fuzzy"). The word "fuzzy" suggests the possibility that the examinee is using texture, as fuzzy implies a tactile sensation. The inquiry results in the examinee indicating the use of texture by touching the card while saying the texture word. The examinee also focuses on the shape of the blot in his response, so a code of FT or TF is appropriate.

In the second case, the examinee again provides a key word ("ice") in the response. Ice could indicate texture, as ice is cold. It also could indicate color or pure shading. In the inquiry, the examinee explains why the blot looks like an ice sculpture ("the shading made me think it would be cold, like ice"), so no query was necessary. In this case, the appropriate coding would be TF or FT, as there is a tactile sensation and form as part of the response. Again, it is not essential to differentiate between TF and FT, as both are interpreted the same way.

Texture Word but No Texture Determinant

Examiners cannot assume that the use of a texture word always warrants the coding of a texture determinant. It is important to remember that the coding of a texture determinant requires both the presence of a tactile sensation *and* the use of shading or a nonverbal response suggesting texture (e.g., touching the card). At times, an examinee will provide a texture word but will not indicate texture in any other way. In these cases, texture is not coded as a determinant. Consider the following example:

> Response (Card VI): It's a cat. Here's the head (points to D3). Looks furry.
> *Examiner repeats examinee's response.*
> Inquiry-1: Yeah, head here (points to D3), whiskers (points to Dd22), body (points to D1), legs (points to Dd24). Looks fat. See how big the body is? *You said it looked furry?*
> Inquiry-2: Yeah, these different lines here (points to Dd29) make it look like fur.
> *Coding: Wo1 Fo A ZW*

In this case, the examinee provides a texture key word in the response ("furry") but does not mention it in the first part of the inquiry. The examiner correctly queries the word, as the examiner needs to determine whether the examinee is using texture as a determinant. The examinee's response (Inquiry-2) indicates that the examinee is using the shape of the blot to indicate texture ("these different lines") rather than the shading. Because the examinee is not using shading to indicate texture, texture is not coded as a determinant. The appropriate determinant for this response is Form (F).

Shading-Based Dimensionality

Shading-based dimensionality is commonly referred to as Vista (V). Vista is used when the examinee is using the shading present in the blot to indicate dimensionality. Simply saying a dimensionality word (see Rapid Reference 3.8) is not sufficient to code Vista. The examinee needs to verbalize that the shading in the blot is resulting in the dimensionality (e.g., "it's darker here so it looks deeper").

It is important to distinguish between shading-based dimensionality (Pure Vista, V) and form-based dimensionality (Form Dimension, FD). The distinguishing factor is the use of shading; V is coded when shading is used to indicate

≡ Rapid Reference 3.8

Examples of Dimensionality Key Words

Above
Behind
Bigger
Deeper
In back
In front
Looking down
Smaller

dimensionality, and FD coding does not involve shading. FD is described in more detail later in this chapter.

V: Pure Vista

Pure Vista (V) is coded when examinees are relying only on shading-based dimensionality to explain their response; they are not using form. Here is an example of this type of response:

> Response (Card VI): It is deep (points to D12).
> *Examiner repeats examinee's response.*
> Inquiry-1: See how it is darker here than it is here? It makes it look deep.
> *Coding: Dv12 V Id*

In this case, form is not used at all; however, the examinee is clearly using shading ("darker here than it is here") and perceives dimensionality ("deep"). The appropriate determinant is V.

VF and FV: Vista-Form and Form-Vista

The Vista-Form (VF) and Form-Vista (FV) codes are used when the examinee is using both the shading of the blot to indicate dimensionality and the shape of the blot to explain why the blot looks like that to them. Again, it is not essential to distinguish between VF and FV because they are interpreted the same way. Here are a couple of examples of these codes:

Example 1 (Card I)

> Response: It is a cone (indicates whole blot). It is shaped like one.
> *Examiner repeats examinee's response.*

Inquiry 1: Here (points). It is shaped like a triangle, but the shading makes it look like this part (points to middle of cone) is closer to me and this part (points to edges) is further away. So I thought it looked 3-D, and a 3-D triangle is a cone.
Coding: Wo1 VF– Id ZW

Example 2 (Card VII)

Response: A totem pole (points to D3).
Examiner repeats examinee's response.
Inquiry-1: Like these are the different animals and here are some wings (points to Dd22). It looks like it has carvings.
I'm not sure I see the carvings yet.
Inquiry-2: See how it is darker here than here? It makes it looked carved.
Coding: D + 3 FVo Ay ZA

In the first example, the examinee describes the object as being three dimensional (i.e., a cone) and also uses shading to justify the dimensionality ("the shading makes it look like this part is closer to me and this part is further away"). In this case, the appropriate coding is either VF or FV; again, both are acceptable as they are interpreted the same way in the CS. In the second example, the examiner recognizes a possible dimensionality key word ("carvings") and appropriately queries it. The examinee then indicates that she saw the carvings because of the shading ("darker here than here"), indicating that shading-based dimensionality influenced what she saw. However, it is clear she is also focused on the structure of the blot ("different animals"), so the appropriate determinant coding is FV or VF. Again, either is acceptable because the two determinants are interpreted the same way.

Diffuse Shading

Diffuse Shading, the final shading determinant, is usually coded by exclusion. It is coded when the examinee is using shading but there is no indication that the shading is associated with texture or vista. Like achromatic color, texture, and vista, Pure Diffuse Shading (Y), Diffuse Shading-Form (YF), and Form-Diffuse Shading (FY) are all interpreted the same way, so it is not essential to distinguish between a YF and an FY. The key words for this type of determinant are the same as the key words for texture and dimensionality. See Rapid References 3.7 and 3.8 for a review of key words for the different shading determinants.

Y: Pure Diffuse Shading

This is a relatively rare code. It occurs when the examinee is using shading without any form. Here is an example of this type of response:

Response Phase (Card I): It looks like evil.
Examiner repeats examinee's response.
Inquiry-1: Yeah, the whole thing.
Remember, I need to see it like you do.
Inquiry-2: See how it's lighter here than it is here? It must be evil.
Coding: Wv1 Y Id ALOG

In this example, the examinee provided only location information in the initial part of the inquiry phase, so the examiner provided a general query for more information. The examinee then responded that it was "lighter here than it is here," indicating the use of shading. Because the examinee did not give any form to the response, the correct determinant coding is Y.

YF and FY: Diffuse Shading-Form and Form-Diffuse Shading

The Diffuse Shading-Form (YF) and Form-Diffuse Shading (FY) codes are used when examinees are using both the shading of the blot and the shape of the blot to explain why the blot looks like that to them. However, there is no indication that they are using shading to indicate dimensionality or texture. Again, it not necessary to distinguish between YF and FY, because they are interpreted the same way. Here are a couple of examples of these codes:

Example 1 (Card IV)

Response: A smoke monster.
Examiner repeats examinee's response.
Inquiry-1: Not this part (points to D1).
Help me see the smoke monster like you do.
Inquiry-2: Yeah, it goes from lighter to darker shades, and it reminded me of smoke. Here are the legs, head, and arms.
Coding: Do7 YFo (H), Fi P GHR

Example 2 (Card VIII)

Response: A lion.
Examiner repeats examinee's response.
Inquiry-1: Here. Legs, 4 of them, head, and a bright eye. It's lighter so it looks bright.
Coding: Do1 FYo A P

In the first example, the examiner queries because the examinee still has not provided the *why* (the determinant). After the query, the examinee focuses on the shading of the blot, then the structure. Additionally, the shading—the "smoke"—is integral to the nature of the response. Without the shading, the monster would not look like a smoke monster; it would be only a monster. Because the examinee is using both diffuse shading and form in his response, a code of YF or FY is appropriate. In the second example, the examinee is also using both the structure of the blot and the shading, although he does not mention the use of shading until the very end. Thus, either a code of FY or YF is appropriate. Again, it is not essential to differentiate between a code of YF and FY, as both are interpreted the same way in the CS.

Querying for Eyes

Often, examinees will point out an object's eye in a lighter or darker shaded part of the blot (see Card VIII area D1 for an example). Beginning Rorschach examiners will often query the eye, thinking that because the person is identifying the eye in a lighter or darker area it is possible that the examinee is using shading. However, this practice often results in an increased number of Y determinants. Viglione (2010) suggested that if the eyes are identified when the person is identifying a series of parts (e.g., "head, lips, eyes, nose"), then the eyes should not be queried. However, if the examinee distinguishes the eyes in some way, such as referring to them as bright, as in the previous example, or dark, then the response should be queried.

FD: Form-Based Dimension

Form-Based Dimension (FD), usually referred to as Form Dimension, or FD, is used when the examinee verbalizes that there is some form of dimensionality in the response but is not using shading. That is, the main difference between the V codes and the FD code is that V, VF, and FV all use shading to indicate dimensionality and FD relies only on the structure of the blot to indicate dimensionality.

FD responses are relatively common and often appear on Card IV. Here is an example:

Response (Card IV): It's a guy sitting on a stump. He is leaning back, relaxing. *Examiner repeats examinee's response.*
Inquiry-1: Yeah, here is the guy, head, legs, body. Stump here (points to D1). *You said he was leaning back?*
Inquiry-2: Yes, the feet are out front (points to D6). I said leaning back because his feet are bigger than his head, so it looks like they are out front.
Coding: W + 1 Mp.FDo H, Bt P ZA GHR

In this example, the examiner notes that "leaning back" could indicate the pos-sibility of dimensionality, warranting a query. The examinee then verbalizes that there is dimensionality, as the feet are bigger than the head. However, there is no indication that the examinee is using shading to indicate dimensionality; the examinee is using only form. Thus, the appropriate determinant is FD.

There is also a human movement determinant (Mp) coded for this example. The examinee sees two movements by the same object ("a guy"): "sitting" and "leaning back, relaxing." Both of these are passive movements, resulting in the code of Mp. It is permissible, and relatively common, to have more than one determi-nant in a response; this is called a blend. Blends are discussed later in this chapter.

Symmetry

There are two symmetry-based codes: reflections and pairs. These codes are recorded in different areas of the coding sheet. Reflections are coded in the determinants section of the coding sheet while pairs have their own column (see Figure 3.1 earlier in this chapter). These codes are exclusive; you *cannot* code both in the same response. If both codes are present in a response, code only the reflection. Both require that the examinee is using the symmetry of the blot to see the reflec-tion or the pair. If the response does not rely on the symmetry of the blot, then these codes are not used. Examples are included in the discussion of each code to help the reader visualize the difference between a coded reflection and a response containing a reflection that is not coded.

CAUTION
· ·

Code reflection or pair only when the reflection or the pair is based on the symmetry of the blot.

r: Reflection

There are two reflection codes: Reflection-Form (rF) and Form-Reflection (Fr). As rF and Fr are interpreted in the same way, it is not important to distinguish between the two. There is no pure reflection code; reflections without form are coded as rF. Key words for reflection include "reflection" and "mirror image."

Here are two examples of responses that contain a reflection. In the first exam-ple, the reflection is based on the symmetry of the blot and is coded as a determi-nant. In the second example, the reflection is not based on the symmetry of the blot and, consequently, the reflection is not coded as a determinant.

Example 1 (Card III)

Response: It's a guy looking at himself in the mirror.

Examiner repeats examinee's response.

Inquiry-1: Yeah, here's the guy (points to D9 on left). Nose, head, legs. Big nose! And here's his reflection in the mirror (points to D9 on right).

Coding: Do9 Mp.Fro H P GHR

Example 2 (Card VI)

Response: It's a duck (points to D3) floating on the water. See, here's the reflection (points to Dd32).

Examiner repeats examinee's response.

Inquiry-1: Here's the duck (points to D3), here's the water (points to D1), here's the reflection (points to Dd32). And before you ask, it looks like a duck because of the shape. Here are the wings. And it looks like water because of the shape. It's round, well sort of, like a pond. Ponds can take any shape. And this is the reflection because of the shape.

Coding: W + 1 FMpu A, Na ZW

In the first example, the reflection is based on the symmetry of the blot. The same location code serves for both the original object ("the guy") and his reflection. In the second example, the object ("duck") and its reflection have different location codes; the reflection is not based on the symmetry of the blot. Thus, reflection is not coded as a determinant.

2: Pairs

Pairs (2) are coded when the examinee verbalizes that there are two of something, based on the symmetry of the blot. However, the examinee does not verbalize that one object is a reflection of the other. Whereas reflections are less common, pairs are very common and frequently appear at least a few times per protocol. Often, examinees indicate a pair by stating that an object is plural (e.g., "bears") or by saying there are two. They do not need to specifically use the word "pair."

Here are two examples of times when an examinee verbalizes seeing a pair. As with the reflection examples, in the first example the examinee indicates that the pair is based on the symmetry of the blot. In the second case, the pair is not based on the symmetry of the blot, so the pair is not coded.

Example 1 (Card II)

Response: Two bunnies (points to D1 on the left and D1 on the right).

Examiner repeats examinee's response.

Inquiry-1: Yeah. Head, cotton tail, body.

Cotton tail?
Inquiry-2: Just the shape.
Coding: Do1 Fo 2 A

Example 2 (Card X)
Response: Crabs.
Examiner repeats examinee's response.
Inquiry-1: One here (points to D1) and one here (points to D7). They are shaped like crabs.
Coding: Do1 Fo A P

In the first example, the examinee, via pointing, indicates that there are two bunnies in the same location area, just on opposite sides of the blot. This is coded as a pair, as the pair is based on the symmetry of the blot. In the second example, the crabs have different location codes, so the pair is not based on the symmetry of the blot. The pair is not coded in this example.

Also, in the first example, the examiner queries "cotton" as it may indicate texture. However, the examinee verbalizes that it is a "cotton tail" because of the shape and not the shading, so texture is not coded as a determinant.

Finally, it is important to note that some things are never coded as pairs. These include things that normally appear as pairs, such as eyes. If the pair is based on the symmetry of a human body or animal (e.g., legs, arms), it is not coded as a pair. It has also become conventional to not code pairs for items that usually appear in pairs, such as shoes and mittens (Viglione, 2010).

Blends

It is permissible, and common, to have more than one determinant per response. In some cases, there will be three, four, or even more. Having more than one determinant in a response is referred to as a blend. When listed, the determinants are separated by periods. Each type of determinant can appear only once in a blend. Thus, a blend can contain both a V and a T, but it cannot contain a TF and an FT. A blend can also include an M, an FM, and an m, as all are considered separate classes of determinants, but it cannot include an Ma and an Mp, as both are in the same class of determinants (human movement).

Consider the following example of a blend:

Response (Card IX): It looks like scoops of melting sherbet.
Examiner repeats examinee's response.

Inquiry-1: (Laughs). Yeah, I thought sherbet because of the different colors—green, pink, and orange (points to colors on blot). Scoops because they are rounded here. Melting because of the different shades of the pink and green; it's making it look like it is melting.

You said they were rounded?

Inquiry-2: Yeah, the shape, see? They are circles (points to D4).

Coding: Wo1 mp.CF.YF– Fd ZW MOR

In this case, the examinee verbalizes using color ("the different colors"), movement ("melting"), and shading ("different shades of pink and green"). All of these contributed to why the examinee saw the blot the way he did, so all are coded as determinants. The examiner queries the word "round" because it might indicate dimensionality. However, the examinee responds that the word "round" was referring only to the shape ("circles") and that the verbalization did not indicate perceiving any dimensionality; so no dimensionality determinant is coded.

Summary of Determinants

Each response will have at least one determinant. Responses with multiple determinants are called blends. A good knowledge of determinants is necessary for a useful administration, as the determinants represent the *why* of the inquiry. In order for the examiner to ensure having the information necessary to code the *why*, the examiner may have to query (see Chapter 2), but in order to know what to query, the examiner must know what to look for. This is why an excellent knowledge of determinants is vital for an accurate administration.

FQ: FORM QUALITY

Form Quality (FQ) is coded in the FQ column of the coding sheet whenever the response contains a determinant with form. If there is no form, there is no form quality. Thus, no form quality is recorded when there are only "pure" determinants in the response (e.g., C, Y, V, C'). Any determinant with a form (e.g., F, CF, FY) will have form quality, as will *most* movement responses. The only movement response that will not have an associated form quality is the disembodied emotions response, when the examinee perceives the blot as being an emotion (e.g., "It's depression").

Unlike determinants, which can be coded in multiples, there can be only one FQ code per response. There are five FQ codes. Rapid Reference 3.9 reviews four of them. The fifth FQ—no form quality—does not have a code assigned to it in

≡ Rapid Reference 3.9

Form Quality Codes

Code	Name	Description
+	Ordinary-Elaborated	FQ is an o, but examinee provides an excessive number of form details (often 6 or more).
o	Ordinary	Response follows the contours of the blot and was commonly seen in the sample of 9,500 protocols used to construct the FQ tables.
u	Unusual	Response follows the contours of the blot but was not commonly seen in the sample of 9,500 protocols used to construct the FQ tables.
–	Minus	Response does not follow the contours of the blot.

Source: Based on information from Exner, 2001, 2003.

the CS. Instead, if there is no FQ, then the FQ column of the coding sheet is left blank.

FQ assesses two things. First, it evaluates how well the response fits the contours of the blot, or whether the object can easily be seen in the area the examinee identifies as the area the object is in. The second thing FQ evaluates is how common the response is.

Like the location codes, the form quality codes to assign for specific objects are located in tables in Exner (2001, 2003). The FQs are listed first by card and then by location area. A caret next to an FQ indicates that the card in question was being held with the top facing either left or right (< or >) or facing down (v).

To determine FQ, the examiner looks in the FQ tables for the object the examinee saw under the location area in which he or she saw it. For example, an examinee states that all of Card I (location = W) looks like a bat. The examiner then looks at the FQ tables for Card I, then looks under the W column(s) for the word "bat." According to the FQ table, a response of bat, using the whole blot, has a FQ code of ordinary (o). So the FQ should be coded as o.

However, there are times when the object the examinee sees is not in the FQ tables. When this happens, the examiner should extrapolate based on the FQ tables. To do this, the examiner should look for objects with a shape similar to the shape in the response; the words themselves do not need to be semantically related.

As an example, an examinee says that Card IV looks like a "scoop of ice cream." "A scoop of ice cream" is not in the FQ tables. Although "ice cream cone" appears in the FQ tables in the W column for Card IV, it should not be used as the basis of the extrapolation because an "ice cream cone" and a "scoop of ice cream" have very different shapes. Instead, it would be better to extrapolate based on something with a rounder shape, such as "helmet," and the coding for that FQ will be –.

FQ should be assessed using the response as a whole, when possible. For example, I have had a few examinees identify Card I as looking like "two strippers pole dancing." This response is not in the form quality tables, as it was not commonly provided by the members of the sample used to derive the FQ tables. However, "Humans (2, facing midline)" is in the FQ tables, and it is reasonable to extrapolate from that item.

When an examiner cannot extrapolate from the whole response, the examiner should then attempt to extrapolate using the various parts of the examinee's response. As an example, on Card X, some examinees have reported seeing "a crab (D1) holding a leaf (D12)." It is impossible to extrapolate from the whole response, as the area being used is a Dd99 area. The examiner should then look at the FQs for each object in the response. The FQ for the crab (area D1) is o and the FQ for the leaf (area D12) is also o. Consequently, it is appropriate to code the FQ as an o.

However, there are times where this process results in FQs that are different. If this occurs, generally the lowest FQ among the objects important to the nature of the response is coded. This does require the examiner to determine which aspects of the response are important and which are not. There are a few things to consider when determining whether an object is important to the response:

1. If the object were different, or did not exist, how much would that affect the response? If the response would still be essentially the same, then the object is not important. If the response would be different, then the object is important.
2. How certain was the examinee about the object? If the examinee seemed uncertain about the object, such as by stating, "I guess it could be," then the examiner should consider that part of the response less important to the nature of the response, as the examinee was less certain about it.
3. Which part of the response did the examinee focus on? If the examinee focuses on one part of the response far more than the rest, that part could be deemed the most important and could be given more weight in the determination of FQ.

There are also times when the examiner cannot extrapolate from the parts of the response. In this case, the examiner should extrapolate based on the shape of the response object(s). For example, if the examinee saw a "snake" but there is no "snake" in the FQ table for that area, the examiner should then look for items in the FQ table with a shape similar to a snake's shape, such as a stick. It is important that the examiner look for items that are similarly shaped and not for conceptually related ones. In the previous example, although a lizard is conceptually more similar to a snake than a stick is, as both are reptiles, it would not be appropriate to extrapolate this FQ from "lizard" in the FQ table because lizards and snakes have very different shapes. Instead, "stick," although not conceptually related to a snake, is a better item to extrapolate from, because sticks and snakes have similar shapes.

Still, there are times when the examiner cannot extrapolate at all from the FQ tables. In this case, the examiner needs to look at the response and determine whether the response object follows the contours of the blot. If it does, then the response should be coded as having unusual (u) FQ. If the object does not follow the contours of the blot, then the response should be coded as having minus (–) FQ.

Summary of FQ codes

Each response will have one FQ code. FQ codes can be found in a variety of sources, including Exner's text (Exner, 2003). Exner identified four FQ codes. Ordinary (o) FQ is assigned to responses that follow the contours of the blot and were commonly seen by the standardization sample. Unusual (u) FQ is assigned to responses that follow the contours of the blot but were not commonly seen by the standardization sample. Minus (–) FQ is assigned when the response does not follow the contours of the blot. Ordinary-Elaborated (+) FQ is assigned when the FQ is an o, but the examinee provided a lot of form details in the response. There is also a fifth FQ, which is no FQ. No FQ is assigned when the response does not contain any objects with form. When no FQ is assigned, the FQ column on the coding sheet is left blank. It is important to remember that only one FQ is assigned per response.

CONTENTS

The contents represent the *what* of the inquiry. These codes represent what the examinee saw. There are multiple content codes, and they are divided into five categories: Human, Animal, Nature, Intellectualization, and Other. As with determinant codes, there can be multiple content codes in the same response. The different content codes are separated by commas (,). Typically, examinees provide this information in the Response Phase; however, they can add contents in the Inquiry Phase. Rapid Reference 3.10 reviews the content codes.

≣Rapid Reference 3.10

Content Codes

Code	Name	When Used	Examples
H	Whole Human	Examinee sees whole, real human; includes historical figures.	Man. Boy. Baby. Hermann Rorschach.
(H)	Fictional/ Mythological Whole Human	Examinee sees whole fictional or mythological human; includes historical figures engaged in supernatural activities.	Hercules. Supergirl. Moses parting the Red Sea.
Hd	Human Detail	Examinee sees part of a real human.	Baby's face. Arm. A guy, he's missing his head.
(Hd)	Fictional/ Mythological Human Detail	Examinee sees partial fictional or mythological human.	Hercules' arm. Dumbledore's face.
Hx	Human Experience	Examinee sees human experience or emotion.	Happiness. Depression.
A	Whole Animal	Examinee sees whole real animal.	Dog. Cat.
(A)	Whole Fictional/ Mythological Animal	Examinee sees whole fictional or mythological animal.	Unicorn. Jackalope.
Ad	Animal detail	Examinee sees partial animal.	Tail. Claw.
(Ad)	Fictional/ Mythological Animal Detail	Examinee sees partial fictional or mythological animal.	Unicorn's horn. Nemo's tail.
Bt	Botany	Examinee sees plant, plant life.	Flower. Apple.
Ls	Landscape	Examinee sees landscape.	Hill. Rock formation.
Na	Nature	Examinee sees natural phenomenon that is not Bt or Ls.	Glacier. Planet.

(continued)

Code	Name	When Used	Examples
Art	Art	Examinee sees art or something decorative.	Statue. Painting. Jewelry.
Ay	Anthropology	Examinee sees something of specific historical or cultural reference.	Totem pole. Joan of Arc.
An	Anatomy	Examinee sees anatomy (including muscles, organs, and bones).	Liver. Femur.
Xy	X-Ray	Examinee sees X-ray, or product of any other method of imaging (e.g., MRI, PET, ultrasound).	X-ray of a pelvis. Ultrasound of a fetus.
Bl	Blood	Examinee sees blood.	Blood.
Cg	Clothing	Examinee sees clothing; typically also includes accessories (e.g., glasses).	Shirt. Shoes.
Cl	Cloud	Examinee sees a cloud.	Cloud. Storm cloud.
Ex	Explosion	Examinee sees an explosion.	Fireworks. Bomb blast.
Fi	Fire	Examinee sees fire or smoke.	Fire. Smoke.
Fd	Food	Examinee sees food; must be native to the species.	Pizza. Lion eating a zebra.
Ge	Geography	Examinee sees a map.	Map of Ireland.
Hh	Household	Examinee sees household items.	Chair. Rug.
Sc	Science	Examinee sees objects associated with science and/or science fiction; includes products of science.	Building. Test tube.
Sx	Sex	Examinee sees sex organs or sexual activity.	Strip tease. Ovary.
Id	Idiographic	Examinee sees objects that do not fit into any other category (use sparingly).	Blob.

Source: Based on information from Exner, 2001, 2003; Viglione, 2010.

Human Content Codes

There are five human content codes. These codes are used when the examinee verbalizes that the blot contains a human, a humanlike figure (e.g., a witch), or a human emotion or experience (e.g., pain, depression). Two of the codes are used when the examinee sees a whole human, two are used when the examinee sees a partial human, and one is used when the examinee perceives a human experience happening in the blot.

When using the two whole human codes, H, Whole Human, is coded when examinees see a complete real human figure in their response. This includes real historical figures, such as Napoleon and Rosa Parks. (H), Fictional Whole Human, is coded when the examinee sees a complete fictional human figure in their response. This includes witches, clowns, spirits, and real historical figures engaging in supernatural activities (e.g., "Jesus turning water into wine").

When using the two partial human codes, Hd, Human Detail, is coded when the examinee sees a part of a real person (e.g., "This is a man's legs"), including parts of historical figures. (Hd), Fictional Human Detail, is coded when examinees see an incomplete fictional person in their response. An example of this is "the devil's head."

Hx is the Human Experience code. This is used when the examinee identifies a human experience, such as an emotion or sensation, in the blot. These codes are rare and are difficult to code correctly. An example of a response that warrants an Hx coding is "It looks like depression." Another example is "They are in love." Note that in order to code an Hx, there has to be an emotion or sensation in the response. Typically, human actions (e.g., "playing cards") do not warrant an Hx code.

Animal Content Codes

There are four animal content codes. These codes are used when the examinee perceives an animal in the blot. As with the human content codes, two of the codes are used when the examinee perceives a whole animal and two of the codes are used when the examinee perceives a partial animal.

When using the two whole animal codes, A, Whole Animal, is coded when examinees perceive a complete real animal in their responses, such as a dog or a cat. (A), Whole Fictional Animal, is coded when examinees report seeing a complete fictional animal, such as Pegasus, in their responses.

When using the two partial animal codes, Ad, Animal Detail, is coded when the examinee reports seeing a partial animal in the response, such as "a rabbit's tail." (Ad), Fictional Animal Detail, is used when the examinee identifies a partial fictional animal in a response, such as "Hedwig's wing."

Natural Codes

Three of the content codes can be classified as natural codes: Botany (Bt), Landscape (Ls), and Nature (Na). These three codes have special rules associated with them. These rules, described later in this section, apply only to these three codes.

Botany is generally easy to identify in a response. Botany (Bt) is used when examinees verbalize that they see a plant or plant life in the blot. This includes flowers, bushes, grass, oranges, and the like.

The other two natural codes—landscape and nature—are more difficult to code. Landscape (Ls) is coded when the examinee perceives a landscape, such as a hill, a valley, or a volcano. In general, the rule is that landscapes are something that you can step on in your current state without causing harm to yourself. There are two exceptions to this rule. The first is a response of "seascape"; seascapes, although we cannot step on them, are coded as landscapes. The second addresses the different states of water. Generally, all water, whatever its physical state (snow, ice, etc.), is coded as nature (Viglione, 2010).

Nature (Na) is the code used when the examinee sees something that is natural but is not botany or landscape. Examples of this are a planet, the ocean, and the sky. It is impossible to stand on the ocean, as we would sink, and we cannot step on the sky without falling. Although we could step on another planet, without life support, we would die due to the lack of oxygen. In other words, in our current state, we would not be able to step on another planet without causing serious harm to ourselves. Thus, a planet is coded as nature.

DON'T FORGET

With only a few exceptions, the difference between landscape and nature is whether you can step on it. If you can step on it, it is probably landscape. If you cannot, it is probably nature.

There is another rule for coding nature, landscape, and botany: only one of these three can be coded per response. This is something unique among the content codes as, generally, multiple content codes can, and should, be coded in the same response. However, because nature, botany, and landscape are all part of the same index (Isolation), only one is coded, so that no one response has undue weight in interpretation. (The indices are discussed in Chapter 4.) There are rules for determining which one to code when multiple natural codes are possible in the same response. These rules can be found in Rapid Reference 3.11.

≡Rapid Reference 3.11

Determining Whether to Code Nature, Botany, or Landscape

1. When nature is present, code nature only. Do not code landscape and/or botany, even if they are present.
2. When only botany and landscape are present, choose only one to code. It does not matter which one you choose.

Intellectualization Codes

Two codes—Art (Art) and Anthropology (Ay)—are classified as intellectualization codes because they are used to calculate the Intellectualization Index. These codes are used when examinees verbalize that they see a form of art or decoration in the blot (e.g., a statue, coded as Art) or that they see a real historical figure or cultural artifact (e.g., a totem pole, coded as Ay).

In general, Art and Ay codes can be coded in the same response, as long as the verbiage that describes each of them does not overlap. For example, "a statue of a dog. Napoleon is looking at it" would be coded both Art ("the statue") and Ay ("Napoleon") because the language associated with each code is separate. Note that this response should also be coded as A ("dog") and H ("Napoleon"). However, "a statue of Napoleon" could only be coded as Art or Ay, because the language used to describe the statue and its subject overlaps. In this case, only one code should be used. This response would also be coded as H, as Napoleon was a real person.

Anatomy and X-Ray

Anatomy and X-ray codes are interpreted together (as described in the next chapter). Anatomy (An) is coded whenever examinees see any form of anatomy in their response. This includes internal organs, bones, and muscle tissue. Anatomy is anything inside the body; human detail should be coded when the examinee describes a body part visible on the outside of the body, such as the skin or an eye.

X-ray (Xy) is coded whenever examinees verbalize that they see some form of imaging. Although Exner (2001, 2003) describes this code solely in terms of X-ray images, it has become commonplace to code any form of imaging, including MRIs, CT scans, and ultrasounds, as X-ray. When examinees verbalize that they see an image of something (e.g., "an ultrasound of a kidney"), only the Xy or the An code is coded; because these codes are interpreted in the same way, only one code is usually recorded per response.

Other Codes

There are a variety of other content codes and they vary in their difficulty to code. Some of the easier ones to code are related to environmental phenomena, like explosions, clouds, and fire. Explosion (Ex) is coded whenever the examinee verbalizes seeing an explosion in the response, such as a bomb blast or a fireworks display. Cloud (Cl) is coded when the examinee verbalizes that there is a cloud in the response. Fire (Fi) is coded whenever the examinee verbalizes seeing fire or smoke in the response.

Three other codes that are typically considered easy to code are blood, clothing, and geography. Blood (Bl) is coded whenever the examinee verbalizes seeing blood in the response. Clothing (Cg) is coded whenever the examinee sees a form of clothing, such as a shirt, pants, or shoes. Typically, clothing also includes accessories, such as glasses. Geography (Ge) is coded whenever the examinee verbalizes seeing a map. While blood and clothing are relatively common codes, geography is a rare code.

Two codes that tend to be more difficult to code correctly are the sex and food codes. Sex (Sx) is typically coded alongside another code and used whenever the person sees objects related to sex, sexual activity, or reproduction. This would include objects like ovaries, sperm, vagina, penis, and stamen. However, it also includes items and activities that are sexually suggestive, like thong underwear, bras, and stripping. For example, a bra would receive a code of Cg (clothing) along with Sx (sex).

The Food (Fd) code also tends to be difficult to code correctly. This code is used only when the person verbalizes that there is an object that is clearly meant to be food. In order to be coded as food, the food needs to be considered native to the species that is eating it. For example, if examinees say they see a cat, a Whole Animal (A), eating a mouse, then the mouse is coded as Food (Fd), because the mouse is a food that a cat would generally eat. However, if they say they see a cat (A) eating a car (Sc), the car would not be coded as food because a car is not something that cats eat normally.

It is important to remember that in order for an object to be coded as food, it has to be obvious that the examinee believes the object is going to be eaten. This causes confusion for some examiners, as there are many objects that humans eat, such as fruits, vegetables, and animals, that could be food, but they also may not be. Consider the following set of responses:

Example 1 (Card IX)

Response: It looks like scoops of melting sherbet.
Examiner repeats examinee's response.

Inquiry-1: (Laughs). Yeah, I thought sherbet because of the different colors—green, pink, and orange (points). Scoops because they are round here. Melting because of the different shades of the pink and green; it's making it look like it is melting.

You said they were round?

Inquiry-2: Yeah, the shape, see? They are circles (points to D4).

Coding: Wo1 mp.CF.YF– Fd ZW MOR

Example 2 (Card VII)

Response: Chicken wings.

Examiner repeats examinee's response.

Inquiry-1: Here and here (points to D2, both sides). The shape reminds me of chicken wings.

Coding: Do2 Fu Ad

Example 3 (Card VII)

Response: Chicken wings.

Examiner repeats examinee's response.

Inquiry-1: Here and here (points to D2, both sides). The shape reminds me of chicken wings. This shape (points around the edge) makes it look like breading. They've been deep fried.

Coding: Do2 Fu 2 Fd

In the first example, the content coding is Food (Fd) because sherbet is only food. Sherbet exists to be eaten. In the second and third examples, the examinees report seeing "chicken wings." Chicken wings could be parts of a chicken, or they could be food. In this case, it is important to look at the Inquiry in order to determine whether the examinee meant the chicken wings as part of a chicken (Animal Detail, Ad) or as Food (Fd). In the second example, the examinee does not provide any indication that the chicken wings are meant as food. In this case, it is best to default to Ad. In the third example, the examinee clearly verbalizes that the chicken wings are intended to be food; the chicken wings have been "deep fried," indicating that they are food.

Two other codes that tend to be difficult to code correctly are Household (Hh) and Science (Sc). The difficulty with these codes lies in choosing between them for certain common objects. Household, on the one hand, is coded whenever the item is a household item, such as a couch, rug, table, bed, or garden hose. Science, on the other hand, is coded whenever the item is related to science or is a product of science. This is a broad category that includes weapons, musical instruments, most things related to science fiction, and transportation items. It is easy to see how these codes can get confusing, as many of our household items (e.g., televisions) are a result of science. In general, anything that is an item that is typical of a household, such as furniture in the United States, should be coded Hh. Things that may be present in households but are generally used for entertainment purposes rather than for running the household, such as gaming systems and televisions, should be coded Sc.

There is one more content code: Idiographic (Id). This is used when the item that the examinee verbalizes cannot be coded under any of the other content codes. This code should be coded rarely, as most items can be coded under one, or more, of the previously mentioned content codes. An example of a proper use of Id code follows.

> Response (Card V): It's a blob. All I see.
> *Examiner repeats examinee's response.*
> Inquiry-1: Yeah. It was all I could think of.
> *I'm not sure I see it like you do.*
> Inquiry-2: Um, the shape makes it look blob-y. That's it. I can't tell you anything else.
> *Coding: Wv1 Fu Id DV1*

Troubleshooting Content Codes

In general, coding content tends to be easier than coding other parts of responses, such as determinants. However, there are some areas that can be confusing. Some of these were mentioned earlier, such as coding something as household versus science and coding anatomy versus human detail. Other common areas of confusion include when to code human versus animal and when to code human versus human detail. Brief discussions of these latter two areas follow. For more detailed information on these topics, and others, I suggest that readers review additional resources, including Viglione (2010).

Hd and Ad: Human Detail Versus Animal Detail

At times, an examinee provides a response that could be considered either Hd or Ad. Examples include "leg," "skin," "foot," and "head." Sometimes, the inquiry will reveal whether the object is more animallike (e.g., contains fur) or more humanlike, and this can guide coding. However, there are times when even after an appropriate inquiry, the examiner is not sure whether the examinee intended the response to be about an animal or a human. We cannot ask whether the examinee intended the response to be about a human or an animal, as that question would be too leading to use in an inquiry. In these cases, where we are not certain whether the examinee meant the object to be more humanlike or animallike, we default to human coding.

H and Hd: Human or Human Detail

Frequently during the Response Phase, examinees will say that they see an entire object (e.g., a person, a dog), but then on the inquiry, verbalize seeing only part of the object. For example:

> Response: A girl. Here (points to D1).
> *Examiner repeats examinee's response.*
> Inquiry-1: Here's her head, hair, nose, and mouth.
> *Coding: Do1 Fo Hd P GHR*

In this case, the appropriate coding is Hd because although the examinee reported it was a girl, it became apparent during the Inquiry that the examinee saw only the girl's head in the blot. Thus, an Hd code is most appropriate.

Another area of confusion with coding H versus Hd occurs when examinees verbalize that part of the person they see is missing. According to Exner (2003), Hd should be coded when there is a clearly incomplete human, such as in the case of a "headless man." Similar rules should be followed for coding A and Ad.

Inappropriate Combinations

At times, the examinee will add an odd object onto a human or an animal, saying, for example, that something looks like a "rabbit with hands." In the case of a "rabbit with hands," the coding should remain A, and Hd should not be coded, as the hands are part of the rabbit and individual parts of an object are not separately coded. For example, if a person says he or she saw "A rabbit. Here is the head, tail, and body," the examiner does not code A for the rabbit and Ad for the head, tail, and body, but only A. Similarly, if an examinee verbalizes seeing "A rabbit. Here are the ears, head, tail, and hands," the examiner should code only A rather than A, Ad, and Hd, as the various parts (ears, etc.) are all seen as part of the animal and, therefore, encompassed under that first code.

POPULARS

Each card has one popular response. These responses were the most common responses in Exner's sample (2003) and, for all but one card, appeared on at least 30 percent of the protocols. In other words, these were extremely common responses. The popular responses for each card can be found in Rapid Reference 3.12. Whenever a popular response is present, the examiner records a P in the Popular column of the coding sheet.

≡Rapid Reference 3.12

Popular Responses

Card	Area	Object
I	W	Bat or butterfly.
II	D1	Bear, dog, elephant, lamb, head or whole animal.
III	D9	Human figure or representation thereof.
IV	W or D7	Human or humanlike figure (e.g., monster). Must be humanlike to be Popular.
V	W	Bat or butterfly.
VI	W or D1	Animal skin, hide, pelt, or rug.
VII	D9	Human head or face, identified as female, child, or Native American, or no gender specified.
VIII	D1	Animal, usually dog, cat, or rodent.
IX	D3	Human or humanlike figure, such as a wizard, giant, monster, etc.
X	D1	Crab or spider.

Source: Adapted from Table 8.3 in J. E. Exner, The Rorschach: A Comprehensive System, vol. I, Basic Foundations and Principles of Interpretation, 4th ed. (Hoboken, NJ: John Wiley & Sons, Inc., 2003). Used with permission of the publisher.

Some of the popular responses use the entire card (e.g., Cards I and V) whereas others use only part of the card (e.g., Card VII). Because some popular responses do not use the entire blot, it is possible for a popular response to be embedded in another response. For example:

Response (Card VII, held upside down): It looks like two girls, hanging upside down.
Examiner repeats examinee's response.
Inquiry-1: Yes, here and here. There are their heads (points to D1), noses, ponytails, body (points to D3), and these are monkey bars or something (points to D4).
Coding: W + 1 Mpo 2 H, Sc P ZW GHR

In this case, the popular response (human head) is embedded in the response. As a result, the response is coded P.

Z SCORES: ORGANIZATIONAL ACTIVITY

Not every response will receive a code for organizational activity, commonly referred to as a Z score. If the response has form (e.g., has a form quality of +, o, u, or –), it may have a Z score. However, it has to meet one of the four sets of criteria presented in Rapid Reference 3.13. Each response can have only one Z score, so if a response meets the criteria for more than one Z score, only the one with the highest value is coded.

As shown in Rapid Reference 3.13, there are four Z scores, each with its own criteria. The values for each type of Z score change with each card; the more difficult it is to achieve a particular Z score, the higher its value. For example, on Card V, it is relatively easy to use the entire blot in a response. Consequently, a ZW score for that blot has a value of 1.0. However, owing to the structure of that blot, it is relatively difficult to obtain a ZD score, so the value of a ZD score is 5.0, which is much higher. The values for the Z scores can be found in a variety of resources, including Exner (2001, 2003).

≡Rapid Reference 3.13

. . . .

Organizational Activity: Z Scores

Code	Name	Criteria
ZW	Whole	1. Has form quality coded as +, o, u, or –. 2. Has developmental quality coded as +, o, or v/+. 3. Location is coded as W.
ZA	Adjacent	1. Has form quality coded as +, o, u, or –. 2. Has developmental quality coded as + or v/+. 3. At least two objects are in a relationship and the parts of the blot they are located in touch.
ZD	Distant	1. Has form quality coded as +, o, u, or –. 2. Has developmental quality coded as + or v/+. 3. At least two objects are in a relationship and the parts of the blot they are located in do not touch.
ZS	Space	1. Has form quality coded as +, o, u, or –. 2. Has developmental quality coded as +, o, or v/+. 3. Location is either WS, DS, or DdS. 4. Response uses both white space and the inked part of the blot.

Source: Based on information from Exner, 2001, 2003.

There will be times when an examinee's response will meet the criteria for two (or more) Z scores. In this case, the examiner should give credit for organizational activity that was most difficult to achieve, that is, the highest Z score value. So if an examinee provides a response to Card V that meets the criteria for both a ZW (1.0) and a ZD (5.0) score, the response should be scored as ZD, since the value of that Z score is higher.

The Book Companion Website Materials contain a flowchart that can help an examiner decide for which Z scores a response is eligible. The examiner can then look up the numbers associated with each Z score and decide which Z score to code.

SPECIAL SCORES

The Special Scores are the most difficult part of coding; however, they are also some of the most important scores, due to the way they are interpreted. Special Scores are coded when there is something odd about the responses. As such, there are multiple types of Special Scores, each with its own interpretation. Interpretation is discussed in the next chapter. It is important to remember that not all responses will have Special Scores.

There are fifteen Special Scores that are coded when unusual verbalizations indicate the following: the examinee is having cognitive mishaps, the examinee is perseverating, there is something unique about the content of the examinee's verbalizations, the examinee is personalizing answers, or the examinee is reporting seeing color where there is none. Each of these Special Scores is discussed in some detail below and in the Rapid Reference Boxes throughout this section of this chapter.

Cognitive Special Scores

Six of the Special Scores (the *critical six*) are related to unusual verbalizations that represent cognitive mishaps. These mishaps range from relatively minor, such as saying the wrong word, to severe, where two percepts are fused into one. It is common to see some of the more minor mishaps on a protocol, and having a few of these minor mishaps is not really a cause for concern. The interpretation of these scores will be discussed in more detail in the next chapter. However, the more severe mishaps, such as fusing two percepts into one, are rare and can be indicative of severe thinking issues.

The Cognitive Special Scores can be subdivided into three categories: deviant verbalizations, inappropriate combinations, and inappropriate logic. Additionally, four of these scores are assigned levels. Levels are discussed later in this section. Rapid Reference 3.14 summarizes the use of each of the cognitive Special Scores.

≡Rapid Reference 3.14

Cognitive Special Scores

Code	Name	When Coded
DV	Deviant Verbalization	An inappropriate word is used, or there is a redundancy.
DR	Deviant Response	The person is either distorting the task or is leaving it.
INCOM	Incongruous Combination	Implausible or impossible features or activities are associated with one object.
FABCOM	Fabulized Combination	At least two objects are in an impossible or implausible relationship.
CONTAM	Contamination	Two or more percepts are fused into one in an unrealistic way.
ALOG	Inappropriate Logic	The person uses strained, concrete reasoning to justify a response.

Source: Based on information from Exner, 2001, 2003.

Level 1 and Level 2

Four of the Cognitive Special Scores—Deviant Verbalization (DV), Deviant Response (DR), Incongruous Combination (INCOM), and Fabulized Combination (FABCOM)—are assigned on each use to one of two levels. The levels are used to differentiate mild cognitive mishaps, such as those that occur even in normally developing individuals, from more severe cognitive mishaps that indicate the possibility of more severe cognitive difficulties.

Unfortunately, Exner did not offer a great deal of guidance in differentiating a Level 1 (mild mishap) from a Level 2 (severe mishap) response. The main difference between a Level 1 and Level 2 score is the degree of bizarreness. However, this can be subjective; what one person considers to be bizarre may not be what another person considers to be bizarre. Viglione (2010) has offered some strategies to differentiate between a Level 1 and a Level 2 score. He emphasizes the importance of considering the entire response, not just the language associated with the Special Score, in determining whether a response meets the criteria for a Level 1 or Level 2 score. For instance, if examinees verbalize that their response is odd, or question their own logic (e.g., "It looks like a bat with hands. Do bats have hands?"), then the response is likely to be a Level 1. For additional assistance, Viglione has provided a series of criteria that can be used to help determine whether a score should be coded as a Level 1 or Level 2 (see his *Rorschach Coding Solutions*, 2010, pp. 7–31 to 7–40).

Another way to differentiate between a Level 1 and a Level 2 score is the cartoon test: Would the examiner consider a particular response bizarre if the examiner saw it in the context of a children's cartoon? If the answer is yes, then that response is likely a Level 2. If the answer is no, then the response is more likely to be a Level 1.

There are a number of examples of Level 1 and Level 2 responses in a variety of resources, including Exner (2001, 2003) and Viglione (2010), and also a few examples in this chapter.

DON'T FORGET
....

Four of the Cognitive Special Scores—DV, DR, INCOM, and FABCOM—have levels. Level 1 is assigned to responses that are less bizarre, and Level 2 is assigned to responses that are more bizarre.

DV and DR: Deviant Verbalizations

There are two types of deviant verbalizations: Deviant Verbalization (DV) and Deviant Response (DR). DV is coded whenever the examinee uses an incorrect word. This can take two forms: a neologism or a redundancy. A neologism is an inappropriate word or a word created by the examinee that is not an actual word in the language that the examinee is being assessed in. Some neologisms are easy to identify, such as "it is a superhero with large *mussels*"; however, other neologisms can appear to be genuine words, such as "caramely." The latter example is a colloquial use of the ending "-y," but nonetheless is not a real word. Redundancy is using two similar words close together, such as "baby infant." As by definition an infant is a baby, so this terminology is redundant. It is not necessary to indicate whether the DV coding reflects a neologism or a redundancy; both receive the DV code.

The two levels of DV codes are coded as DV1 and DV2. When coding, it is vital to differentiate whether the DV code is a Level 1 or Level 2, because they are interpreted differently. DV1 is coded for more benign, less bizarre deviant verbalizations, such as "a *baby puppy*." DV2 is used for more bizarre deviant verbalizations, such as "the blot looks *appendicious*." In general, if people correct themselves in the response, do not code for a DV (Viglione, 2010).

Deviant Response (DR) is coded when the examinee is distorting the task, leaves the task, or uses an inappropriate phrase. As with the DV code, there are two levels of DR codes: DR1 and DR2. In general, a deviant response is easy to identify, as the examinee starts talking about something other than the response to the blot. However, short statements on the nature of the testing process, such as "Wow, this card has a lot of color," are generally not coded as DR, as long as they occur before the examinee begins providing the response. DR is coded only when the examinee starts talking about another topic while providing a response. For example:

It looks like a pizza. My cat likes pizza. Especially pepperoni. (DR1)
It's the devil. You're not religious are you? My pastor enjoys swimming, but only on Wednesdays. (DR2)

Not all asides are coded as deviant responses. When people are trying to remain on task but having difficulty explaining themselves, that should not be coded DR. Viglione (2010) has also recommended that humorous remarks not be coded DR; however, strong emotional reactions to the card can be coded DR. For example:

(Card X) I. . .I can't even. It's horrible (yells and starts shaking). Violence, Pain. (drops card). That's it. (DR2)

This response would be coded DR2 because of the strong emotional reaction to the card, indicating that the person has lost objectivity in relation to the card and is treating it as if what was seen was real. This also represents a distortion of the task.

INCOM, FABCOM, and CONTAM: Inappropriate Combinations

There are three categories for coding inappropriate combinations: Incongruous Combination (INCOM), Fabulized Combination (FABCOM), and Contamination (CONTAM). These represent more serious cognitive mishaps than the DV and the DR codes do. Of the inappropriate combinations, INCOM is generally the least serious while CONTAM is the most serious. The examiner needs to assign levels for INCOM and FABCOM codings; CONTAM codings are not assigned levels.

INCOM is used when the examinee assigns an implausible or impossible features or activities to one object. For example:

A rabbit. Here are his hands. (INCOM1)
A dog with three heads. (INCOM2)
A dog singing. (INCOM1)

In some cases, a response could be coded either as a DV or an INCOM. The first example is an excellent sample of a response that could include either a DV or an INCOM. The use of the word "hands" could be seen as using an inappropriate word; the appropriate word could have been "paws." However, because of the use of the inappropriate word, there is now an impossible feature assigned to the rabbit: the rabbit has hands. The appropriate coding is INCOM1, not DV1.

Like DV and DR, the INCOM code has levels assigned to it. Level 1 codes are typically for more benign responses, assigned to such mishaps as using the incorrect word to describe something, such as referring to "paws" as "hands" or saying "a bat has horns." Level 2 codes tend to be used for strange and unrealistic responses: for example, "a person with eight legs." However, INCOM codes are not assigned if the examinee reports that the object is part of a cartoon, as cartoon objects can take part in many implausible or impossible activities and have implausible features.

DON'T FORGET

If the examinee says that his or her response is a cartoon, do not code INCOM.

FABCOMs are similar to INCOMs, as fabulized combinations involve the examinee assigning an implausible or impossible relationship to two or more objects. The main difference between an INCOM and a FABCOM is that an INCOM involves only one object and a FABCOM involves at least two objects that are in a relationship. Consequently, a FABCOM will typically have a DQ of + or v/+. An INCOM can occur with any DQ.

FABCOMs have two levels, like an INCOM. Some examples of FABCOMs are

Dogs playing poker. (FABCOM1)
These cats were hunting this dragon. See, here, they are feasting on his flesh and toasting their kill. (FABCOM2)

DON'T FORGET

It is easy to confuse an INCOM and a FABCOM. Remember that INCOMs involve only one object while FABCOMs involve two or more objects.

The final inappropriate combination is the Contamination (CONTAM). CONTAM is coded whenever two, or more, objects are fused into one response. It is conceptually similar to a double exposure, where one picture is overlaid onto another picture. Unlike INCOMs and FABCOMs, CONTAMs are not assigned levels.

In general, CONTAMs are relatively easy to code, as these descriptions are generally quite bizarre. For example:

(Card I). It looks like the devil and a cat. It's the devat. Pure evil.

However, there are cases where a response that appears to be a CONTAM should not receive a Cognitive Special Score. These are instances where the examinee perceives that the blot looks like a fictional animal that is a cross between two (or more) animals. For example, on Card IX the examinee may respond by saying it's a "jackalope," because it "looks like a jackrabbit head with antlers." This may not be the fusing of two percepts; it may be a representation of a fictional animal that is part of US folklore. A careful inquiry can help to differentiate whether a person has fused a jackrabbit and an antelope or is referring to the fictional jackalope.

ALOG: Inappropriate Logic

The final Cognitive Special Score is Inappropriate Logic (ALOG). ALOG is coded when, *without prompting*, examinees use strained and/or unconventional logic to justify their response. The examinee may also use extremely concrete reasoning in his or her responses. Concrete reasoning is when the examinee relies on what he or she sees and his or her experiences rather than abstract thought. Individuals who engage in concrete reasoning may not be able to generalize to other situations. Also these examinees appear certain about their response. This is important, as if examinees provide any information to indicate that they are questioning their own response, such as by saying, "I guess it could be," or, "This may be," then ALOG should not be coded. Examinees' verbalizations must indicate that they are certain about their response, and the strained logic that accompanies it, in order to code an ALOG.

Generally, terms like "must be," "has to be," and "because" accompany the strained logic indicative of an ALOG. However, the presence of these terms is not sufficient for coding an ALOG; the logic associated with these terms needs to be strained. For example:

This is a dog and this must be a cat because it is next to the dog. (ALOG)
He must be dead because he is gray. (ALOG)

In both of these cases, the examinee has verbalized that there is no other possibility for what the examinee sees in the blot: the cat needs to be a cat because it is next to the dog. It cannot be anything else. In the second case, "he must be dead" because of the color of the blot. There is no other possibility.

Over-coding ALOG is common (Viglione, 2010). It is important to remember that ALOG cannot be induced and consequently, the verbiage supporting this coding will generally appear in the Response Phase or the first part of an inquiry, before the examiner begins prompting for more information. It is very possible to induce an ALOG during an inquiry; for example:

Response (Card II): It's a rocket ship taking off.
Examiner repeats examinee's response.
Inquiry-1: Here's the ship and the fire.
I'm not sure I see it like you do.
Inquiry-2: Ship is here, wings, front, back. Fire here, the red part.
What makes it look like fire?
Inquiry-3: Here. It's red. It's got to be fire because it's at the bottom of the rocket ship.
Coding: DS + 5 ma.CFo Sc, Fi ZA

In this case, the examinee does not spontaneously offer the strained logic; the examiner needs to prompt twice before the examinee offers it. This should not be coded ALOG.

CAUTION

ALOG is frequently over-coded. Remember, the examinee must offer spontaneously the strained logic to justify the response in order for the examiner to code an ALOG.

Rules for Coding the Cognitive Scores

There are a few rules for coding the Cognitive Special Scores. First, in general, an examiner can code multiple cognitive scores within the same response, as long as the words supporting the different codes do not overlap. Consider the following example:

(Card IX). It looks like two blue apples. They are rolling down this hill here, attacking the villagers below. See all the blood? (INCOM1, FABCOM2)

In this case, both the INCOM1 (blue apples) and the FABCOM2 (attacking the villagers) can be coded because the wording that supports the coding of one does not overlap with the wording for the other.

When wording does overlap, only the more severe cognitive mishap is scored. The examiner determines which cognitive code is more severe by examining the point value for each of the codes; the one with the highest point value is coded. For example, if the examinee states that the blot looks like "a bat with antlers," this meets the criteria for DV1, as "antlers" is an inappropriate word, and also meets the criteria for INCOM1, as bats do not have antlers. In this case, because INCOM1 is assigned more points than DV1, only the INCOM1 is coded. The point values for each of the codes are listed in Rapid Reference 3.15.

The final rule for coding the Cognitive Special Scores is that if a CONTAM is present in the response, no other Cognitive Special Score can be coded, even if the language does not overlap. Rapid Reference 3.16 summarizes the rules for coding these Special Scores.

PSV: Perseveration

Although they all share the same abbreviation, there are three different types of Perseveration (PSV): within card, content, and mechanical. Also each type of PSV is interpreted differently. The interpretation of each type of PSV will be discussed further in the next chapter.

≡Rapid Reference 3.15

Point Values for Cognitive Codes, in Order of Increasing Value

Code	Value
DVI	I
DV2	2
INCOMI	2
DRI	3
INCOM2	4
FABCOMI	4
ALOG	5
DR2	6
FABCOM2	7
CONTAM	7

Source: Based on information in Exner, 2001, 2003.

≡Rapid Reference 3.16

Rules for Coding Multiple Cognitive Special Scores

1. Unless there is a CONTAM present, you can code multiple Cognitive Special Scores in the same response, as long as the wording supporting one code does not overlap with the wording for another code.

2. If the wording supporting multiple Cognitive Special Scores overlaps, code only the score with the highest value (see Rapid Reference 3.15).

3. If a CONTAM is present, code only CONTAM. Do not code any other Cognitive Special Scores.

Source: Based on information from Exner, 2001, 2003.

Within Card PSV is the most common type of PSV. This PSV is coded when two responses on the same card have the same location, DQ, determinants, FQ, contents, and organizational activity (Z scores). Consequently, this PSV can only be coded after the examiner has coded all the responses to the card. It is the second of the two matching responses that is coded PSV, as that is the perseveration. The first response does not get a PSV code.

Content PSVs occur when examinees verbalize that they are seeing the same content they saw previously. It is not sufficient for the examinee to simply name the same content twice, such as reporting seeing a butterfly on both Card I and Card V. Before the response can be coded PSV, the examinee needs to specifically say that it is the same content as before. The examinee may say something like, "Oh, there's that butterfly again," or, "hmm, the man is back," indicating that the examinee is referring back to earlier content.

The final PSV is the Mechanical PSV. This code is scored when the examinee repeatedly provides the same response. This usually results in an invalid Rorschach, as the examinee does not provide a sufficient number of responses.

DON'T FORGET

There are three types of perseverations: Within Card, Content, and Mechanical. All three are coded PSV.

Special Content Characteristics

Four of the Special Scores are classified as special content characteristics. These are coded when there is something unique about the content of the response, involving the use of Abstract Content (AB), Morbid Content (MOR), Aggressive Movement (AG), or Cooperative Movement (COP).

Abstract Content (AB) is coded in two cases. The first case is where examinees clearly state that something in their response, or their entire response, is a representation of something, rather than a direct image of something. For example:

Response (Card III): It's two people, one here and one here (points to D9, both sides). This here (pointing to D3) represents their love for one another. *Examiner repeats examinee's response.*

Inquiry-1: Yes, they are running towards each other to hug each other. The red here (points to D3) reminded me of love because it was red.
Coding: D + 9 Ma.Co 2 H, Id P ZD AB, COP GHR

In this case, the examinee clearly indicates that part of the blot represents something. Specifically, area D3 represents love. Often the examinee will use words like "represents," "symbol," or "symbolize" in this type of response.

The other instance in which AB will be coded is when DQ is vague and the only content code is Hx. These are formless M responses like "It's pain. The colors remind me of pain and anguish." It is not important to distinguish between the two types of AB for coding; both receive the same code.

Morbid Content (MOR) is coded when the examinee reports seeing something that is dead, spoiled, ruined, or sad. Examples of responses warranting a MOR code are

The man is sad.
Two rabbits, bleeding.
A shoe, but the heel is broken off.

In the first example, the examinee identifies that the man is sad, meeting the criteria for a MOR. In the next two examples, the examinee states that the objects are damaged. The rabbits are bleeding, indicating that they were harmed; the shoe's heel was broken.

DON'T FORGET

To easily code MOR, remember the four D's: dead, destroyed, damaged, and dysphoric.

The final two special content characteristics require movement. Consequently, they can only be coded when a movement determinant is coded. These content codes are used when there is an Aggressive Movement (AG) or a Cooperative Movement (COP).

In order to code Aggressive Movement (AG), there must be a movement occurring that is clearly aggressive. This can include movements like "fighting," "stabbing," or "pouncing." It also includes movements that are preparatory to aggressive movement, such as "stalking" and "hunting." Viglione (2010) recommends using a threshold of "stalking"; anything at least as aggressive as "stalking" should be coded AG.

Emotions and looks can also be classified as AG. For example, someone "glaring" at another person is coded AG, as is "a mean look" (see Exner, 2001, for examples). However, an "evil person" is not coded AG because there is no movement involved. Remember, in order to code AG, there must be movement.

Cooperative Movement (COP) is coded whenever there are at least two objects engaged in some form of cooperative or positive movement. The bar for coding cooperative movement is relatively low; as long as the objects are engaged in some form of cooperative movement, such as talking to each other, COP will be coded. Dancing is always coded as cooperative movement, as long as there are two or more objects dancing. Two examples of responses with cooperative movement are

These two people are lifting up this heavy basket.
Two rabbits, playing together.

DON'T FORGET

In order to code AG or COP, there must be a movement determinant. If there is no movement, AG and COP cannot be coded.

The AG and the COP codes are not mutually exclusive; it is possible to have both in the same response. For instance, the response "These two women are working together to destroy this basket. See, there are parts everywhere" would be coded as COP, AG, and MOR. In this response, the women are engaged in a cooperative movement (COP), that is also aggressive (AG, destroying), and the basket has been damaged (MOR). Thus, all three codes should be recorded.

Human Representational Responses

There are two types of human representational responses: Good Human Representational Responses (GHR) and Poor Human Representational Responses (PHR). These codes are mutually exclusive: only one of the two can be coded per response. Not all responses will have a GHR or PHR code. However, any response with any human content code, an M determinant, an FM determinant with a COP code, or an FM determinant with an AG code will receive a human representational response code.

DON'T FORGET

GHR or PHR will be coded if the response has any of the following:

Any human content code

An M determinant

An FM determinant with COP

An FM determinant with AG

There are a series of rules that need to be followed in order to code GHR or PHR; my advice is to let a scoring program code it, because the chance of errors in coding GHR and PHR is high. The coding of GHR and PHR is based on the rest of the coding for the response; thus, it is done last. However, because GHR and PHR are based on the coding for the response, coding of GHR and PHR can be affected by incorrect coding of other variables. This is another reason to make sure that coding is done as accurately as possible and why I strongly recommend allowing a scoring program to code this variable.

PER: Personalized Answers

A Personalized Answer (PER) is coded whenever the examiner is convinced that the examinee is using personal knowledge or experience to justify a response. Often, examinees will say things like "I know this because. . .," I learned this in school," or, "I saw this in. . ." However, PER should not be coded when the examinee is relying on general knowledge, such as in the following example:

> Response (Card X): This part (points to D9), the red part, looks like a poinsettia.
>
> *Examiner repeats examinee's response.*
>
> Inquiry-1: The red color reminded me of a poinsettia. They are red. The bloom is still closed, that's why it is long and skinny. The red, that's why it looks like a poinsettia. I guess I have Christmas on the brain!
>
> *Coding: Do9 CF– Bt*

Examiners sometimes have difficulty determining the difference between DR and PER, as both codes can present as deviating from the task. It is important that an examiner code DR and PER correctly, as the two are interpreted differently. If the examinee is using personal knowledge to justify an off-task response, then the correct code is PER. In contrast, if the examinee is off task and not attempting to justify the response in any way, then the correct code is DR.

CAUTION

Review the difference between PER and DR. Do not code both, unless each is represented by separate verbiage.

CP: Special Color Phenomenon

The final Special Score is a color phenomenon referred to as a Color Projection (CP). CP is a rare score that is applied when an examinee perceives an achromatic part of the blot as being colored. For example:

Response (Card V): It's a butterfly.
Examiner repeats examinee's response.
Inquiry-1: Yes, wings, head, body (points). It's beautiful.
You said it was beautiful?
Inquiry-2: Yes, it is a lovely shade of pink.
Coding: Wo1 FYo A P ZW CP

When an examinee has a color projection, reporting seeing chromatic color where there is none, do not code C, CF, or FC. Instead, it is conventional to code FY, YF, or Y in lieu of a color determinant.

Summary of Special Scores

Special scores are one of the most difficult parts of coding in the CS. However, with practice and review, it is possible to code these scores accurately. There are some resources in the Book Companion Website Materials that can help examiners code more accurately. Additional resources include *Coding Solutions* by Viglione (2010), the 200+ practice codings in the *Rorschach Workbook* (Exner, 2001), and Hilsenroth and Charnas's (2007) training manual. I would advise examiners to review these materials in order to improve their coding of Special Scores.

CONCLUSION

Research (e.g., Allard & Faust, 2000; Hopwood & Richard, 2005; Simons, Goddard, & Patton, 2002) has shown that scoring errors are common in psychological testing. Still, the majority of these errors are small and do not have a significant impact on interpretation. When scoring a test as complex as the Rorschach CS, it is understandable that there will be coding errors. In general, a few small mistakes (e.g., coding an Ma as an Mp) will have little effect on the interpretation; however, patterns of coding errors (e.g., never correctly differentiating between T and Y) can be devastating to an interpretation.

With practice, these errors can be minimized. There are a number of resources, in addition to Exner's (2003) work, that can be used to improve coding. These include Viglione (2010), Exner (2001), and Hilsenroth and Charnas's (2007) training manual. Both beginning and experienced Rorschach examiners should be comfortable consulting with one another over coding; consultation can likely improve reliability and reduce coding errors. Although the Rorschach Comprehensive System, like many other psychological tests, is generally robust enough to handle some minor coding errors, significant errors will affect results, which will influence interpretation.

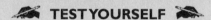

✒ TEST YOURSELF ✒

1. **What is the difference between a D and a Dd area?**
   a. D areas were more commonly used than Dd areas were in the large sample of protocols reviewed by Exner.
   b. D areas use the whole blot while Dd areas use only part of the blot.
   c. D areas use white space while Dd areas do not.
   d. Dd areas use white space while D areas do not.

2. **Your examinee says that Card I looks like "a dog eating a bird." What is the appropriate DQ for this response?**
   a. +
   b. o
   c. v/+
   d. v

3. **Which set of determinants should NOT have an FQ assigned to them?**
   a. CF.Ma.mp
   b. FC.Y
   c. C.Y
   d. C.TF

4. **What does an FQ of u mean?**
   a. The response followed the contours of the blot and was commonly seen.
   b. The response followed the contours of the blot but was not commonly seen.
   c. The response did not follow the contours of the blot.
   d. The response did not follow the contours of the blot but was commonly seen.

5. **What content code(s) should be used for this response: "It looks like a tree, standing on a hill, surrounded by water"?**

   a. Na only

   b. Bt only

   c. Ls only

   d. Bt and Na only

6. **Which of the Cognitive Special Scores is considered to be the most severe?**

   a. DV2

   b. FABCOM1

   c. ALOG

   d. CONTAM

Answers: 1. a; 2. a; 3. c; 4. b; 5. a; 6. d.

Four

Psychological testing should never be interpreted in isolation. Instead, all data provided as part of the psychological testing should be interpreted in light of the other information available, including information from the clinical interview, the results of other tests, collateral information (e.g., interviews with others, medical records, etc.), situational factors (e.g., type of evaluation), and the person's unique cultural background and individual differences. Exner (2000, p. 3) noted some further basic prerequisites for interpreting a Rorschach using the Comprehensive System (CS). These include a "reasonably good understanding of people and the notion of personality," a "good working knowledge of psychopathology and maladjustment," and an "understanding of the test itself." In other words, understanding the CS is not enough for an accurate interpretation. The examiner also needs to have an understanding of personality and psychopathology in order to use the system to its full potential.

CAUTION

Never interpret variables in isolation. Remember that many other factors influence test results, including redundant situational factors and the examinee's mood, culture, and characteristics.

Like many other performance-based measures (e.g., the WAIS-IV; see Wechsler, 2008), interpretation of the CS relies on the deviation principle, or data that are significantly different from the performance data of the normative group. However, focusing solely on deviations can lead us to erroneously take into account only what is aberrant or odd about an examinee and to ignore what is "normal" about the examinee. In order to gain a complete understanding of the person, it is important for us to examine not only what is aberrant but also what is not. Thus, it is very important for examiners to look at all aspects of the CS, rather than focusing just on what is different about the person.

This chapter is designed to help to explain CS interpretation. It is not designed to serve as a replacement for any of the CS interpretation guides, such as Exner (2000, 2003) or Weiner (2003). I recommend that readers use one of those resources to interpret a Rorschach CS and use this book as a resource that can explain or assist you to understand the concepts that inform an interpretation.

Currently, there are a variety of comparison samples available, samples to which you can compare an examinee's performance: the normative data in Exner's *Rorschach Workbook* (2001) and Volume I of *The Rorschach: A Comprehensive System* (2003); the international normative data provided by Meyer, Erdberg, and Shaffer (2007); and also Exner and Erdberg's 450 sample (2005). Other data sets exist as well. Each of these sets of data has strengths and weaknesses, and examiners need to decide to which of these sets of data they want to compare the examinee's performance. I encourage the reader to review each normative data set and consider its strengths and weaknesses before deciding on a comparison standard.

The interpretation of the CS involves three pieces of data: the sequence of scores, the structural summary, and the examinee's verbal responses during the administration. I strongly recommend that examiners using the CS use a computerized scoring program to generate the structural summary. A complete data set can be found in the Appendix, along with reproductions of a computer-generated sequence of scores and a structural summary in Figures A.1, A.2, and A.3.

Although many of these computerized programs also allow users to generate interpretive reports, I would caution readers to avoid doing so, as the computer is unable to take into account the person's individual differences, information from collateral sources, and the like.

Assuming the CS protocol is valid ($R \geq 14$), the first step in interpreting a CS protocol in examinees who are at least 15 years old is to review the Suicide Constellation, or S-CON. The S-CON is a series of variables that have been shown to be predictive of a completed suicide within the next sixty days (Fowler, Piers, Hilsenroth, Holdwick, & Padawer, 2001). Research has shown that S-CON scores of both 8 and 7 can identify individuals who are an increased risk of completing suicide within sixty days after taking the Rorschach. Fowler and colleagues (2001) found that a cutoff score of 7 identified 79 percent of the individuals in a sample who made a near-lethal suicide attempt, accurately distinguishing them from those in the sample who did not make such an attempt. As a result, I would recommend using 7 as a cutoff for the S-CON, not 8 as suggested by Exner (2003).

DON'T FORGET

. . . .

Always interpret the S-CON first for individuals age 15 or older. However, S-CON is not considered valid for examinees under the age of 15.

Traditionally, the interpretation of the CS then proceeds by clusters. However, I would recommend that as a next step the examiner should determine the examinee's coping style. This is important for a number of reasons, including that many variables are interpreted in light of the coping style and that two of the key variables in the Key Variable search require a knowledge of coping style.

The CS categorizes people as having one of three coping styles, using the values for Erlebnistypus (EB): introversive, extratensive, and ambitent. EB is a ratio of the number of M determinants to WSumC. M is a measure of controlled thinking while WSumC relates to emotion. Individuals who have a significantly higher value for M than for WSumC are described as introversive. Individuals who are introversive tend to make decisions by thinking through their options; emotions tend to play a minimal role in their decision making. These individuals can be described as logical and analytical. Extratensive individuals have the opposite pattern; they have a higher value for WSumC than for M. These individuals tend to use both emotions and thinking in decision making and tend to use a trial-and-error approach. They can be described as intuitive. Individuals who are ambitent have similar values for M and WSumC. They do not have a consistent problem-solving style. This will not necessarily be problematic; however, the problem solving of someone with an ambitent style may become less efficient, especially when under stress, because they have no set problem-solving style to fall back on (Exner, 2000, 2003; Weiner, 2003).

There is, technically speaking, a fourth problem-solving style: avoidant. This style is present when the Lambda is higher than 0.99. If Lambda is higher than 0.99, then the examinee will tend to avoid complexity by simplifying it or avoiding it entirely. When this style is present, it supersedes the other three styles. Exner (2000, 2003) does present avoidant-ambitent, avoidant-extratensive, and avoidant-introversive as distinct styles. However, in interpretation, they are all interpreted as avoidant styles. For practicality, there is no reason to differentiate between the different types of avoidant styles. Rapid Reference 4.1 summarizes the four coping styles assessed on the CS.

Determining whether an individual is extratensive, introversive, ambitent, or avoidant is not so simple as looking at whether M or WSumC has a higher value

≡ Rapid Reference 4.1

Types of Coping Styles Assessed on the CS

Style	Examinee Characteristics
Introversive	M > WSumC, L < 1. Thinks through options when problem solving. Emotions play a minimal role in problem solving. Is logical.
Extratensive	WSumC > M, L < 1. Uses trial-and-error approach. Merges emotions with thinking when problem solving. Is intuitive.
Ambitent	M ≈ WSumC, L < 1. Has no set coping style.
Avoidant	L > 0.99. Avoids complexity.

Source: Based on Exner, 2001; 2003; Weiner, 2003.

on the protocol. Exner (2003) discusses the steps to be taken to determine style. Also, the Book Companion Website Materials include a flowchart, designed to be used with a structural summary generated by the Rorschach Interpretation Assistance Program (Exner, Weiner, & PAR staff, 2001), that can help an examiner to easily determine an examinee's coping style.

Test data from the Rorschach is grouped into eight clusters; seven of these are always interpreted: controls and stress tolerance, affect, mediation, ideation, processing, self-perception, and interpersonal perception. The eighth, situation-related stress, is interpreted only when there is evidence in the structural summary that situation-related stress (e.g., transient stress) may be affecting the person to a significant degree. In order to determine the order in which the clusters should be interpreted, readers should carry out a Key Variable search, using the chart in Rapid Reference 4.2. To conduct the Key Variable search, examiners start at the top of this chart and stop at the first positive variable that also appears on the structural summary they are interpreting. That row of the chart displays the cluster search order to follow.

However, there are cases where the examinee's structural summary does not match any of the criteria (the positive variables) in the Key Variable search. In this case, the examiner should move on to the Tertiary Variable search (see Rapid

$\equiv$ *Rapid Reference 4.2*

Key Variable Search

Positive Variable	Typical Cluster Search Routine
PTI > 3	Processing > Mediation > Ideation > Controls > Affect > Self-Perception > Interpersonal Perception
DEPI > 5 and CDI > 3	Interpersonal Perception > Self-Perception > Controls > Affect > Processing > Mediation > Ideation
DEPI > 5	Affect > Controls > Self-Perception > Interpersonal Perception > Processing > Mediation > Ideation
D < Adj D	Controls > Situational Stress (The remaining search routine should be that identified for the next positive Key Variable or the list of Tertiary Variables.)
CDI > 3	Controls > Interpersonal Perception > Self-Perception > Affect > Processing > Mediation > Ideation
Adj D is minus	Controls > (The remaining search routine should be that identified for the next positive Key Variable or the list of Tertiary Variables.)
Lambda > 0.99	Processing > Mediation > Ideation > Controls > Affect > Self-Perception > Interpersonal Perception
FR + RF > 0	Self-Perception > interpersonal Perception > Controls (The remaining search routine should be that identified for the next positive Key Variable or the list of Tertiary Variables.)
EB is introversive	Ideation > Processing > Mediation > Controls > Affect > Self-Perception > Interpersonal Perception
EB is extratensive	Affect > Self-Perception > Interpersonal Perception > Controls > Processing > Mediation > Ideation
p > a + 1	Ideation > Processing > Mediation > Controls > Self-Perception > Interpersonal Perception > Affect
HVI Positive	Ideation > Processing > Mediation > Controls > Self-Perception > Interpersonal Perception > Affect

Source: J. E. Exner & P. Erdberg, *The Rorschach: A Comprehensive System*, vol. 2, *Advanced Interpretation*, 3rd ed. (Hoboken, NJ: John Wiley & Sons, Inc., 2005). Reprinted with permission from the publisher.

Reference 4.3). The process for the Tertiary Variable search is similar to the Key Variable search, in that the examiner goes step by step down the list and stops at the first positive variable that also appears on the structural summary being interpreted.

≡ Rapid Reference 4.3

Tertiary Variable Search

Positive Variable	Typical Cluster Search Routine
OBS Positive	Processing > Mediation > Ideation > Controls > Affect > Self-Perception > Interpersonal Perception
DEPI = 5	Affect > Controls > Self-Perception > Interpersonal Perception > Processing > Mediation > Ideation
EA > 12	Controls > Ideation > Processing > Mediation > Affect > Self-Perception > Interpersonal Perception
M− > 0 or Mp > Ma or Sum6 Sp Sc > 5	Ideation > Mediation > Processing > Controls > Affect > Self-Perception > Interpersonal Perception
Sum Shad > FM + m or (CF + C) > FC + 1 or Afr < 0.46	Affect > Controls > Self-Perception > Interpersonal Perception > Processing > Mediation > Ideation
X−% > 20% or Zd > +3.0 or < −3.0	Processing > Mediation > Ideation > Controls > Affect > Self-Perception > Interpersonal Perception
3r + (2) / R < 0.33	Self-Perception > Interpersonal Perception > Affect > Controls > Processing > Mediation > Ideation
MOR > 2 or AG > 2	Self-Perception > Interpersonal Perception > Controls > Ideation > Processing > Mediation > Affect
T = 0 or > 1	Self-Perception > Interpersonal Perception > Affect > Controls > Processing > Mediation > Ideation

Source: J. E. Exner & P. Erdberg, *The Rorschach: A Comprehensive System*, vol. 2, *Advanced Interpretation*, 3rd ed. (Hoboken, NJ: John Wiley & Sons, Inc., 2005). Reprinted with permission from the publisher.

Examiners may be tempted to skip the Key Variable search. After all, it is much more convenient to simply interpret the clusters in the order they are presented in various interpretation guides (e.g., Exner, 2000, 2003). The purpose of the Key Variable search is to guide the examiner to the clusters that are likely to be most important to the examinee's current personality structure. Thus, interpreting the protocol in the order suggested by the Key Variable search will help to guide the examiner to the most salient parts of the protocol, so that the first two or three clusters are likely to yield the most information about the examinee. Also, the information from the remaining clusters can be interpreted in light of the information obtained from the first few clusters.

Finally, before interpreting a protocol, it is important that examiners are aware of the *barely yield phenomenon* (Exner, 2003). This occurs when an observation barely meets the threshold for a deviant finding. An example of this is having two texture responses in a protocol. One texture response is considered normal, if comparing the examinee's performance to the Exner 600 sample or the Exner 450 sample (Exner, 2001, 2003, 2007; Exner & Erdberg, 2005); however, according to both of these samples, two texture responses are considered a significant deviation from the norm. When there are observations that just meet the criteria for a deviation, such as having two texture responses on a protocol, it is vital that examiners review their coding, to ensure that the items were coded correctly.

The interpretation of the clusters follows a step-by-step process. The following sections, organized by cluster, contain a brief summary of how to interpret a CS protocol; however, readers are strongly encouraged to review one of the available Rorschach interpretation guides (e.g., Choca, 2013; Exner 2000, 2003; Weiner, 2003) in order to gain a broader understanding of the nuances of CS interpretation.

CONTROLS AND STRESS TOLERANCE

Exner defined *control* as the "capacity to form decisions and implement deliberate behaviors that are designed to contend with the demands of a situation" (Exner, 2000, p. 22). In other words, control is the ability of a person to organize and maintain control over her thoughts, behavior, and emotions, to at least some extent, and to remain on task. Individuals' ability to control themselves can change based on their current circumstances. For example, although professors expect most doctoral students to have a high capacity for control, even during comprehensive examinations, it is not abnormal for even the most level-headed student facing such an exam to snap more often at her significant other for things that would normally not be bothersome, such as leaving the cap off the toothpaste. Due to the increased level of stress and demands that the student is experiencing (e.g., a comprehensive examination), her resources are being tapped and her ability to control her behavior, emotions, and thoughts is weakened. However, once the stress is over (e.g., the student successfully completes the comprehensive examination), her ability to control herself returns to normal. It should be noted that the capacity to control oneself varies from person to person; some people have significant capacity to control themselves, whereas others have very little capacity.

It is important to remember that the controls cluster assess only the *capacity* to control. There are people who have the capacity to control but who, for various reasons, do not. In other words, the capacity to control behavior does not mean that the person will always appropriately control her impulses, thoughts, emotions, and behaviors.

DON'T FORGET

Control is the ability of the person to organize and maintain control over her thoughts, behavior, and emotions, and to remain on task.

Stress tolerance, in contrast, is the ability of the person to tolerate stress, which, like control, can fluctuate depending on the demands on the person. The demands on the person can be external (e.g., comprehensive examinations in graduate school) or internal (e.g., depression or anxiety). In times of high demand, the psychological resources are depleted, thus the tolerance for stress is decreased.

A high stress tolerance is thought to be related to a high level of psychological resources. Psychological resources are the reserves the person has; they include the ability to identify feelings and cognitive faculties. There is a relationship between intelligence and psychological resources, in that individuals of average or above average intelligence typically have a higher level of resources available to them than individuals with lower levels of intelligence (Exner, 2000). A person with a high level of resources is better able to handle demands on herself. However, having the resources does not mean that the person is using them appropriately. Most psychologists can recall multiple cases where clients who had high level of psychological resources did not use these resources in a productive or prosocial manner.

DON'T FORGET

Stress tolerance is the ability of the person to tolerate stress. This can fluctuate depending on the demands on the person.

Stress tolerance and capacity for control are related, as both are associated with resources. The level of resources that someone has dictates how much stress she can tolerate at one time. Those with more resources have more capacity to deal with stress, simply because they have more resources. As a result, those with more resources have a higher tolerance for stress and a higher capacity for control; they can deal with more due to their high level of resources. So when under stress, individuals with a high level of psychological resources are less likely to experience difficulty controlling their thoughts, emotions, and behaviors. Still, it is important to remember that having a lower number of resources does not automatically equate to having a poor capacity for control; capacity for control depends not only on the resources but also on the amount of stress the person is under. Someone with a low level of resources may not have any difficulties coping, as long as she is in an environment that minimizes stress and demands on her. On the other hand, even someone with a significant amount of resources may show signs of a reduced capacity for control when placed in high-stress or high-demand situations (e.g., graduate school). Thus, when interpreting this cluster, it is vital to consider the environment that the examinee is in.

Variables

Compared to other clusters, this cluster is relatively short and contains only five steps. However, these five steps include the interpretation of nine variables: the number of responses (R), Adjusted D (Adj D), the Coping Deficit Index (CDI), Experience Actual (EA), Erlebinstypus (EB), Lambda (L), Experienced Stimulation (es), Adjusted es (Adj es), and Experience Base (eb). Rapid Reference 4.4 provides a brief summary of how each variable is calculated and what each of these variables assesses.

Although the cut points for interpretation may change, as the point at which data are considered to have deviated from the normative group depends on what the normative group is, the method of interpretation does not. This information has been designed to be used with any comparison group and is considered to be current as of this writing. Please keep in mind that research may result in changes in the way CS variables are interpreted. Consequently, it is important for test users to remain abreast of the recent research to ensure their interpretations are accurate. As a reminder, this is only a brief summary of the interpretation; I encourage readers to refer to other materials to get additional information regarding the interpretation of the variables.

Recommended Order of Interpretation

Adj D and CDI: Stress Tolerance and Ability to Control Thoughts, Emotions, and Behaviors

The controls and stress tolerance cluster has five steps. The first step involves Adj D and the Coping Deficit Index. Adj D is a measure of the examinee's capacity for control, under the best circumstances. When the CDI is elevated, it suggests

≡ Rapid Reference 4.4

Controls and Stress Tolerance:
How the Variables Are Calculated and Assessed

Variable	How It Is Calculated	What It Assesses in This Cluster
R/	The number of responses the examinee provided.	Validity of protocol, defensiveness.
L	The number of pure form (F) responses divided by the number of all other types of responses $[F / (R - F)]$.	Defensiveness and/or avoidance.
EA	The sum of M and WSumC $(M + WSumC)$.	Available resources.
EB	The ratio of M to WSumC $(M:WSumC)$.	How the examinee approaches tasks.
eb	The ratio of $FM + m$ to $SumC' + SumT + SumY + SumV$ $(FM + m:SumC' + SumT + SumY + SumV)$.	The demands on the person.
es	The sum of everything in eb $(FM + m + SumC' + SumT + SumY + SumV)$.	A summary of the current demands on the person.
Adj es	es—(all but 1Y and 1m).	Helps to determine whether situational stress is affecting the stress tolerance or available resources. It is essentially a measure of the day-to-day demands on the examinee.
CDI	A combination of a variety of variables.	Difficulty coping with situations, especially social situations and those that are highly stressful.
Adj D	EA − Adj es; this value is then compared to a chart to determine Adj D.	Capacity for control and coping abilities, factoring out current situational stress.

Source: Based on information from Choca, 2013; Exner, 2000, 2003; Weiner, 2003.

that the examinee has difficulty coping, especially in interpersonal situations, due to an immature personality organization (see Rapid Reference 4.5 for a definition). For this step, the interpretation relies heavily on Adj D; the CDI is interpreted only when Adj D is 0.

≡ *Rapid Reference 4.5*

· ·

Immature Personality Organization

Kernberg (1967) describes personality organization as a person's typical ways of feeling, thinking, behaving, relating, and coping with stress and difficult circumstances. *Immature personality organization* is a term used to describe someone who has difficulty in one or more areas of functioning, including someone whose reality testing is not intact (e.g., someone experiencing delusions), someone who has difficulty separating self from others, or someone who uses less mature coping strategies, such as avoidance and denial. This is in contrast to more mature coping strategies, such as channeling frustration into work or creative pursuits.

Adj D is a measure of the examinee's capacity for control, assuming no situational stressors. When it is higher than the normal range (i.e., at least one standard deviation above the mean), it suggests that the examinee is better able to tolerate stress and has a higher capacity for control than the average person. Conversely, if the value for Adj D is below the normal range (i.e., at least one standard deviation below mean), then it indicates the examinee's capacity for control and ability to tolerate stress is likely limited. However, the latter examinee will probably be better able to control her behavior in structured environments or environments that she is familiar with. The further below the normal range the examinee's score is, the more difficulty she is likely to experience controlling her behavior.

When Adj D is in the average range (i.e., within one standard deviation from the mean), the CDI becomes an important benchmark. If the CDI value is in the average range, it suggests that the examinee's ability to tolerate stress and capacity for control is similar to that of the average person. However, if the value for the CDI is above the normal range, it may indicate that the examinee's personality organization is less mature and, as a result, she is prone to coping difficulties. These difficulties usually are associated with interpersonal difficulties (Exner, 2003).

EA and Adj D: Validity

The second step involves both EA and Adj D. The interpretation of this step is relatively straightforward, as its purpose is to determine whether these two variables are similar. EA is a measure of resources and Adj D is the capacity for control, which relies on resources, so if Adj D is above average, EA should also be above average. If Adj D is below average, EA should also be below average. However, if the Adj D scores and EA scores are not consistent with each other (e.g., EA is above average while Adj D is average), it suggests that the scores may not adequately capture the examinee's capacity for control. This is explored further in additional steps.

EB and L: Validity of Hypotheses About Resources

The third step examines both EB and Lambda (L). These scores are used to determine the examinee's coping style. However, they also can provide information about the examinee's current state and assess whether the previous hypotheses about the examinee's available resources (EA and Adj D) are supported, which is how they are used in this cluster. EB is the ratio of M to WSumC, or thinking variables to emotional variables. Lambda compares the number of Pure Form (F) responses to the number of other responses [F / (R − F)] and assesses avoidance and defensiveness on the part of the examinee. Collectively, these variables can be used to determine whether there is another factor, such as being overwhelmed by emotions, that may be affecting the ability of the examinee to control her thoughts, emotions, and behavior.

For example, if the left side of EB (M) is 0, it could suggest that the examinee's emotions are overwhelming her. M is controlled thinking. WSumC (right side of EB) relates to emotions. An extremely low value for M and a higher value for WSumC indicate that emotions have taken over; the testing is not showing evidence of a typical level of controlled thinking. As a result, the examinee is at an increased risk of engaging in behaviors that she normally would not. The examinee may also be experiencing difficulty sustaining attention and concentration (M = 0). This pattern suggests that Adj D and EA are not valid. Exner (2003) recommended that when this occurs, interpretation of this cluster should stop.

In contrast, if the value for the right side of EB (WSumC) is 0 and there is a higher value for M (left side EB), it suggests that the examinee is doing everything she can to shut down her emotions. This takes an immense amount of psychological resources; most people do not have the resources available to do this. As a result, there tend to be more demands on the examinee than she can handle, resulting in decreased capacity for control. This pattern suggests that Adj D and EA are not valid. Exner (2003) recommended that when this occurs, interpretation of this cluster should stop.

As the interpretation of these variables can be complex, I strongly recommend that readers review the information in Exner (2003) for additional information regarding interpretation.

Adj es: Daily Demands and the Accuracy of Adj D

The next step relies on the value for Adj es. Adj es is a measure of the daily demands on the person, with current situational stress (if any) removed. If the examinee's available resources (EA) are higher than the demands on the examinee

(Adj es), then the examinee has the capacity to tolerate at least some additional stressors without losing control (Adj D will be in the average range or higher). However, if the demands on the examinee (Adj es) exceed resources (EA), then the examinee is likely to have a low capacity for control and/or be prone to disorganized behavior (Adj D will be below the normal range). Because of the relationship between these variables, the Adj es score can be used to assess whether EA and Adj D are accurate.

The Adj es relates to whether Adj D is an accurate estimate, an underestimate, or an overestimate of the ability to control thoughts, emotions, and behavior and to tolerate stress. If Adj es is in the normal range, then Adj D is likely an accurate reflection of the examinee's ability to control thoughts, emotions, and behaviors and ability to tolerate stress. However, if Adj es is above the normal range, then Adj D may be an underestimate because the elevated Adj es indicates that the person has more demands on her than the average person does (Exner, 2003). This needs to be taken into consideration when determining the examinee's capacity for control. If the examinee has more demands on her than the typical person does (Adj es above average), it is unfair to make assumptions about her capacity to control when her resources are being tapped more than the average person's. Thus, it is reasonable to assume that if the examinee's demands were decreased to those of an average person, her capacity for control and stress tolerance would be increased. That is why an elevated Adj es could indicate that Adj D underestimates the examinee's capacity for control and stress tolerance.

Conversely, if the Adj es is lower than average, this suggests that the examinee has fewer demands than the average person does. Consequently, if the demands on the examinee were increased to those of a typical person, there would be more demands on her than she currently is experiencing, which would tap her resources more than they are currently being tapped. In other words, her capacity for control and stress tolerance would decrease if the demands on her were similar to those of the average person. That is why a low Adj es could indicate that Adj D overestimates the examinee's capacity for control and stress tolerance.

eb: Potential Impact of Other Sources of Stress

The fifth and final step in this cluster examines eb and the variables associated with it that are not typically stress related. Like Adj es, eb is an estimate of the current demands on the examinee. However, Adj es is an overall measure; eb can be broken into its component parts, allowing the examiner to hypothesize which types of demands on the examinee are unusual. Rapid Reference 4.6 describes the variables used in the calculation of eb and possible interpretations.

≡ Rapid Reference 4.6

Interpretation of eb Variables

Variable	Interpretation
FM	*High:* the examinee may be experiencing peripheral thinking that is typically related to a needs state (e.g., hunger, sex, safety, etc.). *Low:* examinee's way of experiencing needs states may be atypical, or the examinee experiences needs states but acts on them more rapidly than do most others (e.g., instant gratification).
SumC'	*High:* the examinee may be holding back emotions that she would like to display. This takes a large amount of resources and can lead to negative emotions, such as anxiety and sadness. It also can cause physical problems, such as headaches and stomach difficulties.
SumV	*High:* the examinee may be examining herself but focusing on negative aspects of herself more than is typical. This also can result from feelings of guilt or shame, so it is important to look at the background information to clarify whether these determinants are more likely due to guilt than to a chronic focus on negative aspects of oneself.
SumT	*High:* the examinee may be experiencing emotional deprivation. This may be chronic or due to more recent events, such as the loss of a loved one, recent divorce, etc.

Source: Based on information from Choca, 2013; Exner, 2000, 2003; Weiner, 2003.

As with EB, the left side of eb relates to thinking. However, while the left side of EB (M) is controlled thinking, the variables that make up the left side of eb relate to thoughts that are outside the examinee's control, either due to needs states (FM) or stress (m). The interpretation of this step focuses on FM. When FM is higher than average, then it suggests that the examinee is experiencing thoughts that interfere with her usual thinking process and that these unintended thoughts are likely related to unfulfilled need states. These needs states could include things like safety and hunger but also could include sexual needs and other types of needs. It is important to examine the examinee's background and situational factors in order to hypothesize what the unfulfilled needs are.

SITUATION-RELATED STRESS

Stress can be chronic or more transient. The situation-related stress cluster assesses the transient stress: the stress that is not always present. Even the most well-adjusted person can be affected by situational stress, which can take many forms, ranging from significant traumas to more common sources of stress such as work or home life. When people experience situational stress, it taxes their available resources. This, in turn, can result in some impulsive behaviors and/or lower control over behavior than is typical. For instance, even the most psychologically healthy person tends to succumb to stress when faced with an unexpected negative event. These individuals are more likely to snap at close friends for relatively minor transgressions, such as being a few minutes late for a planned dinner out. However, once the negative event is over and the situational stress is gone, the individuals return to their normal, psychological healthy state and are no longer as impulsive. This is only one example of the impact that situational stress, especially a high amount of situational stress, can have on a person.

This cluster is unique in that it is not always interpreted. In general, it will be useful only when the D score is less than the Adj D score. This combination of scores suggests that some situational stress is affecting the examinee, as his current capacity for control (D) is lower than it typically is (Adj D). Keep in mind that some people have a naturally higher tolerance for stress and capacity for control than others (their Adj D is higher than average) and others have a lower capacity for control and stress tolerance than others (their Adj D is negative). This can result in the same stressor affecting two people very differently, due to the available resources they have. An individual with more available resources (higher EA) will generally be less affected by stress than someone with a lower level of available resources (lower EA).

DON'T FORGET
. . . .

People will react differently to the same stressor, due to the amount of resources they have. Those with more available resources will typically be less affected by stress than those with fewer resources.

Variables

This cluster is relatively short and contains seven steps. These steps include the interpretation of twelve variables, comprising the D score (D), Adjusted D (Adj D), inanimate object movement (m), the sum of the diffuse shading determinants (SumY), blend complexity, the sum of the texture determinants (SumT), the sum of the vista determinants (SumV), pure color responses (C), human movement determinants with minus form quality (M–), human movement determinants with no form quality (formless M), experience stimulation (es), and adjusted es (Adj es). Rapid Reference 4.7 provides a brief summary of how each variable is calculated and what each of these variables assesses.

≡ Rapid Reference 4.7

Situation-Related Stress:
How Variables Are Calculated and Assessed

Variable	How It Is Calculated	What It Assesses in This Cluster
Adj D	EA – Adj es; the value is then compared to a chart to determine Adj D.	Capacity for control and level of coping abilities, best-case scenario.
D	EA – es; the value is then compared to a chart to determine D.	Capacity for control and coping abilities, current state. Impact of the situational stress.
m	The total number of m determinants.	Unintentional peripheral thoughts, typically due to situational stress. These thoughts can affect thinking and concentration.
SumY	The total number of Y determinants (Y+YF+FY).	Unintended negative feelings and emotions associated with situational stress.
SumT	The total number of T determinants (T+TF+FT).	Whether the Adj D score may have been artificially lowered due to a recent emotional loss.
SumV	The total number of V determinants (V+VF+FV).	Whether the Adj D score may have been artificially lowered due to guilt or remorse.
Blend complexity	The makeup of the blend.	Depends on what determinants are in the blend.
Pure C	The total number of C determinants (does not include CF or FC).	Impulsivity; tends to manifest emotionally.

Variable	How It Is Calculated	What It Assesses in This Cluster
M–	The total number of M determinants with minus form quality.	Difficulty controlling thoughts (note: may actually assess as having a distorted view of others).
Formless M	The total number of M determinants with no form quality.	Difficulty controlling thoughts.
es	The sum of everything in eb.	A summary of the current demands on the person.
Adj es	es – all but 1 Y and 1 m.	Whether situational stress is affecting the stress tolerance or available resources the person has. It is essentially a measure of the day-to-day demands on the examinee.

Source: Based on information from Choca, 2013; Exner, 2000, 2003; Mihura, Meyer, Dumitrascu, & Bombel, 2013; Weiner, 2003.

Recommended Order of Interpretation

Adj D and D: Validity

Interpreting the situation-related stress cluster takes seven steps. The first step involves assessing whether the difference in Adj D and D is an artifact of coding. Incorrect scoring of some variables, specifically m or Y, can result in an artificially low D score. This is due to the way the Adj D and D are calculated. Both rely on EA, but D uses es and Adj D uses Adj es. The difference between Adj es and es is that Adj es is the es with all but 1 m and 1 Y subtracted from it. Thus, if m or Y codes have been incorrectly coded, that can result in changes to the Adj es. As a result, the difference between Adj D and D may be a false positive.

It is important to evaluate whether this is a possibility in order to ensure as accurate an interpretation as possible for the examinee. As long as the difference between es and Adj es is at least 2, then it is likely that the difference between D and Adj D is not due to a false positive. However, if the difference between es and Adj es is less than 2, it is possible that the difference between the D score and the Adj D score could be due to a scoring error. If there is no scoring error, it is important to look at the examinee's history. If there is evidence of situational stress, then the interpretation of this cluster should proceed. However, if there is no evidence of situational stress, then this cluster should either be interpreted with caution or not at all (Exner, 2003).

Adj D and D: Magnitude of the Stress

This step assesses the magnitude of the situational stress that the examinee is experiencing. In general, the larger the difference between D and Adj D, the larger the impact of the situational stress. If there is only 1 point between D and Adj D, then the impact of the situational stress on the examinee is likely to be mild or moderate. However, if the difference is more than 1, there is likely to be a substantial impact on the examinee (Exner, 2003). The impact of the situational stress will likely present itself as affecting the examinee's usual patterns or thinking and behaving (e.g., such as yelling at a partner for a minor transgression that usually does not frustrate the examinee).

m and SumY: Impact of the Stress

The third step assesses the impact of the stress. Stress can affect our thinking (m) and emotions (SumY). For many individuals, stress affects both areas. The goal of this step is to assess if one area is being affected more than the other. This can inform treatment planning, as the strategies to be used with someone who feels uneasy or tense because of stress (SumY) would be different from the strategies for someone with stress that is clouding his thinking (m).

In general, if one variable is significantly higher than the other, then that area is being affected more by the stress. Exner (2003) noted that one variable being more than three times higher constitutes being significantly higher. Rapid Reference 4.8 has the formulas with an example.

⟰ Rapid Reference 4.8

How to Determine Whether Situational Stress Is Affecting Emotions or Thinking More

- If $m > 3 \times SumY$, then thinking (m) is being affected more than emotions (SumY).
- If $SumY > 3 \times m$, then emotions (SumY) are being affected more than thinking (m).
- If neither m nor SumY is more than three times greater than the other one, then the situational stress is affecting both thinking (m) and emotions (SumY) similarly.

For example: the examinee has an m score of 6 and a SumY of 2. In this case, m is equal to 3 times SumY ($3 \times 2 = 6$, $m = 6$), so m is not more than three times greater than SumY. Consequently, situational stress is not affecting thoughts more than emotions. A finding is positive only when either m or SumY is *more* than three times greater than the other score.

Source: Based on information from Exner, 2000, 2003.

Adj D, D, SumT, SumV: Impact on Adj D and D

This step is similar to the first step in that it assesses the validity of the difference between D and Adj D. In this case, two of the variables involved in the calculation of both Adj D and D (SumT and SumV) are evaluated. Generally, elevations in SumT and SumV are due to personality traits. However, their values can also be elevated due to situational variables, such as a recent emotional loss (SumT) or a recent event that has caused the examinee to experience guilt or remorse, which may cause him to focus more on negative aspects of the self (SumV). The purpose of this step is to assess whether any elevations in SumT or SumV may have been due to situational variables and, thus, are contributing to situational stress. If neither SumT nor SumV is elevated, the examiner can move on to the next step (Exner, 2003). However, if either is elevated, it is important to assess whether the elevation is due to situational variables or more chronic, stable characteristics.

If either SumT or SumV is elevated and there is evidence from the background or collateral information to support that this may be due to situational variables (e.g., recent loss), then the Adj D score should be recalculated as if the variables were not elevated. If the Adj D score changes, it suggests that the stressful events are having more of an impact on the examinee than previous steps initially revealed. Keep in mind that due to the way Adj D is calculated, a change of one point for SumT or SumV is unlikely to have a significant impact, but it is possible. Rapid Reference 4.9 demonstrates how to do the calculation and offers an example.

Evaluate the D score: Is Stress Overloading the Resources?
How Stress Could Manifest

The purpose of this fifth step is to determine whether the stress is more than the examinee can handle, based on his available resources. In a previous step, we examined the impact of the stress, whether it was mild/moderate or severe (Adj D – D). However, this did not take into account the examinee's resources. Examinees with more resources can more effectively cope with stress than those who do not have these resources. For example, an examinee with an Adj D score significantly above the average range (e.g., +2, according to Exner's 2003 norms) and a D score in the average range (0, according to Exner's 2003 norms) is experiencing a substantial amount of situational stress. However, there is unlikely to be a significant impact on the examinee's day-to-day functioning, as he has the available resources to appropriately cope with the stress. In contrast, an examinee whose Adj D score is in the normal range (0, per Exner's 2003 norms) and whose D score is below average (–1, according to Exner's 2003 norms) is in a state where his stress is overloading his resources. In other words, he does not have the

≡ Rapid Reference 4.9

How to Recalculate Adj D If SumT or SumV Is Higher Than Expected

Adj D is EA – Adj es. To recalculate this if SumT or SumV is higher than expected, subtract out the extra T codes and V codes from the Adj es. Using Exner's 2003 norms, this would be any SumT higher than 1 and any SumV higher than 0. The examiner should then compare this number to the D/Adj D table (Exner, 2003, p. 152) to recalculate what Adj D would have been without the extra textures and vistas.

For example: the examinee has recently lost her mother to cancer and reported feeling guilty about her mother's death, as she fought with her mother and told her to "Go to hell" shortly before her mother died. She also blames herself for her mother's death. Here are the examinee's scores:

Score	Value
EA	7
Adj es	5
SumT	2
SumV	1
Adj D	0
D	−1

It is possible that the recent loss of her mother may have resulted in a situationally induced elevation to SumT (due to the loss) and SumV (due to her guilt around her mother's death). In order to assess the impact of the likely situationally induced extra texture and vista, we subtract those items from the Adj es (5 − 2 = 3). Our new Adj es is 3. We now subtract that from EA and get a new raw score for Adj D of 4 (7 − 3 = 4). When we compare that to the table, we see that the new Adj D score would be +1, indicating that the situational stress, including the loss of her mother, is having a more significant impact on her functioning than initially indicated.

resources available to cope with his day-to-day life and his stressors. As a result, there are not enough resources to cope with everything, increasing the chance that the examinee may make poor decisions, be impulsive, and have less control over his actions. So even though this second examinee is experiencing less stress than the first examinee, as evidenced by the Adj D-D values, the second examinee is more likely to be experiencing significant difficulties as a result of the stress because the second examinee has fewer available resources than the first examinee does (EA).

In general, if the D score is average or above, then the examinee has the available resources to cope with the situational stress he is experiencing. As a result, it is unlikely that the examinee is at increased risk for losing control of his thoughts, emotions, or behaviors. In other words, his capacity for control is at least average.

However, if the D score is below average, then the demands on the examinee, including the situational stress, are higher than he is capable of handling. Consequently, the examinee is at an increased risk of losing control of his thoughts, emotions, or behaviors. In other words, his capacity for control is lower than it is for the average individual. The lower the D score, the more at risk the examinee is for losing control. In general, the lower the D score, the less likely it is that the examinee can function, even in structured or familiar environments.

When D is below average, it is important to examine the values for pure C and formless M, as this will provide some insight into whether the examinee tends to have emotional impulsiveness or difficulties with thinking. If the pure C value is greater than expected, then it is likely that the examinee's control over his emotions and behaviors is lessened. If formless M values are higher than expected, then it is possible that the stress is affecting the person's thinking and decision making (Exner, 2003). This is different from m, as m assesses unintended peripheral thoughts. The M determinants are thought to assess controlled thoughts, such as decision making.

DON'T FORGET
· ·

The D score is an important benchmark for functioning. As long as the D score is at least average, it is likely that the examinee has the capacity for adequate functioning. It does not mean, however, that he is using that capacity.

Situational Stress Blends: Impact of Stress on Psychological Functioning

The sixth and seventh steps involve blends. Blends are thought to assess psychological complexity. Psychological complexity can be defined as a characteristic of the person that describes how nuanced his patterns of thinking, emoting, and relating are. Theoretically, these concepts are also related to behavior, so individuals with higher levels of psychological complexity may also engage in more complex—or nuanced—behavior. Those who have higher levels of psychological complexity will tend to have more complex thinking and emoting patterns. This is not necessarily a positive or a negative finding; depending on the situation, more complex thinking and emoting patterns could be beneficial. For example, we would expect those in certain professions, like medicine, law, and mental health, to have more complex patterns of thinking because they need to be able to weigh multiple factors at the same time in their work. However, stress can also increase psychological complexity, making thinking and emotions more complex than is typical. This can cause difficulties for a person, especially if he is not accustomed to this level of nuanced thinking and emotional patterns. In more extreme circumstances, this increase complexity can be associated with impulsivity and disorganized thinking, emotions, and behaviors.

The sixth step assesses the impact of stress on the examinee's psychological complexity by examining the number of blends that are blends only because of the presence of an m or a Y determinant—the situational stress variables. In other words, if the m or the Y determinant was not present, the blend would not exist. To do this step, the examiner determines how many blends were created due to the presence of an m or Y determinant and divides this by the total number of blends. For example, if there are 8 blends total, and 3 of these blends are due to the presence of an m or a Y determinant, then 37.5 percent (3/8) of the blends are due to situational stress. The larger this number, the more the situational stress is increasing the psychological complexity. According to Exner (2003), if fewer than 20 percent of the blends are due to situational stress, there is only a mild increase in psychological complexity; a result of 20 percent to 30 percent indicates a moderate increase in complexity; and a result of more than 30 percent indicates a substantial increase.

Color-Shading Blends: Confusion About Feelings

Stress, especially when severe, can cause complex emotions, which can be confusing for people to experience. This step assesses whether situational stress has caused any confusion about feelings (Exner, 2003). This is done by evaluating the number of color-shading blends in the protocol. Rapid Reference 4.10 describes what a color-shading blend is.

≡Rapid Reference 4.10

Color-Shading Blends

Color-shading blends are a combination of a color determinant (C, CF, FC) with any of the shading determinants. There are four categories of shading determinants: Y (Y,YF, FY), T (T,TF, FT), V (V,VF, FV), and C' (C', C'F, FC'). Although C' is not considered to be a shading determinant for coding, it generally is for interpretation. Some examples of color-shading blends are

> VF.C
>
> C'F.FC
>
> TF.CF.Ma

Source: Based on information from Exner, 2000, 2003.

This final step proceeds as the previous one did: first, the examiner determines how many blends were created due to the presence of *both* a color determinant and a shading determinant. The blends are then divided into two categories: those whose shading determinants include a T, V, or C' and those whose shading determinant is a Y. Blends whose shading determinant is a T, V, or C' are indicative of a preexisting confusion about emotions; the confusion about emotions is not due solely to the situational stress. However, blends that include a Y indicate that situational stress is causing confusion about emotions (Exner, 2003). Thus, an examinee with a protocol with both types of color-shading blends would be someone who likely was confused about emotions prior to the stress, but the stress has exacerbated his confusion. Someone whose protocol contains only color-shading blends with Y determinants is experiencing emotional confusion, but it is related to the situational stress and is unlikely to be indicative of a prior condition. Rapid Reference 4.11 provides a chart to assist with the interpretation of this step.

AFFECT

Emotions are an important aspect of psychological functioning, as they are involved in most of our day-to-day activities. Emotions can influence how we

≡Rapid Reference 4.11

Interpretation of Color-Shading Blends

The color-shading blends are divided into two categories: those with a Y determinant and those with a C', V, or T determinant. The categories are interpreted differently, and the following matrix provides an easy-to-understand guide to these interpretations.

	Color-Shading Blend with T, V, or C'	No Color-Shading Blend with T, V, or C'
Color-Shading Blend with Y	Examinee was likely confused about emotions prior to the stress, but the stress is exacerbating the confusion.	Examinee's emotional confusion is likely associated only with the stress.
No Color-Shading Blend with Y	Examinee was likely confused about emotions prior to the stress; the stress does not appear to be exacerbating the situation.	There is no evidence in testing that the examinee is confused by emotions.

Source: Based on information from Exner, 2000, 2003; Weiner, 2003.

behave, think, relate to others, and even how we think about ourselves, although people will differ in the extent to which their emotions influence their behaviors, thoughts, and relationships. Emotions can be positive, like happiness and joy, or negative, like anger and sadness. However, emotions can also be extremely complex and difficult to understand. Consequently, they can cause a great deal of distress. Given the importance and complexity of emotions in everyday life, it is not surprising that the affect cluster is the longest cluster with the most steps.

Variables

This cluster contains sixteen steps, which address the interpretation of twenty-one variables. It also involves the interpretation of three types of blends. Rapid Reference 4.12 lists the variables interpreted with this cluster, how each variable is calculated, and what each of these variables assesses.

≡Rapid Reference 4.12

Interpretation of Affect:
How Variables Are Calculated and Assessed

Variable	How It Is Calculated	What It Assesses in This Cluster
DEPI	A combination of 14 variables.	Affective difficulty, which may include depression.
CDI	A combination of a variety of variables.	Difficulty with social adjustment.
EB	The ratio of M to WSumC.	How the examinee approaches tasks.
L	The number of pure F responses divided by the total number of all other types of responses.	Avoidance and defensiveness.
EBPer	The higher number in the EB ratio divided by the lower; calculated only in specific circumstances.	Whether the examinee is flexible in how she approaches tasks.
eb	The ratio of FM + m to SumC' + SumT + SumY + SumV.	The demands on the person.
SumY	The total number of Y determinants (Y + YF + FY).	Unintended negative feelings and emotions that are associated with situational stress.

Variable	How It Is Calculated	What It Assesses in This Cluster
SumT	The total number of T determinants (T + TF + FT).	Need for interpersonal closeness; elevated scores may be due to a recent emotional loss.
SumV	The total number of V determinants (V + VF + FV).	Presence of guilt or remorse; may be situational. Examinee may also experience excessive negative self-talk and degradation.
SumC'	The total number of C' determinants (C' + C'F + FC').	Tendency to suppress or inhibit emotions that has resulted in negative feelings. Interpreted in conjunction with WSumC.
WSumC	The weighted sum of the color determinants (1.5C + CF + .5FC).	How emotions are released (controlled vs. uninhibited). Interpreted in conjunction with SumC'.
Afr	The number of responses to Cards VIII–X divided by the number of responses to Cards I–VII (i.e., the number of responses to the color cards divided by the number of responses to the achromatic cards).	Willingness to engage and process emotions and emotionally laden situations.
Intellectualization Index	2AB + Art + Ay.	Tendency to use intellectualization to avoid dealing with emotions.
CP	The number of CP responses.	Tendency to cope with negative emotions by substituting a positive emotion instead.
FC:CF + C	FC:CF + C.	How well emotional reactions and displays are controlled.
C	The number of pure C responses.	Severe reduction in emotional control.
S	The number of responses with a WS, DS, or DdS location code.	Individuality, oppositionality.
Blends	The number of blends.	Psychological complexity.

(continued)

(continued)

Variable	How It Is Calculated	What It Assesses in This Cluster
Y and m Blends	The number of blends that are blends due to the presence of a Y or m determinant.	The impact of stress on psychological complexity.
Color-Shading Blends	The number of blends that contain a C determinant with a C',T,Y, or V determinant.	Confusion about emotions.
Shading Blends	The number of blends that contain two shading determinants (C',T,V,Y) in the same blend.	Painful emotions.

Source: Based on information from Choca, 2013; Exner, 2000, 2003; Mihura et al., 2013; Weiner, 2003.

Recommended Order of Interpretation

DEPI and CDI: Affect and Social Adjustment

Some of the sixteen steps in the affect cluster overlap with steps from previous clusters. When this is the case, the text will refer the reader back to the step in the earlier cluster.

The first step involves the interpretation of the Depression Index (DEPI) and the Coping Deficit Index. The DEPI, although called the Depression Index, is not a pure measure of depression. It appears to be related more to difficulties with affect in general. The CDI is a measure of coping deficits, and these coping deficits tend to be related to social adjustment. If someone has difficulty with social adjustment (e.g., an elevated CDI score), it would make sense that she also is at risk of affective difficulties, as social adjustment has been shown to be related to emotional difficulties (e.g., Paykel & Weissman, 1973; Weissman, Paykel, Siegel, & Klerman, 1971).

The DEPI and the CDI are interpreted together. In general, the CDI interpretation will take precedence; the presence of an elevated CDI score will soften the interpretation of any elevated DEPI score. With an elevated CDI, it becomes less likely that an elevated DEPI represents a chronic problem with affect. Instead, the elevated CDI indicates that at least some of the affective difficulties that are present are related to the social difficulties the person is experiencing (Exner, 2003). This has important implications for treatment, as treating the social difficulties, such as through social skills training, group therapy, and so forth, will likely result in a reduction of the affective difficulties as well. The interpretation of the DEPI and the CDI can be found in the matrix in Rapid Reference 4.13

EB and Lambda: Coping Style

The second step involves assessing the examinee's coping style. I recommended earlier that this be one of the examiner's first steps in interpretation, as many variables are interpreted in light of the examinee's coping style. Refer to the Book Companion Website Materials and Exner (2003) for the method of determining coping style.

Interpretation of the coping style is relatively straightforward, but there are a few exceptions. First, there are times when a coping style cannot be determined. When this happens, it seriously limits the interpretability of many variables because of their relationship with the coping style.

The interpretations of the four coping styles—Extratensive, Introversive, Ambient, and Avoidant—can be found in Rapid Reference 4.1, earlier in this chapter.

EBPer: Pervasive Coping Style

When an examinee has either an introversive or extratensive coping style, it is important to determine whether the style is pervasive; that is, whether or not the examinee shows any flexibility in coping. While it can be beneficial to have a

≡Rapid Reference 4.13

Interpretation of CDI and DEPI Scores

	DEPI Within Average Range	DEPI Slightly Above Average	DEPI Higher Than Average
CDI in Average Range	No indications of difficulty with affect or social maladjustment.	Affective difficulties are possible.	Affective difficulties likely, such as depression or anxiety.
CDI Above Average	Some indications of social maladjustment present.	Likely that social adjustment difficulties will predispose the person to having periods of affective difficulties.	Difficulties with affect are likely present, but are being exacerbated by difficulties with social adjustment.

Source: Based on information from Choca, 2013; Exner, 2000, 2003; Mihura et al., 2013; Weiner, 2003.

"set" coping style, it is best if the style is flexible, so the person can use different strategies for different situations. There are times when it is more appropriate to use a more thoughtful style (introversive), and other times when it is more appropriate to use an intuitive style (extratensive). According to Exner (2003), an examinee is considered to have inflexible coping style when EBPer is 2.5 or higher. This indicates that the value in EB that represents the dominant style (WSumC for extratensive, M for introversive) is 2.5 times higher than the other value. When this occurs, it indicates that the examinee will tend to use only her dominant style in decision making, even when the other style may be preferable in a particular situation.

It is important to note that little empirical research has been published supporting the interpretation of EBPer (e.g., see Mihura et al., 2013). I recommend that readers take this into consideration when interpreting this variable.

Right Side eb: Unusual Levels of Distress

The right side of eb (SumT, SumV, SumC', SumY) was interpreted as part of the previous clusters. Right side eb includes variables that could indicate unusual emotional demands on the person, such as a desire for interpersonal closeness (T). The left side of eb indicates the cognitive demands on the person. When the right side is greater than the left side, it indicates that the person is likely experiencing some distress. The form that the distress takes will depend on the variables that are elevated. Nevertheless, even when the left side of eb is greater than the right side, the variables that comprise the right side should still be interpreted, as there may be some unusual emotional demands on the person. The interpretation of the right side eb variables—SumT, SumV, SumC', and SumY—can be found in Rapid Reference 4.12, earlier in this section.

SumC':WSumC (Constriction Ratio): Expression of Emotions

The variables in the Constriction Ratio are related to emotion. SumC' is thought to be related to withholding emotion while WSumC is related to the expression of emotion. It is important to keep in mind that withholding emotions sometimes is normative; however, it can become problematic when there is an excessive withholding of emotion.

Usually, the value for WSumC is higher than the value for SumC'. However, when SumC' is higher than WSumC, it indicates that the examinee is withholding emotions more than is typical (Exner, 2003). Consequently, it is likely that the examinee is experiencing some negative emotions that they would prefer to express.

Examinees may withhold emotions for many reasons, including that they do not believe they can control them, that emotions confuse them, or that they are concerned about how their emotions will be perceived by others. It is important to review the examinee's history in order to put the examinee's inhibition of emotion into context.

Again, there is little published research regarding the validity of this ratio (see Mihura et al., 2013). Consequently, readers should take this into consideration when interpreting this variable.

Affective Ratio: Interest in Emotions and Emotional Situations

The Affective Ratio (Afr) assesses how interested the examinee is in being around emotions and emotionally laden stimuli. This is one of the variables that have different interpretations based on the examinee's coping style. For example, individuals who are extratensive will have a higher Afr than will individuals who are introversive, as extratensives, who use emotions in decision making, should be comfortable around emotion. The expected values for each style for adults and for different age groups of children can be found in Exner (2001, 2003).

The interpretation of Afr is relatively straightforward. If the value for Afr is higher than expected for the examinee's coping style or age, then the examinee is more willing to attend to, process, and be involved with emotions and emotional stimuli than others with her coping style are. If the value for Afr is lower than expected, then the examinee is less willing to be involved with emotional stimuli. If the value is in the expected range, then the examinee is as willing to be involved with emotional stimuli as others with her coping style are (or for children, as others of the same age are).

Regardless of the examinee's style, if she has an abnormally low Afr (>2SD below the mean), then it is likely that the examinee is uncomfortable dealing with emotion. As social interactions, especially romantic ones, can be emotionally laden, this can result in the examinee becoming socially isolated.

Intellectualization Index: Tendency to Intellectualize Emotions

At times, many individuals will use intellectualization, which is a process that can minimize the impact of emotions by dealing with them on an intellectual basis rather than on an emotional one. This can also affect how an examinee perceives a situation, as minimizing the emotion in a situation can distort the meaning of a situation. For example, imagine coping with the death of a loved one without the emotion that goes with it; taking the emotion out of the situation minimizes the impact of the situation and can make it much easier to cope with, at least initially. The occasional use of this strategy is typically not problematic; however, this strategy can become a problem when it is used frequently, as it can result in the impacts of situations being often distorted or minimized.

Some level of intellectualization is expected. However, when the value of the Intellectualization Index (2AB + Art + Ay) is higher than expected, there is evidence to indicate that the examinee is using intellectualization more than is typical. As the value gets higher, it suggests that the examinee is using intellectualization as a way to avoid emotional situations. However, it is important to note that there is also little published research assessing the validity of this interpretation; readers should take this into consideration when interpreting this variable (Mihura et al., 2013).

Color Projections: Positive Emotions Replacing Negative Ones

Color Projections (CP) are extremely rare. According to both Exner's norms and the international norms, protocols are expected to contain no CP codes (Exner, 2001, 2003; Meyer et al., 2007). Thus, the presence of a CP code is noteworthy. The CP code occurs when an examinee perceives an achromatic part of the blot as having chromatic color. The theoretical interpretation of the CP is that the examinee will cope with negative emotions by substituting positive ones for the negative ones. This leads to a gross misunderstanding of the situation, as in order to substitute a positive emotion for a negative one, the examinee needs to distort reality. However, it is important to note that there is very little research regarding color projection (Mihura et al., 2013); this should be taken into consideration when interpreting this variable.

FC:CF + C: Emotional Expression

The color determinants relate to emotional expression. C is associated with an unrestrained expression of emotion. FC is associated with appropriately controlled expression of emotion. CF is in between a C and FC; it indicates less restraint than an FC but better control than a C. The FC:CF + C ratio is essentially a comparison that assesses the frequency of controlled emotional displays in relation to the frequency of less controlled emotional displays. Among healthy adults, we would expect that most emotional expressions are appropriately controlled. Thus, we expect that there would be more FC determinants than CF determinants in a protocol. We also expect no C determinants (Exner, 2003). If the value for FC is greater than the value for CF + C and there are no C determinants in the protocol, the interpretation is that the examinee is controlling her emotional expression as other adults do.

However, it is possible for an individual to have too much control over her emotions. As the difference between FC and CF grows, with FC being the larger number, this indicates that the examinee has strong control over her emotions. The presence of C determinants indicates that the examinee, despite her attempts to control her emotional expression, experiences times where the controls do not work, resulting in a strong expression of emotions. The more C determinants there are, the more likely this is to occur.

When the value of CF + C is greater than FC, with the value for C being above the average range, it indicates that the examinee is less stringent about regulating her emotional expression than other adults are. This is not necessarily an area of concern, as long as the examinee is not under extreme stress or experiencing other significant difficulties, such as delusional thinking. However, as C deviates further and further from the average range, it suggests that the examinee has significant difficulty appropriately controlling her emotions.

DON'T FORGET
. . . .

The C determinants all have to do with the expression of emotion. C is related to an unrestrained expression of emotion, FC is a controlled expression of emotion, and CF is in between.

Pure C Responses: Content Analysis
The tenth step involves reviewing the responses with a C determinant. This involves the use of clinical judgment, as the examiner is tasked with identifying whether the C responses represent more or less mature responses. I recommend that the examiner make these interpretations with caution, as there is a potential for the examiner's own biases and experiences to influence the interpretations.

Space Responses: Oppositionality
Exner (2001, 2003) suggested that Space responses (S) should be interpreted as being indicative of individualism, oppositionality, and anger. However, there has been some recent research (see Mihura et al., 2013) that indicates there is little empirical support for space responses being associated with anger. Instead, some have suggested that the two types of space responses—the integration of white space with the inked parts of the blots and the reversal of figure and ground—should be interpreted differently (see Meyer at al., 2011, discussed in Chapter 8 of this book). Thus, I would recommend a cautious interpretation of S indicating

anger, at least until more research can be conducted to assess the accuracy of this potential interpretation.

Theoretically, using the white space as the focal point of the blot rather than the inked parts of the blot—that is, reversing the figure and the ground—can be interpreted as being indicative of individuality and oppositionality (Bandura, 1954a, 1954b). Thus, the more S location codes in a protocol, the more likely the examinee is to be perceived as being individualistic and/or oppositional. Exner (2003) stated that if the majority of the S responses are to the first couple of cards, the presence of the S responses may represent a reaction to the test, indicating that the examinee was not prepared to take the test and responded to it negatively.

Blends: Psychological Complexity

With this step, the examiner begins interpreting the blends. Blends are considered to be a measure of psychological complexity, which was defined earlier in this chapter. In the CS, the proportion of responses that contain blends on a protocol is interpreted in light of the examinee's coping style. In general, examinees who have an avoidant style (an L score higher than average) have a lower proportion of blends than examinees who are not avoidant. Individuals who have ambitent ($M \approx WSumC$) or extratensive ($M < WSumC$) coping styles tend to have a higher proportion of blends than do individuals who have introversive coping styles ($M > WSumC$) (Exner, 2003).

The interpretation of this variable is straightforward. If the proportion of blends is within the expected range, based on the comparison standard being used, then the examinee's psychological complexity is similar to that found in the comparison group. However, if it is below the expected range, then the examinee's functioning is less complex than that found in the comparison group. If it is higher than the expected range, then her functioning is more complex than expected. It is important to interpret this score in light of the examinee's current circumstances, as having a lower level of psychological complexity is not necessarily a liability, as long as the examinee is not in an environment where she is expected to deal with complex situations and emotions routinely. Similarly, having a higher level of psychological complexity is not necessarily a liability, as long as the examinee has the resources to cope with it.

Situational Stress Blends: Impact of Stress on Psychological Complexity

This step is very similar to a step in the situation-related stress cluster in that the goal of this step is to determine the impact of situational stress on the examinee's current level of psychological complexity. For this step, the examiner subtracts all but one blend created solely due to the presence of a situational stress determinant (m or Y). The examiner then recalculates the proportion of blends, without the extra situational stress blends, and compares that score to the expected ranges for the examinee's coping style (Exner, 2003). If the recalculated proportion of blends falls into a different range, then the interpretation should be that situational stress is causing an increase in psychological complexity, but that the examinee's typical level of complexity is less. An example of this calculation, with an interpretation, can be found in Rapid Reference 4.14.

Blends: Unusual Complexity

The majority of blends will contain only two determinants (Exner, 2003). However, it is not unusual to see the occasional blend containing three determinants on a protocol. It is rare to see blends that contain more than three determinants. The presence of blends with more than three determinants or a significant portion of blends with three determinants is indicative of increased levels of psychological complexity. This indicates that, at times, the examinee's functioning can become extremely complex. Again, this is not necessarily a liability, as long as the examinee has the resources to cope with the increased complexity in thinking and emotional functioning.

Color-Shading Blends: Confused by Emotion

Color-shading blends were interpreted earlier, as part of the situation-related stress cluster. Refer to Rapid Reference 4.11, earlier in this chapter, for a description of color-shading blends. The interpretation of color-shading blends in the affect cluster is somewhat different from their interpretation in the situation-related stress cluster. Regardless of style, the presence of a color-shading blend indicates that the examinee can be confused by emotion (Exner, 2000, 2003). However, this will be less disruptive for people with an extratensive or ambient style than it will be for people with an introversive or avoidant style, as those in the former group are more accustomed to dealing with emotions than those in the latter group. If the color-shading blend includes a Y determinant, then the interpretation is that the emotional confusion is related to situational stress.

Shading Blends: Presence of Painful Emotions

Shading blends are rare and occur when two shading variables (C', T, Y, and V) occur in the same response. The presence of a shading blend indicates that the examinee is experiencing very painful emotions that are affecting her functioning (Exner, 2000, 2003).

⇛Rapid Reference 4.14

Example of Interpretation of Blends Within the Affect Cluster

The examinee is a 47-year-old Caucasian man who was referred by his primary-care physician for an evaluation. His partner of twenty-four years, who had financially supported him for the past three years while the examinee recovered from a serious motor vehicle accident, passed away four months ago in a work-related accident. Since then, the examinee has been struggling, both emotionally and financially. Here are his relevant scores:

R = 24.
EB = 5:3.
L = .50.
EBPer = 1.67.

Blends

m.CF.M.
TF.FM
Y.TF
FC.M
TF.C'F
Y.m
M.Y

The following interpretation uses Exner's 2003 norms.

This examinee's coping style is introversive (M > WSumC, L < 1.0). The expected proportion of blends for someone with an introversive style is between 13 percent and 26 percent (Exner, 2003). The examinee's proportion of blends is 29 percent (7 blends / 24 responses), which is somewhat higher than expected.

Out of the 7 blends, 4 contain situational stress determinants (m.CF.M, Y.TF, Y.m, and M.Y); however, only three of these would become single determinants if the situational stress determinants were taken out. The fourth blend (m.CF.M) would remain a blend even if the situational stress variable were removed. Consequently, there are only three blends that were created exclusively by the presence of situational stress determinants. When we subtract two of these, that leaves us with a total of 5 blends (7 − 2). When we recalculate the blend proportion, taking out the blends caused by the presence of situational stress, the new proportion is 21 percent (5 / 24), which is in the expected range of blends for someone with an introversive style. This indicates that although the examinee's usual psychological functioning is similar to that of other adults, his functioning has become more complex due to recent stressors. This is consistent with his report that he has been struggling since the death of his partner a few months ago.

There are no blends containing more than three determinants and only one of the seven blends has three determinants (14%) so there is no evidence of usual complexity in this protocol.

There are no color-shading blends on this protocol, so there is no evidence to support the hypothesis that the examinee is confused by his emotions.

There is a shading-shading blend (Y.TF), suggesting that the examinee may be experiencing some painful emotions. This is consistent with his report that he has been struggling emotionally since the death of his partner a few months ago.

Taken together, the results suggest that the examinee is experiencing painful emotions, likely associated with the recent sudden death of his long-term partner. The results suggest that the stress the examinee is experiencing has made his thinking and emotional functioning more complex than is typical for him.

INFORMATION PROCESSING

The next three clusters—information processing, cognitive mediation, and idea-tion—are referred to as the Cognitive Triad, as each assesses an aspect of cogni-tion. The variables in the first cluster, information processing, assess how information is input. The variables in the second cluster, cognitive mediation, assess how the information is perceived by the examinee. The variables in the final cluster, ideation, assess how the information is conceptualized and used. A deficit in any of these areas will influence how well the other two areas function. For example, if there is a deficit in how the examinee perceives the information—if the examinee is not perceiving it accurately, for example—this will affect how he conceptualizes and uses the information, as his conceptualization is based on misperceived information.

Information processing involves scanning a situation and placing the informa-tion obtained from the scanning into working memory. It can then be translated (cognitive mediation) into long-term memory and used to make decisions (idea-tion). There are a number of areas in which information can be faulty, including that the examinee misses information or that the examinee is overly focused on small, relatively insignificant details rather than on more important details and the larger picture.

Variables

This cluster has eight steps and a prerequisite step; these steps involve the inter-pretation of fourteen variables. This cluster also involves the interpretation of the location sequence and the DQ sequence. Rapid Reference 4.15 lists the variables interpreted with this cluster, how each variable is calculated, and what each of these variables assesses.

≡Rapid Reference 4.15

Information Processing:
How Variables Are Calculated and Assessed

Variable	How It Is Calculated	What It Assesses in This Cluster
OBS	A combination of multiple variables.	Perfectionism, detail orientation.
HVI	A combination of multiple variables.	Hypervigilance.
Zf	The number of responses with a Z score.	How much effort the examinee puts into processing information, including his environment.
W:D:Dd	The ratio of the number of responses with a W or WS location code to the number of responses with a D or DS location code to the number of responses with a Dd or DdS location code.	Measures processing effort and processing efficiency; interpretation varies depending on the ratio of the variables.
W	The number of responses with a W or WS location code.	When elevated, suggests that the examinee has put more effort into processing than expected.
D	The number of responses with a D or DS location code.	When elevated, suggests that the examinee has been very efficient, possibly overly so, with his processing effort.
Dd	The number of responses with a Dd or DdS location code.	When elevated, suggests that the examinee has a tendency to focus on small details.
Aspirational Ratio	The ratio of the number of responses with a W or WS location code to the number of responses with an M determinant (W:M).	Achievement orientation.
Zd	ZSum − Zest.	How the examinee scans his environment.
Within Card PSV	The number of responses with within card PSV.	Difficulty shifting attention.
DQ+	The number of responses with DQ = +.	Complex processing.

Variable	How It Is Calculated	What It Assesses in This Cluster
DQo	The number of responses with DQ = o.	Adequate processing; examinee may be more conservative in processing efforts than others are.
DQv/+	The number of responses with DQ = v/+.	Attempt at complex processing that has failed.
DQv	The number of responses with DQ = v.	Poor and/or immature processing.

Source: Based on information from Choca, 2013; Exner, 2000, 2003; Mihura et al., 2013; Weiner, 2003.

Prerequisite Step: Examinee's Style, HVI, and OBS

When using the Exner (2003) norms, it is important to consider the individual's coping style (introversive, extratensive, ambitent, or avoidant) prior to starting to interpret the variables in this cluster, as many variables are interpreted in light of the style present. There is some indication that there are differences in how people who use different coping styles process information. Those who tend to have an avoidant style will, by their nature, be avoidant when processing information and, therefore, would be expected to process information at a lower level, due to their tendency to avoid and simplify information. Individuals who are introversive, on the other hand, prefer to review information and think through their options prior to making decisions. Consequently, this group of individuals tends to have a higher level of processing. The consideration of style helps to avoid over- and underidentifying individuals as having difficulties, as it helps to put the results into context.

It is also important to examine whether the examinee is Hypervigilant (HVI) or Perfectionistic/Very Detail Oriented (OBS) prior to starting the interpretation. This is important because individuals who are hypervigilant, perfectionistic, and/or detail oriented will have a tendency to put more effort into processing. For individuals who are hypervigilant, this is usually done to make sure the environment is thoroughly scanned in order to avoid any threats. For individuals who are perfectionistic, the increased effort is generally to ensure that they have thoroughly scanned the environment in order to make sure that they are precise in their assessment of the situation.

Frequency of Z Scores: Processing Effort

In order for a response to have a Z score assigned to it, the examinee has to demonstrate higher order processing on the blot. This may include integrating white space with the chromatic or achromatic parts of the blot, using the entire blot, or seeing at least two objects in some sort of relationship with each other (Exner, 2003). All examinees are expected to engage in some level of organizational processing, and thus, at least some of the responses on a protocol should have Z scores assigned to them.

The Zf score, or the number of responses with a Z score, interpreted in this first step is considered to be a rough measure of processing effort (Exner, 2003). The interpretation of this variable is straightforward: if the examinee's Zf score falls in the expected range derived from the comparison group, then the examinee's processing is probably similar to the processing effort of the individuals in that comparison group. If the examinee's scores are higher than the expected range, the examinee has likely engaged in more processing effort than is typical. If the score is lower than expected, then the examinee is probably putting forth less effort on this task than others typically do. There are many possible reasons for this, including that the examinee was not interested in the task, was being lazy, or was putting forth less effort than others do in processing new information.

W:D:Dd: Focus (Big Picture or Obvious Information or Small Details)

The W:D:Dd variable provides additional hypotheses regarding the examinee's processing efforts (Exner, 2003). Just because an examinee has put a lot of effort into processing, that does not mean that the effort resulted in a better quality of processing. It is difficult to maintain a constant high effort in processing, as that requires a great deal of resources. Additionally, there are times when it is appropriate to put forth less effort in processing, such as when the required response to a situation is obvious or when a situation is straightforward. This step is the first in a series that provides some hypotheses regarding the examinee's processing effort.

Three variables are assessed in this step: W, D, and Dd. In general, most adults will provide more D responses than W responses with only a few Dd responses. There is an expected ratio of W to D responses; when the ratio is not in the expected range, or there are more Dd responses than expected, then the examiner needs to examine the variables individually to assess possible reasons why the ratio was not as expected. The interpretation of each of these variables can be found in Rapid Reference 4.16.

≡Rapid Reference 4.16

Interpretation of Higher Than Expected Values of W, D, and Dd

W	Examinee makes more effort in processing than expected, may be excessive. He may have difficulty seeing the simple or obvious solution to a problem. Likely attempts to see the "big picture."
D	Examinee is more efficient with processing than expected, possibly overly so. This may indicate a tendency to focus only on aspects of situation he is familiar with or that are extremely obvious.
Dd	Examinee has a tendency to focus on small or unusual details, may signify perfectionism or being guarded. He may have dificultly seeing a simple or obvious solution.

Source: Based on information from Choca, 2013; Exner 2001, 2003; Weiner, 2003.

Location Sequence: Consistency in Processing Effort

The purpose of this fourth step is twofold. First, the examiner will determine which blots (if any) resulted in W codes. This can provide important information regarding processing effort, because it is easier to provide a W response to some blots than to others. The second purpose is to examine the sequence of the locations to assess whether the examinee has put forth similar effort across the test or whether the effort has varied. The information gained from this step can become very important when the information generated from the previous two steps does not agree and additional information is needed to clarify the examinee's processing effort.

When reviewing the responses that resulted in W codes, it is important to remember that in general, the more uniform the blot field, the easier it is to provide a W response, and the more broken the blot field, the harder it is to provide a W response. Thus, it is typically easier for an examinee to provide a W response to blots I, IV, and V, which all consist of a solid, unbroken stimulus field. It is relatively difficult for an examinee to provide a W response to blots III, IX, and X; blots III and X have a broken stimulus field, and although blot IX is a solid stimulus field, it is broken up by the different colors. For the remaining blots (II, VI, VII, and VIII), it is moderately difficult to provide a W response. If the examinee provides a significant number of his W responses to "difficult" blots (III, IX, X), that suggests he has put more effort into processing than is typical. However, if the W responses are all to "easy" blots (I, IV, V), that suggests the examinee may not have put forth much effort in processing (Exner, 2003).

For the second part of this step, the location sequence, the examiner should look to see if the examinee has been consistent in how he processes the blots (Exner, 2003). For example, if the majority of an examinee's W responses were the initial response to a blot and the majority of the Dd responses were the last response to a blot, that indicates the examinee's processing was consistent. However, if a quarter of the W responses were the first response, half were the second response, and the remaining quarter were the final response, this is suggestive of inconsistent processing effort over time, because the higher effort processing (the W responses) was not always in the same place. In other words, sometimes the examinee initially put more effort into processing but at other times, he started by putting less effort into processing and later put more effort into processing.

Aspirational Ratio: Overachieving and Underachieving

The Aspirational Ratio (W:M) is thought to assess whether the individual's processing effort (W) is consistent with his cognitive resources (M). It can be seen as a measure of achievement orientation; examinees with a higher than expected number of M codes than W codes in the ratio are not putting forth as much effort as their resources would allow, which may indicate that they are underachieving. In contrast, examinees with a lower than expected number of M codes than W codes in the ratio are putting forth a lot of effort, but they may not have the cognitive resources to support it (Exner, 2003). These individuals may be attempting to overachieve, or to do more than they are capable of at the time of the evaluation. It should be noted that Mihura and colleagues' meta-analysis (2013) indicated that little published research was completed on this variable; as a result, there is little empirical support for the interpretation of this variable.

Zd: Processing Efficiency

In this fifth step, the Zd score provides an estimate of how efficient the examinee is in processing information (Exner, 2003). On the one hand, if an examinee has a higher than expected Zd score, based on the comparison sample the examiner is using, then the examinee is considered to have an overincorporative style: that is, a tendency to try to process all aspects of a situation, no matter how minute or irrelevant they may be. On the other hand, an examinee with lower than expected Zd score is considered to have an underincorporative style, or a tendency to miss information. Both styles have benefits and drawbacks; it is important to consider context when interpreting this variable. Rapid Reference 4.17 provides definitions and possible interpretations of overincorporative and underincorporative.

≡Rapid Reference 4.17

. . . .

Overincorporative and Underincorporative

Overincorporative	The examinee's Zd score is higher than expected. He is likely to take in more information than is necessary. This may not be a liability, depending on the environment, and as long as he has adequate time to review all aspects of a situation.
Underincorporative	The examinee's Zd score is lower than expected. He is likely to take in less information than is necessary. He is at increased risk of making errors because he may miss important information that could influence his decision.

Source: Based on information from Exner, 2001, 2003; Weiner, 2003.

Within Card Perseverations: Difficulty Shifting Attention

There are three types of Within Card Perseveration (PSV): mechanical, content, and within card. This step focuses on the within card PSV only. A within card PSV is associated with difficulties in shifting attention; a higher than expected number of PSV responses could indicate that the examinee is experiencing some difficulties with shifting his attention. In general, the more within card PSV codes there are on a protocol, the more difficulty the examinee may experience with shifting his attention (Exner, 2003).

DQ Distribution: Quality of Processing

It is important to remember that even if someone puts a lot of effort into processing, it does not mean the processing is of good quality. DQ codes relate to the quality of processing. In this step, the examiner reviews the number of each type of DQ code.

The primary focus of this step is the number of synthesized (DQ+) responses and the number of vague (DQv and DQv/+) responses. The DQ+ responses represent high-quality, complex processing. The DQv and DQv/+ responses are on the other end of the DQ spectrum; they represent less mature, more childlike processing. Interpretations of DQ+ and of DQv and DQv/+ can be found in Rapid Reference 4.18.

≡Rapid Reference 4.18

Interpretation of DQ

	Higher Than Expected	Lower Than Expected
DQ+	Examinee uses more sophisticated and/or complex processing than is typical.	Examinee uses less complex processing than is typical. This may be due to engaging in adequate but economical processing; may also be a result of immature processing (see DQv). This may result in difficulty with complex situations.
DQv & DQv/+	Examinee uses less mature processing than expected. Processing may be flawed at times. He may have difficulty with complex situations, especially if DQ+ is low as well.	N/A.

Source: Based on information from Choca, 2013; Exner, 2001, 2003; Weiner, 2003.

DQ Sequencing: Processing Effort

This is the final step in the information processing cluster. Conceptually, this step is similar to the fourth step in this cluster, where we examined the location sequence. The difference with this step is that it examines the DQ sequence. Also similar to the issues involved in identifying the location sequence, on some cards it is easier to obtain a DQ+ score than on others. In general, the more broken the stimulus field is on the blot, the easier it is to obtain a DQ+ score (Exner, 2003). Thus, the cards with more broken fields (II, III, VII, VIII, and X) are the ones where it is easiest to obtain a DQ+ score.

In this step, the examiner reviews the cards where the examinee provided DQ+ responses. If the examinee provided most of his DQ+ responses to cards where it is considered difficult to provide a DQ+ response (e.g., Card I), then it indicates that he may be putting forth an immense effort in order to engage in higher quality processing.

COGNITIVE MEDIATION

Cognitive mediation is the next cluster to be examined in interpreting the cognitive process. After new information is attended to (information processing), an individual must perceive it and translate it so that it can be stored. However, individuals differ in their ability to accurately perceive and translate information, which is an aspect of reality testing. If the individual perceives the information differently than is typical, due to any of a variety of causes ranging from individual differences to delusional thinking patterns, then her translation of the material will also be different from the typical translation of information by the comparison group. Consequently, decisions made based on the information and also thinking that relies on the information may be different from what is customary. In extreme cases, the decisions based on the inaccurate information can be severely flawed. Essentially, the cognitive mediation cluster helps the examiner assess whether the examinee sees the world as others tend to see it (Exner, 2003).

It is very important to remember that many things, besides severe mental illness, can result in a person seeing the world differently from the comparison sample. Someone who is creative may not see the world the same way others do, as a result of her creativity in thinking. An individual who has experienced trauma also may see the world differently, as a result of her trauma. Someone who is a member of a minority group may see the world differently, due to her experiences with prejudice and racism. In short, it is vital to consider the examinee's background, culture, situational factors, and experiences when interpreting this cluster, in order to put the results in context.

CAUTION

It is vital to consider all aspects of the examinee, including her background, culture, situational factors, and experiences, when interpreting the meaning of the variables in the mediation cluster.

Variables

This cluster has six steps and a prerequisite step; these steps address the interpretation of twelve variables. Rapid Reference 4.19 lists the variables interpreted with this cluster, how each variable is calculated, and what each of these variables assesses.

Interpretation of Variables

Prerequisite Step: R, OBS, Lambda

When assessing someone's reality testing, or the accuracy of her perception of their environment and surroundings, it is important to consider a few variables. First, it is important to consider the length of the protocol. In short protocols

≋Rapid Reference 4.19

Cognitive Mediation: How Variables Are Calculated and Assessed

Variable	How It Is Calculated	What It Assesses in This Cluster
OBS	A combination of multiple variables.	Perfectionism, detail orientation.
XA%	The number of FQ+, FQo, and FQu responses divided by R [(FQ+ +FQo + FQu)/R].	Whether the examinee perceives the world accurately.
WDA%	The number of FQ+, FQo, and FQu responses with a W or D location code divided by R.	Whether the examinee perceives the world accurately in situations where the expected responses are obvious.
FQxNone	The number of responses with no FQ.	Interpretation depends on whether these responses occur with M, C, or shading determinants. If with M, then thoughts can affect the ability to perceive situations accurately. If with C or shading, then emotions are affecting the ability to perceive situations accurately.
X–%	The number of responses with FQ– divided by R (FQ– / R).	Whether the examinee perceives the world inaccurately; distorting reality.
FQx–	The number of responses with FQ–.	Whether the examinee perceives the world inaccurately; distorting reality.
S–	The number of responses with a WS, Ds, or DdS location code with FQ–.	Whether oppositionality or individuality may contribute to the examinee perceiving the world inaccurately.
Dd with FQ–	The number of Dd responses with FQ–.	Whether the examinee perceives the world inaccurately or distorting reality, when faced with unusual situations.
P	The number of popular responses on the protocol.	The likelihood that the examinee will make the expected response in situations where the expected response is obvious.

Variable	How It Is Calculated	What It Assesses in This Cluster
FQ+	The number of responses with FQ+.	Whether the examinee strives to be as accurate as possible when perceiving the world.
X+%	The number of responses with FQ+ and FQo divided by R [(FQo+FQ+) / R].	Whether the examinee perceives the world in the same way as others typically do.
Xu%	The number of responses with FQu divided by R (FQu / R).	Whether the examinee perceives the world in a more unique way, but without a distortion of reality (e.g., being individualistic).

Source: Based on information from Choca, 2013; Exner, 2000, 2003; Mihura et al., 2013; Weiner, 2003.

(e.g., fewer than eighteen responses), having four responses with FQ– is more noteworthy than on a protocol that is lengthy, such as one with forty responses. Another variable to consider is OBS. Individuals who have a positive OBS are likely to strive for perfectionism and therefore will likely strive to perceive the world as accurately as possible (high XA%). Finally, Lambda, which assesses for avoidance and defensiveness, also needs to be taken into consideration, as an individual who is avoidant may view the world differently than the comparison sample did. These factors will affect the results of this cluster.

XA% and WDA%: Accuracy in Perception

Both XA% and WDA% assess whether the examinee perceives the world accurately, or at least in the same way that the comparison sample did. Both rely on responses assigned an FQ of +, o, or u. An FQ +, o, or u is assigned when the response follows the contours of the blot; in other words, what the person sees is consistent with the stimulus she is presented with. The difference between the XA% and the WDA% is that the XA% includes all responses while the WDA% includes only the responses that have a W, WS, D, or DS location code (Exner, 2003). The responses with a Dd or DdS location code are not included in the calculation of the WDA%. Typically, the WDA% will be equal to or higher than the XA%. Rapid Reference 4.20 provides some guidance on how to interpret these variables together.

≡Rapid Reference 4.20

Interpretation of XA% and WDA%

	WDA% Higher Than Expected	WDA% Within Expected Range	WDA% Lower Than Expected
XA% Higher Than Expected	Examinee likely works hard in order to ensure that she perceives the world accurately.	This response is unlikely to occur. When XA% is high, WDA% will likely be high as well.	This response is extremely unlikely to occur. When XA% is high, WDA% will likely be high as well.
XA% Within Expected Range	Examinee is likely capable of perceiving the world accurately.	Examinee is likely capable of perceiving the world accurately.	Unexpected processing problem possible or dissimulation. Examinee may also have difficulty separating reality from fantasy.
XA% Lower Than Expected	Examinee is capable of perceiving the world accurately in obvious or familiar situations, but experiences much more difficulty in more subtle or unfamiliar situations.	Examinee is likely capable of perceiving the world accurately in obvious or familiar situations, but has more difficulty in more subtle or unfamiliar situations or when focused on unusual aspects of a situation.	Examinee is likely having difficulty perceiving the world accurately in all situations. The lower the numbers, the greater the level of impairment.

Source: Based on information from Exner, 2001, 2003; Weiner, 2003.

Responses with No FQ

In order to be coded as a no FQ response, the response must have a pure determinant (e.g., one without an F). The interpretation of a no FQ response depends on what the determinant associated with the response. If it was an M, which assesses cognitive resources and controlled thinking, then the lack of FQ with an M indicates that the examinee may have difficulty controlling her own thinking and this is affecting her ability to perceive the world accurately. If a no FQ response has a shading or color determinant, it indicates that the examinee may be having difficulty with her emotions and this is affecting her ability to perceive the world accurately (Exner, 2003). There is little published research on the interpretation of these variables (Mihura et al., 2013); this should be taken into consideration with the interpretation.

Minus Responses: Similarities in Misperceptions

Minus responses (X–%, FQx–, S–, Dd–) indicate that the examinee did not follow the contours of the blot, suggesting that she saw the blot differently from how others typically see it. The interpretation of the minus responses is generally that the examinee is misperceiving the world (Exner, 2003). We all do this at times, and thus, it is expected that there will be a few minus responses in each protocol. However, when the proportion of minus responses is higher than expected, it indicates that the examinee is misperceiving the world more often than is typical, which can be problematic. When this occurs, the examiner needs to examine where the minus responses occur to determine whether there are any similarities among the minus responses, such as whether they all occurred to the first few cards or with color determinants. If there are similarities, it could suggest that the examinee is more likely to misperceive her environment in certain circumstances, such as when strong emotions are present (e.g., most FQ– responses have a C determinant). Rapid Reference 4.21 provides possible interpretations of FQ– responses.

Another part of this step is to review how much distortion is present in the minus response (Exner, 2000, 2003). This part of the step relies heavily on the examiner's clinical judgment, and examiners should take steps to avoid having their own biases and perceptions influence their interpretation of how distorted an examinee's response is.

Populars: Likelihood of Engaging in a Socially Expected Response When Cues Are Present

Each card has a popular response (Exner, 2001, 2003). The popular responses for nine of the ten cards are easy to see and are very common responses. The listed popular response on the remaining card (Card IX) is less commonly seen, and some have questioned whether it should be considered popular anymore (e.g., Meyer et al., 2011).

When the cues in a situation are obvious, it is easier to engage in the expected response. An example of this is a person introducing herself to you, then holding out her hand. In many areas of the United States, the assumption is that the person wants to shake your hand. As long as someone attends to the obvious social

≡Rapid Reference 4.21

Interpretation of FQ– Responses

When all of the minus responses have similar features or are consistent in some way (e.g., most occur with color determinants), it could imply that something about those features is contributing to the examinee's difficulty with perception. Here are some examples and possible interpretations.

Example	Possible Interpretation
All on the first few cards.	Examinee had a reaction to the test.
Most have S location code.	Examinee has a difficulty with perception that may occur primarily due to oppositionality or individuality.
Most have a color determinant.	Examinee has a difficulty with perception that may be more likely when emotion is present. The examinee may not experience the difficulties in situations that are not emotionally laden.
Most have a shading determinant.	Examinee has a difficulty with perception that may be more likely when negative or irritating emotions are present.
Most have an M determinant.	It is possible that the person's patterns of thinking are contributing to the difficulties with perception.
Most have FM or m determinants.	It is possible that unintended peripheral thoughts are contributing to the difficulties with perception.
Most have an rF, Fr, or FD determinant.	It is possible that concern about self-image is affecting the examinee's ability to perceive the world accurately.

Source: Based on information from Exner, 2000, 2003.

cue (another person holding out a hand after an introduction), it is likely she will engage in the socially expected behavior (shaking the hand). Thus, the popular responses indicate how likely it is that the person will make socially expected responses when the cues to engage in that behavior are obvious. It is important to note that the popular responses were based on a sample of over 7,000 protocols from the United States (Exner, 2003). The popular responses may not be the same cross-culturally (e.g., Choca, 2013; Sangro, 1997). It is important to remember this when interpreting this variable.

Like other variables, the interpretation of the number of populars on a protocol is relatively straightforward. If the examinee provides the number of popular responses expected according to the comparison standard, then it is likely that the examinee will engage in the socially expected behavior if cues suggesting that behavior are obvious. If the number of populars is higher than expected, then the examinee may be trying very hard to "fit in" and meet social expectations. There are a number of reasons this could occur, including that the examinee wants to ensure that others approve of her or is striving hard to be socially accepted. She may also be hiding something about herself and the purpose of the socially expected behavior is to make sure that she fits in and does not arouse suspicion.

In contrast, if the number of populars is lower than expected, then this suggests that the examinee is unlikely to engage in the socially expected behavior, even when cues suggesting the behavior are obvious. There are many possible reasons for this, including that the examinee tends to be more individualistic. The examinee may also be from a culture that does not value the same social conventions as the comparison sample did.

FQ+: Preciseness

Ordinary elaborated form quality (FQ+) is a somewhat rare score. In order to warrant a code of FQ+, the response must have FQo and the examinee must provide many form features in her response (Exner, 2001, 2003). If there are more responses with FQ+ than expected, it suggests that the examinee has been very precise with her responses. Low scores are generally not interpreted.

X+ % and Xu%: Perceiving the World Accurately

In order to obtain FQo (X+%) or FQu (Xu%) scores, the examinee must have followed the contours of the blot. The difference between the two scores is that the FQo responses were more commonly provided than the FQu responses were in Exner's (2003) sample of 9,500 protocols used to derive the FQ tables for the CS. In other words, the responses with FQu indicate that the examinee's perception of the blot is not distorted, but the examinee is interpreting it somewhat differently than the comparison sample did; the examinee's response is more individualistic and unique. This suggests that the examinee's behavior in a situation will be appropriate, but not necessarily completely in accordance with social expectations. However, the behavior is unlikely to be viewed as unacceptable. We expect to see at least some FQu responses on a protocol because it does indicate a sense of individuality.

Responses with FQo and FQ+ (X+%) occur when the examinee is not perceiving the blot in a distorted way and in fact, tends to perceive it the same way that others perceived it (Exner, 2000, 2003). In other words, the examinee's reaction to the blot is very similar to others' reactions to the blot. Consequently, the

X + % indicates that the examinee is perceiving the world in a manner very similar to the way others do, which would suggest that the examinee is likely to engage in behaviors that are socially expected. Her behaviors are unlikely to be seen as unacceptable or unique.

It is difficult to interpret X + % and the Xu% without considering the X–%, as collectively, these scores represent the three types of ways an examinee could perceive a blot:

X + % (FQ+ and FQo): The examinee perceived the blot as others did.

Xu% (FQu): Perception was not distorted but the examinee interpreted it differently.

X–% (FQ–): Perception of the blot was distorted.

Rapid Reference 4.22 discusses ways to interpret these three variables together.

≡Rapid Reference 4.22

Interpretation of X + %, Xu%, and X–%

	X + %	**Xu%**	**X–%**
Higher Than Expected	Examinee uses more conventional responses, may be trying very hard to "fit in," may be rigid.	Examinee uses more individualistic responses, may be creativity, may have conflicts with others due to unique behaviors.	Examinee is likely distorting reality. Misperceptions are likely affecting behavior; behaviors unlikely to be appropriate for the situation.
Lower Than Expected	Depends on levels of Xu% and X–% (at least one should be higher than expected); see the interpretations for those.	Depends somewhat on levels of X + % and X–%; examinee is unlikely to engage in individualistic behaviors and instead focuses on ensuring she is engaging in socially acceptable behaviors (see X + %). Behaviors may also be unacceptable (see X–%).	Depends on levels of X + % and Xu%. Examinee has very little distortion in perception.

Source: Based on information from Choca, 2013; Exner, 2001; 2003; Weiner, 2003.

IDEATION

Ideation is the final cluster in the cognitive triad. In this cluster, we are assessing how the information the examinee has obtained is being conceptualized and eventually used in his thinking.

Many things can affect how information is conceptualized. For example, if an individual is depressed, the depression will not only affect how he perceives the world (mediation) but will also affect how he conceptualizes the information he obtains as well (ideation). Specifically, an individual who is depressed may have a tendency to conceptualize things in an overly pessimistic manner. As another example, an individual who has experienced a severe interpersonal trauma may have a tendency to conceptualize everything as a threat. The tendency to conceptualize in a specific way can be strongly influenced by current circumstances, and it is important not to assume that any problems with ideation or conceptualization are permanent.

Variables

The ideation cluster has eleven steps and interprets twenty-two variables. This cluster also involves interpretation of the quality of the responses that have cognitive Special Scores. Rapid Reference 4.23 lists the variables interpreted with this cluster, how each variable is calculated, and what each of these variables assesses.

EB and Lambda: Coping Style

Determination of the coping style was described earlier in this chapter. In brief, individuals with a Lambda score greater than 0.99 are classified as avoidant. The other classifications are ambitent ($M \approx WSumC$), extratensive ($M < WSumC$), and introversive ($M > WSumC$). There are also times when a coping strategy cannot be determined; readers should consult Exner (2003) and the Book Companion Website Materials for how to determine a coping style.

The interpretations of the four coping styles—extratensive, introversive, ambitent, and avoidant—can be found in Rapid Reference 4.1, earlier in this chapter.

EBPer: Pervasive Style

As described above in discussing the affect cluster, when an examinee has either an introversive or extratensive coping style, it is important to determine whether the style is pervasive; that is, does the examinee show any flexibility in coping. There are times when it is more appropriate to use a thoughtful style (introversive), and other times when it is more appropriate to use an intuitive style (extratensive).

≡Rapid Reference 4.23

Ideation: How Variables Are Calculated and Assessed

Variable	How It Is Calculated	What It Assesses in This Cluster
EB	The ratio of the number of M determinants to the WSumC.	Style (extratensive, introversive, ambitent).
L	The number of responses with only form determinants divided by the number of other types of responses.	Style (avoidant vs. not avoidant).
EBPer	The larger side of EB divided by the smaller side of EB.	Flexibility with coping style.
a:p	The ratio of the number of active movement determinants to the number of passive movement determinants, including m, M, and FM.	Fixed attitudes and values.
HVI	A combination of variables.	Hypervigilance, mistrust of others.
OBS	A combination of variables.	Perfectionism.
MOR	The number of MOR Special Scores.	Pessimism.
eb	The ratio of FM and m determinants to the shading variables. Focus is on FM and m in this cluster.	The presence of unintended peripheral thought.
FM	The number of FM determinants.	Unintended peripheral thought caused by the presence of needs states.
m	The number of m determinants.	Unintended peripheral thought that tends to be related to situational stress.
Ma:Mp	The ratio of the number of Ma determinants to the number of Mp determinants.	Whether examinee substitutes fantasy for reality when stressed.
Intellectualization Index	2AB + Art + Ay.	Tendency to intellectualize when faced with emotion.
Sum6	The number of critical six Special Scores (DV, DR, INCOM, FABCOM, CONTAM, ALOG).	(These six scores are interpreted individually; as shown later in this table.)

Variable	How It Is Calculated	What It Assesses in This Cluster
WSum6	Weighted sum of critical 6 Special Scores.	Presence of faulty judgment and possible thought disturbance.
DV	N/A.	Brief cognitive issues; may be due to language; examinee may have difficulty communicating with others.
DR	N/A.	Indecisiveness; difficulty staying on task; may be a tactic used to avoid a task; examinee may have impulse control issues.
ALOG	N/A.	Concrete and/or illogical reasoning.
INCOM	N/A.	Concrete reasoning; bizarre logic.
FABCOM	N/A.	Immature thinking; reality testing is impaired; thinking is distorted.
CONTAM	N/A.	Severe thinking difficulties; examinee likely has difficulty separating concepts, such as reality and fantasy.
M–	The number of M determinants with FQ–.	Distorted view of others, could be associated with psychosis.
Mnone	The number of M determinants with no FQ.	Ability to control thinking is impaired.

Source: Based on information from Choca, 2013; Exner, 2000, 2003; Mihura et al., 2013; Weiner, 2003.

According to Exner (2003), an examinee is considered to have inflexible coping style when EBPer is 2.5 or higher. This indicates that the value in EB that represents the dominant style (WSumC for Extratensive, M for Introversive) is 2.5 times higher than the other value. When this occurs, it indicates that the examinee tends to use only his dominant style in decision making, even when the other style may be preferable in a given situation. It is important to note that, as of this writing, there is little published empirical research supporting this interpretation of this variable (Mihura et al., 2013). Consequently, readers should take this into consideration when interpreting this variable.

a:p ratio: Fixed Attitudes and Beliefs / Active or Passive Role in Relationships

Exner (2003) postulated that the a:p ratio provides some information regarding whether the examinee's values and attitudes are fixed. Individuals with a fixed set of attitudes or values will likely find it difficult to consider other viewpoints or other methods of addressing a problem. Exner (2003) suggested that when one side of the ratio gets much larger than the other, this indicates that the examinee's values and attitudes may be fixed. The larger the discrepancy between the sides, the more likely it is that the examinee's values and attitudes are fixed and the harder it will be to change them. This can have important implications for therapy, as an examinee with fixed attitudes, especially regarding the referral reason for therapy, may be less amenable to change than one who has more malleable attitudes. However, there has been very little research published regarding this interpretation; instead, the main focus of the research on this ratio has been on whether the person tends to be more active or passive in relationships (see Mihura et al., 2013, for a discussion). Consequently, I would not recommend interpreting the a:p ratio as being indicative of fixed attitudes and beliefs.

HVI, OBS, MOR: Hypervigilance, Obsessiveness, and Pessimism

The interpretation of HVI and OBS was discussed earlier in this chapter. However, MOR has not been discussed completely yet. MOR is coded when the examinee perceives something as being one of the four D's: dead, damaged, destroyed, or dysphoric. The interpretation of MOR codes, not surprisingly, is related to pessimism and focusing on the morose (Choca, 2013; Exner, 2000, 2003; Mihura et al., 2013). Having more than the expected number of MOR codes on a protocol could indicate that the examinee has a tendency to conceptualize the world in a pessimistic way. Consequently, the examinee will come to expect negative outcomes.

Left Side eb: Unintended Peripheral Thoughts

In this cluster, the left side of eb (FM, m) assesses how much unwanted peripheral thought the examinee is experiencing (Exner, 2000, 2003). These thoughts are outside the examinee's control. Left side eb contains two variables: FM and m. FM relates to needs states and m relates to situational stress. When the value of left side eb is higher than the average range, according to the comparison standard, then it indicates that the examinee is experiencing more unintended peripheral thought than is typical. A review of the FM and the m values can provide a hypothesis as to whether the increased activity is more likely due to need states or to situational stress.

When the value for the left side eb is lower than expected, then it suggests that the examinee is experiencing a lower level of peripheral thought than is typical. It could suggest that the examinee is reacting faster than is typical to reduce the impact these peripheral thoughts have; in other words, once the examinee starts to experience the thoughts, he instantly addresses the cause, regardless of what he may be doing at the time. The decision to address the need immediately is not necessarily well thought out. As an example, imagine that someone is in a business meeting and starts to get hungry. Rather than wait for the meeting to end, the person gets up and goes to lunch to resolve his hunger need. Although this action addressed the need quickly, it likely caused another difficulty for the examinee; namely, his boss becoming angry with him for leaving the meeting abruptly.

Ma:Mp: Substituting Fantasy for Reality

This ratio is thought to assess whether the examinee has a tendency to substitute fantasy for reality when stressed. If this is the case, then Mp will be greater than Ma. Exner (2000, 2003) referred to this as Snow White Syndrome, as by fleeing into fantasy, the examinee is able to avoid decision making and, instead, relies heavily on others to do it for him. Consequently, he is also prone to being manipulated by others.

It is important to note that there is relatively little recent research on this variable (e.g., Michel & Mormont, 2002). The examiner should take this into consideration when deciding how much emphasis to put on the results of this variable.

Intellectualization Index: Tendency to Intellectualize Emotions

As described in discussing the affect cluster, it is not common to use intellectualization, a process that can minimize the impact of emotions by dealing with them on an intellectual basis rather than an emotional one. The occasional use of this strategy is typically not problematic; however, this strategy can become a problem when it is used frequently, as it can result in the impacts of situations being often distorted or minimized.

Again, some level of intellectualization is expected. However, when the value is higher than expected (>1 SD from the mean), then there is evidence to indicate that the examinee is using intellectualization more than is typical. As the value gets higher, it suggests that the examinee is using intellectualization as a way to avoid emotional situations.

There is very little research on this index (see Mihura et al., 2013, for a discussion). The reader is advised to take this into consideration when interpreting this variable.

WSum6: Possible Presence of Thought Disturbance

The WSum6 is a weighted score constructed from the critical six Special Scores: DV, DR, INCOM, FABCOM, CONTAM, and ALOG. The different critical six Special Scores are weighted according to their relative severity, with DV1 being the least severe and CONTAM and FABCOM2 being the most severe. The Special Scores, ranked from least severe to most severe, can be found in Chapter 3 of this book. Interpretations of each of the Special Scores can also be found in Rapid Reference 4.24.

≋Rapid Reference 4.24

. . . .

Rank Order and Interpretation of the Critical Six Special Scores from Least to Most Severe

Variable	Interpretation
DV1	Examinee has brief cognitive issues. This score may be due to language difficulties (review whether examinee has expressive language disorder or was not tested in his dominant language). Examinee may have difficulty communicating with others.
DV2	Examinee has more severe brief cognitive issues. This score may be due to language difficulties (review whether examinee has expressive language disorder or was not tested in his dominant language). Examinee may have difficulty communicating with others. Examinee may be preoccupied with something to the extent that it is interfering with thought processes.
INCOM1	Examinee uses concrete reasoning. This score may be due to language difficulties (see DV1).
DR1	Examinee shows indecisiveness. Examinee may have difficulty remaining on task. Examinee may be easily distracted. Examinee may have difficulty controlling impulses.
INCOM2	Examinee uses bizarre thinking. Examinee may have strained logic. Examinee may be preoccupied with something to the point that it is interfering with customary patterns of thinking.

Variable	Interpretation
FABCOM1	Examinee's thinking may not be clear. Examinee's thinking may be irrational. Examinee's thinking may be distorted.
ALOG	Examinee uses concrete reasoning. Examinee may make poor decisions.
DR2	Examinee may have significant difficulties remaining on task. Examinee's thinking may be very scattered and fragmented.
FABCOM2	Examinee has severe thinking difficulties. Examinee's thinking is likely to be distorted and not based on reality. Examinee's decision making is likely affected.
CONTAM	Examinee has severe thinking difficulties, unlikely to be reality-based. Examinee likely experiences difficulty separating concepts, like fantasy and reality.

Source: Based on information from Choca, 2013; Exner, 2001, 2003; Weiner, 2003.

In general, the higher the value for WSum6, the more bizarre and detached from reality the examinee's thinking is (Choca, 2013; Exner, 2003). However, when considering the value for WSum6, it is also important to consider which Special Scores contributed to the WSum6. If the WSum6 is elevated, but the scores are primarily DV and/or INCOM1 scores, it implies that there may be a difficulty with language rather than with thinking. However, if the WSum6 is elevated due to the presence of Level 2 scores, an ALOG, or a CONTAM, then it indicates that there are more serious difficulties with thinking, as these scores are not common in the general population. When thinking is impaired to this extent, decision making and behaviors are also likely to be affected, resulting in atypical and bizarre behaviors.

Evaluation of Critical Special Scores: Content Analysis

The purpose of this step is to review the responses that have critical six Special Score codes associated with them in order to put the scores into context. This provides a chance for examiners to account for individual differences (e.g., culture, language differences, speech disabilities) in their interpretations. For instance, if the individual has an elevated WSum6, but a review of all the critical six Special Scores indicates that they were due to an inappropriate word use, such as substituting "paws" for "hands," and there is information in the examinee's background to suggest that he experiences word finding difficulties (e.g., he was not tested in his dominant language, or he has an expressive language disorder), then this should be taken into account in the interpretation. Conversely, if the responses that led to the elevation of WSum6 were very bizarre, then there should also be evidence of bizarre behavior in the examinee's history.

Mnone and M–: Difficulty with Thinking and Distorted Perceptions About Others

M determinants assess cognitive resources, which include the ability to think, plan, and organize (Choca, 2013; Exner, 2000, 2003; Mihura et al., 2013). Conceptually, the presence of a FQ– or FQnone with an M determinant indicates that thinking is seriously impaired. However, recent research has suggested that M determinants with FQ– are strongly associated with having a distorted view of others (Mihura et al., 2013). Formless M responses—M determinants with no FQ—are thought to indicate impaired control over thinking; however, the meta-analysis by Mihura and colleagues (2013) revealed that little research has been done on this variable. Additionally, a survey by Meyer, Hsiao, Viglione, Mihura, and Abraham (2013) indicated that practicing clinicians who used the Rorschach did not believe the formless M responses were clinically valid. Consequently, examiners should take this into consideration when deciding how much emphasis to put on the presence of formless M variables on a protocol.

Quality of M Responses: Content Analysis

In this final step, the examiner reviews the quality of the M responses in order to determine whether the examinee's thinking was concrete and/or impaired. This process, too, relies heavily on the examiner's clinical judgment. Examiners should take steps to avoid having their own biases and perceptions influence their interpretation of the quality of the M responses.

SELF-PERCEPTION

Simply put, self-perception is how one views the self. On the CS, self-perception is conceptualized as having two parts: self-image and self-involvement. Self-image is how the person views the self and the various aspects of the self. Ideally, a person's self-image is based on real experiences and incorporates reality-based perceptions about herself, but this is not always the case. It is easy to see how misperceptions, distortions of reality, and faulty conceptualizations could result in an inaccurate self-image. For example, if a person is experiencing depression and, as a result, tends to have a very negative view of herself, she may tend to think the difficulties she is experiencing are a result of negative aspects of the self.

As a result, her self-image becomes more negative, which, in turn, could negatively affect her depression.

Self-involvement, conversely, is how concerned individuals are with themselves. In other words, it is how focused they are on themselves, rather than on others, the environment, and so forth. Usually, someone who is considered to be highly focused on herself is considered to be narcissistic, but this may not be the case. Consider someone with an eating disorder: typically, an individual with an eating disorder is highly focused on perceived negative aspects of the self (e.g., her body) and this becomes an overriding focus for her. This high level of self-involvement is not due to narcissism; it is due to a negative self-focus.

Variables

This cluster has eight steps that involve the interpretation of nine variables. This cluster also involves searching for projected material. Rapid Reference 4.25 lists the variables interpreted with this cluster, how each variable is calculated, and what each of these variables assesses.

≡ Rapid Reference 4.25

Self-Perception: How Variables Are Calculated and Assessed

Variable	How It Is Calculated	What It Assesses in This Cluster
OBS	A combination of variables.	Perfectionism; insecurity.
HVI	A combination of variables.	Focus on vulnerability.
rF and Fr	The number of rF and Fr determinants.	Whether the examinee overvalues her own worth; focuses on her own needs rather than the needs of others.
Egocentricity Index	$3r + (2) / R$.	Self-esteem; the balance between focus on the self and focus on others.
FD	The number of FD determinants.	Tendency toward self-examination.
V	The number of V, VF, and FV determinants.	Tendency to focus on negative aspects of the self.

(continued)

(continued)

Variable	How It Is Calculated	What It Assesses in This Cluster
An + Xy	The number of An and Xy content codes.	Unusual focus on the body, could also include focus on body functioning.
MOR	The number of MOR Special Scores.	Pessimistic view of the self.
H:(H) + Hd + (Hd)	The ratio of the number of whole human content codes to the other human content codes, not including Hx.	Whether self-image is based on real or distorted experiences.

Source: Based on information from Choca, 2013; Exner, 2000, 2003; Mihura et al., 2013; Weiner, 2003.

Interpretation of Variables

OBS and HVI: Obsessiveness or Perfectionism and Hypervigilance
The OBS and HVI variables both assess constructs that could influence a person's perception of herself. According to Exner (2001, 2003), individuals with a positive OBS are thought to be overly focused on being perfect. This focus on being perfect may be a way to avoid failure and to compensate for feeling insecure. According to Exner (2003), these individuals are at an increased risk of experiencing difficulty when they fail at a task. Rather than move on, these individuals will be prone to overstate the impact of the mistake and its consequences. In other words, they will tend to place the blame for the difficulties on themselves.

Also according to Exner (2000, 2003), a positive HVI indicates that the examinee does not trust the environment. This is thought to be due to concerns about being vulnerable. It takes an incredible amount of resources in order to maintain a heightened state. Unlike individuals with a high OBS, individuals with a high HVI will tend to blame external circumstances for their difficulties.

However, it is important to note that there is little research on either of these indices and a recent survey of experienced clinicians has questioned their accuracy (Meyer et al., 2013; Mihura et al., 2013). The examiner should take this into consideration when making interpretations.

Reflection: Narcissism
Reflections (Fr + rF) are suggestive of narcissism and an inflated sense of self-worth (Exner, 2000, 2003; Mihura et al., 2013). Having an inflated sense of

self-worth is not necessarily problematic, as long as the environment is providing feedback that supports it. However, if the environment is not providing feedback supportive of the high sense of self-worth, then the examinee is at risk of psychological difficulties. In other words, if there is a good person-environment fit, then psychological difficulties are unlikely to occur. However, if there is a disconnect between the person's characteristics and the environment, psychological difficulties are more likely to occur.

Reflections are typically interpreted only when there are more reflections than expected. If the number of reflections is higher than expected, based on the comparison sample, it indicates that the examinee may have an inflated sense of self-worth.

Egocentricity Index: Involvement with the Self

The Egocentricity Index [3r + (2) / R] is thought to provide an assessment of how involved individuals are with themselves (Exner, 2003). However, an increased level of self-involvement does not necessarily equate to high self-esteem or narcissism; it is very possible to have a high level of self-involvement and a very negative sense of self.

In general, when the Egocentricity Index is higher than expected, the examinee is more focused on herself than is typical. Again, this could be positive or negative. When the Egocentricity Index is lower than expected, then the examinee is less focused on herself and typically more focused on others. This could be due to a low sense of self-worth (e.g., low self-esteem).

The Egocentricity Index is often interpreted in conjunction with the number of reflections in the protocol. Possible interpretations for the Egocentricity Index and reflections are displayed in Rapid Reference 4.26.

FD and Sum V: Self-Examination

According to Exner (2003), both FD and V determinants are thought to relate to self-examination, including examining one's thoughts, emotions, and behaviors. The difference between the interpretations of these variables is that the presence of a few FD determinants is thought to be associated with general self-examination, which can be positive. The presence of a few FD determinants may also be a positive prognostic sign for therapy, as it suggests that the examinee is already engaging is some self-examination and may already have some insight into their thoughts, emotions, and behaviors. However, Exner (2000, 2003) suggested that the presence of more FD determinants than is typical indicates that the examinee may be overly concerned with their self-image. Still, given recent research suggesting that there is little support for this interpretation of FD, I would suggest that examiners focus their interpretation on V rather than FD, as the interpretation of V has shown to have some empirical support (Mihura et al., 2013).

≡Rapid Reference 4.26

Possible Interpretations of the Egocentricity Index and Reflections

	Egocentricity Higher Than Expected	Egocentricity Within Expected Range	Egocentricity Lower Than Expected
Reflection Responses Present	The presence of narcissism is likely.	Examinee may be aware that her high view of herself may not be warranted. May be doubting herself.	Examinee may be engaging in a "compensatory narcissism" in order to compensate for her low sense of self-worth. May also be experiencing a great deal of conflict about her self-image and worth.
Reflection Responses Absent	Examinee may have a high level of self-focus, but not taking pleasure from it.	Examinee is focused on self about as much as others typically are.	Examinee is less focused on herself than others typically are; likely due to a low sense of self-worth.

Source: Based on information from Exner, 2000, 2003; Weiner, 2003.

The presence of V, VF, and FV determinants, on the other hand, is associated with more negative self-examination and a focus on the negative features of the self. When there are more V determinants than is typical (e.g., >1SD above the mean), then it suggests that the examinee is more focused on the negative aspects of the self than is usual.

An + Xy: Body Focus

The An and Xy determinants have been associated with being focused on the body and bodily functioning (Exner, 2003). This variable can be interpreted only when its value is higher than expected (>1SD above the mean). When this is the case, it indicates that the examinee may be more focused on his body and/or its functioning than is typical. There is strong empirical support for the interpretation of this variable (Mihura et al., 2013).

It is important to keep in mind that there are many reasons why someone may be focused on the body/its functioning. Those who are body conscious may elevate this scale. However, those who also work with the human body on a regular basis (e.g., paramedics, surgeons) may also elevate this scale, because their work focuses on body functioning. An elevation on this scale does not necessarily mean that the person is body conscious.

MOR: Focus on Morose, Pessimism

MOR Special Scores are associated with pessimism, especially about the self (Exner, 2003). Like many other variables in the CS, the presence of MOR Special Scores is interpretable only when it is higher than expected. When this occurs, it indicates that the examinee is more pessimistic about herself than others are about themselves.

Human Response Codings: Relating to Others

This step has two substeps. The first focuses on the human interest ratio [H:(H) + Hd + (Hd)]; Exner stated that this ratio can be interpreted only when the examinee provides a sufficient number of human response content codes (three for the CS). Exner (2000, 2003) also noted that the expected number of human responses varies based on style.

In general, if a person has many more H content codes than the other types of human content codes combined, then it indicates the examinee is able to relate to others and see them as distinct, complete human beings, rather than as extensions of the examinee or as partial individuals (e.g., the examinee is able to see that her teacher is not only her teacher and does have other interests). This can be very positive, as it suggests that the examinee has the ability to form a self-concept that is based in real interactions with other people.

However, if an examinee has fewer H content codes than other types of human content codes, that suggests the examinee is more likely to see others as fragmented and not as distinct, complete humans. It is also possible that the examinee is identifying with individuals in fantasy (e.g., in books and other media) rather than in reality. This can affect the development of a self-image, as it may be based not on real interactions but rather on fantasy interactions.

The second part of this step involves a review of the responses with human content codes. This involves clinical judgment on the part of the examiner.

Search for Projected Material

The final step in this cluster involves searching for projected material. This, too, involves clinical judgment on the part of the examiner. Again, it is important to take steps to minimize the impact of the examiner's own biases and perceptions on this aspect of interpretation.

INTERPERSONAL PERCEPTION

The interpersonal perception cluster addresses how people perceive others. How someone perceives others will affect how that person acts in a social situation. Ideally, the perception of others is based on reality; however, there are times when it is not. For example, if an examinee perceives others to be threats, even if they are not, the examinee will act as though other people are threatening to him. Conversely, if an examinee perceives someone to be trustworthy, even if that person is not, the examinee will act as though the other person is trustworthy.

Many factors determine how someone perceives others. They include individual characteristics, such as personality traits, the presence of narcissistic tendencies, and current mood, to name just a few. Environmental factors will play a role as well. For example, if you see someone holding a baseball bat on a baseball field, your perception of that person will likely be neutral or positive, as your conceptualization of the individual is likely that the person is playing baseball. However, if you see that same person holding a baseball bat in a dark alley, your perception of that person is likely to be much more negative, due to the environment in which the person appears.

Variables

This cluster has eleven steps that result in the interpretation of thirteen variables. This cluster also involves reviewing the M and FM responses that include pairs. Rapid Reference 4.27 lists the variables interpreted with this cluster, how each variable is calculated, and what each of these variables assesses.

Interpretation of Variables

CDI: Social Difficulty
The Coping Deficit Index has been examined in the discussions of other clusters. Elevations on the CDI have been associated with social immaturity and social difficulty. Examinees who have scores that are higher than expected on this index are often seen as having fewer social skills than would be expected for an adult.

HVI: Hypervigilance
The HVI score has also been examined in the discussions of other clusters. Individuals with a high HVI may not trust others, and this will affect the nature of their interpersonal relationships and how they perceive others. This mistrust of others can lead to being guarded and suspicious around others, which makes it difficult to form close relationships.

≡Rapid Reference 4.27

Interpersonal Perception:
How Variables Are Calculated and Assessed

Variable	How It Is Calculated	What It Assesses in This Cluster
CDI	A combination of variables.	Social immaturity; difficulty with social interactions.
HVI	A combination of variables.	Hypervigilance; mistrust of others.
a:p	The ratio of the number of Ma, FMa, and ma determinants compared to the number of Mp, FMp, and mp determinants.	Whether the examinee is passive in relationships.
Fd	The number of food determinants.	Dependency.
SumT	The number of T, FT, and TF determinants.	Needs for emotional closeness; openness to close relationships.
Interpersonal Interest Sum	The sum of all human content codes, except Hx [H + (H) + Hd + (Hd)].	Interest in others; conceptualization of others.
H	The number of pure H content codes.	Understanding of others.
GHR	Calculated via an algorithm.	Tendency to engage in appropriate interpersonal behaviors.
PHR	Calculated via an algorithm.	Tendency to engage in less appropriate interpersonal behaviors.
COP	The number of COP Special Scores.	Expectation of positive interpersonal exchanges.
AG	The number of AG Special Scores.	Expectation of aggressive and/or competitive interpersonal exchanges.
PER	The number of PER Special Scores.	Defensiveness in interpersonal interactions.
Isolation Index	The sum of Bt, 2 × Cl, Ge, Ls, and 2 × Na, divided by the number of responses [(Bt + 2Cl + Ge + Ls + 2Na) / R].	Social isolation; how active the examinee is in social interactions.

Source: Based on information from Choca, 2013; Exner, 2000, 2003; Mihura et al., 2013; Weiner, 2003.

a:p: Active or Passive Role in Relationships

The use of the a:p ratio was discussed in the ideation cluster, where it assesses the presence of fixed attitudes and beliefs. In this cluster, the a:p ratio is thought to offer some information about how the examinee approaches interpersonal relationships. Exner (2001, 2003) noted that this ratio is interpreted only when p is higher than a, which suggests that the examinee may be passive in relationships. However, Choca (2013) has suggested that this ratio can also be interpreted when a is much higher than p; he notes that when a is much higher than p, it suggests that the examinee may respond to all situations with action, even when it is not warranted. He also suggested that when a and p are similar, it indicates that the examinee may be indecisive.

It is important to note that a recent meta-analysis indicated little empirical support for the interpretation of this variable (Mihura et al., 2013). Consequently, I would caution against putting too much emphasis on this variable, at least until more research is completed on it.

Food: Dependency

Food content codes are relatively rare. This variable is part of the Rorschach Oral Dependency Scale (ROD), which will be discussed in more detail in Chapter 8, as a variant of it is included on the R-PAS. Both Exner (2001, 2003) and Choca (2013) suggest that the presence of any food content codes on a protocol indicates that the examinee is dependent on others. However, Mihura and colleagues' meta-analysis (2013) and Meyer and colleagues' survey (2013) do not support this interpretation. Consequently, I would caution against putting too much emphasis on this interpretation. If a measure of dependency is desired, the ROD has a great deal of empirical support (Bornstein, 1996; Masling, Rabie, & Blondheim, 1967).

SumT: Interest in Others

Texture responses have been interpreted in previous clusters as a measure of internal demands on the person. For this cluster, this variable is thought to relate to needs for interpersonal closeness. If it is higher than expected, then the examinee has more needs for closeness than are typical. When this is the case, then it is important to review the examinee's history in order to determine whether the increased needs for closeness are due to a recent loss, which could include a death, a divorce, or a move. Both Exner (2000, 2003) and Weiner (2003) recommend a possible interpretation for SumT scores that are below the expected range as well; specifically, individuals with a lower than expected SumT score may be expressing their needs for closeness differently than others typically do, possibly due to being uncomfortable with physical contact.

Interpersonal Interest and H: Interest in Others, Accuracy of Perceptions of Others

Human response variables were discussed as part of the interpretation of the self-perception cluster. In the interpersonal perception cluster, these variables are used to offer some hypotheses regarding the examinee's interest and understanding of others (Exner, 2003). The sum of the interpersonal interest variables is associated with interest in others and is interpretable when values are both higher and lower than expected. If the value is higher than expected, based on the comparison sample, then the person is more interested in others than is typical. If it is lower than expected, then the person is less interested in others than expected.

The H score assesses whether the examinee understands others and is capable of seeing others as complex, whole beings. Like the sum of the interpersonal interest variables, it is interpretable when values are both higher and lower than expected. Thus, an examinee whose H score is lower than expected likely does not understand others well. An examinee whose H score is equal to or greater than expected likely does understand others well.

Exner (2000, 2003) did note that different ranges were expected for these variables, based on style. When using Exner's norms as a comparison (Exner, 2000, 2001, 2003), it is important to take this into consideration when interpreting these variables.

It is also important to note that Mihura and colleagues' (2013) meta-analysis indicated that there was sufficient research to support this interpretation of H. However, there was little research on the interpersonal interest sum.

GHR and PHR: Understanding of Others

GHR and PHR are dichotomous. Good human representational responses (GHRs) are associated with engaging in positive interpersonal behaviors, and poor human representational responses (PHRs) are associated with engaging in negative, maladaptive interpersonal behaviors (Choca, 2013; Exner, 2003; Weiner, 2003). In general, when there are more responses with GHR codes than with PHR codes, the examinee's interpersonal behaviors are likely to be seen by others as being adaptive and appropriate. The opposite is true when there are more responses with PHR codes than GHR codes; in this case, the examinee's interpersonal behaviors may be seen as less adaptive and inappropriate.

COP and AG: Perceptions of Interpersonal Interactions

COP and AG both are thought to relate to how the examinee perceives interpersonal interactions. Specifically, COP responses indicate that the examinee is likely to perceive interpersonal interactions to be positive, while AG responses indicate that the examinee probably perceives interpersonal interactions to be aggressive or competitive (Exner, 2003). In general, these variables are interpreted only when they are in the expected ranges or higher; low scores are not interpreted. There is much stronger support in the published literature for the interpretation of COP than for the interpretation of AG (Mihura et al., 2013).

PER: Defensiveness in Interpersonal Interactions

Personalized Answers (PERs) are associated with defensiveness in interpersonal interactions (Exner, 2003). Occasional defensiveness in interpersonal interactions is typical; it is a way for individuals to support their opinion and to keep others from questioning them. However, doing this excessively can alienate people, as it presents as if the individual is trying to dominate over others or is not open to others' opinions and experience.

This variable is generally interpreted only when the number of PER responses exceeds the expected range. Higher than expected scores indicate that the examinee tends to be more defensive in interpersonal interactions than is typical.

Isolation Index: Social Isolation

Like many other CS variables, the Isolation Index $[(Bt + 2Cl + Ge + Ls + 2Na) / R]$ is interpreted only when its value exceeds the expected range (Exner, 2003). Individuals with an elevated Isolation Index tend to be more socially isolated than others. This is not necessarily a negative finding, especially if the examinee is not interested in social interactions. Still, it is important to note that there is little published empirical support for this interpretation (Mihura et al., 2013). I would advise against focusing an interpretation on this variable.

M and FM Responses with Pairs: Content Analysis

This final step involves a review of the human and animal movement responses that have pairs. This step involves a great deal of clinical judgment. As with all content analysis steps, I would advise the examiner to take steps to minimize the influence that the examiner's own preconceived notions and biases might have on the interpretation.

CONCLUSION

There is not one right way to interpret test results. Consistent with this, there are many guides available to assist with the interpretation of variable personality tests, including the Rorschach CS (e.g., Choca, 2013; Exner, 2000, 2003; Weiner, 2003). These texts differ somewhat in their interpretations. This is acceptable; personality assessment interpretation is not an exact science and involves clinical judgment and opinion, which will differ from examiner to examiner. It is most important that the interpretation provided is consistent with the data available.

It is also important to remember that the information obtained from testing is simply a group of hypotheses. These hypotheses need to be placed in some sort of context in order to make sense of them. Consequently, test interpretation is not something that can be done in isolation. In order to put the hypotheses generated by the test results into some context, it is important to consider all aspects of the examinee, including culture. It is also important to consider the potential impact of the testing situation, as this can influence the test results.

The next chapter is a CS case. The examinee's responses, sequence of scores, and the structural summary are included, with an interpretation. The same case is used for the R-PAS discussion later in this book; this allows the reader to compare the administration, coding, and interpretation of both systems using the same case.

🐟 TEST YOURSELF 🐟

1. **What should you do first when interpreting a valid coded and scored CS protocol for an adult?**
   a. Determine coping style.
   b. Do a Key Variable search.
   c. Evaluate S-CON.
   d. Interpret the ideation cluster.

2. **Which CS cluster is not always interpreted?**
   a. Situation-related stress
   b. Controls
   c. Affect
   d. Ideation

3. **Which variables are associated with the presence of situational stress?**
   a. M, FM
   b. m, Y
   c. T, r
   d. F, 2

4. **Which clusters make up the cognitive triad?**
   a. Affect, situation-related stress, controls and stress tolerance.
   b. Interpersonal perception, self-perception, controls and stress tolerance.
   c. Ideation, interpersonal perception, mediation.
   d. Ideation, mediation, information processing.

5. **Which Special Score could be due to language difficulties rather than thought disturbance?**

   a. DV1

   b. FABCOM2

   c. CONTAM

   d. INCOM2

6. **True or False: It is important to consider the possible impact of the circumstances surrounding testing on how the examinee approached the test.**

   a. True

   b. False

   Answers: 1. c; 2. a; 3. b; 4. d; 5. a; 6. a.

Five

COMPREHENSIVE SYSTEM CASE SAMPLE

This book uses the same case sample for both the CS and R-PAS. This allows the reader to compare the systems to one another. This chapter includes background history and referral information for the case, a Rorschach protocol administered according to the Comprehensive System, the sequence of scores (coding), and an interpretation based on the data provided. The structural summary for the protocol can be found in the Appendix. The Book Companion Website Materials contain additional materials, including an annotated administration, an annotated coding, and an annotated interpretation. The annotated administration provides information that is designed to explain why some responses were queried and why others were not. The annotated coding explains why the responses were coded the way that they were. Finally, the annotated interpretation is designed to explain which test data and/or observations support the interpretation statements.

BACKGROUND INFORMATION

Identifying Information and Reason for Referral

Sarah Frazier is a 25-year-old Caucasian female, currently residing in the Mid-Atlantic region of the United States. In September 2015, Ms. Frazier began a graduate program in criminology. Despite doing extremely well in both high school and college, she said she struggled with her first semester of graduate school, but still passed all her classes with grades of B– or above. She went to her advisor for advice, but began "crying uncontrollably," at which point her advisor encouraged her to seek assistance at the university clinic, where she was tested for a learning disorder. However, the results of that testing did not support a diagnosis of a learning disorder. The evaluator at the university suggested that Ms. Frazier participate in follow-up testing to identify possible reasons for her difficulty in classes.

The purpose of this evaluation is to identify possible contributing factors to Ms. Frazier's reported difficulty in graduate school and to make recommendations to improve her performance.

Relevant Background Information

Sarah Frazier provided the following background information. She was born and raised in the southwestern United States in an intact family and is the older of two children. Her younger brother is 17 and resides with their parents. Her father is self-employed and reportedly "does well." Her mother is a homemaker and volunteers with a local animal shelter. Ms. Frazier described her childhood as "typical," recalling that her parents were always very supportive of her decisions. She recalled feeling closer to her father than her mother, which she attributed to shared interests (e.g., martial arts, marksmanship). She said that she "tolerated" her younger brother when she was younger, but now has regular contact with him via text messages. She also talks to her parents "a few times per week," but said that they were not aware of the difficulties she has been having in graduate school, because "It would devastate them."

Ms. Frazier said that she did "extremely well" in high school and was offered "a full ride" to multiple colleges on a marksmanship scholarship. She opted to attend a school in the southwest United States, where she majored in criminal justice. She said that she was on the dean's list each semester in college and was able to balance her academic work with her training schedule for the marksmanship team. She also was the first member of her family to attend college, saying that it was typical for the women in her family to get married young and to have at least one child by the time they were 22.

During her freshman year in college, she met Greg Radnor (pseudonym), a senior at the university, at a party. She recalled that her roommate "strongly encouraged" her to go to the party and that she went only because her roommate promised to "stop harassing" her if she went. Ms. Frazier said that she and Mr. Radnor were both standing in the corner and he commented about how much he hated parties. The two talked about how much they hated parties and then started dating. They were married a few months after Ms. Frazier graduated with her BS degree in criminal justice. Shortly after they were married, Mr. Radnor was offered employment with a biotechnology firm in the Mid-Atlantic region of the United States, and the two moved. Her family initially opposed the move, saying that "family needs to stay together." However, Ms. Frazier has said that while it was difficult to move away from her parents, as she was the first in the family to leave the area, she does not believe it has negatively impacted their relationship, as she speaks with her family a few times per week.

Ms. Frazier sought work with the federal government and with local state agencies, but was told by recruiters that her application was not competitive because she lacked graduate education. She found employment with a school district, working in the main office, and planned to save money in order to pay for graduate school. However, after three years of working, Ms. Frazier and Mr. Radnor had not saved enough money for Ms. Frazier to go to school full time as they were focusing on paying off Mr. Radnor's student loans. Rather than wait longer to start graduate school, Ms. Frazier said that she decided to continue working full time while attending graduate school full time; she said that she believed she would be able to handle the stress. However, she noted that graduate school was "more difficult" than she thought it would be. She said that school has not interfered with her work and, in fact, her boss has praised the quality of her work. However, her grades last semester were lower than she was accustomed to; her GPA was a 3.0. As an undergraduate, her average GPA was reported to be a 3.8.

Ms. Frazier stated that she and Mr. Radnor have discussed having children. At this point, they are unsure if they want children. Still, Ms. Frazier has said that both her mother and her mother-in-law are encouraging them to start a family because they want grandchildren. When asked about her mother's and mother-in-law's comments, she stated that the comments do not bother her because "I am in a different place than they were when they were my age. Neither one attended college, let alone graduate school. They do not understand that I do not have time for children now. I'm only 25; I have plenty of time, if Greg and I choose to have kids."

Ms. Frazier said that she has friends but that she does not discuss "serious issues" with them because she does not believe they will understand this topic. She elaborated by stating that many of her friends from high school "are in a different place than I am" as they are married with multiple children. However, she does discuss other topics with them, including frustrations with work and with family. Most of her friends from college, in contrast, are in graduate school but are "far along in their programs" and busy with comprehensive examinations and working on research. She did say that she has sought support from some of them in the past, but that she does not want to be seen as incapable, so she does not ask for assistance. Ms. Frazier said that her husband knows she has been struggling but that she does not want to "burden him" because his work is stressful, so she has not spoken to him directly about it. Ms. Frazier added that she wants her husband to ask her how he can help, but he has not.

Ms. Frazier denied any significant medical or mental health history. She also denied any significant family mental health history, although she did note that her mother has type 2 diabetes. She also denied any history of substance abuse and stated she prefers to be in control of her own thoughts and actions.

Results of Previous Testing

During October 2015, Ms. Frazier was referred to the university clinic by her academic advisor for testing. According to Ms. Frazier, she "freaked out" and "sobbed" after getting a B– on her first paper and went to her advisor. Her advisor recommended an evaluation. She does feel that her advisor was "overreacting" and she did not believe that she needed testing. However, she reported that she went to the clinic because she was concerned about how her academic advisor would view her if she did not follow his advice, given that she will likely be asking him for a letter of recommendation in the future.

Ms. Frazier said that she was having difficulty concentrating on her reading, which was resulting in her taking an excessive amount of time to complete assignments. In addition, Ms. Frazier was working 40 hours per week and sharing household duties with Mr. Radnor. She said that she "squeezes in" reading when she can, which includes reading her assignments during her lunch hour and breaks while working. However, Ms. Frazier insisted that she was able to handle everything.

The university clinic conducted cognitive and academic achievement testing with Ms. Frazier. The results placed her cognitive abilities in the high average range, with scores ranging from 112 to 117. Her academic achievement scores were consistent with her cognitive abilities and with her academic attainment as a first-year graduate student. The clinic also had Ms. Frazier complete a self-report measure of personality and emotional functioning; all scores were within normal limits.

The evaluation concluded that Ms. Frazier did not meet diagnostic criteria for a learning disorder and that test results were not consistent with the presence of anxiety or depression. The evaluator recommended that Ms. Frazier consider using the tutoring services available on campus and consider participating in additional testing to identify possible contributing factors to her reported difficulty in classes.

Mental Status and Behavioral Observations

Ms. Frazier arrived to the appointment approximately 30 minutes early and was appropriately dressed and well groomed. She was poised and made appropriate eye contact with the evaluator. Her speech was normal in rate and in tone. Her responses to the questions asked of her were appropriate but tended to be very direct, with little elaboration unless she was specifically asked to elaborate on her response. When asked questions regarding emotions or typically emotionally laden situations (e.g., her wedding, death of a close family member), Ms. Frazier had a tendency to discuss factual aspects of the situation rather than her emotional reactions. Consistent with this, she reported her mood was "fine" and she did not display many emotions during the evaluation. The emotions she did display were limited to positive emotions (e.g., happiness) and even then, the display was limited. As an example, she did smile when discussing her wedding and her husband. However, she did not demonstrate any emotion when discussing the incident with her advisor that led to his referring her to the university clinic.

Ms. Frazier denied symptoms consistent with mood disturbance and anxiety. She denied experiencing difficulty sustaining attention, except with some of her statistics readings, which she reported finding "dreadfully boring." She also denied experiencing symptoms consistent with thought disorders, including visual, auditory, and tactile hallucinations. There was no evidence of disorganized or tangential speech. She also firmly denied any past or current history of suicidal, homicidal, or self-harming thoughts or behaviors.

Ms. Frazier actively participated in all aspects of testing. Thus, these results are considered to be an accurate reflection of her personality and emotional functioning at the time of the evaluation. Please be advised that this interpretation was based on the information available to the evaluator at the time of the evaluation.

ADMINISTRATION

Table 5.1 displays the CS administration for Ms. Frazier. The locations (e.g., D1, D2) that the examinee identified are embedded in the responses.

CODING

The complete data set for this case study can be found in the Appendix, and reproductions of the computer-generated sequence of scores and of the structural summary can be found in Figures A.1, A.2, and A.3 in the Appendix. Table 5.2 reproduces the CS code sequence for Ms. Frazier.

Table 5.1 CS Administration for Ms. Frazier (pseudonym)

Card	#	Response	Inquiry
I	1	A bug. *Take your time and look some more, I'm sure you'll see something else too.*	These (D1) look like little antennas. These (D2) looked like wings and these (DdS26) reminded me of markings that could be on an insect. That's why I thought bug. Area: WS
	2	A bat.	Wings (D2), body (D4), the wings are out, like it's flying. Area: W
II	3	A ladybug.	The red made me think of a ladybug (points to D2, D3 and red spots on D6). Ladybugs also have black too on them, like this picture. The wings are out, it's flying. Area: W
	4	It kind of looks like ribs and chest, like anatomy.	It's like you are looking down through the ribcage. This part (D6) is the ribcage and this part is the pelvis (D3). See how it's smaller? It looks further away. This reminded me of anatomy because this (D3) looked like the shape of a pelvis. Area: D6 & D3
	5	In the white space there is a ballet dancer.	Right here (DS5). *Help me see the ballerina.* She is dancing. She has her arms straight up and this is her fluffy white tutu. *You said it was fluffy?* Yeah, the shape makes it look fluffy. Area: DS5
III	6	Oh I definitely see two people here (D9). Women, because they have boobs. They are fighting over this basket, here (D7).	Ok, so it looks like they are bending over, grabbing, and pulling at this basket here. Both of them want it. You can see the basket is starting to break from being pulled, see how it looks like it is coming apart? These red spots are blood; they cut themselves on the basket shreds. It kind of looks like shopping on Thanksgiving when they have those really great deals and people fight over items. Area: W

Card	#	Response	Inquiry
	7	I see a fetus.	Right here (D2). Head, body, and this is the umbilical cord. I would guess it is a second semester fetus because you can see all the different parts but it is still small. Area: D2
IV	8	v I don't really see anything. . .oh wait, it kind of looks like the monster from Fantasia, what was his name?	Chernabog! That was his name! Anyway, here is the head (D1), horns, wings (D6), the wings are spread out, like a show of strength. He is really buff, the shading makes it look like muscles. Area: W
	9	(turned card 360 degrees) Umm, it kind of looks like Hagrid riding on his motorcycle when I look at it this way.	You know, like from Harry Potter? So he's leaning back on his motorcycle because his feet (D6) are big and his head (D3) is small, so it looks like the feet are closer. This (D1) is the wheel of the motorcycle and these (D4) are the handlebars. Area: W
V	10	Another bug. I keep seeing bugs!	Antenna (Dd34), legs (D9), wings (D4). The wings are out, it's flying. Area: W
	11	It also kind of looks like a pterodactyl.	It's basically the same thing, but not this part (points to Dd34). Legs (D9), Wings (d4). It's also flying. Head is here (Dd30). Area: Dd99
VI	12	Cowhide rug. Looks furry.	You know, like one of those rugs you put on your floor? This is the head (D3), the body and legs (D1), here's the butt (Dd33). *You said it was furry?* Just the shape. Reminds me of fur. Area: W
	13	>It looks like a ship. Just this part (D4).	This is the front, the smokestack, and the back. The shape reminds me of a ship. Area: D4
VII	14	2 people with their hair up. I don't know what kind of style that would be. Maybe a beehive?	They are girls. Here is the face and head (D9), that crazy hairstyle (D5), the shape just reminds me of hair I guess. They are hunched over a bit, see how it looks like the head is forward (points to D2)? Area: D2

(continued)

Table 5.1 Continued

Card	#	Response	Inquiry
	15	Right here (DS10) looks like a bowl.	Just the shape reminds me of it. Area: DS10
VIII	16	> Oh this one is easy. It's an animal, maybe a wolf, walking in the Arctic.	There's the wolf (D1). He's walking over these glaciers, here (D6). I thought glaciers because it looked like ice to me. *Ice?* Yeah, because you can see the reflection of the animal here. Area: W
	17	An ugly dress.	Just this part (D2). This is the top (Dd33) and this is the skirt (D7). *You said it was ugly?* The color combination. It's hideous. Area: D2
IX	18	A waterfall. That's it.	It's the whole thing, except for this (D6). The faint blue here (D8) is water falling. These are the lush green plants that are growing around the waterfall (D11), they are growing quickly because it is a good environment to grow. These are the cliffs (D3). It is really a beautiful picture. Area: D2
X	19	A woman.	She's old. She's here (outlines area that includes DdS29, D6, and D10). This is her head (top of DdS29), these are her boobs (D6), her boobs are really low, like what happens when you get old and your bra is not supportive. She is wearing colorful stockings, here (D10). This (D8), is her gray hair. Area: Dd99
	20	< Another bug! This one is a caterpillar. No, a banana slug. It's definitely a banana slug.	I had to eat a banana slug at camp, so I know what they look like. This looks just like it (D9). It's the same shape, but this is not the right color. Banana slugs are yellow, not red. Area: D9

Table 5.2 Sequence of Scores

			Sequence of Scores					
Card	Resp. No.	Location and DQ	Loc. No.	Determinant(s) and Form Quality	(2)	Content(s)	Pop	Z Score	Special Scores
I	1	WSo	1	Fo		A		3.5	
	2	Wo	1	FMao		A	P	1.0	
II	3	Wo	1	CF.C'.F.FMau		A		4.5	
	4	Do	3	FD–		An			
	5	DS+	5	Ma.FC'u		Cg,H		3.0	GHR
III	6	W+	1	Ma.C.mpo	2	H,Sx,Bl,Hh	P	5.5	AG, MOR, PHR
	7	Do	2	Fu		H,An			DV, GHR
IV	8	Wo	1	Ma.FYo		(H)		2.0	GHR
	9	W+	1	Ma.FDo		(H),Sc	P	4.0	GHR
V	10	Wo	1	FMao		A		1.0	
	11	Ddo	99	FMau		A			
VI	12	Wo	1	Fo		Ad,Hh,Sx	P	2.5	
	13	Do	4	Fo		Sc			
VII	14	Do	2	Mpo	2	Hd	P		GHR
	15	DSo	10	Fo		Hh			
VIII	16	W+	1	FMa.rFo		A,Na	P	4.5	
	17	Do	2	FCu		Cg			
IX	18	Dv/+	2	map.CFo		Na		2.5	
X	19	DdSo	99	FC'.FC–		H,Sx,Cg		6.0	PHR
	20	Do	9	Fo		A			PER

Source: Rorschach Interpretation Assistance Program: Version 5, Copyright 1999, 2001 by PAR Inc.

INTERPRETATION

Ms. Frazier was administered the Rorschach using the Comprehensive System. She provided enough responses for the Rorschach to be scored and interpreted using the Comprehensive System. Results also indicated that she was not overly defensive during the administration of the instrument. Thus, the following interpretation is considered to be an accurate reflection of her personality and emotional functioning at the time of the evaluation.

The results of testing indicated that Ms. Frazier is not at an increased risk of a lethal suicide attempt in the near future. This is consistent with her denial of suicidal ideation during the clinical interview.

Emotional Functioning

The results of the Rorschach suggest that Ms. Frazier is uncomfortable around emotions and does her best to avoid situations where strong emotions may be present. This observation is consistent with the evaluator's observation that Ms. Frazier tended to avoid talking about emotions during the clinical interview. Moreover, when specifically asked about emotionally laden situations, such as the death of a close family member, Ms. Frazier had a tendency to focus on the factual aspects of the situation rather than the emotional aspects. This is consistent with a marked tendency to avoid emotions.

The results of the Rorschach offer several hypotheses that could help to explain why Ms. Frazier avoids emotions. First, the results of the Rorschach suggested that Ms. Frazier is experiencing negative emotions, which could include depression, anger, and fear. Given her report of her struggles in graduate school, including that she needs to work full time while attending her graduate program full time, and that she is finding graduate school to be more difficult than she initially thought it would be, it would not be unexpected for her to be experiencing some negative emotions, including anxiety, depression, and anger. Additionally, the results of testing indicated that Ms. Frazier is prone to strong emotional displays rather than controlled ones. Although this observation seems at odds with her tightly controlled presentation during the evaluation, it is consistent with her report of her strong emotional display in her advisor's office. Taken together, this could suggest that Ms. Frazier is avoiding emotions in an effort to reduce the risk of experiencing a strong negative emotional display, like the one she reportedly experienced in her advisor's office ("sobbing").

The results of the Rorschach also suggest that Ms. Frazier has a tendency to be confused by emotions. It is also possible that she is avoiding emotions because she does not understand them, or is not clear on how to appropriately cope with them.

Coping/Functioning

The results of the Rorschach indicate that Ms. Frazier is not experiencing any significant distress at this time that is interfering with her ability to function adequately. This is consistent with Ms. Frazier's report that she is "fine" and that she believes she can handle the stressors she is experiencing. Still, it is important to note that while Ms. Frazier has been able to maintain her employment while passing her graduate school classes, she has been experiencing difficulty concentrating, which could be related to an increase in complex thinking and emotional patterns due to the stressors she is experiencing. While she is able to cope with maintaining full-time employment while attending graduate school at this time, her current methods of coping, which include a tendency to avoid emotions and not seeking assistance from others, may not be sufficient if additional stressors present themselves.

Self-Perception

The results of the Rorschach suggested that Ms. Frazier has a high level of self-focus. This is consistent with her reported focus on advancing her career. However, the results also indicated that Ms. Frazier is experiencing some doubt about her self-image and is focusing on negative aspects of herself. This is consistent with her report that she did "extremely well" in high school and college, yet is "struggling" in graduate school, leading her to seek out reasons why she is having difficulty (e.g., talking to her advisor, the evaluations). Taken together, these results imply that Ms. Frazier is conflicted about her current self-image. This can be extremely disconcerting, especially for someone who is strongly self-involved and focusing on the negative aspects of self, like Ms. Frazier. A focus on negative aspects of the self can evoke strong negative emotions; this may be another contributing factor to her avoidance of emotions.

The results of the Rorschach also indicated that Ms. Frazier is experiencing some concern about her body. She made no mention of this in her clinical interview.

Interpersonal Perception

Testing suggested that Ms. Frazier is able to view others as complex beings. However, testing indicated that she does not expect positive interactions with others and is not comfortable in interpersonal interactions. This is consistent with Ms. Frazier's report that she tended to keep to herself during college and is continuing to do so during graduate school. Additionally, the evaluator's observations of Ms. Frazier suggest that Ms. Frazier tended to be direct; it is possible that this directness was related to Ms. Frazier's discomfort with the testing situation.

The results of testing also indicated that Ms. Frazier has a tendency to express her needs for closeness differently than others typically do. This is consistent with Ms. Frazier's report that she is not reaching out for assistance from others, such as family and friends, and instead, prefers to deal with difficult situations on her own. Still, it is important to note that Ms. Frazier's interpersonal differences do not appear to be impeding her ability to act appropriately in social situations; testing indicated that she is typically able to engage in appropriate behaviors. This is consistent with her appropriate behavior during the testing session. Still, it is important to note that there is some indication from testing that Ms. Frazier tends to be oppositional and/or independent. This may be related to her tendency toward interests that are not traditionally feminine (e.g., martial arts, marksmanship) and her not following family traditions of having children early and staying in close proximity to the rest of the family.

Cognition

Testing did not reveal any significant difficulties with thinking. This is consistent with the evaluator's observations that Ms. Frazier's speech was consistent with the questions asked of her and goal directed; it is also consistent with Ms. Frazier's report that she did not experience hallucinations.

Overall, Ms. Frazier tends to put forth as much effort in processing new information as others typically do. However, when presented with information, Ms. Frazier has a tendency to focus on the entire situation, or the "big picture." Her effort to see the entire situation can result in her sometimes missing the obvious answer. This tendency to see the "big picture" could benefit her in her future desired career as a criminologist, as it would be important for her to consider the whole situation before offering a conclusion.

Testing also indicated that Ms. Frazier makes a strong effort to ensure that she is perceiving a situation the ways that others typically do. Still, she has a tendency to make decisions that disregard social convention more often than others do. This is consistent with her report that she is in a "different place" than many of her friends from high school, who are reportedly married with children. Instead, Ms. Frazier has opted to pursue a graduate degree. Her tendency to disregard social convention was present in high school, as she pursued interests that reportedly were not traditionally engaged in by women in the area she grew up (e.g., marksmanship). This is not to say that her decisions are unacceptable; they are acceptable, but are not consistent with the traditional expectations of the area she grew up in.

SUMMARY AND RECOMMENDATIONS

Ms. Frazier is a 25-year-old Caucasian female who was referred by her university clinic for additional testing. Ms. Frazier reported that she has been struggling with graduate school, although it is important to note that she is receiving passing marks in her classes. The previous testing was not consistent with the presence of a learning disorder, depressive disorder, or anxiety disorder, and additional testing was recommended.

The results of this evaluation suggest that Ms. Frazier is a conservative individual who tends to keep to herself. She is used to a high level of achievement, as she did "extremely well" in both high school and college and, per her report, was able to balance multiple demands on her time during college. However, she is currently attempting to balance a full-time graduate program with full-time work. She is successful, as her boss has reportedly praised her work and she is passing all of her courses, albeit with lower grades than she is used to receiving.

According to the results of this evaluation, Ms. Frazier is accustomed to being successful in her endeavors. As an example, she was able to attend college on a scholarship, was on the dean's list, and has been doing well at work. This consistent positive feedback could have resulted in her feeling strongly positive about her own attributes. However, her recent difficulty in graduate school has resulted in her questioning whether her high view of herself is accurate. As Ms. Frazier works through her rectifying her high view of herself with the negative feedback she has received from the environment, she is at risk of experiencing symptoms of anxiety and depression.

Perhaps in an effort to avoid negative emotionality, Ms. Frazier has a tendency to avoid emotionally laden situations and topics. When she does experience emotion, her emotional displays tend to be less controlled. This combination of her avoidance of emotion and her tendency to have strong emotional displays could result in her becoming isolated, as emotions and emotional interactions tend to be an important aspect in interpersonal interactions. Consistent with this, Ms. Frazier has not reached out for support from friends or family at this time.

In conclusion, there is no evidence from testing to suggest that Ms. Frazier's reported difficulty in classes is due to the presence of psychopathology. Instead, testing indicates that Ms. Frazier's reported difficulty in classes is most likely secondary to her balancing working full time with graduate school and her being accustomed to a higher level of academic achievement. Another influencing factor could be that there is evidence to suggest Ms. Frazier is questioning her own sense of self-worth due to her receiving lower than expected, yet still passing, grades on assignments and in class. Ms. Frazier is accustomed to a high level of achievement and positive feedback about her achievement from the environment (e.g., feedback from her boss, high grades), and now that the feedback is less positive, there are indications that she is starting to question her self-worth.

The following recommendations may help Ms. Frazier at this time:

1. **Counseling.** Ms. Frazier may benefit from counseling that focuses on the following areas:
   a. **Emotions.** Ms. Frazier has a tendency to avoid emotions yet is experiencing some negative emotionality. She could benefit from counseling to help her work through the negative emotions she

is experiencing. Another, related, focus could be working with Ms. Frazier to help her develop coping strategies to compensate for her tendency to display her emotions strongly.

b. **Self-acceptance.** Another focus of counseling could be to help Ms. Frazier work through rectifying her high view of herself with the negative feedback she has been receiving from the environment (e.g., average grades).

c. **Providing support.** Counseling could also serve to provide Ms. Frazier with some additional support as she works to balance her work and school requirements.

d. **Monitor for depression and anxiety.** Her therapist should also monitor Ms. Frazier for signs of depression and anxiety, as testing suggested that Ms. Frazier is prone to both.

2. **Self-care.** Ms. Frazier is working to balance working full time with attending school full time. This can be stressful. In order to reduce her stress level, Ms. Frazier could benefit from ensuring that self-care is an important aspect of her daily routine. This can take many forms, such as exercise and relaxation strategies.

3. **Organization/time management.** Ms. Frazier is attempting to balance working full time with graduate school and household duties. She could benefit from learning and using additional organizational and time management strategies, such as the use of checklists and breaking down larger tasks into smaller, more manageable ones.

🐟 TEST YOURSELF 🐟

1. **What does Ms. Frazier's S-CON score of 6 suggest?**
   a. She is at increased risk of attempting suicide in the next two months.
   b. She is not at increased risk of a lethal suicide attempt in the near future.
   c. She will never commit suicide.
   d. She is considering suicide about 60 percent of the time.

2. **Given the background information, which of the following interpretations of Ms. Frazier's An + Xy score of 2 is most accurate?**
   a. She has an eating disorder.
   b. She should be a doctor.
   c. She believes she is overweight.
   d. None of the above.

3. **Ms. Frazier had one color-shading blend on her protocol. What are color-shading blends thought to be associated with?**
   a. Positive emotionality
   b. Negative emotionality
   c. Confusion about feelings
   d. Trauma

4. **Which variables on the structural summary were used to determine Ms. Frazier's coping style?**
   a. EB, L
   b. EA, es
   c. a:p, SumC'
   d. XA%, X–%

5. **True or False: The presence of one DV on Ms. Frazier's protocol indicates that she has severe difficulties with thinking clearly.**
   a. True
   b. False

Answers: 1. b; 2. d; 3. c; 4. a; 5. b.

Six

R-PAS ADMINISTRATION

This chapter focuses on the accurate administration of the Rorschach Performance Assessment System (R-PAS) (Meyer et al., 2011). The discussion of the administration of the Comprehensive System in Chapter 2 covered basic information for test administration, including the importance of accurate administration and the determination of whether the Rorschach is an appropriate test to use, given the referral question. Readers may wish to use Chapter 2 to review that information.

Four principles underlie R-PAS administration (Meyer et al., 2011). The first is that the administration follows standard procedures. This is important, because interpretation of standardized instruments assumes that the administration has been completed according to the standard procedures. The second principle is that the administration is nondirective. This is especially important, as being too directive during an administration can significantly influence the administration, causing it to reflect the examiner's strong guidance during the administration rather the examinee's actual performance.

The third and four principles are that the purpose of the administration is to accurately record the examinee's performance (verbalizations and gestures) and that there should be a focus on the "problem solving" and "visual-perceptual aspects of the task" (Meyer et al., 2011, p. 5). Recording the examinee's performance accurately is vital, as accurate coding and, eventually, interpretation assume that the administration accurately recorded the examinee's verbalizations and relevant behaviors. If these have not been accurately recorded, they cannot be accurately coded. Finally, the focus on the "problem solving" and "visual-perceptual aspects of the task" helps to guide the Clarification Phase, focusing it on the most important aspects of the task.

PREPARING TO ADMINISTER R-PAS

There are only a few required materials for R-PAS administration. The examiner needs a copy of the Rorschach blots, a few location sheets, pens, and something to record the examinee's responses on, such as a computer or paper. Location sheets can be purchased from a variety of testing companies and via the R-PAS online store. The blots should not have any marks on them. For those who are handwriting the examinee's responses, a form for this purpose is available in the Book Companion Website Materials. For those who prefer to use a computer to record the examinee's responses, electronic forms can be downloaded, free of charge for those with an account, from the R-PAS website (www.r-pas.org, under "Handy downloads"). If examiners choose to use a computer or tablet to record responses, I strongly advise them to have the AutoSave function activated on their word processor; to shut off the laptop or tablet speaker and any sounds associated with messaging functions and the like, to minimize the chance of a technology-based interruption; and to have paper at hand to use in case the technology fails. I also recommend that the AutoCorrect function on the word processor be turned off, as it may alter what the examinee has said. For example, I once had an examinee refer to Card IV as the "Abdominal Snowman" (because he had "washboard abs") and AutoCorrect changed it to "Abominable Snowman." This was a significant change to the response and had I not noticed it, would have likely resulted in a change to the coding. Finally, examiners should make sure that their laptop or tablet is fully charged before the administration.

Those examiners who are recording the examinee's verbalizations and behaviors using pen and paper should be sure to have multiple copies of the recording form they plan to use or a lot of paper with them to record a complete record. The maximum number of R-PAS responses is forty (four per card), so twenty sheets of paper should be sufficient. The record for each card should start on a new page; there should never be responses from two different cards on the same page. This is done to keep the responses properly organized. Additionally, I recommend having no more than two responses per page and having the form organized in such a way that the records for the two phases of administration (Response Phase and Clarification Phase) are aligned for each response. The easiest way to do this is to divide the form into five columns, with the two widest columns used to report responses and clarifications (see Figure 6.1 for an example).

It is also important that the examiner number everything correctly. Cards have Roman numerals (e.g., I, II, III) whereas the responses have Arabic numerals

Card	Resp#	Response	Clarification	Pr/Pu

Figure 6.1 Example of a Protocol to Use for an R-PAS Administration

(e.g., 1, 2, 3). Responses are numbered consecutively across the cards. This allows the examiner to easily determine whether the examinee has provided enough responses for the administration to be valid (sixteen responses).

DON'T FORGET

You need 16 responses for a valid R-PAS administration.

As R-PAS measures both personality states and traits, it needs to be administered in one sitting. A typical R-PAS administration takes about an hour, but this will vary depending on the skill of the examiner and the characteristics of the examinee. In order to ensure enough time to complete the administration, I recommend scheduling ninety minutes for the administration. The room being used for the testing session should be quiet and free from distractions. The room should have a table for the examiner to keep the cards on. Some examiners prefer to have a table in front of them, while others prefer to have the table to the side; either way, it is important that the cards be kept out of the reach of the examinee and face down. The room should also have two chairs that can be moved so the examiner and the examinee can sit next to each other. This setup allows the examiner to easily see where the examinee is pointing on the blots and also makes it difficult for the examinee to see the examiner's nonverbal reactions to the examinee's responses. This is important—if the examinee sees the examiner respond negatively to a response, such as by raising an eyebrow, rolling his or her eyes, or seeming surprised, it can cause the examinee to censor the subsequent responses so as to not elicit anymore negative reactions from the examiner (Magnussen, 1960; Masling, 1965). Some examiners prefer to sit slightly behind the examinee, as it facilitates being able to see where on the blot the examinee is pointing. See Figure 6.2 for possible room setups.

R-PAS administration requires that the examiner record all of the examinee's responses verbatim, as well as all of the examinee's relevant behaviors, such as pointing to or touching the card. This is done to facilitate coding (scoring). The examiner should also record his or her own verbalizations. This will allow the examiner to determine whether anything the examiner said may have induced a pattern of responding by the examinee.

Because of the requirement that everything the examinee says must be recorded verbatim, in my experience, many individuals choose to type the record during R-PAS administration, as many of us type faster (and more neatly) than we write. For those who choose to write, there are abbreviations that can be used; these can be found in Rapid Reference 6.1. Those who type can also use these abbreviations; however, many find that it is faster to simply type the whole word rather than to use the abbreviations.

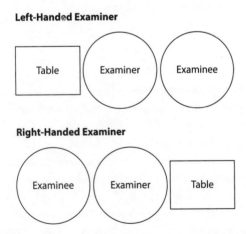

Figure 6.2 Examples of Ways to Set Up a Room for an R-PAS Administration

≡ Rapid Reference 6.1

Abbreviations That Can be Used During R-PAS Administration

Term	Abbreviation
Be	b
See	c
Are	r
You	u
Your	ur
About	abt, @
Around	ard
Anything	at
Because	Bec; b/c
Don't know	DK
Everything	et
Whole	W
Looks like	ll
Maybe	mb
Some sort	ss
-ing	-g
Human	H
Animal	A
Blood	Bl
Clothing	Cg
Cloud	Cl
What Makes it Look Like	WMILL
To	2
In my opinion	IMO
On the other hand	OTOH
Extraterrestrial	ET
Help me see it	HMSI
Reminds me of	RMO
People	ppl
Examiner repeats response	ERR

Source: Based on information from Exner, 2001; 2003; Meyer et al., 2011.

It is permissible for an examiner to slow down an examinee in order to ensure accurate transcription. Meyer and colleagues (2011, p.25) suggest that an examiner say something like "I am writing down everything you say, go a little slower please," or "I am having trouble keeping up with you; can you slow down some? Thanks." However, continuously slowing down an examinee could affect rapport as well as significantly slow down the pace of testing, so examiners should do their best to keep up with the examinee if possible.

I also advise against making an audio or video recording of the administration for many reasons. First, there is the possibility that examinees may react differently knowing that they are being recorded, so it is possible that examinees' recorded responses will be different from what the unrecorded responses would have been. (Constantinou et al., 2005). It is unethical, and in some states illegal, to record individuals without their permission, so examinees would have to be informed that they are being recorded. There may also be a tendency for examiners to over-rely on the recording, and consequently, these examiners may not pay sufficient attention to the administration and may miss necessary queries or gestures. There is also the issue that technology can fail, and may not be available to fill in any information that an examiner missed.

WHAT IS NEEDED FOR A VALID ADMINISTRATION

In order for an administration to be valid, an examinee must provide at least sixteen responses, with at least one response to each card. However, because of the administration procedures, most R-PAS protocols will have between twenty and thirty responses, with two to three responses per card. The maximum number of responses for an R-PAS protocol is forty, as a maximum of four responses are allowed per card. The administration procedures are described in more detail in the next section.

ADMINISTERING R-PAS

R-Optimized Administration

R-PAS uses a method of administration referred to as *R-Optimized*. As its name suggests, the purpose of R-Optimized administration is to optimize the number of responses in a protocol. Research has shown that there are problems with short protocols yielding too little information and there may be issues with long protocols providing too much information (e.g., Dean, Viglione, Perry, & Meyer, 2007; Sultan & Meyer, 2009). The latter could possibly lead to an overpathologizing of the examinee, if the length of the protocol is not taken into account.

The R-Optimized administration was designed, based on the results of empirical studies, to produce protocols with a sufficient number of responses to provide usable data regarding the examinee's performance, but not to provide so much information that the protocol becomes overwhelming or unwieldy. Studies using earlier versions of the R-Optimized system with the CS have been promising, indicating that there rarely, if ever, is a need to readminister the CS due to having too few responses when this system is used (Dean et al., 2007; Reese, Viglione, & Giromini, 2014; Viglione et al., 2015).

R-PAS administration differs from traditional CS administration in a number of ways. First, unlike traditional CS administration, R-PAS administration allows the examiner to prompt for additional responses on each card. Second, R-PAS administration allows the examiner to stop the examinee from providing additional responses on each card, rather than only under certain circumstances, as in the CS. Finally, the instructions for R-PAS administration are longer and more specific than the instructions for the CS, as previous research has shown that longer instructions are associated with a decrease in the number of invalid protocols due to having too few responses (Hartmann, 2001; Hartmann & Vanem, 2003). The combination of these three empirically supported interventions should result in fewer too short and too long protocols.

Prior to administering R-PAS, the examiner should ensure that the examinee is properly prepared for testing. This includes obtaining informed consent—and assent if the examinee cannot legally provide consent or does not have to provide consent—and developing a working rapport. The examiner should also have all required materials readily available and the room should be set up appropriately.

R-PAS administration has two parts: the Response Phase and the Clarification Phase (Meyer et al., 2011). For individuals familiar with the CS, these phases are conceptually similar to the Response Phase and the Inquiry Phase, respectively, but there are some differences. Generally, the complete administration takes no more than sixty minutes, with the Response Phase taking less time than the Clarification Phase. During the Response Phase, the examinees' job is to tell the examiner *what* the blots look like to them. In the Clarification Phase, the examinees' job is to explain *why* the blots look like that to them and *where* in the blots they saw what they saw. The ultimate goal of the Clarification Phase is to code the protocol accurately.

Response Phase

For this part of the administration, the examiner will need something to record the examinee's responses with (paper or a computer or tablet with word-processing capabilities) and the Rorschach inkblots. The location sheets that will be used later should be placed out of the examinee's view. For examiners who choose to use a laptop, the location sheets can be placed under the laptop. For those who are using paper, the location sheets can be placed under the paper that the examiner is writing on.

Prior to starting the test, the examiner should introduce the procedures. This sets the stage for the administration so the examinee knows what to expect. To start, Meyer and colleagues (2011, p. 8) recommend saying, "We're ready for the Rorschach (or inkblot) test now, have you heard of it, seen it, or taken it?" If the examinee says no, the examiner should then explain the parameters of the task by saying, "It's a series of inkblot designs that I'll show you and I want you to tell me what they look like to you" (Meyer et al., 2011, p. 9). However, if the examinee indicates having some knowledge of the Rorschach, it is important to explore the examinee's knowledge of the Rorschach and if he or she took it. If the examinee has taken the test before, it is important to ask when the examinee took it and why he or she took it. After this, the examiner should say, "As you know then, it is a series of inkblot designs that I will show you. All I want you to do is to tell me what they look like to you" (Meyer et al., 2011, p. 9).

After this initial introduction, the examiner provides the specific instructions for the task by saying, "OK, now we are ready to start. I will hand the inkblots to you one at a time. Your task is to look at each card to answer the question What might this be? Does that make sense?" (Meyer et al., 2011, p. 8). If the examinee does not have any questions, the examiner follows up this statement by saying, "Good, we can get started then. Try to give two responses or maybe three to each card. That is, for each card try to see two different things, possibly three. What might this be?" (Meyer et al., 2011, p. 8). When making this statement, the examiner should focus on the word "two" rather than "three," in order to encourage the examinee to provide about twenty responses altogether, or two per card. This number of responses should provide sufficient information to interpret, without providing an overwhelming amount of information.

Prior to asking, "What might this be?" the examiner should hand the examinee the first card upright. The examiner should record the examinee's responses verbatim. The examinee is allowed to rotate the card; if this occurs, the examiner should note this on the record form, including how the examinee rotated the card. For example, if the examinee turned the card upside down, then upright, then upside down again, the examiner should note, "v ^ v" to show the card turning. This differs somewhat from the CS, where the examiner typically notes only the final position of the card. As in the CS, the examiner should record the final position of the card when the response is provided. Rapid Reference 6.2 displays the symbols that can be used to indicate card rotation. The examiner should also

≡ *Rapid Reference 6.2*

Symbols Used to Denote Card Turning

Symbol	Description
@	Card was turned at least 90 degrees, but examinee provided the response with the card in the upright position.
v	Card was turned 180 degrees.
>	Card was turned so that the right side was up.
<	Card was turned so that the left side was up.
^	Card was turned so that it was upright.

Source: Meyer et al., 2011.

note if the examinee takes time to provide the response, by estimating and noting the amount of time (e.g., "~45 seconds").

Troubleshooting the Response Phase

During the Response Phase, the examiner can prompt if the examinee provides only one response on a card. One prompt can be used on each card; this differs from the CS, where prompts can only be used in certain circumstances. The use of the prompts helps to improve the chance that the protocol will be valid and will contain around twenty responses. An example of a prompt is, "We would like two, or maybe three, responses to each card, so please try to give another" (Meyer et al., 2011, p. 13).

The examiner can also prevent the examinee from providing too many responses by "pulling" the card. In truth, the examiner does not actually pull the card away from the examinee, but rather provides an intervention requesting that the examinee return the card to the examiner. A pull occurs once the examinee provides four responses to the same card. At this point, the examiner could say something like, "Okay, that's good. Remember, try to give two responses to each card, maybe three" (Meyer et al., 2011, p. 14). The examiner is permitted to offer this instruction on each card. Again, this differs from the CS, where the examiner can pull the card only under very specific circumstances.

The examiner should note each prompt or a pull on the record form. If examiners are recording their own verbalizations, then there will be a record of each prompt and pull. If they are not recording their verbalizations, which is ill-advised, then they should note on the response form when they have to prompt ("Pr") or pull ("Pu") (see Figure 6.1 earlier in this chapter). Still, because of the explicit instructions at the start of the administration that specifically request the examinee to provide two or three responses to each card, prompts and pulls should not be very common.

The examiner also needs to intervene if the examinee attempts to reject a card. In order to have a valid administration, the examinee needs to provide at least one response to every card. If the examinee rejects a card and does not provide any response to that card, the administration is not valid. If the examinee attempts to reject one of the first few cards, the examiner should stop testing, review the purpose of testing, and ensure that there is a good working rapport. Once these issues are corrected, testing should restart. If the examinee attempts to reject a later card, generally Card IX, the examiner should not accept the card and should encourage the examinee to provide a response. Generally, after receiving this encouragement, examinees will provide a response.

The final time an examiner may need to intervene during the Response Phase is if the examinee finishes the phase but provides fewer than sixteen responses. Given the specific instructions provided by the examiner at the start of the Response Phase (e.g., asking for two to three responses per card), this should be rare. However, it can happen, especially in the case of an extremely resistant examinee. When the examinee provides fewer than sixteen responses, the examiner should then go through the cards one more time, to elicit additional responses in order to get a valid protocol. This is not a retest, as it would be with the CS. Instead, the new responses are added in with the old responses to make a complete protocol.

DON'T FORGET

If the examinee provides fewer than 16 responses during the Response Phase, go through the cards again with him or her to elicit more responses.

To introduce this second step, the examiner should say, "That was fine. However, we need a few more responses for the test to be helpful. So let's go through the cards again. Take your time when looking at them and see what other things you can come up with. What else might this be?" (Meyer et al., 2011, p. 15). The examiner hands the examinee each of the cards again, omitting any cards where the examinee has already provided four responses.

This second step proceeds a bit differently from the traditional R-PAS Response Phase. No prompts are provided; the examiner should not ask for an additional response on a card, even if the examinee does not provide any additional responses. The examiner can still pull any card once the examinee has provided a total of four responses to it. Remember, the total number of responses includes the responses generated in the Response Phase and in this second step, so if the examinee provided two responses in the first Response Phase and two more responses in the second step, the examiner should then pull the card. All the responses generated will then be queried in the next phase, the Clarification Phase.

Clarification Phase

Like the Inquiry Phase in the CS, the Clarification Phase is arguably the more important of the two phases of R-PAS. The goal of the Clarification Phase is to obtain the necessary information to properly code the *what* (content), the *where* (location), and the *why* (determinants). Remember, for each response the examiner needs to know *what* examinees saw, *where* they saw it, and *why* it looked like that to them. If there is missing information, it will affect coding and, therefore, interpretation (Lis et al., 2007).

DON'T FORGET

The main purpose of the Clarification Phase is to ensure that the examiner has the information needed to code for content (*what* the examinee saw), location (*where* the examinee saw it), and determinants (*why* it looked like that to the examinee).

In order to conduct a useful inquiry, the examiner needs to have an excellent understanding of coding. R-PAS coding is discussed in the next chapter. Briefly, during coding the examiner will be scoring the contents (*what* the examinee saw), the location (*where* the examinee saw it), and determinants (*why* it looked like that to the examinee). Generally, the examinee provides most, if not all, of the information necessary to code the contents (the *what*) during the Response Phase. Consequently, much of the Clarification Phase is focused on obtaining the information necessary to code the location (the *where*) and the determinants (the *why*). This is also the time when the examiner will resolve any coding ambiguities, such as whether an examinee provided one response or two on a card (Meyer et al., 2011). This is not a time for new responses; only the responses that the examinee provided during the Response Phase should be clarified.

Administration of the Clarification Phase

The Clarification Phase begins immediately after the completion of the Response Phase. Examiners will need the same materials for the Clarification Phase as they did for the Response Phase, with the addition of the location sheets so that they can identify the location of the responses. The first step of the Clarification Phase is to introduce it. The standard introduction of the Clarification Phase is this:

> Now we are going to start the final step. While looking at the cards I want to review your responses with you to clarify what it is that you saw and how you saw it. So we will look at the cards one by one. I will read your responses back to you and I want to know where on the card you were looking and what about the inkblot made it look like that to you. Does that make sense? [Meyer et al., 2011, p. 16].

After providing this introduction, the examiner should then answer any questions that the examinee has. Once the examinee has no further questions, the examiner should then hand the examinee the first card and read the examinee's first response verbatim. The examiner should ask questions, as necessary, to help to resolve any questions about coding he or she has. It is important that examiners' questions address only coding ambiguities; prior to asking a question, examiners should ask themselves, "Will this question help me code contents, determinants, or location, or clarify if this is one response or two?" If the answer is no, then the examiner should not ask the question.

DON'T FORGET
. . . .

Prior to asking a question in the Clarification Phase, ask yourself, "Will this question help me code contents, determinants, or location, or clarify whether this is one response or two?" If the answer is no, do not ask the question!

Once the examiner has the information necessary to code the *what* (contents), the *where* (location), and the *why* (determinants), then the examiner should move onto the next response, unless there is an indication that there may be another code associated with the current response due to the presence of key words. Key words are words or phrases that suggest the presence of another code, usually a determinant. These are words like "pretty" (color) and "behind" (dimensionality). A list of some key words can be found in Rapid Reference 6.3.

≡ Rapid Reference 6.3

Examples of Key Words

Determinant	Key Words
Color	Pretty, bright, happy, party, blood, sad, dreary, paint
Achromatic color	Night, evil, dark, tuxedo, dreary, depressing, snow, bright, lighter, darker
Dimensionality	Hole, deeper, behind, looking up, mountain, valley, carved, bumpy
Texture	Soft, fluffy, hairy, hot, cold, smooth, rough, bumpy
Shading	Smoky, darker, lighter

Source: Based on information from Exner, 2001, 2003; Meyer et al., 2011.

Querying on R-PAS tends to be very direct. Often, it is sufficient to simply repeat the key word that could indicate the presence of another code, such as, "Pretty?" Other ways to phrase the question are to say, "You said it was pretty?" and "What makes it look pretty?" Here is an example of a response clarification:

Response (Card I): It is the devil. He looks evil.
Examiner repeats examinee's response.
Clarification-1: It is the whole thing. Here are his horns, legs, wings. He has his wings spread out (demonstrates with hands), maybe a show of force, so people know he means business.
You said he looks evil?
Clarification-2: He's black.

In this case, the examinee provided the content in the Response Phase ("the devil") and provided the location in the first part of the Clarification Phase ("it is the whole thing"). The examinee also provided some information regarding possible determinants in the first part of the Clarification Phase ("He has his wings spread out," indicating movement); however, there was a key word present in the initial response that was not addressed: "evil." The examiner correctly clarified this by asking about it in the Clarification Phase. This led to the examinee's stating that the devil looked "evil" because the blot was black, indicative of another determinant (achromatic color). Had the examiner not questioned this, the information would not have been coded and, therefore, not interpreted.

However, the presence of a key word does not always mean that the determinant is present. The following example has the same response as above, but with a different result in the Clarification Phase:

Response (Card I): It is the devil. He looks evil.
Examiner repeats examinee's response.
Clarification-1: It is the whole thing. Here are his horns, legs, wings. He has his wings spread out (demonstrates with hands), maybe a show of force, so people know he means business.
You said he looks evil?
Clarification-2: Yeah, the horns make him look evil (points).

In this case, the examiner correctly identified that the word "evil" could indicate the presence of another determinant and correctly asked the examinee about it. However, the examinee did not provide any information indicating another determinant. Instead the devil was evil because of the horns, not because of the presence of achromatic color or shading.

Key words have to be queried only when the examinee does not spontaneously explain them. If the examinee explains the key word during the Response or Clarification Phase, there is no reason to question the examinee further. For example:

Response (Card II): It looks like two bears fighting. This red is blood.
Examiner repeats examinee's response.
Clarification-1: Yeah, here is one bear, here is the other (points to D1, both sides). Blood here (points to D3).

At this point, there is no need to clarify further. The examinee provided *what* he or she saw (contents) in the Response Phase ("bears" and "blood") and *why* it looked like that to him or her (determinants: "fighting"—movement; "red is blood"—color). In the Clarification Phase, the examinee provided where he or she saw it (location) by pointing. There is no indication that the examinee perceived any objects or any additional reasons why the blot looked like two bears fighting to him or her, thus, there is no need to ask any additional questions.

This example is also a good model of the *color convergence principle*. The color convergence principle applies when the characteristics of the blot and the examinee's verbalizations or gestures about the blot converge in such a way to strongly indicate the presence of a determinant, even without the examinee directly stating that the determinant is present. In the previous example, the examinee never verbalized that the D3 area was blood because it was red, rather, the examinee stated that the red was blood. Given the qualities of that part of the blot (it is red) and that the examinee verbalized that part of the blot was something that is typically red (blood), it is reasonable to assume that the examinee perceived that spot to be blood due to the color, indicating the presence of a determinant.

The color convergence principle can be used whenever the examinee verbalizes the color and an object that is prototypically that color. Examples would be grass in a green-colored part of the blot, teeth in a white part of the blot, and water in a blue part of the blot. The rules for using the color convergence principle are that the examinee verbalizes the color in some way and that the object seen in the color is typically that color (e.g., blood is red, grass is green, night is black). If the object the examinee sees can be that color but is typically other colors as well, the color convergence principle does not apply. For example, if an examinee pointed to the D1 area of Card X, which is blue, and said "This blue is a crab," that is not sufficient to code color, because although crabs can be blue, they can be other colors as well. At this point, it is unclear that blue is being used as a determinant or a location; further clarification may be necessary. However, if the examinee had said "This is a blue crab" the use of color would be unequivocal, and no further clarification would be necessary.

DON'T FORGET

In order for the color convergence principle to apply, examinees must verbalize the color, and the object they report seeing in that area must be prototypically that color.

There are times when clarification is unnecessary and inappropriate. First and foremost, if the question being asked does not help the examiner code content, location, or determinants, then it is likely unnecessary. Second, clarification is not necessary when the examinees have already verbalized or gestured to indicate why it looked like that to them, such as by rubbing a card when saying a texture word, indicating the presence of a texture. Finally, the examiner should never ask a leading question, such as "Did you use color?" or "Is it moving?" as this may introduce a determinant that the examinee did not originally perceive. In general, any question that can be answered with a yes or a no is an inappropriate question to use during the Clarification Phase.

It is also possible for the examiner to over-clarify. This usually happens with novice examiners who are striving to ensure that they get all of the determinants and get the location "exactly" right. In general, the examiner should question only key words that are present in the Response Phase and the first part of the Clarification Phase. Additionally, it is important to remember that the purpose of the Clarification Phase is to code accurately, not to see the response the same way the examinee saw it. There will be times when the examiner will be absolutely unable to see the response the same way the examinee saw it—or at all. This is fine, as long as the examiner has the information necessary to correctly code the response. The following is an example of a response that the examiner has enough information to code, but still cannot "see" the way the examinee saw it.

Response (Card V): It's a soldier in a bunker.

Examiner repeats examinee's response.

Clarification-1: It's like in the Gulf. There is no water there. Dehydration runs rampant.

You said the solider was in a bunker?

Clarification-2: All soldiers are in bunkers.

Show me the soldier in the bunker.

Clarification-3: All is the bunker, hiding the soldier (waves hand over entire card). Soldier's head here (points to Dd99). Bunker is covering the rest, hiding him from the truth.

In this case, the examinee provided the content (the *what*) in the Response Phase ("a soldier in a bunker"). However, the examiner had to ask a few questions in order to get the location and the determinants. The examinee did not provide the location (the *where*) until Clarification-3 ("all" with the gesture indicates the examinee was using the whole card). The examinee also confirmed the determinant (the *why*) in Clarification-3 ("bunker is covering the rest").

Recording Location and Location Clarification

Usually, the examinee will provide the location by pointing to it during the Clarification Phase. This is one of the reasons why it is so important for the examiner to attend to examinee's gestures as well as verbalizations. However, there are times where the examinee does not indicate location during either the Response Phase or the Clarification Phase. In order to get this information (the *where*), the examiner then needs to query. The examiner could say something like "Where do you see that?" or "Show me the (insert response here)." The examiner should avoid asking the examinee to trace the location with a finger, as this introduces too much focus on form and boundaries; the Rorschach (R-PAS and CS) was not intended to have this level of location precision (Exner, 2003; Meyer et al., 2011).

For each response, the examiner needs to record on the location sheet the location the examinee used. This is done by circling the area of the blot used, identifying the number of the response the location is associated with, and identifying a few parts of the response to aid with coding. If the examinee is using the whole blot (coded as W) in a response, rather than circling the whole blot, the examiner simply needs to write that this response equals W (e.g., for Response 3, the coding would be 3 = W). I recommend recording no more than two or three responses per blot, because the blots on the location sheets are small and can get crowded with information; this makes it difficult to determine which areas are associated with which response. An example of recorded locations on a simulated blot can be seen in Figure 6.3.

NOTE

In Figure 6.3, neither Response 1 nor Response 2 uses the entire blot. For each response, a few aspects of the response are labeled to aid with coding (e.g., for Response 1, "head" and "wing" are labeled).

Troubleshooting the Clarification Phase

Usually, the problems that arise in the Clarification Phase are due to the examiner having difficulty knowing which questions to ask and when. However, there are times when the Clarification Phase becomes difficult because the examinee is being resistant. If the examinee is having difficulty understanding the directions and is not providing the *what*, *where*, and *why*, then the examiner should reexplain

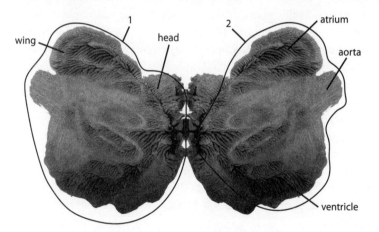

Figure 6.3 Example of Locations Recorded on a Simulated Blot
Note: Blot created by Zachary Hasson

the purpose of the Clarification Phase as necessary. Sometimes, examinees state that they can no longer see a response they provided in the Response Phase. If this happens, the examiner should encourage the examinee to take a look and, usually, the examinee is able to see the response again and explain it. In the case where examinees are unable to locate what they saw in the Response Phase, the examiner should code based on the information provided in the Response Phase. If there is not enough information to code location (*where*), then Dd99 should be entered as the location code. If there is not enough information to code the determinants (*why*), then a code of F should be used. R-PAS coding is described in more detail in the next chapter.

There are other times when examinees may state that they did not provide an answer. If this occurs, the examiner should be tactful, yet firm. If examinees continue to insist that they did not provide that response, the response should be coded based on the information provided in the Response Phase, if possible. If location cannot be coded based on the information provided, it should be coded as Dd99. If the determinants cannot be coded based on the information provided, then a code of F should be entered.

ACCOMMODATING DISABILITIES AND USING INTERPRETERS

Although examiners strive to follow standard procedure whenever possible, there are times when standard procedure needs to be altered to accommodate the examinee. Any alterations to standard procedure should be documented in progress notes and in the report produced based on the test results. The examiner also needs to keep in mind that interpretations that result from administrations based on altered procedures may not be accurate, as they are not based on standard procedures. This is true for any standardized test.

Like any other psychological test administration, R-PAS administration can be altered in order to accommodate testing for individuals with disabilities. For example, if the person being tested has severe attentional or memory deficits, and thus after a delay may not remember where he or she saw the response, the examiner may want to conduct the clarification on the response right after the examinee provides the response. In other words, there would be a mini-clarification after each response, rather than going through the entire Response Phase, then the entire Clarification Phase. This tactic can also be used with young children.

Although it is not ideal, R-PAS can be used with an interpreter. It is preferable to administer R-PAS in the examinee's dominant language, with a practitioner who speaks that language. However, this is not always an option and an interpreter is used instead. If an interpreter is going to be used, the examiner should make sure that the interpreter is aware that everything needs to be translated as close to verbatim as possible. In most cases, the interpreter should be placed behind the examinee to reduce the chance that the interpreter's nonverbal reactions could influence testing. However, when a sign language interpreter is required, the interpreter needs to sit across from the examinee, so that the examinee can see the interpreter. If a sign language interpreter is not available, some research suggests that having the examinee write out the responses is a viable option (Schwartz et al., 1990).

CONCLUSION

R-PAS administration can seem daunting, especially for a beginning examiner. With practice, administration will become more automatic and fluid. Administration also improves when the examiner has a thorough understanding of scoring, known as *coding* in the Rorschach. Coding is discussed in the following chapter.

🖋 TEST YOURSELF 🖋

1. **How many responses are needed for a valid R-PAS administration?**
   a. 12
   b. 14
   c. 16
   d. 18

2. **What is the first phase of the R-PAS administration called?**
   a. Free Response Phase
   b. Response Phase
   c. Answer Phase
   d. Location Phase

3. **What is the second phase of the R-PAS administration called?**
   a. Clarification Phase
   b. Inquiry Phase
   c. Determinant Phase
   d. Response Phase

4. **Which of the following is an example of an inappropriate query?**
   a. You said it was beautiful?
   b. What makes it look like a tiger?
   c. Was it moving?
   d. Show me the dog.

5. **True or False: You can use a computer during the administration of R-PAS.**
   a. True
   b. False

6. **True or False: You can prompt for an additional response only three times during an R-PAS administration.**
   a. True
   b. False

7. **True or False: Examinees are allowed to provide only five responses per card.**
   a. True
   b. False

Answers: 1. c; 2. b; 3. a; 4. c; 5. a; 6. b; 7. b.

Seven

R-PAS CODING

S coring, in Rorschach circles, is known as coding. For those familiar with the CS, learning to code according to R-PAS should not be difficult, as many of the variables coded in the CS are also coded in R-PAS. However, CS users should be aware that there are some subtle differences between R-PAS and the CS in how some of the variables are coded; consequently, CS users should not automatically assume they can code according to R-PAS without reviewing the R-PAS manual and practicing. CS users are strongly advised to thoroughly review Chapters 3 ("Basic Coding") and 4 ("Advanced Coding") in the R-PAS manual (Meyer et al., 2011) and to practice using the example responses in Chapter 7 of the manual (Meyer et al., 2011) prior to coding according to R-PAS.

One of the goals of the development of R-PAS was to create a streamlined system and to remove redundant variables from the CS (Meyer et al., 2011). This is very evident in the coding, as many variables that were present in the CS are not present in R-PAS. There were also significant changes to some variables that simplify coding; these are discussed throughout this chapter. There are some new variables as well. The additions, deletions, and changes to the variables are discussed in the category where each changed variable occurs.

For those not familiar with the CS, learning to code according to R-PAS is like learning a new language. There are multiple categories to code, including contents and Special Scores; and each category has its own set of variables. There are over sixty variables that can be coded. This, combined with the need to use clinical judgment to code some variables, can make coding seem overwhelming, especially to someone new to the Rorschach. However, with review, practice, and training or consultation with someone who knows the system, it is very possible to code the system with a reasonable degree of accuracy.

In this chapter, there is a description of each of the coding categories on R-PAS, with their respective variables. There are also hints throughout each subsequent chapter to help examiners code as accurately as possible, along with resources to increase the likelihood of accurate coding. There are also examples throughout this chapter to demonstrate the different aspects of coding. See Rapid Reference 7.1 for an explanation of the R-PAS coding categories, roughly in the order they appear on the coding form. Table 7.1 lists all of the R-PAS coding categories along with the possible variables for each one. The categories are presented in the same order that they appear on the R-PAS code sequence sheet, which is where examiners record their codes. A completed R-PAS Coding Sequence can be found in Table 9.2 later in this book. Additionally, blank Coding Sequence sheets can be downloaded from the R-PAS website (www.r-pas.org, under "Handy Downloads").

≡ Rapid Reference 7.1

Name and Description of Coding Categories

Category	Description
Coded response behaviors	Final orientation of the card when the response was provided and whether the examiner needed to prompt for more responses or pull the card.
Location	Where the examinee saw the response.
Space	Whether the examinee used space in the response and how the examinee used that space (integrated it with the chromatic parts of the blot, or saw the white space as the primary focus of the response).
Content	What the examinee saw.
Object qualities and pairs	The quality of the processing present in the examinee's response, and whether the examinee saw a pair of objects.
Form quality	How accurately the examinee perceived the structure of the blot.
Populars	Whether the examinee's response was the same as what others frequently see.
Determinants	Why the blot looked like what the examinee reported seeing in it.
Special Scores	The presence or absence of any odd or bizarre language or perceptions.

Source: Based on information in Exner, 2003; Meyer et al., 2011.

Table 7.1 R-PAS Response Level Codes: Table 3.1 in the R-PAS Manual

What is the card angle?	Where is it seen?	Is white space used? How?		What is seen?	Are any objects meaning-fully related?	Are all objects in the percept vague?	Are there two identical objects?	How well does it fit the blot?	Do many people see it?	What makes it look like that?	Are there issues with thought processes?	What themes are present?	Were steps taken to manage R?
Card Orientation	Location*	Space Reversal	Space Integration	Content Class*	Synthesis	Vagueness	Pair	Form Quality*	Popular	Determinants*	Cognitive Codes	Thematic Codes	R-Optimized
@ <v >	W, D, Dd Loc#(s)	SR	SI	H An (H) Art Hd Ay (Hd) Bl A Cg (A) Ex Ad Fi (Ad) Sx NC	Sy	Vg	2	o, u, −, n	P	M FM m (a, p, a-p) FC, CF, C C' Y T V FD r F	DV1, DV2 DR1, DR2 INC1, INC2 FAB1, FAB2 PEC CON	ABS PER COP MAH AGM AGC MOR MAP GHR, PHR ODL	Pr, Pu

*Scored for every response.

More than one of Determinants, Content, Cognitive, or Thematic codes can be assigned to each response.

Entries on the same row within a column are mutually exclusive options; only one can be assigned to a response.

Source: Reproduced from the Rorschach Performance Assessment System®: Administration, Coding, Interpretation, and Technical Manual (©2011) with copyright by Rorschach Performance Assessment System, LLC. All rights reserved. Used by permission of Rorschach Performance Assessment System, LLC.

THINGS TO REMEMBER BEFORE CODING AN R-PAS PROTOCOL

There are a few things to remember before an examiner starts coding a protocol. First, it is important to remember that only the examinee's verbalizations and gestures can be coded. At no time should an examiner make any assumptions about what the examinee "meant" to say. The only exception to this rule occurs when the examiner applies the *determinant convergence principle* at the time when the characteristics of the blot and what the examinee says or gestures, when combined with prototypic imagery, strongly suggest the presence of a determinant, even if the examinee did not explicitly say he or she was using the determinant. For example, an examinee may say, "this red is blood" while pointing to a red-colored spot on the card. At this point, there is enough information to code a color determinant, even though the examinee did not explicitly say, "This is blood because it is red." Instead, the combination of the prototypic imagery of blood (red), with the characteristics of the blot area the examinee is using (colored red), combined with the examinee's verbalization that the spot is red, all strongly suggest that the examinee is using color as a determinant. Thus, a color determinant can be coded, using the determinant convergence principle.

CAUTION

Don't overuse the determinant convergence principle. It applies only when the object the examinee perceives in the blot has prototypical features (e.g., blood is red, water is blue, grass is green).

The second thing to remember about coding is that the examiner should code only what the examinee perceives on the card. For example, if on Card VI the examinee says, "It looks like a cat that has been run over by a car," only the cat is coded because the examinee did not perceive the car as being part of the blot.

The final thing to remember about coding is that it can be difficult. It is normal to feel confused at times, especially when first learning the Rorschach. Consult with others as needed on coding.

CODED RESPONSE BEHAVIORS

Three types of behavior are coded and scored on R-PAS; see Rapid Reference 7.2 for a summary of these behaviors. The first is card turning, which is coded in the Card Orientation column of the code sequence page. Only the final orientation of each card is input into the internet-based scoring platform; the one exception

═ Rapid Reference 7.2

Coded Response Behaviors

Variable	Possible Codes	Summary	Where Coded
Orientation of the card when the response was provided	<	Left side of card was facing up.	Card Orientation column
	>	Right side of card was facing up.	
	v	Bottom of card was facing up.	
	@	Card was turned, but was held upright when the response was provided.	
Prompt	Pr	Examiner had to prompt for a second response.	R-Optimized column
Pull	Pu	Examiner had to request the card back (after 4 responses to the same card).	

Source: Based on information from Meyer et al., 2011.

to this rule is when examinees turn the card but then return the card to the upright position before providing their response. In this case, an @ should be recorded, to show that the examinee rotated the card before providing a response with the card in the upright position. Not all responses will have a code in the Card Orientation column.

The second behavior that is coded and scored consists of the prompts (Pr). Remember that examiners should prompt for a second response when the examinee provides only one response to a card. In addition to recording the wording of their prompt on their verbatim transcript of the administration, examiners should record a Pr in the R-Optimized column of the code sequence page. Only one Pr can be recorded per response, as examiners are allowed to prompt only once per response. However, not all responses will have a Pr code, because not all cards will require a prompt for the examinee to provide two responses. In fact, given the nature of R-PAS's administration instructions, examiners should expect to see very few, if any, prompts on a protocol.

The final behavior that is coded and scored is providing a pull (Pu) during the Response Phase. This should occur only when the examinee has provided four responses to a card. In addition to recording the pull on their verbatim transcript of the administration, examiners should record a Pu in the R-Optimized column of the code sequence page. Only one Pu can be coded per response, but not all responses will have a Pu code. Again, given the nature of R-PAS's administration instructions, examiners should expect to see very few, if any, pulls on a protocol.

It is possible to have both a Pr and a Pu for the same response, although this should be exceedingly rare.

LOCATION CODES AND NUMBERS

The location is *where* the examinee saw what he or she saw in the card. Typically, the examinee provides this information during the Clarification Phase, but occasionally, an examinee may provide it during the Response Phase. Often the examinee communicates this information by pointing or gesturing. Each response will have one location code.

The location codes are used to identify whether the examinee used the whole blot (W), a common detail (D), or an uncommon detail (Dd) for the response. Each D and Dd area is signified by a number. The D areas are typically numbered 1 through 15, while the Dd areas are numbered 21 and above.

The location codes, with numbers, are located in the R-PAS manual (Meyer et al., 2011). These are very similar to the location codes supplied in resources for the CS, such as Exner (2001, 2003, 2005) and Viglione (2010); however, there are some minor differences. For example, according to the CS location areas, Area D6 on Card II does not contain any part of the D3 area; however, according to the R-PAS tables, area D6 on Card II can contain the D3 area (Exner, 2003; Meyer et al., 2011). Still, these differences are minute.

There is no need to memorize the numbers associated with the different locations. However, practitioners who use the Rorschach frequently will likely find that they start to memorize location numbers for commonly used areas.

W: Whole Blot

A W is coded whenever examinees use the whole blot for their response. The response does not have to use any of the white space to receive a code of W. However, the response does need to use the whole blot; if the examinee excludes any part of the blot, no matter how small, then the response is no longer a W. Instead, the response will be coded either D or Dd, depending on the areas being used.

Sometimes, examinees will verbalize that they are using the whole blot in their response, by saying something like "It's the whole thing." More frequently, examinees use gestures, including pointing, to indicate that they are using the entire blot. For example:

Response (Card X): It's an underwater scene.

Examiner repeats examinee's response.

Clarification-1: There's fish everywhere! Mermaids here (points to D9), crabs here (points to D1), here (D7), and here (D13), a little yellow fish here (points to D2). Eels here (points to D4). The rest is coral and seaweed and stuff (gestures over entire card). It reminds me of the irregular shapes seen in the ocean.

Coding: W (H),A,NC Sy 2 o P FC

In this example, the examinee never specifically mentions using the entire blot. However, the verbalizations and gestures (see above) indicate that the examinee is likely using the entire blot. In this case, it is appropriate to score this response as a W.

DON'T FORGET

Code W only if the examinee is using the entire blot. If the examinee excludes any of the blot, do not code W. Instead code a D or a Dd, depending on the area used.

D: Common Detail

If the response does not meet the criteria for a W location code, it will be either a D or a Dd. The D codes, or common details, are areas of a blot that were used in at least 5 percent of the responses in Exner's large sample of protocols. These areas tend to be large, but are not always so. Do *not* make an assumption that a large area is a D area; some large areas are Dd areas while others are D. It is important that examiners check the location areas in the R-PAS manual (Meyer et al., 2011) to determine whether an area is a D or a Dd area.

Dd: Uncommon Detail

Uncommon details, in contrast, are areas of a blot that were used in fewer than 5 percent of the responses in Exner's large sample of protocols. These areas, with their associated numbers, can be found in the R-PAS manual (Meyer et al., 2011). If a response does not meet the criteria for a W or a D code, it will be a Dd.

Multiple Objects in the Same Response

Usually, locations are fairly straightforward to code. However, there are times when coding location can become difficult. This occurs when multiple objects in the same response do not use the entire blot. At this point, the code will have to be either a D or a Dd. In order to determine whether to code D or Dd, the examiner must review the areas that each discrete object in the response occupies. If each object occupies a D area, then the location code should be D. If each object occupies a Dd area, then the location code should be Dd.

The difficulty arises when the examinee sees the separate objects occupying discrete space located in both D and Dd areas. The R-PAS manual provides a great deal of guidance to assist with this situation. According to the manual, if any of the objects are in a Dd area, and are not half of a symmetrical pair, then the response should be coded as Dd.

CODING ALL LOCATION NUMBERS

Unlike in the CS where only one location number is recorded, in R-PAS, all location numbers are recorded in the Location Numbers column of the code sequence sheet. Consider the following example:

Response (Card II): Ballerina in love.
Examiner repeats examinee's response.
Clarification-1: She's here (points to DS5), wearing a white tutu. She's happy and dancing and twirling around. This (points to D3) is the stage she is dancing on.
You said she was in love?
Clarification-2: The stage is red to symbolize her love.
Code: D 5,3 SR SI H,Cg,NC Sy u Ma,C',CF ABS GH

In this case, the examiner should code a D area, because both of the objects the examinee reported (ballerina and stage) were in D areas. Both numbers should be recorded as well.

SR AND SI: SPACE RESPONSES

Unlike on the CS, where space is coded only alongside a location code (e.g., WS, DS, DdS), space is also a stand-alone code on R-PAS. There are two types of space responses on R-PAS: Space Reversal (SR) and Space Integration (SI). Both of these were included under the S code on the CS, and on the CS there was no differentiation between the two.

The SR and SI codes are coded in different circumstances. SR is coded when the examinee views a white part of the blot as being a main object, such as seeing a "ballerina" in area DS5 on Card II. Conceptually, this represents a reversal of figure and ground. The figure, or the focus of the cards, is usually seen in the colored part of the blots. The ground, or the background of the blots, is usually seen as the white part of the blots. An SR occurs when the usual background (white space) becomes the focus, or the figure, of the response.

SI is coded when white space is integrated with the colored part of a blot. The white part of the blot and the chromatic part of the blot are then on the same plane. For example, an examinee who says Card I looks like "A face. The whole thing. These (points to DdS30) are the eyes" is integrating the white part of the blot (DdS30) with the colored part of the blot.

These two codes are not mutually exclusive; it is possible to have both types of space responses in a response. The previous example—the ballerina dancing on the red stage—is an example of this. In this response, the ballerina, a main focus, is in the white space. This represents an SR, or a reversal of the figure and the ground. At the same time, the white space/ballerina is integrated with the stage, which is colored. This is an SI. This response would be coded for both SR and SI.

Space Reversal and Space Integration have separate columns on the code sequence sheet. If SR is present, put an SR in the SR column. If SI is present, put an SI in the SI column.

CONTENT CODES

The content codes represent the *what* of the Clarification Phase: they describe what the examinee perceived on the blot. Each response will have at least one content code. Some responses will have multiple content codes. When this occurs, the different content codes should be separated with a comma.

Typically, the examinee will provide the information necessary to code content in the Response Phase; however, there are times where an examinee will add additional codes during the Clarification Phase.

There are seventeen content codes in total, many fewer than there are on the CS. The seventeen content codes can be divided into five categories: human content, animal content, intellectualized content, critical content, and other. Rapid Reference 7.3 lists all the content codes and their full names, provides a brief description of when each is coded, and gives an example. Rapid Reference 7.4 lists the content codes that are coded in the CS but are not coded in R-PAS.

≡ Rapid Reference 7.3

R-PAS Content Codes

Classification	Code	Name	When Coded	Example
Human	H	Whole Human	Whole real human figure	Man
	Hd	Human Detail	Partial real human figure	Child's face
	(H)	Fictional Whole Human	Whole fictional human figure	Captain America
	(Hd)	Fictional Human Detail	Partial fictional human figure	Clown's nose
Animal	A	Whole Animal	Whole real animal figure	Cat
	Ad	Animal Detail	Partial real animal figure	Dog's tail
	(A)	Fictional Whole Animal	Whole fictional animal figure	Hippogriff
	(Ad)	Fictional Partial Animal	Partial fictional animal figure	Jackalope's head
Intellectualized	Art	Art	Works of art and decorative objects, including jewelry	Statue
	Ay	Anthropology	Anything that is from a culture or historical context different from the examinee's current context (e.g., if the examinee is in the UK, anything related to the culture of the UK would not be coded Ay).	Shofar (for a non-Jewish examinee)
Critical	An	Anatomy	Anatomy, including when it is visualized using imaging techniques, such as X-ray or MRI	Pelvis
	Bl	Blood	Blood or red wounds	Blood
	Ex	Explosion	Any explosion	Fireworks
	Fi	Fire	Fire, embers, or smoke	Smoke

Classification	Code	Name	When Coded	Example
	Sx	Sex	Sex organs, sexual activity, sexually suggestive clothing	Thong underwear
Other	Cg	Clothing	Clothing, including accessories	Shirt
	NC	Not Classified Content	Anything else	Tree

Source: Based on information from Meyer et al., 2011. The reader is encouraged to review Chapter 4 in the R-PAS manual for more information on coding content.

Human and Animal Content Codes

There are four human content codes. These codes are used when examinees state that a blot looks like a human or a humanlike figure (e.g., a ghost). Two codes, H and (H), are used when examinees say they see a whole human figure, and two codes, Hd and (Hd), are used when examinees say they see a partial human figure. One difference between the codes is that the H and the Hd codes are used when examinees perceive a real human figure, such as a person, while the (H) and (Hd) codes are used when examinees perceive a fictional or mythological human figure, such as a ghost or an angel. The other difference between the codes is that the H and (H) codes are used when examinees say they see a whole human figure, whereas Hd is used when they say they see a partial human figure, such as a head, and (Hd) is used when they say they see a partial fictional human figure, such as

≡ *Rapid Reference 7.4*

Content Codes Used in the CS but Not Used in R-PAS

Ten content codes that are coded in the CS are not coded in R-PAS. These are Human Experience (Hx), Nature (Na), Botany (Bt), Landscape (Ls), X-ray (Xy), Clouds (Cl), Geography (Ge), Food (Fd), Science (Sc), and Idiographic (Id). Items that would have been coded Xy in the CS are typically coded An in R-PAS. Some items that could have been coded Fd on the CS (e.g., fried chicken wings) can be coded A or Ad on R-PAS. Otherwise, items that would have fit these codes on the CS are coded as Not Classified Content (NC) on R-PAS.

Source: Based on information from Exner, 2001, 2003; Meyer et al., 2011.

a ghost's legs. Real deceased individuals (e.g., George Washington) should be coded as H. Depending on the examinee's current context, these types of responses may also warrant a secondary coding of Ay.

There are also four animal content codes. These codes are used when examinees state that a blot looks like an animal or animallike figure, such as a horse, coded A, or frog's legs, coded Ad. Two codes, A and (A), are used when examinees verbalize that they see a whole animal figure. A is coded whenever examinees say they see a real whole animal, such as a mouse or a dog. (A) is coded whenever examinees say they see a fictional whole animal, such as a dragon. The other two codes, Ad and (Ad), are used when examinees verbalize that they see a partial animal figure. Ad should be coded whenever examinees say they saw a partial animal figure, such as a chicken's wing. (Ad) should be coded when examinees say they saw a partial fictional animal, such as the Loch Ness monster's head.

Distinguishing Between Human and Animal Content Codes

There are times when it is unclear whether the examinee perceived a human or an animal. For example, if an examinee says that he or she sees a leg, it is unclear whether this is a human leg or an animal leg. Sometimes, examinees provide information indicating whether they intended it to be either human or animal (e.g., "It's got a lot of fur on it" would indicate an animal leg). However, there are times when this level of elaboration is not present and it is not at all clear whether the examinee was perceiving a human or an animal. When this occurs, the general rule is to default to the human code, unless the examinee elaborates more animal features than human ones, such as in the following example:

Response (Card IV): It's a monster.
Examiner repeats examinee's response.
Clarification-1: Legs here, paws, head, tail. It looks furry (touches card).
Coding: W (A) o T

DON'T FORGET

If you are unclear whether the examinee saw a human or an animal, default to human unless the information the examinee provided strongly suggests more animallike features.

Intellectualized Content Codes

Two codes, Art and Ay, can be classified as intellectualized content codes, because they are used to calculate the Intellectualized Content Composite. These codes are used when examinees verbalize that they see a form of art or decoration in the blot, such as a statue or jewelry (coded Art); or when they see a real historical figure or cultural artifact that is not part of their current context (coded Anthropology, Ay). An example of a response that would warrant an Ay code is "Napoleon." Note that this response would also warrant a code of H.

In general, because the Art and Ay content codes are interpreted as part of the same composite score, they are generally not scored in the same response. However, there are exceptions to this rule, including when a different verbalization for each object supports coding both content codes. For example:

Response (Card X, ∨): The Sistine Chapel and Michelangelo.
Examiner repeats examinee's response.
Clarification-1: It's the whole thing. It is reminiscent of the artwork on the ceiling of the Sistine Chapel, specifically the Separation of Light from Darkness. The red is like the red robe God was wearing, this is God (points to D9), the white is the light because it is bright (points to DdS30). Here is Michelangelo, standing back, admiring his work (points to D5).
Coding: W SI H,(H),Art,Ay,Cg Sy – CF,C',Mp PH

In this example, the Sistine Chapel and the artwork are the same percept; it is the Sistine Chapel because it looks like the artwork on the ceiling of the Sistine Chapel. However, Michelangelo is a distinct percept; the Sistine Chapel and Michelangelo can be supported by different verbalizations. So both Ay (Michelangelo) and Art (artwork on the Sistine Chapel ceiling) should be coded.

Critical Content Codes

Five content codes can be classified as critical content codes because they are used in the calculation of the Critical Content %. These codes are An, Bl, Ex, Fi, and Sx.

The An (anatomy) code is used whenever the examinee reports seeing anatomy, such as internal organs and bones, in the card. This includes seeing these types of objects as products of imaging techniques, such as MRI scans and X-rays. It is important to remember that An should be coded whenever the object is typically inside the body (e.g., kidney, femur), while Hd should be coded whenever the object is typically outside of the body (e.g., skin, arm).

DON'T FORGET

....

The difference between An and Hd is that An is coded when the object is typically inside the body and Hd is coded when the object is typically outside the body.

The Bl (blood) code is used whenever examinees say they see blood on the card. It is also used whenever the examinees describe a wound as being red, because the wound is presumably red owing to blood. This is the only time Bl should be coded as content without the examinee specifically stating that he or she sees blood on the card.

Ex and Fi are coded whenever the examinee sees an explosion (Ex), or fire or smoke (Fi) on the card. As with other codes, the examinee does not need to say the specific word "explosion" for an Ex code. Other words for explosions, such as "nuclear blast," "fireworks," and "eruption," are sufficient for Ex to be coded. The same is true for the Fi code; the examinee does not need to use the word "fire" in order for it to be coded. Words like "blaze," "flame," and "smoke" are sufficient to code Fi, as all strongly indicate the presence of fire.

The final critical content code is sex (Sx). It is coded whenever examinees say they saw anything related to sex, including sexual or reproductive organs (e.g., penis, ovaries), sexual or sexually related activities (e.g., stripping), and sexually suggestive clothing, such as underwear (e.g., lingerie). Sx is often coded in conjunction with other codes, including the human codes and An.

Other Codes

There are two other content codes. The first, Clothing (Cg), is interpreted as part of the Vigilance Composite, along with the human and the animal content codes. Cg is coded whenever the examinee reports seeing clothing in the blots, such as shirts, dresses, and pants. Cg is also coded when the examinee reports seeing other objects that people often wear, such as shoes, hats, and glasses.

The final content code, Not Classified Content (NC), is coded when the content that the examinee sees in the blot does not fit any other category. This would include things like buildings, plant life, and land, to name just a few. NC is coded only once per response, even if there are multiple contents that would have met for NC in the response.

DON'T FORGET

Responses can have multiple content codes. Separate content codes with commas.

OBJECT QUALITIES

Object qualities are the quality of the cognitive organization of the responses. Conceptually, the concept of object qualities is similar to the concept of Developmental Quality (DQ) on the CS (see Rapid Reference 7.5). On R-PAS, two types of object qualities are coded: Synthesis (Sy) and Vagueness (Vg). Each type has its own column on the code sequence page (see Table 9.2, later, for a completed code sequence page). These codes are not mutually exclusive; a response can meet the criteria for only one, both, or none.

Vagueness (Vg) is coded when none of the objects in the response has form demand or an easily recognizable typical shape. An item has form demand if an outline of it would be easily recognizable, like a structural prototype. For example, "laptop" would have a form demand because there is a structural prototype for a laptop: when open, it is two rectangles that are perpendicular to one another with a screen, a keyboard, a touchpad, and so forth. A specific set of features is associated with all laptops. Having specific features, however, does not

≣ *Rapid Reference 7.5*

R-PAS Object Qualities Compared to CS Developmental Quality

Object qualities on R-PAS are conceptually similar to DQs on the CS. The following table shows the equivalent codes for the variables used in each system.

CS Code	Equivalent R-PAS Code(s)
v	Vg
v/+	Vg, Sy
o	No code
+	Sy

Source: Based on information from Exner, 2003; Meyer et al., 2011.

mean that an object always takes on the same exact shape. Laptops obviously differ from one another in a number of ways, including size, color, and brand, but all have the same basic set of features described here. Anything that has form demand will not be coded as having Vagueness. Thus, there will be no code in the Vg column for these types of responses.

Responses where none of the objects have any form demand, or a set of specific features, will be coded as having Vagueness (Vg). Examples of these types of responses include things like blood, lakes, and forest. Each of these objects has some defining characteristics; blood is usually red, lakes are usually seen as being blue, and a forest is usually green (depending on the season). However, none of these have a specific shape. No one will look at an outline of a forest and say, "That's definitely a forest" because forests have no set shape. However, someone can look at a drawn outline of a laptop, table, chair, or a person and easily recognize what the outline represents, because all of these items have form demand. Vg is coded only when none of the objects in the response have form demand.

An examinee can interject form demand into an object. For example, "a lake" typically does not have form demand; it can take on many shapes. However, "Lake Michigan" has form demand; Lake Michigan has one set shape. Here is an example of an examinee interjecting form demand into a response:

Response (Card X): This one is hard . . . a coffee spill I guess because of the color.
Examiner repeats examinee's response.
Clarification-1: Yeah, it is a coffee spill. The color and it's shaped like a circle, so it reminded me of it. Just this part (points to D13), not the rest.
Coding: D13 NC – CF ODL

During the Response Phase, the examinee provides a response of "coffee spill" which is normally coded Vg, under object qualities. However, in the Clarification Phase the examinee elaborated and said it was "shaped like a circle." Because "circle" indicates an easily recognizable shape, it is no longer a vague response, so Vg should not be coded. The examinee's elaboration interjected a form demand.

DON'T FORGET

An object with an easily recognizable shape has form demand. In order to determine if something has form demand, imagine the outline of the object. If you can easily recognize it without any other features (color, texture, etc.), then the object likely has form demand. If you cannot, then it probably does not have form demand.

Synthesis (Sy) can be coded only when there are at least two objects in the response that are in some sort of relationship with each other. Having two objects in a response is not sufficient to code Sy; the objects must be in some sort of relationship or interacting with each other to code Sy. The objects do not need to have form demand; objects can include things like music and love, as long as they are visualized on the card. Examples of Sy responses include "these two people are talking to each other" and "these aliens are holding up the Eiffel Tower." In the first example, the two people are interacting with each other (talking), and in the second example the aliens are in a relationship with each other, as they are both holding up the Eiffel Tower, and they are also in a relationship with the Eiffel Tower (holding it up). The object qualities coding for both of the previous two examples would be Sy.

It is possible for a response to have both Sy and Vg codes. In order for this to occur, examinees must say that they saw at least two objects in some sort of relationship with each other, and none of the objects can have form demand. This could include responses like "water hitting the shore" and "two clouds merging." In both examples, the objects in the response are interacting in some way, but neither of the objects has a form demand. The appropriate code for object qualities for these responses would be Sy, Vg.

2: PAIRS

Pairs (2) are coded when examinees verbalize that they see a pair of objects. The pair of objects must be based on the symmetry of the blot and the objects must be identical.

Sometimes examinees will say that they saw a pair of objects (e.g., "a pair of bears"), but generally, they usually just use the plural of the word to indicate the members of the pair (e.g., "bears"). Examinees rarely say that the objects in the pair are the same; it is appropriate for the examiner to assume the objects are the same unless the examinee says otherwise, such as in the following example:

> Response (Card VII): Two girls. One here and one here (points to D1, both sides).
> *Examiner repeats examinee's response.*
> Clarification-1: It's just their heads. This one is older (points to right side D1) because she is taller. Nose, eyes, mouth here.
> *Coding: D 1 Hd o P F GH*

In this example, the examinee verbalized seeing two girls; however, the examinee differentiated between the girls by saying one is taller. Because of this, the response is not coded as a pair. Had the examinee not said that one was taller, the response would have been coded as a pair because the assumption would be that the two objects were the same.

FQ: FORM QUALITY

Form Quality (FQ) is a combination of two factors on R-PAS: how well the object or response follows the contours of the blot and how commonly the object has been seen. Responses that more closely follow the contours of the blot and/ or have been more commonly reported on Rorschach administrations have higher FQ values than those that do not follow the contours of the blot and/or have rarely been seen.

R-PAS and the CS form quality tables are different. R-PAS's FQ tables are based on the ratings of over 13,000 objects by 569 raters, and also on comparisons among the FQ ratings of the objects on various FQ tables (Meyer et al., 2011). Each response has one FQ code. Rapid Reference 7.6 displays the four FQ codes, ordered from highest to lowest quality.

The FQ codes can be found in the FQ tables in the R-PAS manual. It is very important to identify whether you are using the CS tables or R-PAS tables to

≡ *Rapid Reference 7.6*

. . . .

R-PAS FQ Codes

Code	Name	Description
o	Ordinary	The response has at least one determinant with form.* The object follows the contours of the blot and has been frequently reported by others in that area.
u	Unusual	The response has at least one object with form.* The coding falls between ordinary and minus.
–	Minus	Response has at least one object with form.* The object does not follow the contours of the blot and has rarely been seen by others in that area.
n	None	Response does not have an object with form.

*It may be C', T, Y, V, or r, because form can be present in these determinants.

Source: Based on Meyer et al., 2011, p. 85.

identify FQ on R-PAS, because the FQs are different and represent different things on the two systems. For example, an FQu response on the CS (coded as u in the FQ column of the CS coding sheets) follows the contour of the blot but is less commonly seen than the FQo responses (Exner, 2003). However, on R-PAS, a response can be assigned FQu (coded as u in the Form Quality column of the R-PAS code sequence page) if the fit is less accurate but not "grossly inconsistent" with the shape of the blot (Meyer et al., 2011, p. 85). Although the concepts of FQ are similar for the CS and R-PAS, they are not exactly the same. Meyer and colleagues (2011) point out that about 40 percent of items have different FQs in R-PAS than they do in the CS.

CAUTION

For R-PAS, be sure to identify whether the CS (Exner, 2003) or R-PAS (Meyer et al., 2011) FQ tables were used to code FQ. This will be important for scoring when using the online scoring platform.

To determine FQ, the examiner looks in the FQ tables for the object the examinee saw under the location area where he or she saw it. For example, an examinee might state that all of Card I (location = W) looks like a jack-o'lantern. The examiner will then look at the FQ tables for Card I, specifically looking under the W column(s) for the word "jack-o'lantern." According to the FQ table, a response of jack-o'lantern using the whole blot has an FQ code of ordinary (o). So the FQ should be coded as o.

However, there are times when the object the examinee sees is not in the FQ tables. When this happens, the examiner should extrapolate based on the FQ tables. To do this, the examiner looks for objects with a shape similar to the object seen in the response; the words themselves do not need to be semantically related. As an example, an examinee might report seeing "a worm" in area D3 of Card I. While this is not in the FQ tables as an option, a "snake" is. Given that worms and snakes have a similar shape, it would be reasonable to extrapolate FQ from "snake." The FQ for worm should be a u.

FQ should be assessed using the response as a whole, when possible. However, this is not always possible. When an examiner cannot extrapolate from the whole response, the examiner should then attempt to extrapolate using the various parts of the examinee's response. As an example, on Card X, some examinees have reported seeing "a crab (D1) holding a leaf (D10)." It is impossible to extrapolate from the whole response, as the area being used is a Dd99 area. The examiner should then look at the FQ for each object in the response. The FQ for the crab (area D1) is o and the FQ for the leaf (area D12) is also o. Consequently, it is appropriate to code the FQ as o.

However, there are times where this process results in FQs that are different. If this occurs, generally the lowest FQ among the objects important to the nature of the response is coded. This does require the examiner to determine which aspects of the response are important and which are not. There are a few things to consider when determining whether an object is important to the response:

1. If the object were different, or did not exist, how much would that affect the response? If the response would still be essentially the same, then the object is not important. If the response would be different, then the object is important.
2. How certain was the examinee about the object? If the examinee seemed uncertain about the object, such as by stating, "I guess it could be," then the examiner should consider that part of the response as being less important to the nature of the response, as the examinee was less certain about it.
3. Which part of the response did the examinee focus on? If the examinee focuses on one part of the response far more than the rest, that part could be deemed the most important and could be given more weight in the determination of FQ.

There are also times when the examiner cannot extrapolate from the parts of the response. In this case, the examiner should extrapolate based on the shape of the response object(s). For example, if the examinee saw a "snake" but there is no "snake" in the FQ table for that area, the examiner should then look for items in the FQ table that have a shape similar to a snake's shape, such as a stick. It is important that the examiner look for items that are similarly shaped and not conceptually related. In the previous example, although a lizard is conceptually more similar to a snake than a stick is, as both are reptiles, it would not be appropriate to extrapolate FQ from "lizard" in the FQ table because lizards and snakes have very different shapes. Instead, "stick," although not conceptually related to a snake, is a better item to extrapolate from, because sticks and snakes have similar shapes.

Still, there are times when the examiner cannot extrapolate at all from the FQ tables. In this case, the examiner needs to look at the response and determine whether the response object follows the contours of the blot. If it does, then the response should be coded as having unusual FQ (u). If the object does not follow the contours of the blot, then the response should be coded as having minus FQ (−).

P: POPULARS

Each card has one popular response (Exner, 2003; Meyer et al., 2011). These responses were the most common responses and, for all but one card, appeared on at least 30 percent of the protocols. In other words, these were extremely common responses. The popular responses for each card can be found in Rapid Reference 7.7. Whenever a popular response is present, the examiner should code a P in the popular column.

Some of the popular responses require the use of the entire card (e.g., Cards I, V) whereas others use only part of the card (e.g., Card VII). Because some

≡ Rapid Reference 7.7

Popular Responses

Card	Area	Object
I	W	Bat or butterfly.
II	D1	Bear, dog, elephant, lamb, head or whole animal.
III	D9	Human figure or representation thereof.
IV	W or D7	Human or humanlike figure (e.g., monster). Must be humanlike to be popular.
V	W	Bat or butterfly.
VI	W or D1	Animal skin, hide, pelt, or rug.
VII	D9	Human head or face, identified as female, child, or Native American, or no gender specified.
VIII	D1	Animal, usually dog, cat, or rodent.
IX	D3	Human or humanlike figure, such as a wizard, giant, monster, etc.
X	D1	Crab or spider.

Source: Adapted from Table 8.3 in J. E. Exner, *The Rorschach: A Comprehensive System*, vol. 1, *Basic Foundations and Principles of Interpretation*, 4th ed. (Hoboken, NJ: John Wiley & Sons, Inc., 2003). Used with permission of the publisher.

popular responses do not use the entire blot, it is possible for a popular response to be embedded in another response. For example:

Response (Card VIII): It looks like two animals climbing up a mountain.
Examiner repeats examinee's response.
Clarification-1: Animals are here (points to D1, both sides). Head, four legs. The green is the grassy mountain top (points to D4). This is the rest of the mountain (points to D6).
Coding: W A,NC Sy 2 o P FMa,CF

In this case, the popular response (animal) is embedded in the response. As a result, the response is coded as popular.

DETERMINANTS

Determinants answer the question "Why did it look like that to you?" The determinants are the characteristics of the blot that the examinee attended to in coming up with a response. There are multiple determinants, and they can be divided into six categories: form, movement, color/achromatic color, shading, dimensionality, and symmetry. A list and brief description of each of the R-PAS determinants is in Rapid Reference 7.8.

≡ *Rapid Reference 7.8*

R-PAS Determinants

This table includes a list of all the types of R-PAS determinants, with their names and a brief description. There are also examples of key words that could indicate the presence of the determinant.

Code	Name	Description	Examples of Key Words
F	Form	Examinee sees a shape.	Shape Form
Ma Mp Ma-p	Human Movement	Examinee sees human movement, or supernatural movement of any species.	Any movement word

Code	Name	Description	Examples of Key Words
FMa FMp FMa-p	Animal Movement	Examinee sees animal movement that is consistent with the way an animal would move (e.g., an animal reciting a poem would not be coded FM, it would be M).	Any movement word
ma mp ma-p	Inanimate Object Movement	Examinee sees inanimate object movement that is consistent with the way an inanimate object would move (e.g., a flower flying would not be coded m, it would be M).	Any movement word
C CF FC	Color	Examinee sees chromatic color, which includes all colors except white, black, and gray.	Happy Beautiful
C'	Achromatic Color	Examinee sees achromatic color, which includes white, black, and gray only.	Evil Bright
T	Texture	Examinee uses shading of the blot to indicate the presence of a tactile sensation.	Furry Cold
V	Vista	Examinee uses shading of the blot to indicate the presence of depth or dimensionality.	Deep Behind
Y	Diffuse Shading	Examinee uses shading of the blot, but it does not indicate the presence of a tactile sensation or dimensionality.	Dark Bright
FD	Form Dimension	Examinee uses the form, or shape, of the blot to indicate dimensionality.	Behind Under
r	Reflection	Examinee sees a reflection or mirror image (image must be based on the symmetry of the blot).	Reflection Mirror

Source: Based on information from Meyer et al., 2011.

There can be multiple determinants in a response. A response with multiple determinants is referred to as a *blend* and the different determinants are separated by commas (,). The rules for blends can be found in Rapid Reference 7.9.

≡ Rapid Reference 7.9

Rules for Blends

Blends occur when the examinee uses multiple determinants in the same response. There are some rules governing the use of blends:

1. Separate the different determinants in a blend with commas (,).
2. Only one of each determinant can be present in a blend. There cannot be two T codes, two m codes, both a CF and an FC, and so forth. However, you can have an m and an FM, because these are different determinants.
3. Form is never in a blend.

Source: Based on information from Meyer et al., 2011.

DON'T FORGET

It is possible to have more than one determinant in a response. This is referred to as a blend. The different determinants in a blend are separated by commas.

An excellent understanding of determinants is necessary for a good clarification, as the determinants represent the *why* of the clarification. The key words referenced in Chapters 2 and 6 of this book are words that could indicate a presence of a determinant (e.g., "night" may indicate the use of achromatic color). Similarly, a good understanding of determinants will assist the examiner to better identify key words.

There are some important differences between the coding of determinants on the CS and on R-PAS. These are highlighted throughout this section, in order to help ease the transition between the CS and R-PAS. However, I would still strongly encourage that any practitioner transitioning from the CS to R-PAS or from R-PAS to the CS to review the systems in detail, as there are many subtle differences between coding determinants on the CS and R-PAS that are beyond the purview of this book.

F: Form

When examinees are relying on the shape of the blot to explain why the blot looks that way to them, they are using Form (F). Occasionally, examinees will state that the response looks that way to them because of the shape, but more often, they point out parts of the blot that look like parts of their response. Consider the following response:

Response (Card V): Bat.
Examiner repeats examinee's response.
Clarification-1: Head, ears, legs, wings.
Coding: W A o P F

Although the examinee never mentions using the shape, the fact that he or she pointed out different aspects of the response—in this case the head, ears, legs, and wings—indicates that the examinee is using form.

Form is rarely involved in a blend. Instead, form is usually subsumed in another determinant. These instances are described throughout this section.

M, FM, and m: Movement

Examinees sometimes verbalize that they see movement in the blot. This does not mean that they actually see the inked areas physically moving; rather, it means that something about the blot causes them to perceive movement. This can involve Human Movement (M), Animal Movement (FM), and Inanimate Object Movement (m). All movement is also classified as either being Active (a) or Passive (p), which traditionally was coded as a superscript next to the movement determinant. For example, an active human movement response would be coded M^a; however, it has become customary to no longer use the superscript when typing (e.g., M^a is often typed Ma instead, as is the practice in this book). The active-passive distinction is discussed later in this section. Form is assumed with movement, so there is no need to code F when there is a movement code.

In order to be coded, the movement needs to be happening currently. Any movements that occurred in the past (e.g., "The car ran over this cat") are not coded as movements. Only present-tense movements are coded.

CAUTION

When using the online scoring platform for R-PAS (www.r-pas.org), it is important to enter inanimate object movement as IM and human movement as HM, because the platform does not distinguish between a small m and a capital M. The platform also allows animal movement to be entered as AM or FM.

Human Movement (M) is coded whenever the examinee reports seeing human movement, such as a person walking, in a response. However, the human movement code is used in other cases as well. Emotions, such as depression, are usually coded as human movement; however, there are some exceptions to this rule, as discussed below. Animals and inanimate objects that are engaged in typically human activities, such as dancing, are coded as human movement rather than animal or inanimate object movement. This is done to reflect the human fantasy that went into the response.

Supernatural activities, such as "this bear is shooting repulsor rays from its paws," or, "this man is running at the speed of light," are coded as human movement, regardless of whether they are being completed by a human, animal, or inanimate object. Refer to Rapid Reference 7.10 for examples of responses that should be coded as having human movement.

Animal Movement (FM) is coded whenever an animal is identified in the response. However, in order to be coded as animal movement on R-PAS, the animal needs to be engaging in a movement that is typical animal movement, such as digging, running, and the like. This differs significantly from the CS, where only movements that are consistent with the species are coded as animal movement. So, "a snake slithering on the ground" would be coded as FMa on R-PAS, as would "a snake flying through the air," even though snakes do not fly. On the CS, only the first example would be coded FMa; the second example would be coded Ma.

When determining whether a movement is appropriate for an animal, it is important to consider context. For example:

Response (Card II): Two bears, dancing. They are wearing hats, here (points to D2).
Examiner repeats examinee's response.

≡ *Rapid Reference 7.10*

Examples of Movements That Should Be Coded M

These bears are talking to each other. (Mp)
A tree, killing all of these squirrels that are annoying him. (Ma)
A man, flying through the air, like Superman. (Ma)
Oh! Dancing water. See how beautifully it moves together, like a couple in love. So graceful! (Ma)
Two mermaids, whispering to each other. (Mp)

Clarification-1: Here's one bear, here's the other (points to D1). They are in the circus, performing. They are doing a little dance together.
Coding: W A, Cg Sy 2 o P FMa COP MAH GH

In the Response Phase, the examinee reported seeing "two bears, dancing" which would have been coded as M, because dancing is a typically human activity. However, in the Clarification Phase, the examinee elaborated that the bears were doing the dance as part of a performance for a circus. This context is reasonable; bears could be trained to dance as part of a circus performance, so an FM code is used instead.

Animal emotional expressions that are appropriate for that animal are also coded as FM. So "an angry cat clawing a couch" would be coded FMa. However, if the emotion and the movement are not appropriate for the animal, such as "a happy cat skipping in a circle," then the response should be coded M.

Inanimate Object Movement (m) is coded whenever the examinee verbalizes that an inanimate object is moving in the blot. Inanimate objects are anything that is not either human or an animal and include a variety of things, such as plants, rocks, buildings, and weapons. As an example, "a flag flying in the wind" would be coded ma. However, if the inanimate object is engaging in an activity that is not consistent with the object, such as "a flower dancing," the response is coded as a human movement response to reflect the fantasy that went into the creation of the response. Unconscious, automatic movements, such as bleeding and digestion, are usually coded as m. Rapid Reference 7.11 contains a summary of the movement determinants.

≣ *Rapid Reference 7.11*

Summary of Movement Determinants

Code	Name	Description
M	Human Movement	Used when there is any human movement (realistic or supernatural) or when an animal or object engages in a typically human or supernatural movement.
FM	Animal Movement	Used when there is an animal movement, including when animals are engaging in non-species-specific animal movement (e.g., a snake flying).
m	Inanimate Object Movement	Used when an inanimate object (e.g., a rock) is moving.

Source: Based on information from Meyer et al., 2011.

Active Versus Passive Movement

Determining whether a movement is active or passive is one of the more difficult aspects of coding. The rule is that "talking" is the most active of the passive movements. Thus, "talking" would be coded as passive and anything more active than talking, such as "yelling" would be coded as active. Exner (2003, pp. 92–94) and others (e.g., Holaday, 1997) have conducted research on the determination of active and passive movement and have provided lists of movement responses and how their participants coded them. These lists can be beneficial in determining whether a movement is active or passive. The R-PAS manual also has a number of examples that can assist with this determination (Meyer et al., 2011, pp. 101–103).

It is important to evaluate the whole response when deciding whether a movement is active or passive and not just the movement word. For example, "praying" is generally coded as passive. However, a "person praying, look how excited they are! They are waving their arms in the air" has an active component to it ("waving their arms in the air"), so a code of Ma is appropriate.

Multiple Movements in the Same Response

There are times when an examinee reports seeing multiple movements in a response. In general, if they are different types of movement and from different objects, such as an animal and a human, then both types of movement will be coded. For example, the response "It looks like a person petting a dog. The dog is wagging his tail" has two different types of movements. There is the human movement of a person petting a dog (Ma) and the animal movement of the dog "wagging his tail" (FMa). As a result, both are coded.

There are also times when one object is said to be engaging in two different movements, such as "these two people are talking while running a marathon." In this case, typically only one movement is coded, and it is important to give credit for the active movement when it is present, so for the response "these two people are talking while running a marathon," the correct determinant is Ma, as one of the movements (running) is active. The other movement, talking, is passive.

There is a set of rarely used movement codes: Ma-p, FMa-p, and ma-p. These codes are used when there are two objects of the same type, such as two humans, engaging in different movements in the same response. This code is rarely used, as it requires two separate objects in the same response engaging in different movements. Here is an example: "It looks like a mother bear and her cub. See here, the cub is sleeping (FMp). The mother bear is protecting her cub, see, she's growling (FMa)."

Because there are two separate objects, each engaging in its own movement, the correct code for this response is FMa-p.

C, CF, and FC: Color Determinants

There are three color chromatic determinants that are used when the examinee is relying on the chromatic parts of the blots to explain a response. These codes are used only when the examinee explicitly states that color was important to the nature of the response; simply seeing something that is typically colored, such as a flower, is not enough to code color. Examinees need to state or strongly imply (via the *color convergence principle*) that the color was a factor in their seeing the item. These codes are not used when the examinee is relying on the colors white, black, or gray in the response; white, black, and gray are referred to as achromatic colors and are discussed in the next section of this chapter.

There are three color determinants: Pure Color (C), Color-Form (CF), and Form-Color (FC). It is important to accurately distinguish between the three color determinants, as they are interpreted differently. It is generally fairly easy to determine whether a response should be coded as C or as either CF or FC; however, the CF or FC determination tends to be more difficult. Rapid Reference 7.12 outlines when each of the color determinants should be coded.

Pure Color (C) is coded when the examinee is relying only on color for a response; there is no indication that the examinee is using the form or the shape of the blot in any way. Often, these objects will have Vg object quality. Two examples of this type of response follow.

≡ *Rapid Reference 7.12*

Color Determinants

Code	Name	Description
C	Pure Color	Used when the examinee is relying only on color; there is no mention of shape or form in the response.
CF	Color-Form	Used when the examinee is relying on both color and form; color is more important to the nature of the response than the form is.
FC	Form-Color	Used when the examinee is relying on both color and form; form is more important to the nature of the response than the color is.

Source: Based on information from Exner, 2001, 2003; Meyer et al., 2011.

Example 1 (Card X)

Response: Sadness.

Examiner repeats examinee's response.

Clarification-1: The yellow (points to D2). It is yellow so it must be sadness.

Coding: D2 NC Vg n C,Mp PEC MOR PH

Example 2 (Card X)

Response: Blood.

Examiner repeats examinee's response.

Clarification-1: The red here (points to D9). The color is the color of blood.

Coding: D9 Bl Vg n C

In both examples, the examinee is relying only on the color of the blot to explain why the blot looked like it did; there is no indication that the examinee is using form in the response.

Color-Form (CF) is coded when examinees are using both the color and the form or shape of the area to explain why they saw what they saw, and when the color is more important to the response than the shape is. Unfortunately, examinees rarely specifically state whether color or form is more influential in the creation of their response. Generally, the examiner will need to determine whether color or form is more important based on the examinee's verbalizations and gestures. For example:

Response (Card IX): A beautiful lake.

Examiner repeats examinee's response.

Clarification-1: The light blue color here reminds me of a lake. It kind of has the shape of a lake too.

Coding: D8 NC Vg u CF

In this case, the examinee clearly is focusing more on color than form. A color key word ("beautiful") is mentioned in the Response Phase, and color is also the first thing mentioned in the Clarification Phase. There is a mention of form ("the shape") but it is the last thing mentioned. Thus, CF is the most appropriate determinant.

The final color determinant, Form-Color (FC), is used when examinees are using both the color and the form or shape of the area to explain why they saw what they saw. However, the form is more important to the response than the color is. For example:

Response (Card IX): It's a pool (points to D8).

Examiner repeats examinee's response.

Clarification-1: The shape reminds me of the pool I had in my backyard when I was a kid. See the two rounded areas? It's also kind of blue colored and a lot of times pools can be blue.

Coding: D8 NC u FC PER

In this case, the examinee is focusing more on the shape than on the color. The appropriate code in this example is FC.

Color is sometimes coded even when examinees do not specifically state that the reason the object looks like it does to them is due to the color. This is due to the color convergence principle. This principle can be applied only under specific circumstances. Specifically, the object the examinee reports seeing is commonly associated with a specific color, the color of the area of the blot the examinee is using is strongly associated with the object, and the examinee mentions color in the response. For example, if an examinee says, "This red could be blood," in reference to area D3 on Card II (which is red), there is enough to code color, even though the examinee did not specifically say that the object was blood because it was red. Nonetheless, because the examinee mentioned color and used a spot that had a color strongly associated with the object (e.g., blood is usually red), it is appropriate to code a color determinant.

CAUTION

Do not over-apply the color convergence principle. In order for the color convergence principle to be applied, the object must be associated with a specific color. The principle cannot be applied to objects that can be many colors, such as insects, buildings, clothing, and so forth.

Step-Down Principle

Coding color can become even more difficult due to a concept known as the *step-down principle*. This principle applies when an object that would typically be coded as a C touches something with form. When this happens, the C determinant is stepped down to a CF. For example:

Response (Card II): It is two grizzly bears fighting.

Examiner repeats examinee's response.

Clarification-1: The whole thing. Here's one bear (points to D1) and here's the other. Their paws are up like they are fighting.

You said they were fighting?

Clarfication-2: Yes, there is fresh blood everywhere, see, the red (points to D2, D3, and red spots on D1).

Coding: D 1,3 A,Bl Sy 2 o P FMa,CF AGC,AGM,MAP,MOR PH

Normally, blood would be coded C; the examinee stated that it was blood because of the color only. There is no indication that the examinee is using form at all. However, because the red touches something with form, namely the bears, the determinant is stepped down to a CF.

Color as a Locator

Color can also be used as a locator rather than as a determinant. For example, an examinee can say, "This red could be a flower." It is unclear whether the examinee is using color as a determinant to support the response of a flower or if the examinee is using color simply as a locator code (e.g., this spot, which happens to be red, looks like a flower). In order to determine whether the examinee is using color as a determinant or a locator, the examiner would need to query. An appropriate query could be "You said it was red?"

C': Achromatic Color

There is one achromatic color determinant (C') that is used when the examinee states that achromatic color—black, white, or gray—was an important factor in the determination of a response. The examinee needs to state that the achromatic color was important to the nature of the response, or strongly imply it via the color convergence principle. Simply using white space is not sufficient to code C'.

Unlike the multiple color codes, there is only one achromatic color code: C'. Thus, it is not vital to determine whether form or achromatic color was more important to the response, unlike the color determinants where it is very important to determine whether color or form was more important. Even if form is used in the response, it is incorrect to blend F with C'; the C' codes assume form and it is not necessary to code F separately. For example:

Response (Card I): It's a woman in a gray dress.
Examiner repeats examinee's response.
Clarification-1: Here (points to D4). Her hands are up (points to D1). This is the dress, see the outline? It is an A-line dress (traces). Here are her legs (points).
Coding: D4 H,Cg Sy o C',Mp GH

In this response, the examinee is clearly using both achromatic color ("gray") and shape ("the outline") to explain why the object looks like a dress. However, because form is assumed with C', there is no need to separately code for form.

For those who know the CS, this is a significant change. In the CS, there are three C' codes: C', C'F, and FC'. Anything that would be coded as C'F or FC' on the CS is coded as C' on R-PAS.

Color Convergence with Achromatic Color

The color convergence principle can be applied to objects that are typically white, black, or gray. This could include objects like "night" (black), "teeth" (white), and "elephant" (gray). This principle can be applied when the examinee reports seeing something that is commonly associated with a specific color, the color of the area of the blot the examinee is using is strongly associated with the object, and the examinee mentions color in the response. As an example:

Response (Card I): This white could be a snow-covered tree.
Examiner repeats examinee's response.
Clarification-1: Here (points to DdS99, half of DdS30). It's shaped like an evergreen tree.
Coding: Dd99 SR NC – C'

In this case, the examinee verbalizes using achromatic color ("white") and associates it with something that is typically white ("snow-covered"), and the object is located in the area of the blot that is white. Collectively, this information strongly suggests that achromatic color influenced the examinee's perceptions of the blot, so it is appropriate to code C'.

Achromatic Color as a Locator

Achromatic color can also be used as a locator rather than as a determinant. For example, an examinee might say, "This white could be a ballerina." It is unclear whether the examinee is using color as a determinant to support the response of a ballerina, or using color simply as a locator code (e.g., this spot, which happens to be white, looks like a ballerina). In order to determine whether the examinee is using color as a determinant or a locator, the examiner would need to query. An appropriate query could be "You said it was white?"

Light or Dark

When using achromatic color, examinees do not always use the words "black," "gray," or "white." Instead, they sometimes use the terms "light" and "dark." However, these terms can also be used to indicate shading. If the examiner is confident that the use of the term "light" or "dark" is meant to indicate achromatic color, then the response should be coded as C'. However, if the examiner is not certain, then the response should be queried. If even after querying it is still not clear, then the response should be coded as diffuse shading (Y, discussed in next section). Here are two examples to demonstrate the difference:

Example 1 (Card I)

Response: It is an evil woman (points to D4).

Examiner repeats examinee's response.
Clarification-1: Body, hands, head should be here but it's missing (points to Dd22).
You said she was evil?
Clarification-2: She's wearing dark clothes. The dress flares out.
Coding: D4 Hd,Cg Sy o C' AGC,MOR PH

Example 2 (Card I)
Response: It looks like smoke (indicates whole card).
Examiner repeats examinee's response.
Clarification-1: The light and the dark colors make it look like smoke.
You said it was smoke?
Clarification-2: Yes. The light and dark of the blot remind me of smoke.
Coding: W Fi Vg Y

In the first example, the way the examinee explains the response indicates that "dark" is being used as a color. There is no indication that the examinee is using shading. In the second example, it is still unclear whether "the light and the dark" refer to colors or shading. In this case, a code of diffuse shading is appropriate.

Shading Determinants

There are three shading determinants: Texture (T), Dimensionality (Vista, V), and Diffuse (Y). Although they are all interpreted differently, they do have a few things in common. First, all require the use of shading in order to be coded. For instance, an examinee simply stating that she saw a texture is not sufficient to code T; the examinee needs to somehow indicate that the shading of the blot is the reason she is seeing the texture, rather than something else, such as the shape of the blot. Another thing all these codes have in common is that like the achromatic code, form is assumed with the shading determinants and there is no need to code F with them. These codes are listed in Rapid Reference 7.13.

T: Texture
Texture (T) is coded when the examinee is using the shading present in the blot to indicate a texture or tactile sensation (e.g., soft, hard, heat, cold). Simply saying a texture word is not sufficient to code T. Examinees need either to verbalize that the shading in the blot is resulting in their seeing texture (e.g., "the different hues make it look furry") or to touch the card while saying the texture

≡ Rapid Reference 7.13

• •

Achromatic and Shading Determinants

Code	Name	Description	Key Word Examples
C'	Achromatic Color	Black, white, or gray colors in the blot influence the examinee's perception of the objects in the blot.	Night Snow Bright Evil
T	Texture	Examinee perceives the shading in the blot to indicate a tactile sensation.	Cotton Soft Hot Hard
V	Dimensionality/Vista	Examinee perceives the shading in the blot to indicate dimensionality.	Deep Behind Valley Covered
Y	Diffuse Shading	Examinee uses the shading in the blot, but does not indicate either texture or dimensionality.	Lighter Darker Hues

Source: Based on information from Exner, 2001, 2003; Meyer et al., 2011.

word (e.g., "it looks soft" [pets card]). The nonverbal indication of a tactile sensation combined with the use of a texture word, such as stroking the card in the case of something the examinee says is soft, is sufficient to code T. For example:

Response (Card VII): It's Anna from *Frozen*.
Examiner repeats examinee's response.
Clarification-1: She's here (points to Dd22). Here is her face (points to D9), hair (D1), and body (D3 & Dd24). She looks cold (touches card).
Coding: Dd22 (H) o P T GH

In this case, the examinee used a word to indicate a tactile sensation ("cold") while touching the card. Even though the examinee never specifically states that the shading indicates texture, the examinee's touching the card while saying the texture word is sufficient to indicate the use of texture.

It is important to never assume that the use of a texture word always warrants coding a T determinant. The coding of a texture determinant requires both the presence of a tactile sensation *and* the use of shading or a nonverbal response suggesting texture (e.g., touching of card). At times, an examinee will provide a texture word but will not indicate texture in any other way. In these cases, texture is not coded as a determinant. Consider the following example:

Response (Card IV): It's a hairy monster. He's looking down from high above.
Examiner repeats examinee's response.
Clarification-1: See, the feet are bigger than the head, here (points to D6 and D3). Makes the head look further away. Here's the body. This isn't part of it (points to D1).
You said he was hairy?
Clarification-2: Yeah the lines around him look like hair.
Coding: D7 (H) o P Mp,FD AGC GH

In this case, the examinee uses a word that could indicate texture ("hairy"), but there is no indication that the examinee is using shading to indicate texture and the examinee does not engage in any gestures that indicate texture. Consequently, texture is not coded as a determinant.

CAUTION

Code T only when the examinee uses a texture word and either states that the shading indicates texture or uses gestures that indicate texture, such as stroking the card. Simply saying the texture word is not sufficient to code T.

V: Shading-Based Dimensionality

Shading-based dimensionality is commonly referred to as Vista (V). Vista is used when the examinee is using the shading present in the blot to indicate dimensionality. Simply saying a dimensionality word is not sufficient to code vista. Examinees need to verbalize that the shading in the blot is resulting in their seeing the dimensionality (e.g., "it's darker here so it looks deeper"). For example:

Response (Card VI): A canyon.
Examiner repeats examinee's response.
Clarification-1: See how it gets darker here (points to D12)? It makes it look deeper, like a canyon.
Coding: D12 NC Vg o V

In this example, the examinee indicates the possible presence of dimensionality in the Response Phase (e.g., "a canyon") and confirms its presence in the Clarification Phase by stating that the darker color makes it look deeper. The appropriate determinant code for this response is V.

It is important to distinguish between shading-based dimensionality (V) and form-based dimensionality (Form Dimension, FD). The distinguishing factor between the two is the use of shading; V uses shading to indicate dimensionality, and FD does not. FD is described in more detail later in this chapter.

Y: Diffuse Shading

Diffuse Shading (Y), the final shading determinant, is usually coded by exclusion. It is coded when the examinee is using shading, but there is no indication that the shading is associated with texture or vista. For example:

Response (Card IV): The smoke monster from *Lost*.
Examiner repeats examinee's response.
Clarification-1: It's everything but this part (points to D1). It kind of is shaped like a man, see the head here (points to D3) and legs here (D6), but it is made of smoke.
What makes it look like smoke?
Clarification-2: The different shades.
Coding: D7 (H), Fi o P Y AGC GH

In this case, the examinee verbalizes using shading to indicate smoke; however, the examinee is not using it to indicate dimensionality or texture. The appropriate determinant for this response is Y.

FD: Form Dimension or Shape-Based Dimensionality

The Form Dimension (FD) determinant is coded when the examinee indicates the presence of dimensionality in the response and the dimensionality is based on the structure of the blot rather than the shading. Unlike the V code, FD does not rely on shading to indicate dimensionality. This determinant is commonly seen on Card IV:

Response (Card IV): It's a man relaxing on a stump.
Examiner repeats examinee's response.
Clarification-1: This is the stump (points to D1), head, legs, arms. See how the head is smaller than the feet, it looks further away, like he is sitting back and relaxing on the stump.
Coding: W H,NC Sy o P Mp,FD GH

The examinee indicates seeing some form of dimensionality in the response ("looks further away"), but there is no indication that the examinee is using shading at all in the response. Instead, the dimensionality is due to the structure of the blot. Specifically, because the "head" is smaller than the "feet," the examinee perceives this as indicating that the feet are closer than the head is. The appropriate determinant is FD. There is also a movement code (Mp), because the man is "relaxing" and "sitting back" on the stump.

r: Reflection

The reflection determinant (r) is coded when the examinee verbalizes that there is an object with its reflection or mirror image in the blot. The reflection needs to be based on the symmetry of the blot. If the examinee verbalizes seeing a reflection that is not based on the symmetry of the blot, then the reflection is not coded.

Like many of the other determinants, the reflection codes can assume form. Thus, if there is a reflection coded when form is also present, there is no need to code for form. In addition, Pairs (2) cannot be coded when there is a reflection present. If there are a pair and a reflection in the same response, the reflection takes precedence. Only the reflection should be coded. For example:

Response (Card X): It is a crab getting ready for a date. She's looking at herself in the mirror.

Examiner repeats examinee's response.

Clarification-1: It's a cartoon. So this crab is getting ready for the big dance and her friends are helping her. See, she's looking at herself in the mirror and twirling around, here is the reflection, here (points to D1). These two fish are twins (points to D2) and they are giving her advice on what to wear.
Coding: D1,2 (A) Sy u P Ma,r COP GH

In this example, there is a reflection (the crab) and a pair (the twin fish). However, only the reflection is coded, due to the rule that when there is a pair and reflection in the same response, only the reflection is coded.

CAUTION

Never code a pair with a reflection. If there is a pair and a reflection in the same response, code only the reflection.

SPECIAL SCORES

On R-PAS, the Special Scores are divided into two categories: cognitive codes and thematic codes. The cognitive codes represent odd thought processes and are subdivided into language and reasoning cognitive codes and perceptual cognitive codes. The thematic codes relate to content.

Cognitive Codes

Three cognitive codes are classified as language and reasoning codes and three are classified as perceptual codes, making six categories of cognitive codes in all. All the codes are weighted in terms of severity. Those that represent more serious cognitive problems are weighted more heavily than those that represent less severe, typically more common, cognitive lapses.

Four of the codes have levels assigned to them that separate more benign cognitive lapses (such as saying an incorrect but related word) from more severe cognitive difficulties. This results in a total of ten cognitive codes that can be coded in a response. The codes, with their names, definitions, and an example of each, are displayed in Rapid Reference 7.14. The order of the codes, in terms of severity, can be found in Rapid Reference 7.15.

≡ *Rapid Reference 7.14*

R-PAS Cognitive Codes

These tables list all the cognitive codes by category, giving the code name, a description, and an example for each.

Language and Reasoning Codes

Code	Name	Description	Example
DV1	Deviant Verbalization Level 1	Inappropriate word use, easy to understand what the intent likely was.	A third-semester fetus.
DV2	Deviant Verbalization Level 2	Inappropriate word use, difficult to understand what the intent likely was.	A digrie top.
DR1	Deviant Response Level 1	Off-task communication.	Did you see that episode of *Homeland*? It was awesome!

(continued)

(continued)

Code	Name	Description	Example
DR2	Deviant Response Level 2	More severe off-task communication.	It's coffee, but not from a coffee shop. It was created specifically for this purpose. For life, for all of us.
PEC	Peculiar Logic	Strained, concrete logic.	She must be older because her hair is darker.

Perceptual Codes			
Code	Name	Description	Example
INC1	Incongruous Combination Level 1	One object, either doing something implausible or with implausible attributes.	A pink tiger.
INC2	Incongruous Combination Level 2	One object, either doing something implausible or with implausible attributes, more bizarre than INC1.	A woman with bug heads for hands.
FAB1	Fabulized Combination Level 1	Two objects in an implausible relationship.	Two bunnies doing a high five.
FAB2	Fabulized Combination Level 2	Two objects in an implausible relationship, more bizarre than FAB1.	A man running a marathon. See here, you can see his heart beating hard through his chest.
CON	Contamination	Seeing two percepts at the same time, occupying the same blot area (double exposure).	A baby-apple.

Source: Based on information from Meyer et al., 2011.

Levels

The four cognitive codes that have levels assigned to them are DV, DR, INC, and FAB. Level 1 is assigned when the verbiage in the response is not bizarre. Usually, these represent simple verbal "goofs" that are somewhat common among even psychologically healthy individuals. Level 2 codes, in contrast, are assigned to much more severe and bizarre responses. The R-PAS manual provides a number of criteria that can be used to help determine whether a response should be coded as a level 1 or level 2 response; Viglione (2010) is also an excellent resource.

☰ Rapid Reference 7.15

Cognitive Codes in Order of Severity

The cognitive codes in order, from the least severe to the most severe:

DV1
DV2
INC1
DR1
INC2
FAB1
PEC
DR2
FAB2
CON

Source: Based on information from Exner, 2003; Meyer et al., 2011.

A quick rule to guide coding a level 1 or a level 2 is the cartoon rule: If you saw it in a cartoon, would you think it was bizarre? If the answer is yes, then it is likely a level 2. If the answer is no, then it is probably a level 1. However, this is intended only as a guide; the final coding should be based on a thorough review of the criteria in the manual.

Rules for Coding Cognitive Special Scores

There are rules governing the coding of the Cognitive Special Scores. First and foremost, each cognitive code can be coded only once per response. If there are multiple instances of a cognitive code in the same response, code only the most severe. For example, if there is an INC1 and an INC2 in the response, only the INC2 should be coded. The second rule is that when coding multiple cognitive codes, each needs to have its own unique verbiage or image. If the wording overlaps, then only one should be coded, even if the response meets the criteria for multiple cognitive codes. Again, only the most severe code should be recorded. Finally, if there is a CON present, then only CON is coded.

DV: Deviant Verbalizations

Deviant Verbalizations (DV) occur when the examinee uses an incorrect word in the response. For instance, rather than saying "hands," the examinee may say "paws." These tend to be simple, somewhat common verbal "goofs" that occur even in psychologically healthy people.

DV codes have two levels. Generally, DV1 is coded when the examiner can easily determine the examinee's probable intent. For example:

Response (Card III v): It's a public arch.
Examiner repeats examinee's response.
Clarification-1: Here, it's shaped like an arch. Reminds me of a pelvis. See, the shape?
Coding: D1 NC o F DV1

In the Clarification Phase, it became obvious that the examinee likely meant the card was reminiscent of a "pubic arch" rather than a "public arch." This is a simple miscommunication, whose content was easily determined when placed in context.

A level 2 DV is more bizarre. Even in context, it is difficult to discern what the examinee's likely intent was. For example:

Response (Card IV): It's a borborygmus giant.
Examiner repeats examinee's response.
Clarification-1: His head, feet, legs.
What makes the giant look borborygmus?
Clarification-2: I'm not sure. He just seemed that way to me.
Coding: W (H) o P F DV2 PH

In this case, it is completely unclear why the giant was seen as "borborygmus"; in fact, even the examinee was not clear why it looked that way. The appropriate coding here is DV2.

CAUTION

For CS users: Do *not* code colloquial use of "–y" and "–ish" endings added to words and trivial redundancies (e.g., "little tiny") as DVs on R-PAS. On R-PAS these are not considered DVs.

DR: Deviant Response

A Deviant Response (DR) is coded when the examinee goes off task or distorts the task in some way. DRs can be difficult to code, as proper coding requires that the examiner determine whether the examinee has left the task or is simply making a comment about the task. In general, the difference between a brief aside (no DR) and a response warranting a DR is whether the examinee's verbalizations are still related to the task, which is to tell the examiner what the blot looks like and explain why it looks that way. Brief asides that should *not* be coded as DR on R-PAS include phrases like "Boy, I am hungry," and "Wow, look at all of the colors!" These statements are brief and do not represent a distortion of the task, as long as the examinee returns to the task. If the examinee continues to elaborate and does not return to the task, then a DR should be coded.

Meyer and colleagues (2011) have suggested using the "two step" rule for coding DR's. In order to code a DR, the examinee must be "two steps" away from the task. For example:

Response (Card VIII): It's a tiger (points to D1). Tigers are beautiful.
Examiner repeats examinee's response
Clarification-1: Head here, legs, it's climbing. Did you know tigers are endangered? It's a shame. They are such lovely creatures.
You said they were beautiful?
Clarification-2: Yes, they are beautiful creatures. So muscular!
Coding: D1 A o P FMa DR1

In this example, the examinee "stepped away" from the task twice: the first step was "tigers are beautiful." The second step away was the discussion about tigers being endangered; neither was relevant to the task. Consequently, a DR1 code is appropriate. However, if the examinee had said only "tigers are beautiful," there would be no DR coding, as the examinee would then have stepped away from the task only once.

Like DV, the DR code has two levels. Generally, DR1 is coded when the examinee is off task but has not strayed far. Typically, the examinee's phrases are logical and related to one another; there should not be a lot of evidence of tangential or circumstantial thought. In other words, the examinee's verbalizations are easy to understand. However, in a DR2, the communication is often difficult to follow and/or understand. An example of a DR2 is "clearly it is a bug, the savior of mankind. All need to pay respects, or else be smitten." In this response, there is strong evidence of tangential thought, warranting a code of DR2.

PEC: Peculiar Logic
The final language and reasoning cognitive code is Peculiar Logic (PEC). This code is known as Inappropriate Logic (ALOG) on the CS. PEC is coded when the examinee spontaneously uses strained or concrete logic to explain a response. If the examiner in any way prompts the language that is used to code PEC, then PEC cannot be coded. In general, the language justifying the PEC code will be used in the Response Phase or the first part of the Clarification Phase.

Often, examinees will use phrasing like "has to be," "it must be," or "because" in the verbiage that supports the PEC. The presence of this language is not sufficient to code peculiar logic, but it does indicate that PEC may be present. PEC is coded only when the explanation is illogical. If there is a logical reason for the response (e.g., "These animals are fighting. This is blood because it's red."), then PEC is not coded.

The examinee also needs to be certain of the response in order to code a PEC. If the examinee is tentative or uncertain about the response, then PEC should not be coded. For example, if the examinee says, "This could be lettuce because it is next to a tomato," that would not be coded as PEC because the examinee is tentative. However, if the examinee says, "This must be lettuce because it is next to a tomato," then PEC should be coded because the examinee is certain and the logic is strained. In the latter example, the examinee is essentially saying there is nothing else possible the object could be because of its relationship to the tomato. This is the strained and illogical thinking that is characteristic of a PEC code.

INC: Incongruous Combinations

An Incongruous Combination (INC) is coded when the examinee perceives one object that either has implausible features assigned to it or is engaging in an implausible activity. For example, "a dog laughing" would be coded as INC1, as it is highly unlikely that a dog would laugh. Another example would be "a pink bear," as bears are not usually pink. This response would also be coded as INC1.

In general, INC1 responses are more benign while INC2 responses are more bizarre. Examples of INC2 statements would include "a woman with bug heads for hands" and "a sad flying bra."

At times, an examinee may use the wrong word (DV) and, as a result of that word, the response will contain an object that has implausible features assigned to it (INC). Meyer and colleagues (2011) provide a few guidelines to help determine whether an item should be coded DV or INC. These guidelines are listed in Rapid Reference 7.16.

CAUTION

Be careful when coding INC. Some INCs may actually be DVs; that is, the examinee may simply be using the wrong word to describe something (e.g., saying "antlers" instead of "antenna").

≡ Rapid Reference 7.16

DV Versus INC

Meyer and colleagues (2011, p. 127) provide some guidance to determine whether a response that meets the criteria for both DV and INC should be coded as DV or INC:

Code DV

1. When the examinee uses an anatomical term similar to the one expected (e.g., uses "arms" to describe the front legs of a raccoon).
2. When the examinee uses the wrong word but appears to be visualizing the correct word (e.g., says "claws" but describes hands when "hands" is the correct term).

Code INC

1. When the examinee uses the wrong word and appears to be visualizing the wrong word (e.g., says "claws" when "hands" is the correct word, but then continues on to describe claws in some detail).
2. When the examiner is unclear whether the examinee meant to use the correct term or the incorrect term.

FAB: Fabulized Combination

A Fabulized Combination (FAB) is comparable to an Incongruous Combination (INC), except that a FAB involves two or more objects in an implausible relationship. Examples of FABs are "these two divers are underwater sharing a smoke" (FAB1), and "carnivorous trees, trapping and eating these squirrels" (FAB2).

In general, FAB1 responses are less bizarre while FAB2 responses are very bizarre. The second example, "carnivorous trees, trapping and eating these squirrels," is very bizarre and, as a result, is coded FAB2.

DON'T FORGET

An INC code involves only one object, while a FAB code involves two or more.

CON: Contamination

Contamination (CON) is the rarest of the cognitive codes. This occurs when the examinee sees two different objects in the same blot area. Conceptually, this is like a double exposure—the examinee is seeing two discrete objects at the same time in the same area. For example:

> Response (Card IX): A baby-apple.
> *Examiner repeats examinee's response.*
> Clarification-1: Here is the baby, the head (points to D4), legs (Dd30), body (one half of Dd35), and the face. And it looks like an apple too, see the red circular shape? Apples are red.
> *Coding: Dd99 H,NC – FC CON PH*

In the Response Phase, it was not clear that the examinee was seeing two objects in the same area; based on the language, it was possible that the examinee was seeing a small apple or the early stages of an apple. However, during the Clarification Phase, it became clear that the examinee was seeing both a baby ("head, legs, and face") and an apple ("red circular shape") in the same part of the blot. This is a fusing of two separate percepts in the same area, which is indicative of a CON.

Thematic Codes

There are nine Thematic Special Scores. The thematic codes are used when there is something unique about the content of the response, such as the use of abstract language or an aggressive content. Multiple thematic codes can be coded for the same response. The thematic codes, with descriptions and examples of each, are presented in Rapid Reference 7.17.

ABS: Abstract Representation

Abstract Representation (ABS) is coded when the examinee says that something in the blot represents something abstract, such as an emotion. For example, an examinee could say, "This yellow is pain." This is an example of an ABS because the yellow is representing or symbolizing pain.

PER: Personal Knowledge Justification

Personal Knowledge Justification (PER) is coded when examinees are using their own knowledge or experience to justify what they are reporting they see in the blot. Use of general, or common, knowledge does not meet the criteria for a code of PER. For example, an examinee might say, "It is a pelvis. It looks just like the picture in my anatomy text." Or someone could say, "It looks like my dog Delilah's face." Both of these are examples of PER because the examinee is supporting the response with information that the examiner is unlikely to have. However, if an examinee said, "It is a jack-o'lantern. It looks like one people carve

≡ *Rapid Reference 7.17*

Thematic Codes

Code	Name	Description	Example
ABS	Abstract Representation	Something in the blot, or the entire blot, represents or symbolizes something else.	This red symbolizes their love for one another.
PER	Personal Knowledge Justification	Examinee is using his or her personal knowledge to justify the response.	It looks just like the pictures in my biology textbook.
COP	Cooperative Movement	Two objects are engaging in a cooperative or positive interaction with one another.	These two people are picking up this heavy pot, here.
MAH	Mutuality of Autonomy–Health	Two objects are involved in a mutually beneficial activity. Both objects have to be acting independently.	They are building a house together to live in.
MAP	Mutuality of Autonomy–Pathology	An object is causing damage or harm to another or is compromising another object's independence.	This cat was run over by a car.
AGM	Aggressive Movement	Aggressive or hostile activity is occurring, includes thoughts.	The Evil Queen, planning to destroy Snow White's happiness.
AGC	Aggressive Content	Examinee sees items or objects that are typically seen as aggressive or harmful toward humans.	Shark.
MOR	Morbid Content	Object is dead, destroyed, damaged, or dysphoric.	A crumpled leaf.
ODL	Oral Dependency Language	In the Response Phase, the examinee uses language indicative of oral or dependent content.	He's sticking his tongue out.

Source: Based on information from Meyer et al., 2011.

at Halloween," the response would not be coded as PER, because the justification ("people carve at Halloween") is considered to be common knowledge.

It is possible to code both a DR and a PER in the same response. Coding one does not prohibit the examiner from coding the other; however, the verbiage supporting one should be separate from the verbiage for the other.

COP: Cooperative Movement

Cooperative Movement (COP) should be coded when two objects, animals or humans, are engaged in a positive movement with one another. There must be a movement in order to code COP. Examples include "praying," "partying," and "discussing." COP should also be coded when two or more objects are working together to achieve a goal, such as "two men carrying this pot" or "people building a house." However, the goal does not need to be positive. COP should also be coded for statements like "two wolves attacking this man" and "these aliens are plotting to take over the world."

AGM: Aggressive Movement

Aggressive movement (AGM) is coded whenever the examinee verbalizes that there is aggressive activity in the response. Aggressive thoughts are also considered to be aggressive activity. There must be movement in the response in order to code AGM, so all responses with an AGM code will have a movement determinant. Examples of AGM are "fighting," "scheming to take over the world," and "punching."

DON'T FORGET

In order to code COP or AGM, there must be movement. If there is no movement in the response, do not code COP or AGM.

AGC: Aggressive Content

Aggressive Content (AGC) is coded whenever there is an object that is typically seen as being dangerous, harmful, or a predator. Animals that are typically perceived as being dangerous to people—regardless of whether or not they are actually dangerous to people—are also coded as AGC. Examples of AGC are weapons, an earthquake, a shark, "evil people," and claws. A number of other examples of AGC objects are given in the R-PAS manual (Meyer et al., 2011, pp. 138–139). Still, as with many other codes, context is extremely important for this code. Thus, if an examinee says that he or she sees a "cuddly bear," it should not be coded AGC.

It is possible to code both AGM and AGC in the same response. For example, if the examinee reported seeing "an alligator, see its teeth? It is attacking something," this would meet the criteria for both AGC (alligator, teeth) and AGM (attacking).

MOR: Morbid Content

Morbid content (MOR) is coded when an object is characterized by one of the four D's: dead, destroyed, damaged, or dysphoric. Here are some examples:

He's missing a leg.
A sad fish.
A man. He's very sick.
A dead lobster.

DON'T FORGET

The object does not need to be physically damaged to meet the criteria for a MOR code. Sad and dysphoric objects also meet the criteria for a MOR code.

MAH and MAP: Mutuality of Autonomy Codes

The Mutuality of Autonomy codes on R-PAS—Mutuality of Autonomy–Health (MAH) and Mutuality of Autonomy–Pathology (MAP)—are derived from Urist's (1977) Mutuality of Autonomy Scale. This scale is designed to assess object relations, or a person's schemas or prototypes for relationships, and is psychodynamically derived. However, research has suggested that the scale assesses both object relations and psychopathology (Bombel, Mihura, & Meyer, 2009). This is not surprising, given that an individual's schema for relationships will likely affect how he or she interacts with others, which can influence mood, personality, and the like.

MAH and MAP can be coded whenever there is a relationship between two or more objects. However, MAH and MAP are mutually exclusive codes; if one is coded, the other cannot be. If both MAH and MAP are present in a response, only MAP is coded (Meyer et al., 2011).

Mutuality of Autonomy–Health (MAH) is coded whenever the examinee verbalizes seeing two autonomous objects engaging in an activity that is reciprocal; both should be participating equally in the activity and gaining enjoyment or another benefit from it. In other words, the objects must be doing the action together and there cannot be an imbalance of power. The objects have to be equals and have to be cooperating in some way. Thus, in order to code MAH, there must be a movement determinant and there must be a COP code. If these conditions are not met, MAH cannot be coded (Meyer et al., 2011).

Because of these criteria, it can be difficult to determine when to code MAH. Meyer and colleagues provide some threshold examples for coding MAH (2011, p. 136). Examples include "two friends waving at each other" and "two men bowing toward each other. They are picking this up." Conversely, "two people waving at each other" would not be sufficient to code MAH because it is not clear that these two individuals are getting any benefit from the action; they may simply be engaging in a socially expected interaction rather than a mutually beneficial interaction. However, in the case of the two friends, it is more likely, because they are friends, that the action (waving) is reciprocal and beneficial, as they already have a positive relationship (friendship). Another threshold example is "two people having a conversation." Again, conversely, "two people talking with each other" would not be sufficient to code MAH because there is no indication that the activity is reciprocal; one person could be dominating the talking. However, in the case of a conversation, there is the suggestion that there is some reciprocity between the two parties.

Mutuality of Autonomy–Pathology (MAP) is coded whenever there is a relationship between two objects and one object is damaging the other object or preventing it from doing something. There does not need to be an imbalance to code MAP; if one object is severely damaging the other, that is generally sufficient for an MAP code. Sometimes, the destructive object is not seen on the blot; in this case, it is still permissible to code MAP. Examples of responses that should be coded MAP are "a cat that has been run over" and "two bears fighting. See, there's the blood, one's injured" (Meyer et al., 2011).

Not surprisingly, MAP is often coded with MOR. MOR was described earlier in this section.

There are times when responses meet the criteria for both MAH and MAP. For example:

Response (Card I): Two witches, casting a spell.
Examiner repeats examinee's response.
Clarification-1: Here's one witch (points to D2, right side), the other (D2, left side). These are their hats (points to D7). They are working together and casting a spell to destroy this man here piece by piece (points to D4). See, his head is already missing.
Coding: W (H),Hd Sy 2 o Ma AGC,AGM,COP,MOR,MAP PH

In this response, there is an MAH (the witches working together to cast a spell) and an MAP (destroying the man, piece by piece). When both MAH and MAP are present in a response, code only MAP (Meyer et al., 2011).

DON'T FORGET
. . . .

If a response meets the criteria for both MAH and MAP, code only MAP.

ODL: Oral Dependent Language

Oral Dependent Language (ODL) is also a psychodynamically derived variable. It is the lone variable that is coded only in the Response Phase. Any verbalizations in the Response Phase that have some sort of oral association or indicate dependency are coded for ODL. There is a separate ODL column on the code sequence sheet (see Table 9.2, later, for an example); ODL is not coded alongside the other Thematic Special Scores.

The R-PAS manual (Meyer et al., 2011) includes a table that provides examples of verbalizations in the Response Phase that warrant an ODL code. These feature responses of foods (pizza), organs used to eat foods (tongue), activities that the mouth is used for (smiling), and objects that are used with the mouth (flute). They also include verbalizations that indicate dependency and should also be coded as ODL, such as gift givers (genie), helplessness (baby birds), and good luck objects (rabbit's foot).

When coding ODL, it is important to focus on the words and not the imagery. If a person says the blot looks like a "tongue on a shoe," for example, this should still be coded for ODL because of the word "tongue." Additionally, it is not necessary to distinguish between an oral response and a dependent response. Both are coded under ODL and weighed equally in scoring.

Good or Poor Human Representation

Good human representation and poor human representation are scored by the online scoring platform and are based on other codes. There is an algorithm for coding them that can be found in the R-PAS manual for those who want to hand score. I would strongly advise against hand scoring, as there are many variables that are used to score this variable, which increases the risk of errors.

CAUTION
. . . .

For CS users transitioning to R-PAS: CP and PSV are not coded as part of R-PAS.

SCORING PLATFORM

At this point, an R-PAS protocol can be hand scored using the forms available via the R-PAS website or electronically scored via the online scoring platform, located at www.r-pas.org. Due to the number of errors possible when hand scoring, I would strongly advise against it. Instead, I strongly recommend that R-PAS users score their protocols via the online scoring platform. When using the online scoring platform, it is important not to enter any of your client's identifying information or the client's protected health information. This includes the client's name, address, email, phone number, social security number, and birth date. In fact, there is no place to add any of this information; there is space only for an identification code and the client's age, gender, and years of education. Do not use any of the client's protected health or identifying information (e.g., name, birth date, social security number, or health care ID number) as the identification code.

CONCLUSION

The thought of coding a protocol can seem intimidating, especially for a new Rorschach examiner, due to the amount of clinical judgment involved. Meyer and colleagues (2011) do an excellent job of providing organized guidelines to assist with scoring; this should serve to increase the accuracy and ease of coding. Still, it is necessary to review the manual and practice. With practice, and feedback from someone who knows the system well, it is very possible to code R-PAS protocols with a reasonable degree of accuracy.

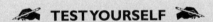

◢ TEST YOURSELF ◣

1. **What is the most active of the passive movements?**
   a. Sitting
   b. Standing
   c. Talking
   d. Dancing

2. **Your examinee sees a "house standing on a beautiful field, covered with daises." Should this response be coded Sy, Vg, both, or neither?**
   a. Sy only
   b. Vg only
   c. Sy and Vg
   d. Neither Sy nor Vg

3. **Which Special Score is coded based only on verbalizations present in the Response Phase?**

   a. ODL

   b. MAH and MAP

   c. COP

   d. AGC

4. **Your examinee provides a response that should be coded as both an MAH and an MAP. What should you code?**

   a. MAH only

   b. MAP only

   c. Both the MAH and the MAP

   d. Neither the MAH nor the MAP

5. **Which standard scores have levels assigned to them (select all that apply)?**

   a. DV

   b. DR

   c. INC

   d. FAB

   e. PEC

   f. CON

   g. MAH and MAP

   h. AGM

   i. AGC

   Answers: 1. c; 2. a; 3. a; 4. b; 5. a, b, c, d.

Eight

R-PAS INTERPRETATION

Interpretation of an R-PAS protocol, like that many other psychological tests, relies on the deviation principle; the focus is generally on characteristics that deviate from the norm. As it is impossible to know the characteristics of everyone, we rely on a normative group to provide us with that norm. The normative group should be representative of the population being assessed; this is why many normative samples are stratified in order to match various demographics of the target population, including gender, racial background, ethnicity, and educational level, to name a few.

The normative sample for R-PAS uses a subset of the international normative data collected by various examiners in different countries (Meyer et al., 2007, 2011). A subset of 640 protocols from the international norms was used to calculate the majority of the R-PAS norms. These 640 protocols were collected using CS administration procedures; however, the protocols were then modeled to look like protocols administered using R-PAS administration procedures.

Multiple countries are represented in the normative sample for R-PAS, with the United States being the most heavily represented (about 21% of the protocols). The European countries represented are Belgium, Denmark, Finland, France, Greece, Italy, Portugal, and Romania. Two South American countries are represented: Argentina and Brazil. Finally, Israel is represented. There are no African or Asian countries in the normative sample. Additionally, Australia is not represented.

The R-PAS normative sample includes only adults. The average age of the normative sample was 37.3 (SD = 13.4). The members of the normative sample had an average of 13.3 years of education (SD = 3.6), which is equivalent to just over a year of college. The sample was mostly female (55.3%) and white (66.8%, with 19.4% being other/multiracial, 8.7% Hispanic/Latino, 2.6% Asian, and 2.6% black). The majority of the sample members were married or with a partner (53.9%, with 35.5% being single, 6.8% divorced, 2.3% widowed, and 1.6% separated).

Children were not represented in the original R-PAS norms. However, there are now transitional child and adolescent norms available (Meyer, Viglione, & Giromini, 2016). The sample for these norms was derived using protocols from the United States (137), Brazil (197), and Italy (11). The sample was predominately female (51.7%, and 45.1% male) and included individuals ranging in age from 6 to 17.

INTERPRETATION

Interpretation of an R-PAS variable follows the deviation principle. In general, interpretation using the deviation principle focuses on scores that deviate from the mean. Scores that deviate from the mean are seen as unusual. However, it is up to the examiner to determine what clinical impact, if any, these unusual scores have.

Still, over-applying the deviation principle can result in an examiner over-focusing on the atypical parts of the protocol and disregarding the "normal" parts of the protocol. Sometimes what is not there is just as important as what is. For example, if you are evaluating someone who has been diagnosed with PTSD, yet the person's protocol does not show any evidence of hypervigilance, this is an odd finding that is inconsistent with what would be expected, given the previous diagnosis. In this case, a score in the typical range of functioning becomes an important point. This is only one example of why it is important to focus not only on what is atypical about the protocol but also on what is typical.

Unlike the CS, R-PAS converts the raw scores into standard scores. This makes interpretation more straightforward, as all scores have the same mean (100) and standard deviation (15). Additionally, the online scoring platform uses color coding for the variables on the scored protocol in the Summary Scores and Profiles section. Scores that are between 90 and 110 are identified with a green dot. Scores between 80 and 89 and between 111 and 120 are identified with a yellow dot. Scores between 70 and 79 and between 121 and 130 have red dots. Any score below 70 or above 130 (>2 SD from the mean) has a black dot.

The scored R-PAS protocol is divided into four parts, as shown in Rapid Reference 8.1.

The first part, the Code Sequence, contains the coded responses. The next part, Protocol Level Counts and Calculations, contains information about the individual variables on R-PAS, including the ones calculated from other variables (e.g., CritCont%). The third part contains the Summary Scores and Profiles. These are the primary sources for the interpretation and are the focus of the majority of this chapter. The final part contains the EII-3 and Composite

≡ Rapid Reference 8.1

The Parts of a Scored R-PAS Protocol

Name	What It Contains
Code Sequence	Coded responses
Protocol Level Counts and Calculations	Raw data on each variable
Summary Scores and Profiles	Standard score and percentile ranks for the recommended interpreted variables.
EII-3 and Composite Calculations	Calculation of EII-3 and composite scores
Appendix	Standard scores and percentile ranks for all variables.

Source: Based on information from Meyer et al., 2011.

Calculations; this is where all the information regarding the calculation of the composite scores can be found. The scored protocol also contains an appendix, which includes summary scores for all the variables. An example of an R-PAS Code Sequence can be found in the Appendix (Table A.25). The Protocol Level Counts and Calculations for this example are also in the Appendix (Figure A.4), as are the two pages of the Summary Score and Profiles (Figures A.5 and A.6).

Interpretation of R-PAS focuses on the two Summary Scores and Profiles pages, referred to as Page 1 and Page 2. The Page 1 variables are the primary variables; the Page 2 variables are secondary. Interpretation should proceed down Page 1 and then down Page 2, going in the order of the variables. Meyer and colleagues (2011) recommend that the variables on Page 1 of the Summary Scores and Profiles should be interpreted when they are less than about 90 or greater than about 110 (25th and 75th percentiles, respectively). The variables on Page 2 should be interpreted when they are below about 85 or above about 115 (16th and 84th percentiles, respectively). These scores represent a deviation of one standard deviation from the mean. Of course, these are not strict cut points; examiners should use their clinical judgment when determining whether to interpret a variable. It is also important to remember that scores in the average range (between 90 and 110) can provide information as well; it is important not to ignore those scores.

R-PAS also allows the examiner to adjust the protocol for complexity. Complexity appears to be related to the amount of psychological activity, both positive and negative, the examinee is engaging in (Meyer et al., 2011). Interpretation of Complexity is not straightforward because elevations (in either direction) can be due to a combination of factors that are affected by both the individual characteristics and the situational demands of the examinee. In other words, it can be hard to tease apart what part of an elevated Complexity score is due to personal characteristics, what part is due to the testing situation, and what part is due to an interaction between the two.

Personal characteristics that are thought to influence the Complexity score include intelligence, being curious, being open to new experiences, and psychological resources (Meyer et al., 2011). Thus, those with higher levels of intelligence should have higher Complexity scores and those who have fewer cognitive resources should have lower Complexity scores. Other individual characteristics that are associated with lower Complexity scores include severe anxiety that is associated with rigid thinking and concreteness, depression, and the numbing associated with trauma. Thus, it is conceivable that lower Complexity scores could be associated with severe mental illness, including the cognitive decline that can be associated with schizophrenia.

Situational factors can also influence Complexity scores. Because Complexity scores are calculated, at least in part, on the basis of the multiple contents and determinants in a response, high Complexity scores are thought to be associated with someone who is trying to impress the examiner or exaggerate psychological distress (Meyer et al., 2011). Low Complexity scores, in contrast, have been associated with defensiveness and low levels of motivation. In other words, examinees who are not engaged in the test, presumably, would provide fewer responses and the responses they provide would tend to be simplistic. This would result in a lower Complexity score.

DON'T FORGET

The Complexity score is thought to be influenced by both situational and personal factors. Both of these need to be taken into account with interpretation.

In deciding whether to adjust a variable due to Complexity, the examiner should consider the influence of both personal and situational factors on the results. For example, on the one hand, if the examinee has a higher Complexity score than expected and is being tested as part of an evaluation regarding his or her mental status at the time of a criminal offense (or regarding an insanity plea), then there is some indication that an increased Complexity score could be due to the examinee attempting to exaggerate psychological distress. On the other hand, if the examinee was participating in a court-ordered evaluation and did not seemed to be engaged, a lower Complexity score may be related to the examinee's lack of engagement in the testing. Meyer and colleagues (2011) recommended that the examiner consider adjusting for Complexity only when the scores are more than one standard deviation from the mean (>115 or < 85). Ultimately, the decision on whether to adjust for Complexity lies with the examiner.

DON'T FORGET

Variables on Page 1 should be considered atypical when they are below about 90 or above about 110.

The following is a brief summary of the variables, organized by page and by domain. Each domain discussion also contains a Rapid Reference box with the variable abbreviations, their full names, how they are calculated, and what they are thought to measure.

PAGE 1 VARIABLES

Administration Behaviors and Observations

Interpretation begins with an evaluation of the Administration Behaviors and Observations. This section has only three variables: Prompts (Pr), Pulls (Pu), and Card Turns (CT). These are behaviors that the examinee engaged in during testing (Meyer et al., 2011). Rapid Reference 8.2 describes these variables and their interpretation. Figure A.5, in the Appendix, contains an example of Page 1 of the R-PAS Summary Scores and Profiles.

The first two variables, Pr and Pu, assess to what extent the examinee "followed the rules" of the test. These two variables are generally only interpreted when high, because when an examinee "followed the rules" and did not require the examiner to prompt or pull, her scores will be in (or very close to) the average range. Having a score in the average range simply means that the examinee followed the rules. However, if the score is higher than expected (e.g., above about 110), then it suggests that the examinee was not following the rules set forth in the introduction to the Response Phase. There are a number of possible reasons

≡ Rapid Reference 8.2

Administration Behaviors and Observations: How the Variables Are Calculated and What They Assess

Variable	Name	How It Is Calculated	What It Assesses
Pr	Prompt	The number of times the examiner had to prompt.	Whether the examinee is following the rules of the test; her engagement with testing.
Pu	Pull	The number of times the examiner had to pull.	Whether the examinee is following the rules of the test.
CT	Card Turn	The number of responses in which the examinee turned the card.	Examinee's curiosity, flexibility, oppositionality; avoidance of something the examinee finds disturbing.

Source: Based on information from Meyer et al., 2011.

for this, including limited cognitive ability (Pr), being uncooperative (Pr), and trying to please the examiner (Pu) (Meyer et al., 2011).

Unlike Pr and Pu, the final variable in this section—CT—is not a violation of the rules of the test; examinees are never told they cannot turn the card. Consequently, the interpretation of CT is somewhat different. Elevated scores on CT are thought to be associated with curiosity and flexibility. However, they have also been associated with anxiety and hostility. As with all variables, the exact interpretation will depend as well on other factors, including situational factors and the characteristics of the examinee.

Engagement and Cognitive Processing

The Engagement and Cognitive Processing domain on Page 1 of the Summary and Scores assesses the examinee's engagement in the testing, including motivation, and her psychological resources (Meyer et al., 2011). This domain addresses ten variables. These variables, along with how they are calculated and an overview of their interpretation, can be found in Rapid Reference 8.3.

≡ Rapid Reference 8.3

Engagement and Processing, Page 1:
How the Variables Are Calculated and What They Assess

Variable	Name	How It Is Calculated	What It Assesses
Complexity	Complexity	A combination of factors, including object qualities, location codes, space codes, the number of content codes, and the number of determinants.	Examinee's effort and resources applied during testing.
R	Responses	The number of responses the examinee provided during testing.	Examinee's engagement with testing, cognitive flexibility.
F%	Form%	The number of responses with only an F determinant divided by the total number of responses multiplied by 100.	Examinee's ability to identify and interact with different aspects of her world, including both simple features and more complex ones.
Blend	Blends	The number of responses that have blends (multiple determinants).	Examinee's ability to identify and interact with multiple, different aspects of her world.
Sy	Synthesis	The number of responses that have an object quality of Sy or Sy, Vg.	Examinee's complex thinking patterns. Her ability to integrate different concepts at the same time.
MC	Human Movement and Weighted Sum of Color	The sum of the number of M determinants and WSumC (1.5C + CF + .5FC).	Examinee's psychological resources.
MC – PPD	Human Movement and Weighted Sum of Color – Potentially Problematic Determinants	The value for MC minus the sum of the number of FM, m, Y, T, V, and C' determinants [MC – (FM + m + Y + T V + C')].	Examinee's potential to be able to cope with current stressors.

(continued)

(continued)

Variable	Name	How It Is Calculated	What It Assesses
M	Human Movement	The number of human movement determinants (Ma + Mp + Ma-p).	Examinee's cognitive resources, including intelligence.
M / MC	M proportion	The value for M divided by value for MC, multiplied by 100.	Whether thought or emotion affects the examinee's decisions more.
(CF + C) / SumC	CFC proportion	The sum of the number of CF and C determinants divided by the total number of color determinants, multiplied by 100.	How much emotional control the examinee has.

Source: Based on information from Meyer et al., 2011.

Complexity

The Complexity variable was described in some detail earlier in this chapter. In general, the Complexity variable is associated with the effort and the resources the examinee applied to the testing situation. As such, it is associated with both individual (e.g., cognitive resources) and situational (e.g., poor rapport with examiner) factors. The interpretation of high scores can be both positive and negative. For example, high scores on this variable have been associated with intelligence and high levels of education, as individuals with high levels of intelligence and education tend to have more complex thinking patterns (Meyer et al., 2011). However, high Complexity scores can also be associated with psychological disturbance, as trauma, depression, and thought disorders can all cause more complex thinking than is typical for the examinee. High Complexity scores can also be associated with an exaggeration of psychological distress. Of course, high Complexity scores can also result from a combination of these factors (e.g., someone with a high level of cognitive resources who recently experienced a trauma). In order to differentiate between these hypotheses, the examiner should evaluate the client's background history, the examiner's own testing observations, and the results of other tests administered as part of the evaluation.

Low Complexity scores, conversely, are associated with lower levels of cognitive resources, such as would be seen in individuals experiencing a cognitive decline secondary to schizophrenia or those with a moderate to severe traumatic brain injury. An examinee who is highly defensive, whether due to individual factors (e.g., paranoia) or to situational factors (e.g., a child custody evaluation), can also have low scores on Complexity. Low scores can also represent a disengagement from the environment, such as could happen with severe trauma, anxiety, and depression. In other words, both high Complexity scores and low Complexity scores can be associated with psychological distress (Meyer et al., 2011).

R: Number of Responses

R, or the number of responses, is associated with the examinee's motivation in testing and her ability to follow the "rules" of testing that were introduced during the Response Phase (e.g., the request to give 2 or 3 responses to each card). Individuals who have higher levels of cognitive flexibility and can see multiple aspects of a situation, or see a situation in different ways, will tend to have higher scores on R than will individuals who have lower levels of flexibility. High scores can also occur due to the examinee not following the guidelines and providing more than the requested number of responses per card. When this is the case, it is possible that the examinee was trying to overachieve or had difficulty inhibiting her impulses.

Low R scores could indicate that the examinee was not engaged in testing, especially if the value for Pr is high. It also could suggest that the examinee was defensive during the testing or that she is inflexible and has difficulty seeing things from multiple perspectives. It is important to remember that defensiveness can be an individual trait of the examinee and it can also be influenced by the situation.

F%: Form%

Form% (F%) is associated with how the person views the world. Specifically, people with high F% have a tendency to focus on the more simplistic, concrete aspects of the world, including their environment and other people (Meyer et al., 2011). As a result, they are at risk of missing the more complex and nuanced features of their environment and of others. This disengagement could be conscious or unconscious; the examinee may not be aware of the degree to which she is simplifying the environment.

Examinees with a low F% have a tendency to see the world in a complex way. In general, this is a positive finding. However, this can also be a liability, as the examinee can get "caught up" in all of the subtleties and miss the big picture. Additionally, it is possible that the examinee will spend her energy focusing on the subtleties of the environment rather than other things, such as herself. This can take an immense amount of psychological resources; if the examinee has a high amount of resources, as evidenced by an above-average MC score, then this focus on the complexity of the world may not be so problematic, because the examinee has the psychological resources to compensate.

Blends

Like F%, blends are related to the examinee's ability to identify complexities in the environment. Blends are also one of the factors contributing to the Complexity score (Meyer et al., 2011).

Examinees with a high blends score tend to focus on various aspects of a situation at the same time. Depending on other characteristics of the examinee, such as psychological resources and the presence of psychopathology, this could be a positive finding or a negative finding. It is possible to be "too complex" and to focus too much on subtleties. When this happens, the examinee is at risk of missing the big picture. The adage "can't see the forest for the trees" applies here. The examinees with very high blends are tree people; they see the trees but miss that when all the trees are together, they make a forest.

Low scores on blends, in contrast, are associated with simplistic processing and a tendency to miss detail. These individuals are forest people. They see the forest but not any of the trees that make it up.

Sy: Synthesis

Synthesis (Sy) responses are associated with complex processing, specifically the ability to integrate different concepts (Meyer et al., 2011). This differs from seeing blends and having a low F% because those scores are more related to the ability to see multiple features of the environment. Sy is the ability of the examinee to bring it all together. High scores are associated with the ability to integrate concepts and relate them to one another. Low scores are associated with simple, more straightforward processing. The latter is not necessarily a negative finding, depending on the examinee's environment and the demands on her.

MC: Psychological Resources

MC is a measure of the person's psychological resources, which are the reserves the person has to cope with stressors in the environment, including the ability to identify feelings and her cognitive faculties (Exner, 2003; Meyer et al., 2011). In general, someone with more psychological resources will be better able to cope with stressful situations than someone with fewer resources will. Still, there are exceptions to this, as it depends on how these resources are being used. Having the resources does not mean they are being used in an adaptive way. Additionally, having a low level of resources is not necessarily a negative finding; if the examinee is in an environment where there are few stressors and the available resources are being used appropriately, then it is likely the examinee can function adequately.

MC – PPD: Coping Effectiveness

MC – PPD is a measure of coping effectiveness. It is a measure of the examinee's psychological resources that remain available after accounting for the various stressors that the examinee is likely experiencing, including stress and depression (Meyer et al., 2011). When MC – PPD is high, it suggests that the examinee has available psychological resources to cope with everyday life. Conversely, when it is low, it suggests that the examinee lacks the resources to cope with everyday life, so these individuals may be more affected by stress than those with a higher level of resources.

M: Human Movement

Human Movement (M) is related to thinking that is under the examinee's control. Individuals with high M scores tend to be better able to understand the different factors (individual and situational) that affect behavior (Meyer et al., 2011).

M Proportion

This variable provides information regarding the processes the examinee tends to use to make decisions and cope with stress (Meyer et al., 2011). Individuals with a high score for the M Proportion have more M determinants than C determinants on their protocol. M determinants relate to thinking while C determinants relate to emotions. Consequently, individuals with a high M Proportion tend to be dominated by thinking. These examinees tend to think through their options before making a decision, with emotions playing less of a role in that process. On the CS, this is referred to as an introversive style.

Examinees with a low score on the M Proportion have more C determinants than M determinants. C determinants are related to emotions; consequently, these examinees tend to make decisions and cope with stress by relying on intuition and their emotions. On the CS, this is referred to as an extratensive style.

Examinees with an average score (between 90 and 110) use both thinking, or logic, and emotions to cope with stressors and make decisions.

CFC Proportion: Color Dominance Proportion

The Color Dominance Proportion (CFC Proportion) provides hypotheses regarding the amount of control the examinee has over her emotions (Meyer et al., 2011). In general, the less form present in a color determinant, the less control the examinee has over her emotions. High scores on this variable are associated with less restrained emotional expression. Depending on the examinee's environment and other characteristics, this may not be a liability. However, when this variable is very high, it indicates that the examinee's emotional reactions may be dramatic.

Low scores on the Color Dominance Proportion are associated with emotional control. In general, this is a positive finding, as it suggests that the examinee's emotional expressions are appropriately modulated. However, very low scores suggest that the examinee may be inhibiting almost all emotional expression.

Perception and Thinking

The Perception and Thinking domain on Page 1 assesses problems in thinking (Meyer et al., 2011). Some of the variables in this section assess for reality testing, or whether the examinee perceives the world accurately. There are eight variables in this section. These variables, along with how they are calculated and an overview of their interpretation, can be found in Rapid Reference 8.4.

≋ Rapid Reference 8.4

Perception and Thinking, Page 1: How the Variables Are Calculated and What They Assess

Variable	Name	How It Is Calculated	What It Assesses
EII-3	Ego Impairment Index–3	A combination of factors, including FQ–, WSumCog, CritCont%, M–, GHR, PHR, and R.	Thinking disturbance and how severe the psychopathology (if present) is.
TP-Comp	Thought and Perception Composite	A combination of factors, including WD–%, FQ–%, FAB2, WSumCog, M–, and R.	Reality testing; disorganized thinking.
WSumCog	Weighted Sum of the Six Cognitive Codes	$DV1 + 2 \times DV2 + 2 \times INC1 = 4 \times INC2 + 3 \times DR1 + 6 \times DR2 + 4 \times FAB1 + 7 \times FAB2 + 5 \times PEC + 7 \times CON.$	Disordered and disturbing thinking.
SevCog	Severe Cognitive Codes	All level 2 cognitive codes, CON, and PEC $(DV2 + DR2 + INC2 + FAB2 + PEC + CON).$	Evidence of severe problems with thinking.

Variable	Name	How It Is Calculated	What It Assesses
FQ–%	FQ–%	The number of responses with FQ–, divided by R, multiplied by 100.	Distortions of reality; not perceiving the world as others do.
WD–%	WD–%	The number of responses with a W or D location code with FQ–, divided by the number of responses with a W or D location code, multiplied by 100.	Distortions of reality are present, even in conventional or common situations.
FQo%	FQo%	The number of responses with FQo, divided by R, multiplied by 100.	Seeing the world in the ways that others do.
P	Popular	The number of popular responses that the examinee provided.	Seeing the world in the ways others do, but also in highly conventional ways.

Source: Based on information from Exner, 2000, 2003; Meyer et al., 2011; Weiner, 2003.

EII-3: Ego Impairment Index–3

The Ego Impairment Index–3 (EII-3) is derived from variables that have historically been associated with thinking disturbance, including FQ– and WSumCog. Research has indicated that scores on an earlier iteration of the EII are associated with psychiatric severity (Diener, Hilsenroth, Shaffer, & Sexton, 2011). Thus, high scores on the EII-3 are indicative of thinking disturbance and severe psychopathology. Low scores may indicate the absence of severe psychopathology, or good mental health (Meyer et al., 2011).

TP-Comp: Thought and Perception Composite

The Thought and Perception Composite (TP-Comp) is made up of variables associated with thinking disturbance, including some of the same variables used in the calculation of EII-3. While the two composite scores overlap, there are some differences. Specifically, EII-3 includes the human representation responses and critical contents while TP-Comp does not (Meyer et al., 2011).

High scores on TP-Comp are associated with thought disturbance and difficulties with reality testing (Meyer et al., 2011). Although these are typically associated with schizophrenia, there can be other factors that result in reality testing difficulties, including other types of severe mental illness, trauma, or substance abuse. High scores may also be associated with exaggeration of psychopathology. Low scores can be indicative of good mental health.

DON'T FORGET

The TP-Comp and EII-3 are calculated using some of the same variables. If one is elevated but the other is not, consider the makeup of each variable to determine why the elevation occurred.

WSumCog: Weighted Sum of the Six Cognitive Codes

The weighted sum of the six cognitive codes (WSumCog) is a combination of the six Cognitive Special Scores (DV, DR, INC, FAB, PEC, CON), weighted according to their severity. It is a measure of difficulties with thinking (Exner, 2003; Meyer et al., 2011). On the extreme end, high scores can be indicative of a thought disturbance. Lower elevations are typically associated with more minor thinking difficulties. It is important to review the scores that contributed to an elevated WSumCog to gather additional information about the severity of the thinking problems. It is possible to elevate this variable through frequent, minor verbal goofs. However, it is also possible to elevate through evidence of more severe thinking difficulties. This is why it is important to rely not only on the score but also on the variables that went into the score. Rapid Reference 8.5 provides possible interpretations of each of the six Cognitive Special Scores.

SevCog: Severe Cognitive Codes

SevCog (Severe Cognitive Codes), like WSumC, is a measure of disordered thinking. However, this variable focuses on only the severe cognitive codes, namely, the level 2 codes and also PEC and CON. As these codes are evidence of more severe difficulties in thinking, elevations on this variable are frequently associated with severe psychopathology (Meyer et al., 2011).

On most profiles of individuals without thinking disturbance, the standard score for SevCog should be below 100 (Meyer et al., 2011). However, it is possible for someone without severe psychopathology to elevate this variable.

≋ Rapid Reference 8.5

. . . .

Interpretation of the Individual Cognitive Special Scores

Variable	Possible Interpretations
DV1	Examinee has mild difficulties with verbal expression. Examinee may have difficulties with language (e.g., being tested in a nondominant language, expressive language disorder). Unlikely to cause significant difficulties with communication.
DV2	Examinee has moderate to severe difficulties with verbal expression. Examinee may have difficulties with language (e.g., being tested in a nondominant language, expressive language disorder). Likely to cause difficulties with communication.
DR1	Examinee may have a tendency to get slightly off topic in conversations. Off topic speech is not bizarre and is likely to be at least somewhat related to the topic being addressed. This makes it fairly easy to redirect the examinee to the original topic. Unlikely to cause difficulties with communication.
DR2	Examinee has a tendency to get very off topic in conversations. Diversion may be bizarre or incomprehensible. Difficult to redirect examinee back because there is no logical way to connect the diversion back to the original topic. Likely interferes with communication.
INC1	Examinee uses concrete reasoning. May indicate creativity. Not bizarre.
INC2	Examinee uses bizarre reasoning and combinations of stimuli.
FAB1	May indicate creativity. Not bizarre.
FAB2	Examinee uses bizarre combinations. Examinee displays illogical thought.
PEC	Examinee uses concrete reasoning. Examinee displays illogical thought. May be evidence of thinking disturbance.
CON	Suggestive of severe thought disturbance. Examinee may have difficulty separating fantasy from reality.

Source: Based on information from Exner, 2003; Meyer et al., 2011; Weiner, 2003.

Specifically, someone who tends to be very concrete could elevate SevCog due to a high number of PECs in the record. Additionally, someone who has difficulty with language could elevate this due to having multiple DV2s in the record. Thus, when interpreting this variable, it is important to examine why this variable was elevated.

CAUTION

When interpreting WSumCog and SevCog, it is important to review the variables that are used in their calculations (the Cognitive Special Scores) to determine exactly why the variables were elevated. There is a difference between someone who has elevated scores owing to a large number of DV1 and DV2 codes and someone who has elevated scores owing to having FAB2 and CON codes in his record.

FQ–: Form Quality Minus

Form Quality Minus (FQ–) codes indicate that the examinee was not following the contours of the blot when providing his response. This is interpreted to be a misinterpretation or a distortion of reality. Even in healthy individuals, there can be instances of distortion, thus having a few FQ– codes in a record is not a large concern. Having only a few will typically yield a low FQ–% score (Meyer et al., 2011). However, when the value for the variable goes above 100, that is an indication that the examinee is distorting reality more often than is typical. The main concern with this is that the examinee is more prone to perceiving the environment, others, and the like inaccurately, and this can lead to poor decisions and inappropriate behavior.

WD–%: Whole and Common Detail with FQ–

To reiterate, FQ– codes indicate that the examinee was not following the contours of the blot when providing his response. The W and the D location codes represent areas that are usually easily and commonly seen by others. An elevated WD–% indicates that even in common situations, the examinee is more prone than others to misperceive the environment, people, and so forth. High scores on this variable are suggestive of psychopathology, as these individuals' misperceptions of reality are pervasive and occur even in common situations (Meyer et al., 2011).

WD–% and FQ–% can be interpreted together. Some possible interpretations are given in Rapid Reference 8.6.

⚋ Rapid Reference 8.6

. . . .

Interpretation of WD–% and FQ–%

	WD–% High	WD–% Average or Lower
FQ–% High	Evidence that the examinee has severe, pervasive difficulty with seeing the world accurately.	The examinee is more likely than others to misperceive a situation when presented with a less common, more ambiguous situation.
FQ–% Average or Lower	This combination is unlikely to occur. If this happens, the examinee must have provided a large number of Dd responses. This combination indicates that when presented with an uncommon, ambiguous situation, the examinee likely perceives the situation accurately, but will tend to misperceive the situation when it is a common, less ambiguous situation.	The examinee does not misperceive situations more often than is typical.

Source: Based on information from Exner, 2003; Meyer et al., 2011; Weiner, 2003.

FQo%: Ordinary Form Quality Percentage

Ordinary Form Quality (FQo) is coded when the examinee's response is consistent with the contours of the blot and the examinee reports an object that has been commonly seen in that area. This suggests that the individual is perceiving the world as others do, which increases the likelihood that he will engage in behaviors that are appropriate, given the situation. In other words, because the examinee is perceiving the world accurately, his assessment and interpretation of a situation is likely to be accurate and not distorted. Thus, the behaviors that result from his judgments are likely to be seen by others as being reality based and consistent with social expectations (Meyer et al., 2011).

Low scores on the Ordinary Form Quality Percentage (FQo%) indicate that the examinee is not perceiving the world the same way that others do. However, this may not be indicative of psychopathology. It is possible to view the world differently than others do, but still do so in a socially acceptable way. There is a difference between an examinee who perceives the world in an unrealistic, possibly psychotic way and may have severe disturbance (FQ–%) and an examinee who tends to make unconventional but still socially acceptable decisions (FQu%).

P: Popular

Popular (P) responses were present on about one third of the protocols in a large sample of Rorschach protocols examined by Exner (2003). When an examinee provides a popular response, it indicates that the examinee perceived the blot the same way many others did: that is, in a highly conventional way. When scores on this variable are higher than expected, it indicates that the examinee is making a huge effort to see the world the same way others do (Meyer et al., 2011). Depending on other characteristics, this could be a positive finding. However, this could also be indicative of the examinee making an effort to hide something about himself by trying hard to fit in with social expectations. When this happens, the examinee may be sacrificing individuality for the sake of fitting in with others.

Low scores are indicative that the individual did not perceive the blots in a highly conventional way. Again, this finding may be positive or negative; an examinee may have a low score on this variable due to his being individualistic. Another possibility is that the examinee may not be perceiving situations accurately.

Stress and Distress

The Stress and Distress domain on Page 1, which includes the experience of stress (Meyer et al., 2011), has five variables. These variables, along with how they are calculated and an overview of interpretation, can be found in Rapid Reference 8.7.

YTVC': Sum of Shading and Achromatic Color

Historically, the shading and achromatic color variables have been associated with stress and distress, and the sum of shading and achromatic color (YTVC') assesses such stress and distress (Exner, 2003; Meyer et al., 2011). Specifically, Y is associated with feeling helpless due to stressors, C' is associated with the experience of negative emotions that the examinee finds irritating, T is related to a desire for emotional closeness with others, and V is related to self-deprecating behaviors. The presence of a few of these variables in a protocol is typical; it would be practically impossible for an examinee to have no evidence of stress in her life. However, as the score for this variable increases, it suggests that the examinee is attending to these nuances in the environment. This is not necessarily a negative finding, as it could indicate that the examinee is aware of these stressors and is appropriately coping with them. Still, attending to these areas could cause distress.

≡ Rapid Reference 8.7

· ·

Stress and Distress, Page 1: How the Variables Are Calculated and What They Assess

Variable	Name	How It Is Calculated	What It Assesses
YTVC'	Sum of Shading and Achromatic Color	The total number of shading and achromatic color determinants $(Y+T+V+C')$.	Attraction to nuances and inconsistencies in the environment, especially those related to stress and distress.
m	Inanimate Object Movement	The total number of inanimate object movement determinants.	Stress-related evidence; usually associated with stress manifesting as unwanted or uncontrolled peripheral thoughts.
Y	Diffuse Shading	The total number of diffuse shading determinants.	Stress-related evidence; usually associated with feeling nervous or helpless.
MOR	Morbid Content	The total number of MOR codes.	Pessimism; seeing self as damaged; aggressive tendencies.
SC-Comp	Suicide Concern Composite	A combination of variables, includes V, FD, CBlends, r, pairs, MOR, Complexity, space responses, MC − PPD, CF + C Proportion, FQo%, P, H.	Suicide risk.

Source: Based on information from Choca, 2013; Exner, 2003; Meyer et al., 2011; Mihura et al., 2013; Weiner, 2003.

m: Inanimate Object Movement

Inanimate Object Movement (m) is associated with stress. Specifically, the presence of m determinants indicates that the stress the examinee is experiencing is associated with unwanted peripheral thoughts that are interfering with her ability to concentrate (Meyer et al., 2011). As with other variables, the presence of some of these determinants is considered to be typical; however, as the score for this variable becomes elevated, it is strong evidence to suggest that stress the examinee is experiencing is manifesting in unwanted peripheral thoughts that can interfere with functioning.

Y: Diffuse Shading

Diffuse Shading (Y) is also associated with stress. While m determinants are associated with the cognitive impact of stress, Y determinants are associated with the emotional impact of distress, namely, feeling distressed and helpless. As the score for this variable becomes more and more elevated, it indicates that the examinee is experiencing stress that is resulting in distress or feelings of helplessness (Meyer et al., 2011).

MOR: Morbid Content

Morbid Content (MOR) is typically associated with pessimism and viewing the self as damaged (Meyer et al., 2011).

SC-Comp: Suicide Concern Composite

The Suicide Concern Composite (SC-Comp) is associated with a risk of suicide. Elevations on this scale have been associated only with lethal attempts; there is no indication in the literature that elevations on this composite variable, or on its precursor (S-CON in the CS), are associated with suicidal gestures or self-mutilation (Fowler et al., 2001).

Self and Other Representation

The variables in the Self and Other Representation domain on Page 1 relate to how the examinee views and understands himself, others, and relationships (Meyer et al., 2011). There are nine variables in this category. The variables, along with how they are calculated and an overview of interpretation, can be found in Rapid Reference 8.8.

ODL: Oral Dependent Language

The percentage of Oral Dependent Language (ODL%) is a measure of dependency, including dependent attitudes and dependent behaviors. Research supports its use as a measure of dependency (e.g., Bornstein & O'Neill, 1997; Fowler, Brunnschweiler, Swales, & Brock, 2005). Individuals with high scores on this variable may have high dependency needs. This can affect many areas of functioning, including interpersonal functioning, as they may rely heavily on others.

SR: Space Reversal

Space Reversal (SR) is thought to be a measure of oppositionality. However, the research on this is somewhat mixed (Bandura, 1954a, 1954b; Fonda, 1951; Frank, 1993; Mihura et al., 2013). Theoretically, the interpretation makes sense,

≡ *Rapid Reference 8.8*

Self and Other Representation, Page 1:
How the Variables Are Calculated and What They Assess

Variable	Name	How It Is Calculated	What It Assesses
ODL%	Oral Dependent Language	The number of responses with an ODL code divided by the total number of responses (ODL / R).	Dependency.
SR	Space Reversal	The number of SR codes on the protocol.	Oppositionality, independence.
MAP / MAHP	MAP Proportion	The number of responses with an MAP code divided by the number of responses with an MAH or an MAP code [MAP / (MAH + MAP)].	Whether a person's schema for relationships is healthy or unhealthy.
PHR / GPHR	PHR Proportion	The number of responses with a PHR code divided by the number of responses with a PHR or a GHR code [PHR / (PHR + GHR)].	How well a person understands himself, others, and relationships.
M–	M with FQ–	The number of M determinants with FQ–.	Distorted views of others.
AGC	Aggressive Content	The number of responses with AGC codes.	Aggressive concerns or focus.
H	Whole Human	The number of responses with an H content code.	Ability to see others as whole people, with strengths and weaknesses.
COP	Cooperative Movement	The number of responses with a COP code.	Proneness to see relationships as positive, cooperative, or supportive.
MAH	Mutuality of Autonomy– Health	The number of responses with an MAH code.	Existence of potential for mature, healthy relationships.

Source: Based on information from Choca, 2013; Exner, 2003; Meyer et al., 2011; Mihura et al., 2013; Weiner, 2003.

as the SR represents a reversal of the figure and the ground, which could be linked with oppositionality.

MAP / (MAH + MAP): MAP Proportion

The MAP Proportion [MAP / (MAH + MAP)] is a measure of whether the examinee's schema, or his mental representation, for relationships is healthy or unhealthy. This variable was derived from Urist's Mutuality of Autonomy Scale (Urist, 1977), which has some empirical support in the literature (Graceffo, Mihura, & Meyer, 2014). When the score for this variable is high, it suggests that the examinee's schema for relationships is unhealthy; the examinee may be prone to expect relationships to be negative, damaged, or unequal. When the score for this variable is low, then the opposite should be true: the examinee may be prone to expect relationships to be balanced and healthy. Having a low score does not necessarily mean that the examinee's relationships are healthy, just as having a high score does not mean that the examinee's relationships are unhealthy. Instead, these scores relate to the mental representation of relationships; it is possible to have a positive relationship schema yet participate in a negative, unbalanced relationship. Having a positive relationship schema simply means that the examinee may be more likely to expect balanced, reciprocal relationships; it does not mean that he has them.

PHR / (PHR + GHR): PHR Proportion

The PHR Proportion [PHR / (PHR + GHR)] is a measure of how well the examinee understands himself, others, and relationships (Meyer et al., 2011). On the one hand, high scores indicate that the examinee does not understand himself and others well, which can result in difficulties with interpersonal relationships. Low scores, on the other hand, are indicative of a good understanding of self, others, and relationships. They suggest that the examinee has the skills necessary to maintain good, reality-based relationships; however, this does not mean that he is using those skills.

M–: M Determinants with FQ–

The number of M determinants with FQ– (M–) is empirically supported as a measure of having a distorted view of people (Mihura et al., 2013). This can cause difficulty with relationships. High scores are suggestive that the examinee has a distorted view of others; it is important to remember that this could be indicative of psychosis, but it also could be related to trauma, abuse, anxiety, or depression.

AGC: Aggressive Content

Aggressive Content (AGC) is a measure of aggression in the examinee. There is strong evidence in the literature for the relationship of this variable with aggression (e.g., Baity & Hilsenroth, 2002). Aggression can take many forms, ranging from physical acting out to competitiveness, so high scores on this variable could be associated with someone who is competitive and not necessarily physically aggressive, such as a person who is a competitive athlete.

H: Whole Human Content Codes

The number of Whole Human content codes (H) is related to the ability to see the self and others as psychologically complete people rather than as parts (Choca, 2013; Exner, 2003; Meyer et al., 2011; Mihura et al., 2013). High scores on this variable indicate that the examinee is able to see himself and others for who they are, to integrate the positive and the negative aspects of a person together into a whole. Examinees with high scores are unlikely to see others as only a part of the whole. For example, they recognize that the barista who makes their latte in the morning is more than a barista; she has other interests besides coffee and a life beyond the coffee shop. Low scores on this variable imply that the examinee has trouble seeing others, or perhaps even himself, as whole people. Rather, he tends to understand people in only one context, such as their employment. He will tend to understand someone as being only one part, rather than as a sum of his or her parts.

An excellent example of an examinee with a low score on H is someone who categorizes people as being either "good" or "bad." This person is unable to see that "good" people can do "bad" things, thus when someone who was on his "good" list does something "bad," that person is moved from the "good" list to the "bad" list. There is no understanding that someone who is generally a good person can engage in "bad" behavior.

COP: Cooperative Movement

Cooperative Movement (COP) is coded when the examinee perceives a positive interaction occurring on the blot. This variable is associated with perceiving interactions as being positive; there is strong empirical support for this assertion (e.g., Del Giudice & Brabender, 2012; Mihura et al., 2013). High scores are associated with a tendency to perceive interpersonal interactions as being reciprocal and helpful.

MAH: Mutuality of Autonomy–Health

The Mutuality of Autonomy–Health (MAH) variable is a relatively rare code. High scores on this variable indicate that the examinee tends to expect relationships to be balanced and healthy (Meyer et al., 2011). Again, this does not mean that the examinee's relationships are healthy; it only suggests that there is a potential for healthy relationships.

PAGE 2 VARIABLES

The Page 2 variables should be given less weight in the interpretation than the Page 1 variables (Meyer et al., 2011). In general, the Page 2 variables have less empirical support than the Page 1 variables do. Meyer and colleagues recommend that the variables on Page 2 should not be considered to be elevated unless they are below 85 or above 115.

The Page 2 variables are divided into the same categories as the Page 1 variables are, except that there is no "Administration Behaviors and Observations" section on Page 2. The following sections describe each of the Page 2 variables with possible interpretations. Figure A.6, in the Appendix, presents an example of Page 2 of the R-PAS Summary Scores and Profiles.

Engagement and Cognitive Processing

There are eleven variables in the Engagement and Cognitive Processing domain on Page 2 of the Summary and Scores. Rapid Reference 8.9 contains a brief summary of these variables, along with how they are calculated and an overview of their interpretation.

≋ Rapid Reference 8.9

Engagement and Cognitive Processing, Page 2:
How the Variables Are Calculated and What They Assess

Variable	Name	How It Is Calculated	What It Assesses
W%	Whole Percentage	The number of responses with W locations divided by the number of responses (W / R).	Holistic processing; may also reflect high effort.
Dd%	Uncommon Detail Percentage	The number of responses with Dd locations divided by the number of responses (Dd / R).	A focus on small, uncommon details.
SI	Space Integration	The number of responses with SI codes.	Complex, flexible thinking.

Variable	Name	How It Is Calculated	What It Assesses
2ABS + Art+Ay	Intellectualized Content	The number of ABS codes multiplied by 2, plus the number of Art and Ay codes (2ABS + Art + Ay).	Tendency to intellectualize, especially with emotions.
Vg%	Vagueness Percentage	The number of responses with Vg object quality divided by the number of responses (Vg / R).	Vague processing.
V	Vista	The number of responses with a V code.	Perspective taking; if the examinee has symptoms of depression, presence of this variable could indicate negative self-evaluation.
FD	Form-Based Dimension	The number of responses with an FD code.	Perspective taking.
R8910%	Percentage of total Responses that were provided to the Color Cards	The number of responses to Cards VIII, IX, and X, divided by the number of responses [(VIII + IX + X) / R].	Responsiveness to compelling situations, possibly including emotional interactions.
WSumC	Weighted Sum of Color	$.5 \times FC + CF + 1.5\ CF$	Attention and interest in compelling aspects of the environment; may include emotional reactivity.
C	Pure Color	The number of responses with a C determinant.	Unmodulated emotions; may suggest the potential for emotional reactivity.
Mp Proportion	Mp Proportion	The number of responses with Mp determinants divided by the total number of responses with Mp and Ma determinants [Mp / (Mp + Ma)].	Possible tendency to experience passive fantasy; person may withdraw into fantasy.

Source: Based on information from Choca, 2013; Exner, 2003; Meyer et al., 2011; Mihura et al., 2013; Weiner, 2003.

W%: Whole Percentage

Whole Percentage (W%) is thought to be a measure of global processing. It also could indicate that the examinee has a tendency to make sure that she attends to and understands all aspects of a situation (Meyer et al., 2011). This can be beneficial in some circumstances and it could be a liability in others. Whether it is beneficial or a liability depends on other factors, including situational factors. For example, a high W% could also suggest that the examinee has difficulty seeing the easy, practical situation (D codes). This could result in the examinee working harder to complete a task than is necessary, as she is attempting to incorporate all the data rather than just the most relevant data.

When interpreting this variable, it is important to consider on which blots the examinee used the whole blot in the response, as it is easier to use the whole blot for some cards than it is for others. In general, the more segmented the blot, the more difficult it is to use the entire blot in a response.

Dd%: Uncommon Detail Percentage

Uncommon Detail Percentage (Dd%) is thought to be a measure of a tendency to focus on small details (Meyer et al., 2011). This could result from an examinee being detail oriented, obsessive, or hypervigilant or it could be due to paranoia. There are times when being detail oriented can be beneficial, such as when preparing a tax return; however, if there is too much focus on details, it is possible to miss the "big picture" or the straightforward solution to a problem.

SI: Space Integration

As is the case for most of the other Page 2 variables, there is little research on Space Integration (SI). It is thought to be associated with complex thinking patterns and flexibility in thinking. Meyer and colleagues (2011) report that research has suggested that SI responses are associated with educational level and creativity.

2ABS + Art + Ay: Intellectualized Content

Intellectualized Content (2ABS + Art + Ay) is associated with a tendency to intellectualize (Exner, 2003; Meyer et al., 2011). Intellectualization is usually associated with emotions or emotionally laden situations, as it is a way to avoid addressing emotions. Intellectualization is something that is used by many individuals from time to time; however, it becomes problematic when it is used more frequently, as it is a way for them to avoid experiencing or coping with emotions.

Vg%: Vagueness Percentage

The Vagueness Percentage (Vg%) is thought to be associated with a less sophisticated form of processing (Meyer et al., 2011). In order to obtain a vague score, the examinee has to see something without form demand, such as "happiness" or "blood." This can be seen as a very superficial type of processing, where the examinee avoids processing at a deeper level (e.g., seeing people who are happy). There are multiple reasons why examinees could engage in this level of processing, including cognitive limitations and defensiveness.

V: Vista

Historically, Vista (V) codes have been associated with the presence of painful emotions, such as guilt or remorse, that result in self-deprecation (Exner, 2003). There is some empirical support for this interpretation. Additionally, V codes are thought to be associated with perspective taking (Meyer et al., 2011). More recently, Choca (2013) has suggested that the presence of V determinants could indicate feelings of inferiority.

FD: Form-Based Dimension

Form-Based Dimension (FD) codes have been associated with the ability to engage in self-reflection and introspection (Exner, 2003). However, this interpretation has not been supported by the literature. Instead, FD codes are now thought to be associated with perspective taking (Meyer et al., 2011).

R8910%: Percentage of Responses to the Color Cards

Percentage of responses to the color cards (R8910%) is a measure of how attracted the examinee is to interesting and bright stimuli, like emotions. It is thought that individuals with a high R8910% are more attracted to and inspired by emotion than those with lower scores. However, little research has been completed on this variable or on its counterpart on the CS, the Affective Ratio (Afr) (Mihura et al., 2013).

WSumC: Weighted Sum of Color

Historically, color has been associated with emotion; the less form the color determinant had, the less control the examinee was thought to have over her emotions (Exner, 2003; Meyer et al., 2011). Essentially, the higher the weighted sum of color (WSumC) value, the stronger the individual's emotional reactions. FC determinants were considered to represent a more controlled form of emotional expression, while CF and C determinants were thought to represent a less controlled form of emotional expression.

WSumC is thought to be associated with being aware of, and perhaps seeking out, stimulation from the environment. It may also include how the examinee responds to environmental stimuli, which would include how much control the examinee has over her emotions. Again, this could be a positive or a negative finding, depending on other variables, the examinee's unique characteristics, and so forth. For example, if the examinee is in a supportive environment, is appropriately seeking out support, and is experiencing positive emotions, like happiness and joy, this is not necessarily a negative finding. In contrast, if the examinee is in a nonsupportive environment and is experiencing primarily negative emotions, such as anger, this finding could indicate the possible presence of psychopathology, or, at the very least, a poor person-environment fit.

C: C Determinants

The number of responses with a C determinant (C) is thought to be related to an unbridled, unconstrained expression of emotion (Exner, 2003; Meyer et al., 2011). It is important to consider the environment when interpreting C; if the examinee is in a positive environment, experiencing positive emotions, and there is no evidence of psychopathology, then an elevated C could indicate a willingness to experience and engage with positive emotions. However, if there is evidence of a severe psychopathology or personality disturbance, the elevated C could suggest that the examinee has a tendency to engage in over-the-top displays of emotion.

Mp / (Ma + Mp): Mp Proportion

Individuals with a high Mp Proportion [Mp / (Ma + Mp)] are thought to have a strong tendency to engage in passive fantasy, perhaps as a way to escape from reality (Meyer et al., 2011). Actively engaging in fantasies, such as rehearsal for an event, can be positive, as it is a way to prepare for the future or to work through difficult situations. However, passive engagement in fantasies does not help the person work through anything; it is as though she is an observer in the fantasy, rather than an active participant.

Although active fantasy is often considered to be more positive than passive fantasy, both can be overused. As with other coping strategies, occasionally using fantasy as a defense is generally not a concern. However, when this becomes the predominant way that an examinee copes with stressful situations, then it is something that would likely need to be addressed.

Perception and Thinking

There is only one variable in the Perception and Thinking domain on Page 2. Rapid Reference 8.10 contains a brief summary of the variable, along with how it is calculated and an overview of interpretation.

FQu%: Unusual Form Quality Percentage

On R-PAS, Unusual Form Quality Percentage (FQu%) indicates either that the examinee saw something that was not commonly seen by others or that what he saw did not fit the blot exactly, but the contours of the objects were not completely

≡ Rapid Reference 8.10

Perception and Thinking, Page 2:
How the Variable Is Calculated and What It Assesses

Variable	Name	How It Is Calculated	What It Assesses
FQu%	Unusual Form Quality Percentage	The number of responses with FQu divided by the number of responses (FQu / R).	A tendency to see the world in unusual, but not distorted, ways.

Source: Based on information from Choca, 2013; Exner, 2003; Meyer et al., 2011; Mihura et al., 2013; Weiner, 2003.

inconsistent with the contours of the blot. In other words, a code of FQu "fits" but others responses could "fit better" (Meyer et al., 2011).

Consistent with this, the interpretation of a high FQu is that the examinee sees the world in a somewhat different way than others do and, as a result, has a tendency to engage in more individualistic behaviors. In general, the examinee's behaviors are not seen as unacceptable, but they are not necessarily conventional either.

Stress and Distress

There are five variables in the Stress and Distress domain on Page 2. Rapid Reference 8.11 contains a brief summary of the variables, along with how they are calculated and an overview of interpretation.

PPD: Potentially Problematic Determinants

The Potentially Problematic Determinants (PPD) are a combination of determinants that, historically, have been associated with increased demands on the person. There is some empirical support for this variable that indicates the presence of these determinants can be associated with irritating or distressing thoughts and experiences (Meyer et al., 2011). Most of the variables that make up the PPD are interpreted elsewhere individually (e.g., m, Y, T, V, C'); one is not (FM).

Although the presence of the states that are associated with these determinants can tap psychological resources, the presence of the PPD does not necessarily

⇛ Rapid Reference 8.11

Stress and Distress, Page 2:
How the Variables Are Calculated and What They Assess

Variable	Name	How It Is Calculated	What It Assesses
PPD	Potentially Problematic Determinants	The sum of FM, m, Y, T, V, and C' (FM + m + Y + T + V + C').	Psychological demands on the person.
CBlend	Color Blended with Shading and Achromatic Color	The number of blends that have both a C determinant (C, CF, FC) and a shading or achromatic color determinant (T, V, Y, C').	Tendency to mix positive emotional experiences with negative ones.
C'	Achromatic Color	The number of C' determinants on the protocol.	Tendency to inhibit reactions to emotions.
V	Vista	The number of V determinants on the protocol.	Presence of self-evaluation; the person could be overly self-critical.
CrtiCont%	Critical Contents Percentage	The number of critical content codes (MOR, AGM, An, Bl, Ex, Fi, and Sx) divided by the number of responses [(MOR + AGM + An + Bl + Ex + Fi + Sx) / R].	Trauma, failing to censor self, and/or exaggeration of symptoms.

Source: Based on information from Choca, 2013; Exner, 2003; Meyer et al., 2011; Mihura et al., 2013; Weiner, 2003.

mean that the examinee is unable to deal with the increased demands. For example, Y and m are both associated with situational stress. If the examinee has the psychological resources to cope with the situational stress, then she is unlikely to manifest signs of distress. Instead, she may simply be more attuned to and aware of the various nuances in the world, rather than experiencing distress. It is important to examine the rest of the protocol and consider the examinee's background and other assessment data, before coming to the conclusion that the presence of these determinants is associated with distress.

DON'T FORGET
....

PPD assesses for *potentially* problematic determinants. The presence of these determinants in a protocol does not necessarily mean that the examinee is experiencing significant distress.

CBlend: Color Blended with Shading or Achromatic Color

There is little research on the Color Blended with Shading or Achromatic Color (CBlend) variable. Theoretically, this variable is a combination of emotions (color) and painful or distressful experiences (shading or achromatic color). Consequently, one possible interpretation of this variable has been that painful emotions, such as severe anxiety or depression, are likely to be present (Choca, 2013; Exner, 2013). Meyer and colleagues (2011) have suggested that an elevated CBlend score could indicate that the examinee is acutely aware of her environment and emotions, which can result in her experiencing complex emotions that include both positive and negative emotions. For example, the examinee could experience something very positive (e.g., getting a promotion), but rather than focus on the positive emotionality and experience, such as the excitement and the new experiences the promotion could bring, the examinee is also acutely aware of the aspects of the promotion that could be negative, such as the increased responsibility and the anxiety that is associated with it. Consequently, positive emotions tend to get intermixed with negative emotions.

C': Achromatic Color

Achromatic Color (C') is associated with the presence of negative emotions and with the tendency to be drawn toward dreary stimuli (Meyer et al., 2011; Mihura et al., 2013). Consequently, the traditional interpretation of this variable is that the examinee may have a tendency to inhibit emotions, as this is one way to prevent oneself from experiencing anxiety, depression, and the like (Exner, 2003).

V: Vista

Vista (V) responses are theoretically associated with perspective taking. They have also been associated with a tendency to engage in negative self-evaluation, and there is some speculation that they could be associated with a tendency to evaluate others as well (Meyer et al., 2011; Mihura et al., 2013). This is not necessarily a negative finding, as long as this evaluation is carried out in an appropriate, and ideally constructive, manner. For example, a supervisor who is evaluating employees should attempt to evaluate their weaknesses, too, as part of her assessment of her staff. Additionally, someone who is in therapy will likely be aware of negative aspects of the self, which is possibly why that individual sought therapy.

CritCont%: Critical Contents

The Critical Contents (CritCont%) variable comprises two Thematic Special Scores (MOR and AGM) and five content codes (An, Bl, Ex, Fi, and Sx) that may be coded for responses seen as socially inappropriate. According to the social conventions within many cultures in the United States, there are certain topics that are not appropriate for discussion, especially when meeting with someone for the first time. These topics include morbid themes (death, destruction, blood), sex, and aggression. There are many reasons why individuals might bring up these topics, including that they are unable to stop thinking about them, as in the case of trauma, they experience a failure to censor (e.g., they have a personality disturbance), or they are attempting to look more psychopathological than they actually are (Meyer et al., 2011). Because the presence of these variables is associated with a number of different potential interpretations, it is important to consider all aspects of the examinee while interpreting elevations on this variable.

Self and Other Representation

There are nine variables in the Self and Other Representation domain on Page 2. Rapid Reference 8.12 contains a brief summary of the variables, along with how they are calculated and an overview of interpretation.

SumH: All Human Content Codes

The sum of all the human content codes (SumH) is considered to be a rough measure of the examinee's interest in others (Exner, 2003; Meyer et al., 2011). In general, elevated scores indicate that the examinee is more interested in others than is typical, while low scores indicate that the examinee is less interested in others than is typical. Interest in others does not equate to an understanding of others, however. For example, someone can be very interested in engaging with others but may still lack the requisite social skills to do so. As a result, this individual may engage in a number of "social blunders" that make it difficult to make and sustain relationships. Conversely, someone who is not interested in others may be socially adept, but may simply choose not to engage for a variety of reasons.

It is important to note that there is limited research on this variable. In a recent survey, clinicians perceived that it was valid; however, the empirical research that supports the validity of this variable is very limited (Meyer et al., 2013; Mihura et al., 2013). The interpretations for this variable are theoretical only and, as of this writing, are not empirically supported.

≡ Rapid Reference 8.12

. . . .

Self and Other Representation, Page 2:
How the Variables Are Calculated and What They Assess

Variable	Name	How It Is Calculated	What It Assesses
SumH	All Human Content	The sum of all human content codes [H + (H) + Hd + (Hd)].	Awareness of and interest in others.
NPH / SumH	Non-Pure H Proportion	The sum of all of the human content codes except for H, divided by the sum of all of the human content codes [(H) + Hd + (Hd)] / [H + (H) + Hd + (Hd)] or [(SumH – H) / SumH].	Having an unrealistic view of self and others; could suggest that the examinee is more comfortable relating to fantasy characters than to real humans.
V-Comp	Vigilance Composite	Calculation based on a variety of variables.	Vigilance, being guarded.
p / (p + a)	Passive Proportion	The number of Mp, FMp, and mp determinants divided by the total number of movement determinants.	Tendency to engage with the world in a passive way rather than to actively take part in it.
AGM	Aggressive Movement	The number of AGM Special Scores on the protocol.	Awareness of, and possible interest in, aggression.
T	Texture	The number of texture determinants on the protocol.	Desire for interpersonal closeness (e.g., tactile closeness).
PER	Personal Knowledge Justification	The number of PER Special Scores on the protocol.	Tendency to justify responses by citing personal knowledge; may be defensive.
An	Anatomy	The number of An content codes on the protocol.	Body focus.
r	Reflections	The number of r determinants on the protocol.	Narcissism.

Source: Based on information from Choca, 2013; Exner, 2003; Meyer et al., 2011; Mihura et al., 2013; Weiner, 2003.

NPH / SumH: Non-Pure H Proportion

On the one hand, Pure H responses are associated with a tendency to see a person as a sum of his or her parts, as a whole person. Hd, on the other hand, is associated with a tendency to see a person as only a part of who they truly are. For example, a kindergarten student may be surprised to see his teacher out at a restaurant on a date. For the student, the teacher only exists in one context—as his teacher. In other words, the student sees his teacher as only part of who that person really is. That is why it was surprising for the student to see his teacher outside the typical context (classroom) and engaging in some nontypical teacher behavior (a date). However, older students, who have realized that people have different parts, roles, and so forth, tend to be less surprised to see a teacher out socializing.

In general, high scores on the Non-Pure H Proportion (NPH / SumH) suggest that the examinee may view others in unrealistic ways (Meyer et al., 2011). This is not necessarily associated with psychosis. For example, someone who reads a lot of fantasy novels may have a high NPH proportion because he may be better able to relate to the characters in the books he reads than to other people. However, as with SumH, there is little empirical evidence to support the validity of this variable; more research is needed to examine the construct validity of this variable (Mihura et al., 2013).

V-Comp: Vigilance Composite

V-Comp's precursor was the HVI on the CS. V-Comp is designed to be a measure of vigilance, which includes being guarded, wary around others, and being alert to the possibility of danger in the environment. Although these traits are typically associated with paranoia, they can result from other sources as well, including trauma. Individuals who are vigilant also tend to be detail oriented, especially as they scan their environment for indications of danger (Meyer et al., 2011).

r: Reflections

The presence of Reflections (r) has been theoretically linked with narcissistic tendencies. There is empirical support for this assertion (Mihura et al., 2013). Elevated scores are thought to be indicative of narcissism. This may not be a liability, as long as the examinee is receiving appropriate feedback from the environment to maintain his high sense of self-worth.

p / (p + a): Passive Proportion

There is limited empirical support for the interpretation of the Passive Proportion [p / (p+a)] variable (Mihura et al., 2013). Theoretically, elevated scores on this variable are associated with a tendency to take a passive stance in life. This would include an examinee allowing others to make decisions for him or assuming that luck or fate controls his destiny. It is vital to consider the possible impact of culture on the interpretation of this variable, as for some cultures, certain groups are expected to be passive and to not engage in decision making.

AGM: Aggressive Movement

As is the case with many other Page 2 variables, there is limited empirical support for the validity of this Aggressive Movement (AGM) variable. However, clinicians have reported that they found this variable to be useful (Meyer et al., 2013).

Theoretically, AGM Special Scores are associated with an awareness of, and perhaps attraction to, aggression. This does not necessarily mean that the examinee has a tendency to engage in aggressive acts; in fact, research does not support this assertion (Mihura et al., 2013). When interpreting this score, it is important to consider the examinee's context; if the examinee resides in an area with a great deal of violence, an elevated AGM score could simply reflect the examinee's current environment.

T: Texture

Texture (T) codes are a measure of the examinee's desire for closeness with others. Theoretically, textures are linked with interpersonal closeness due to the tactile interactions that will tend to occur between individuals who are close (e.g., hugs, holding hands). There is also good support in the peer-reviewed literature for this interpretation (Mihura et al., 2013). Generally, high scores are associated with a strong desire for interpersonal closeness (Meyer et al., 2011). It is important to examine the examinee's history to identify why this may be present; this finding could represent someone who has recently lost someone close to him and, thus, has unfulfilled needs for closeness. In other words, the elevated T may be situational. Conversely, the elevated T could be more chronic; it could also indicate that the examinee has a stronger desire than is typical to be close to people.

PER: Personal Knowledge Justification

Personal Knowledge Justification (PER) is coded whenever the examiner is convinced that the examinee is relying on his personal knowledge or experience to support his response. The interpretation is similar; when PER is elevated, it suggests that the examinee uses his own knowledge more often than is typical to support his opinions and conclusions (Meyer et al., 2011). There is some empirical support for this interpretation of the variable (Mihura et al., 2013).

The use of personal knowledge to support a conclusion or opinion can be defensive. However, it is possible that the examinee is attempting to share some interesting information about himself as well (e.g., "It's a Yorkie. I have a Yorkie at home that looks just like this").

An: Anatomy

The presence of Anatomy (An) content codes is indicative of the examinee being focused on bodily functioning (Meyer et al., 2011). This interpretation is extremely well supported in the literature (Mihura et al., 2013). It is possible that individuals in the medical profession and first responders may have elevated scores on this variable due to their frequent exposure to anatomy. These groups, by nature of their work, would be more focused on bodily functioning than is typical.

CONCLUSION

There is no one right way to interpret test results; however, there is a wrong way. Specifically, personality test results should never be interpreted in isolation. Personality tests provide us with hypotheses from which to work. In order to make sense of the data from the tests, it is vital to consider all other available pieces of data, including the examinee's background, culture (broadly defined), other assessment data, and the potential impact of situational factors.

Personality assessment interpretation is not an exact science and involves clinical judgment and opinion, which will differ from examiner to examiner. It is most important that the interpretation provided is consistent with the data available.

🖋 TEST YOURSELF 🖋

1. **What cut point for interpretation do Meyer and colleagues (2011) recommend using for the Page 1 variables?**
   a. Anything above or below 110
   b. Below 90 or above 110
   c. Below 85 or above 115
   d. Below 70 or above 130

2. **What cut point for interpretation do Meyer and colleagues (2011) recommend using for the Page 2 variables?**
   a. Anything above or below 110
   b. Below 90 or above 110
   c. Below 85 or above 115
   d. Below 70 or above 130

3. **Which of the following statements is true about Complexity?**
    a. It is influenced only by personal factors.
    b. It is influenced only by situational factors.
    c. It is influenced by both personal and situational factors.
    d. It is not influenced by either personal or situational factors.

4. **Your client has elevated PPD, but does not appear to be experiencing a significant amount of stress. Your client also has an elevated MC. What is the best interpretation of these data?**
    a. Your client is in denial about his problems.
    b. Your client is so distressed he is no longer able to cope.
    c. Your client has a lot of resources but is not experiencing any demands on himself.
    d. Your client is likely able to cope with the increased demands on him due to the above-average number of resources he has.

5. **Your client has elevated S-Comp. What does this mean?**
    a. Your client reported experiencing suicidal ideation on R-PAS.
    b. Your client denied experiencing suicidal ideation on R-PAS.
    c. Your client may be at risk for a lethal suicide attempt in the near future.
    d. Your client is at an extremely low risk of a lethal suicide attempt.

Answers: 1. b; 2. c; 3. c; 4. d; 5. c.

Nine

R-PAS CASE SAMPLE

his book uses the same case sample for both the CS and the R-PAS discussions. This allows the reader to compare the systems to one another. This chapter includes the examinee's background history and referral information, a Rorschach protocol administered according to the R-PAS, the coded responses, relevant scoring information for the protocol, and an interpretation based on the data provided. Please see Figures A.4, A.5, and A.6 in the Appendix for some of the materials produced by the R-PAS computerized scoring program: the R-PAS Protocol Level Counts and Calculations and the Summary Scores and Profiles for this examinee. The Book Companion Website Materials provided online for this book contain additional materials, including an annotated administration, an annotated coding, and an annotated interpretation. The annotated administration provides information that is designed to explain why some responses were queried and why others were not. The annotated coding explains why the responses were coded the way that they were. Finally, the annotated interpretation is designed to explain which test data and/or observations support the interpretative statements.

BACKGROUND INFORMATION

Identifying Information and Reason for Referral

Sarah Frazier is a 25-year-old Caucasian female, currently residing in the Mid-Atlantic region of the United States. In September 2015, Ms. Frazier began a graduate program in criminology. Despite doing extremely well in both high school and college, she said she struggled with her first semester of graduate school, but still passed all her classes with grades of B– or above. She went to her advisor for advice, but began "crying uncontrollably," at which point her advisor encouraged her to seek assistance at the university clinic, where she was tested for a learning disorder. However, the results of that testing did not support a diagnosis of a learning disorder. The evaluator at the university suggested that Ms. Frazier participate in follow-up testing to identify possible reasons for her difficulty in classes.

The purpose of this evaluation is to identify possible contributing factors to Ms. Frazier's reported difficulty in graduate school and to make recommendations to improve her performance.

Relevant Background Information

Sarah Frazier provided the following background information. She was born and raised in the southwestern United States in an intact family and is the older of two children. Her younger brother is 17 and resides with their parents. Her father is self-employed and reportedly "does well." Her mother is a homemaker and volunteers with a local animal shelter. Ms. Frazier described her childhood as "typical," recalling that her parents were always very supportive of her decisions. She recalled feeling closer to her father than her mother, which she attributed to shared interests (e.g., martial arts, marksmanship). She said that she "tolerated" her younger brother when she was younger, but now has regular contact with him via text messages. She also talks to her parents "a few times per week" but said that they were not aware of the difficulties she has been having in graduate school, because "It would devastate them."

Ms. Frazier said that she did "extremely well" in high school and was offered "a full ride" to multiple colleges on a marksmanship scholarship. She opted to attend a school in the southwest United States, where she majored in criminal justice. She said that she was on the dean's list each semester in college and was able to balance her academic work with her training schedule for the marksmanship team. She also was the first member of her family to attend college, saying that it was typical for the women in her family to get married young and to have at least one child by the time they were 22.

During her freshman year in college, she met Greg Radnor (pseudonym), a senior at the university, at a party. She recalled that her roommate "strongly encouraged" her to go to the party and that she went only because her roommate promised to "stop harassing" her if she went. Ms. Frazier said that she and Mr. Radnor were both standing in the corner and he commented about how much he hated parties. The two talked about how much they hated parties and then started dating. They were married a few months after Ms. Frazier graduated with her BS degree in criminal justice. Shortly after they were married, Mr. Radnor was offered employment with a biotechnology firm in the Mid-Atlantic region of the United States, and the two moved. Her family initially opposed the move, saying that "family needs to stay together." However, Ms. Frazier has said that while it was difficult to move away from her parents, as she was the first in the family to leave the area, she does not believe it has negatively impacted their relationship, as she speaks with her family a few times per week.

Ms. Frazier sought work with the federal government and with local state agencies, but was told by recruiters that her application was not competitive because she lacked graduate education. She found employment with a school district, working in the main office, and planned to save money in order to pay for graduate school. However, after three years of working, Ms. Frazier and Mr. Radnor had not saved enough money for Ms. Frazier to go to school full time as they were focusing on paying off Mr. Radnor's student loans. Rather than wait longer to start graduate school, Ms. Frazier said that she decided to continue working full time while attending graduate school full time; she said that she believed she would be able to handle the stress. However, she noted that graduate school was "more difficult" than she thought it would be. She said that school has not interfered with her work and, in fact, her boss has praised the quality of her work. However, her grades last semester were lower than she was accustomed to; her GPA was a 3.0. As an undergraduate, her average GPA was reported to be a 3.8.

Ms. Frazier stated that she and Mr. Radnor have discussed having children. At this point, they are unsure if they want children. Still, Ms. Frazier has said that both her mother and her mother-in-law are encouraging them to start a family because they want grandchildren. When asked about her mother's and mother-in-law's comments, she stated that the comments do not bother her because "I am in a different place than they were when they were my age. Neither one attended college, let alone graduate school. They do not understand that I do not have time for children now. I'm only 25; I have plenty of time, if Greg and I choose to have kids."

Ms. Frazier said that she has friends but that she does not discuss "serious issues" with them because she does not believe they will understand this topic. She elaborated by stating that many of her friends from high school "are in a different place than I am" as they are married with multiple children. However, she does discuss other topics with them, including frustrations with work and with family. Most of her friends from college, in contrast, are in graduate school but are "far along in their programs" and busy with comprehensive examinations and working on research. She did say that she has sought support from some of them in the past, but that she does not want to be seen as incapable, so she does not ask for assistance. Ms. Frazier said that her husband knows she has been struggling but that she does not want to "burden him" because his work is stressful, so she has not spoken to him directly about it. Ms. Frazier added that she wants her husband to ask her how he can help, but he has not.

Ms. Frazier denied any significant medical or mental health history. She also denied any significant family mental health history, although she did note that her mother has type 2 diabetes. She also denied any history of substance abuse and stated she prefers to be in control of her own thoughts and actions.

Results of Previous Testing

During October 2015, Ms. Frazier was referred to the university clinic by her academic advisor for testing. According to Ms. Frazier, she "freaked out" and "sobbed" after getting a B– on her first paper and went to her advisor. Her advisor recommended an evaluation. She does feel that her advisor was "overreacting" and she did not believe that she needed testing. However, she reported that she went to the clinic because she was concerned about how her academic advisor would view her if she did not follow his advice, given that she will likely be asking him for a letter of recommendation in the future.

Ms. Frazier said that she was having difficulty concentrating on her reading, which was resulting in her taking an excessive amount of time to complete assignments. In addition, Ms. Frazier was working 40 hours per week and sharing household duties with Mr. Radnor. She said that she "squeezes in" reading when she can, which includes reading her assignments during her lunch hour and breaks while working. However, Ms. Frazier insisted that she was able to handle everything.

The university clinic conducted cognitive and academic achievement testing with Ms. Frazier. The results placed her cognitive abilities in the High Average range, with scores ranging from 112 to 117. Her academic achievement scores were consistent with her cognitive abilities and with her academic attainment as a first-year graduate student. The clinic also had Ms. Frazier complete a self-report measure of personality and emotional functioning; all scores were within normal limits.

The evaluation concluded that Ms. Frazier did not meet diagnostic criteria for a learning disorder and that the test results were not consistent with the presence of anxiety or depression. The evaluator recommended that Ms. Frazier consider using the tutoring services available on campus and consider participating in additional testing to identify possible contributing factors to her reported difficulty in classes.

Mental Status and Behavioral Observations

Ms. Frazier arrived to the appointment approximately 30 minutes early and was appropriately dressed and well groomed. She was poised and made appropriate eye contact with the evaluator. Her speech was normal in rate and in tone. Her responses to the questions asked of her were appropriate but tended to be very direct, with little elaboration unless she was specifically asked to elaborate on her response. When asked questions regarding emotions or typically emotionally laden situations (e.g., her wedding, death of a close family member), Ms. Frazier had a tendency to discuss factual aspects of the situation rather than her emotional reactions. Consistent with this, she reported her mood was "fine" and she did not display many emotions during the evaluation. The emotions she did display were limited to positive emotions (e.g., happiness) and even then, the display was limited. As an example, she did smile when discussing her wedding and her husband. However, she did not demonstrate any emotion when discussing the incident with her advisor that led to his referring her to the university clinic.

Ms. Frazier denied symptoms consistent with mood disturbance and anxiety. She denied experiencing difficulty sustaining attention, except with some of her statistics readings, which she reported finding "dreadfully boring." She also denied experiencing symptoms consistent with thought disorders, including visual, auditory, and tactile hallucinations. There was no evidence of disorganized or tangential speech. She also firmly denied any past or current history of suicidal, homicidal, or self-harming thoughts or behaviors.

Ms. Frazier actively participated in all aspects of testing. Thus, these results are considered to be an accurate reflection of her personality and emotional functioning at the time of the evaluation. Please be advised that this interpretation was based on the information available to the evaluator at the time of the evaluation.

ADMINISTRATION

Table 9.1 displays the R-PAS administration for Ms. Frazier. The locations (e.g., D1, D2) that the examinee identified are embedded in the responses.

Scoring

Table 9.2 reproduces the R-PAS code sequence for Ms. Frazier; this can also be seen in the Appendix (Table A.25). For her Protocol Level Counts and Calculations and her Summary Scores and Profiles see Figures A.4, A.5, and A.6 in the Appendix.

Table 9.1 R-PAS Administration for Ms. Frazier (pseudonym)

Card	#	Response	Inquiry
I	1	A bug. *Remember to try to give two, maybe three responses to each card. Please try to give another.*	These (D1) look like little antennas. These (D2) looked like wings and these (DdS26) reminded me of markings that could be on an insect. That's why I thought bug. Area: WS
	2	A bat.	Wings (D2), body (D4), the wings are out, like it's flying. Area: W
II	3	A ladybug.	The red made me think of a ladybug (points to D2, D3 and red spots on D6). Ladybugs also have black too on them, like this picture. The wings are out, it's flying. Area: W
	4	It kind of looks like ribs and chest, like anatomy.	It's like you are looking down through the ribcage. This part (D6) is the ribcage and this part is the pelvis (D3). See how it's smaller? It looks further away. This reminded me of anatomy because this (D3) looked like the shape of a pelvis. Area: D6 & D3
	5	In the white space there is a ballet dancer.	Right here (DS5). *Help me see the ballerina like you do.* She is dancing. She has her arms straight up and this is her fluffy white tutu. *You said it was fluffy?* Yeah, the shape makes it look fluffy. Area: DS5
III	6	Oh I definitely see two people here (D9). Women, because they have boobs. They are fighting over this basket, here (D7).	OK, so it looks like they are bending over, grabbing, and pulling at this basket here. Both of them want it. You can see the basket is starting to break from being pulled, see how it looks like it is coming apart? These red spots are blood; they cut themselves on the basket shreds. It kind of looks like shopping on Thanksgiving when they have those really great deals and people fight over items. Area: W
	7	I see a fetus.	Right here (D2). Head, body, and this is the umbilical cord. I would guess it is a second semester fetus because you can see all the different parts but it is still small. Area: D2

Card	#	Response	Inquiry
IV	8	v I don't really see anything. . .oh wait, it kind of looks like the monster from Fantasia, what was his name?	Chernabog! That was his name! Anyway, here is the head (D1), horns, wings (D6), the wings are spread out, like a show of strength. He is really buff, the shading makes it look like muscles. Area: W
	9	(turned card 360 degrees) Umm, it kind of looks like Hagrid riding on his motorcycle when I look at it this way.	You know, like from Harry Potter? So he's leaning back on his motorcycle because his feet (D6) are big and his head (D3) is small, so it looks like the feet are closer. This (D1) is the wheel of the motorcycle and these (D4) are the handlebars. Area: W
V	10	Another bug. I keep seeing bugs!	Antenna (Dd34), legs (D9), wings (D4). The wings are out, it's flying. Area: W
	11	It also kind of looks like a pterodactyl.	It's basically the same thing, but not this part (points to Dd34). Legs (D9), Wings (d4). It's also flying. Head is here (Dd30). Area: Dd99
VI	12	Cowhide rug. Looks furry.	You know, like one of those rugs you put on your floor? This is the head (D3), the body and legs (D1), here's the butt (Dd33). *You said it was furry?* Just the shape. Reminds me of fur. Area: W
	13	>It looks like a ship. Just this part (D4).	This is the front, the smokestack, and the back. The shape reminds me of a ship. Area: D4
VII	14	2 people with their hair up. I don't know what kind of style that would be. Maybe a beehive?	They are girls. Here is the face and head (D9), that crazy hairstyle (D5), the shape just reminds me of hair I guess. They are hunched over a bit, see how it looks like the head is forward (points to D2)? Area: D2
	15	Right here (DS10) looks like a bowl.	Just the shape reminds of me it. Area: DS10
VIII	16	> Oh this one is easy. It's an animal, maybe a wolf, walking in the Arctic.	There's the wolf (D1). He's walking over these glaciers, here (D6). I thought glaciers because it looked like ice to me. *Ice?* Yeah, because you can see the reflection of the animal here. Area: W

(*continued*)

Table 9.1 Continued

Card	#	Response	Inquiry
	17	An ugly dress.	Just this part (D2). This is the top (Dd33) and this is the skirt (D7). *What makes it look ugly?* The color combination. It's hideous. Area: D2
IX	18	A waterfall. That's it. *I wonder if you can see something else there too.* (turns cards around, 30 second delay) No, that's it, just the waterfall. It's all I see now.	It's the whole thing, except for this (D6). The faint blue here (D8) is water falling. These are the lush green plants that are growing around the waterfall (D11), they are growing quickly because it is a good environment to grow. These are the cliffs (D3). It is really a beautiful picture. Area: D2
X	19	A woman.	She's old. She's here (outlines area that includes DdS29, D6, and D10). This is her head (top of DdS29), these are her boobs (D6), her boobs are really low, like what happens when you get old and your bra is not supportive. She is wearing colorful stockings, here (D10). This (D8), is her gray hair. Area: Dd99
	20	< Another bug! This one is a caterpillar. No, a banana slug. It's definitely a banana slug.	I had to eat a banana slug at camp, so I know what they look like. This looks just like it (D9). It's the same shape, but this is not the right color. Banana slugs are yellow, not red. Area: D9

IMPORTANT
· ·

Table 9.2 was reproduced from the Rorschach Performance Assessment System® (R–PAS®) Scoring Program (© 2010–2016) and excerpted from the Rorschach Performance Assessment System: Administration, Coding, Interpretation, and Technical Manual (©2011) with copyrights by Rorschach Performance Assessment System, LLC. All rights reserved. Used by permission of Rorschach Performance Assessment System, LLC.

Table 9.2 R-PAS Code Sequence for Ms. Frazier (pseudonym)

C-ID: Sarah Frazier (pseudonym) P-ID: 7 Age: 25 Gender: Female Education: 16

Cd	#	Or	Loc	Loc #	SR	SI	Content	Sy	Vg	2	FQ	P	Determinants	Cognitive	Thematic	HR	ODL (RP)	R-Opt
I	1		W			SI	A				o		F					Pr
II	2		W				A				o		FMa					
	3	@	W				A				−		FMa, CF, C'					
	4		D	6, 3			An				−		FD					
III	5		D	5	SR		H, Cg	Sy			u		Ma, C'			GH		
	6		W				H, Bl, NC	Sy		2	o	P	Ma, mp, C		AGM, MOR, MAP	PH		
IV	7		D	2			H, An				o		F			GH	ODL	
	8	v	W				(H)				u		Ma, Y	DV1	AGC	GH		
V	9	@	W				(H), NC	Sy			o	P	Ma, FD			GH		
	10		W				A				o		FMa					
	11		Dd	99			A				o		FMa					
VI	12		W				Ad, NC				o	P	F					
VII	13	>	D	4			NC				o		F					
	14		D	2			Hd			2	o	P	Mp			GH		
	15		D	10	SR		NC				o		F					
VIII	16		W				A, NC	Sy			o	P	FMa, r		AGC			
	17		D	2			NC				u		FC					
IX	18		D	2			NC	Sy	Vg		u		ma-p, CF					
X	19		Dd	99	SR	SI	H, Cg				−		FC, C'		PER	PH		Pr
	20		D	9			A				u		F				ODL	

Source: ©2010–2016 R-PAS. Used by permission of Rorschach Performance Assessment System, LLC.

INTERPRETATION

Ms. Frazier was administered the Rorschach using Rorschach Performance Assessment System (R-PAS). She provided enough responses for the Rorschach to be scored and interpreted using R-PAS. There was also no evidence to suggest that Ms. Frazier may have been exaggerating her problems. Thus, the following interpretation is considered to be an accurate reflection of her personality and emotional functioning at the time of the evaluation.

The results of testing indicated that Ms. Frazier is not at a significantly increased risk of a lethal suicide attempt in the near future. This is consistent with her denial of suicidal ideation during the clinical interview.

Coping and Emotional Functioning

Based on her report, Ms. Frazier has been able to cope with the stressors of working full time and attending graduate school full time. However, there are some indications that her current coping strategies are inefficient when it comes to dealing with the stressors she is experiencing, as evidenced by her feeling "overwhelmed" and her "sobbing" in her advisor's office. Although the results of this R-PAS administration indicated that it is unlikely she is experiencing difficulties with coping, there is some indication that she may be less able to cope with stressors than others with her level of cognitive abilities and her educational attainment. This is not to say that she is unable to cope with stressors, but rather, her ability to cope with stress is not so developed as one would expect given her cognitive abilities and her resources. It is possible that Ms. Frazier's report of feeling "overwhelmed" could be related to her tendency to focus on multiple aspects of a situation. This could result in an "information overload," or feeling overwhelmed. As an example, Ms. Frazier said that she studies when she is able to, in between the other demands on her time. This has included studying at work during breaks. This requires being able to focus on multiple things at the same time (e.g., work and school) and being able to switch from one task to another. In other words, Ms. Frazier does not focus on only one task at a time; she focuses on many.

It is also important to note that there are some indications from testing that Ms. Frazier is better able to cope with situations that require thinking rather than emotional reaction. Consequently, Ms. Frazier may have a tendency to shy away from emotionally laden situations. Consistent with this, Ms. Frazier showed very little emotion during the evaluation and, instead, tended to focus on "facts" rather than the emotional aspects of a situation. Still, the results of testing suggested that Ms. Frazier is aware of emotional stimuli and is interested in them as much as others typically are. This apparent paradox may be due to Ms. Frazier being prone to experiencing unmodulated emotional responses, such as occurred in her advisor's office. In order to avoid experiencing the high level of emotional reactivity she is prone to, she strives to avoid emotions altogether. This could explain her lack of emotional reactivity and her avoidance of emotion during the evaluation.

Testing has also suggested that Ms. Frazier has a tendency to focus on the nuances of a situation when experiencing positive emotions, which could lead to a mixed emotional reaction, where positive emotions (e.g., joy) are mixed with negative ones (e.g., anger). Her avoidance of emotionally laden situations may be related; she may be attempting to avoid experiencing a potentially confusing emotional state where positive emotions are mixed with negative ones.

Cognitions

When presented with a situation, Ms. Frazier is accustomed to a high level of processing in that she tends to attend to multiple aspects of a situation at the same time and is capable of thinking through her options before acting. However, there is no evidence from testing to suggest that this high level of processing she is capable of engaging in results in complex thinking; in fact, testing suggests that Ms. Frazier's thinking tends to be straightforward. Still, there is also evidence that she can engage in perspective taking. This could suggest that while Ms. Frazier is capable of seeing multiple aspects of a problem, she strives to find a simple straightforward solution, when possible.

It is important to note that testing did not reveal any evidence of a severe thinking disturbance. This is consistent with the examiner's observations that there was no evidence of disorganized thought or speech during the evaluation. Still, there is some evidence that Ms. Frazier is prone to make poor decisions at times, especially in emotionally laden situations. In general, her perceptions of the world are similar to those of others and are not out of touch with reality.

Self-Perception

The results of this R-PAS administration suggest that Ms. Frazier has a high opinion of herself that requires positive feedback from the environment if it is to be maintained. Based on her report, she has typically received the necessary positive feedback to maintain her high sense of self-worth, via excelling at school, obtaining a full scholarship to college based on her marksmanship skills, and receiving positive feedback from work. However, the feedback she has been getting from graduate school is not so positive as she is accustomed to. This can be jarring, especially for someone who has historically received extremely positive feedback from others.

Interpersonal Perception

In regard to interpersonal relationships, testing indicated that Ms. Frazier is interested in others and is able to view other individuals for the complex beings that they are; it is unlikely that she categorizes people into "good" and "bad." Consistent with this, she reported that she has friends and family that she cares about and that she talks to on a regular basis. Although she reported she has not sought out support from family or friends recently, it is possible that she is avoiding them because she is concerned about looking less than perfect; she has always been a high achiever and has said that she does not want to be seen as "less than capable."

The results of testing indicate that Ms. Frazier's social skills are similar to those of others, and thus she is capable of engaging in appropriate interpersonal relationships with others. Consistent with this, she is married and reported having good relationships with family and friends. However, testing suggested that she may have a tendency to be more formal and reserved in interpersonal relationships than is typical. This is consistent with her presentation during this evaluation in that she presented as very poised and focused on factual aspects of situations rather than emotional ones. Testing also suggested that Ms. Frazier may not view relationships as supportive or cooperative; this, coupled with her reported desire to look "capable," may help to explain why she has not sought out support from others recently.

Interestingly, testing revealed that Ms. Frazier has a strong tendency toward being oppositional and independent. This seems somewhat counter to her presentation during the evaluation, as there was no evidence of oppositionality. However, her decision to violate her family's traditional social customs (e.g., to not have children, to work outside the home, and to attend graduate school), can be seen as evidence of her being somewhat oppositional, at least when it comes to family traditions.

SUMMARY AND RECOMMENDATIONS

Ms. Frazier is a 25-year-old Caucasian female who was referred by her university clinic for additional testing. Ms. Frazier reported that she has been "struggling" with graduate school. The previous testing was not consistent with the presence of a learning disorder, depressive disorder, or anxiety disorder, and additional testing was recommended.

Based on the results of this evaluation and her report, Ms. Frazier has had some difficulty coping with balancing working full time with being a full-time student. Although testing has suggested that she is able to cope as well as most individuals, given that Ms. Frazier has more cognitive resources available to her than the average individual (e.g., a high level of education, above-average cognitive abilities), one would expect that she would be better able to cope with stressors than others are typically able to. Consequently, this may be why she feels "overwhelmed" attempting to work full time while attending graduate school. This is a higher level of stress, requiring more resources, than is typical, causing her to use all her available resources. As a result, she has no additional resources to use when more stressors present themselves, such as was the case when she received a lower than expected grade on an assignment. It is likely that because her resources were all dedicated to other areas, such as graduate study and work, she was unable to appropriately cope with this additional stressor, resulting in her reportedly strong display of emotion in her advisor's office. Additionally, results indicated that Ms. Frazier is better able to cope when focusing on information rather than emotion, so the negative emotionality she likely experienced when receiving the B– likely contributed to her use of less adaptive coping methods (e.g., strong emotional reaction) to deal with the negative feedback.

Testing indicated that Ms. Frazier is accustomed to receiving positive feedback that she uses to support her high sense of self-worth. However, she is very sensitive to criticism and has taken steps to avoid being seen as "less capable" by others (e.g., does not discuss difficulties with her friends). This could help to explain why Ms. Frazier reacted so strongly to experiencing some difficulty in graduate school; she is used to achieving at a high level, which supported her strong, positive view of herself. However, her reported difficulties in graduate school provided her with some negative feedback about herself, causing distress.

Consistent with the results of previous testing, there was no evidence of severe difficulties with thinking. There is some evidence of anxiety and stress, per Ms. Frazier's report. The following recommendations may help Ms. Frazier at this time:

1. **Self-Care.** Ms. Frazier is working to balance working full time with attending school full time. This can be stressful. In order to reduce her stress level, Ms. Frazier could benefit from ensuring that self-care is an important aspect of her daily routine. This can take many forms, such as exercise and relaxation strategies.

2. **Counseling.** Ms. Frazier may benefit from counseling that focuses on the following areas:

   a. **Coping with Stressors.** Ms. Frazier is experiencing many demands on her time. Although she reported completing all to at least a satisfactory level (e.g., she is passing her classes and receiving positive feedback at work), she reported feeling "overwhelmed." She could benefit from learning additional coping strategies to help her appropriately cope with the stressors she is experiencing. Another focus could be helping Ms. Frazier learn to more appropriately cope with her emotions, as testing revealed she has more difficulty coping with emotions than with facts.

   b. **Self-Acceptance.** Another focus of counseling could be to help Ms. Frazier work through rectifying her high view of herself with the negative feedback she has been receiving from the environment (e.g., average grades).

   c. **Providing Support.** Counseling could also serve to provide Ms. Frazier with some additional support as she works to balance her work and school requirements.

3. **Organization and Time Management.** Ms. Frazier is attempting to balance working full time with graduate school and household duties. She could benefit from learning and using additional organizational and time management strategies, such as using checklists and breaking down larger tasks into smaller, more manageable ones.

🐟 TEST YOURSELF 🐟

1. **Which variable on Ms. Frazier's profile is thought to be associated with independence and oppositionality?**
   a. SR = 122.
   b. SI = 96.
   c. r = 113.
   d. COP = 88.

2. **Ms. Frazier's score on MC was a 110. Which of the following observations is most consistent with that score?**
   a. Ms. Frazier has fewer resources than is typical.
   b. Ms. Frazier has somewhat more resources than is typical.
   c. Ms. Frazier's allocation of her resources is atypical.
   d. Ms. Frazier is experiencing a great deal of stress.

3. **What does Ms. Frazier's score of 100 on ODL% suggest?**

   a. She is self-centered.

   b. She has a high level of cognitive abilities.

   c. She is highly stressed.

   d. She is as dependent on others as is typical.

4. **True or False: Ms. Frazier's MOR score of 100 suggests that she is strongly focused on negative aspects of her environment.**

   a. True

   b. False

5. **True or False: Ms. Frazier's (CF+C) / SumC of 104 indicates that she is significantly more emotional than others are.**

   a. True

   b. False

Answers: 1. a; 2. b; 3. d; 4. b; 5. b.

Ten

COMPARISON OF THE CS AND R-PAS: STRENGTHS AND WEAKNESSES OF BOTH SYSTEMS

No psychological test divides the field as much as the Rorschach does. When reading the literature, it seems as if the field of psychology can be divided into two groups: those who adore the Rorschach and those who despise it. This differentiation is not limited to the Rorschach, as some other tests are similarly divisive; however, individuals seem to be more vocal about the Rorschach than they are about other psychological tests. I suggest that this may have to do with the Rorschach's lack of face validity; it can be difficult for anyone, including a seasoned clinician, to consider that a series of inkblots can elicit information regarding the examinee's problem-solving capabilities, personality, and emotional functioning, to name just a few things the Rorschach assesses. There was even a call for a moratorium on the use of the Rorschach in clinical and forensic settings, which is indicative of the level of doubt some in the field have about the instrument's validity (Garb, 1999). Yet research continues to support the validity of many Rorschach variables (e.g., Hiller, Rosenthal, Bornstein, Berry, & Brunell-Neuleib, 1999; Mihura et al., 2013). The promising results of Mihura and colleagues' recent meta-analysis resulted in Wood, Garb, Nezworski, Lilienfeld, and Duke (2015) altering Garb's previous recommendation on the moratorium; they noted that they believe there is sufficient evidence to support the validity of the cognitive scores of the Rorschach (e.g., FQ). Still, they stated that their suggestion applies only to the cognitive scores, and not to other scores, such as affect-related scores (e.g., WSumC, CFC Proportion).

It is easy to get caught up in the back-and-forth that occurs between the Rorschach advocates and the Rorschach critics. However, it is important for test users to examine the Rorschach on their own to determine whether it would be useful with a specific client and referral question. Like any test, the Rorschach has strengths and weaknesses and may not be applicable to all referral questions or be the ideal test for all clients. This chapter provides a summary, arranged by topic, of some of the strengths and weaknesses of various aspects of both the

Rorschach CS and R-PAS. The final section of the chapter discusses the similarities and the differences between the two systems. The Book Companion Website Materials contain additional materials for this comparison, including a variable comparison sheet. These materials are designed to help clinicians switch between the two systems.

STANDARDIZATION AND NORMS

The accuracy of the norms and standardization practices associated with both systems have been questioned by individuals in the field. In fact, one of the biggest concerns about the Rorschach is its norms; some individuals have suggested that Exner's norms have a tendency to "overpathologize," or to make otherwise healthy individuals appear as if they have pathology (e.g., Wood, Nezworski, Garb, & Lilienfeld, 2006). Others have suggested that Exner's norms are flawed, given that there are differences in scores between Exner's (2003) norms and other comparison samples, including the international norms (Meyer et al., 2007; Wood, Nezworski, Garb, & Lilienfeld, 2001). There could be many reasons for these discrepancies between groups, including differences in group composition. It would be naïve to suggest that all collected comparison group data should produce the same results, so the differences between Exner's norms and other comparison groups may not be so problematic as critics suggest. Instead, the differences among the various comparison samples highlight the importance of choosing the comparison sample that can help the examiner to best assess the examinee's functioning. If the examinee is a thirty-seven-year-old Caucasian male factory worker born in the United States, then Exner's norms could be the appropriate comparison group norms to use. However, if the examinee is a nineteen-year-old biracial female who has recently immigrated to the United States from Brazil, then Exner's norms may not be the appropriate comparison sample to use, given that Exner's samples did not include individuals similar to the examinee as part of the normative group. Instead, another comparison sample may be more appropriate. It is also possible that the Rorschach would not be an appropriate test to use with this client and that, instead, another instrument, or set of instruments, should be used.

There have been specific concerns raised about the international norms. Some concerns have come from Rorschach critics (e.g., Hunsley, Lee, Wood, & Taylor, 2014), while others have come from Rorschach proponents (e.g., Ritzler & Sciara, 2009). Both sides have similar concerns, including whether the international norms are truly representative of the countries included, as the samples used for the international norms were recruited through word of mouth and were not stratified to ensure that they adequately represented the country in which they were collected. Other concerns have included the use of graduate student examiners in the data collection and the use of small sample sizes for some of the countries. The use of graduate student examiners may be particularly problematic, as studies have underscored the importance of a high-quality administration and of well-conducted Inquiry and Clarification Phases on the quality of the data obtained (e.g., Lis et al., 2007). Graduate student examiners generally have less experience and less training than seasoned professionals, and this lack of experience can be reflected in the quality of their administration and inquiry, as was evidenced in the study by Lis and colleagues (2007).

The concerns about the international norms affect both the CS and R-PAS, as R-PAS norms were derived using the international norms. The use of the international norms to derive R-PAS norms is problematic because the international norms were collected using CS administration procedures and, as of this writing, the research and data supporting the equivalency of the CS and R-PAS are limited (e.g., Reese et al., 2014). At this time, it is unclear whether the two different administration types produce the same quality of responses.

R-PAS norms have both strengths and weaknesses. First, R-PAS norms represent individuals from a variety of countries, rather than just the United States. Additionally, R-PAS norms relied on the use of multiple examiners. Both of these can be strengths. However, the quality of the examiners' training differed from sample to sample, and this could have affected the quality of the data obtained. Another weakness in R-PAS norms is that, as mentioned above, they were collected using CS administration procedures, and the data sets obtained from the two administration procedures have yet to be shown to be equivalent, at least in adult samples. In order to make the data appear as they would for an R-PAS administered protocol, the data were modeled.

It is important to note that there is an ongoing R-PAS normative sample data collection, and this process is using trained and certified examiners. Once these norms are published, they could present a significant strength for R-PAS and should address many of the concerns with the current normative sample noted earlier.

The final weakness, which affects both the CS and R-PAS, is the relatively small normative sample available for both systems. Exner's 2003 norms are based on a sample of 600 people, while R-PAS comparison norms are based on the results of 640 individuals (Meyer et al., 2011). To put this in perspective, the Personality Assessment Inventory (PAI) compares an individual's test performance to a sample of over 2,000 individuals in the United States, the MMPI-2 normative group consisted of over 2,500 adults in the United States, and the MCMI-IV used over 1,500 adults (Butcher et al., 2001; Millon et al., 2015; Morey, 2007). The strengths and weaknesses of the normative samples used in the CS and R-PAS are summarized in Rapid References 10.1, 10.2, and 10.3.

≡Rapid Reference 10.1

Strengths and Weaknesses of the Comprehensive System Norms

Strengths	Weaknesses
• Data were collected using experienced examiners. • Data were collected using standardized procedures for the CS.	• Normative group is small. • Data may "overpathologize" examinees.

≡Rapid Reference 10.2

Strengths and Weaknesses of the International Norms

Strengths	Weaknesses
• Multiple countries are represented. • Overall sample size is large. • Multiple examiners were used.	• Countries represented are predominately European; minimal representation of Asian and South American countries and no representation of African countries. • Sample sizes for individual countries are small. • Graduate student examiners were used. • Reliance on word of mouth to recruit participants.

≡Rapid Reference 10.3

Strengths and Weaknesses of R-PAS Norms

Strengths	Weaknesses
• Multiple countries are represented. • Existence of an ongoing process of collecting new normative data, using trained and certified examiners.	• The sample size is small. • Data were collected using CS administration procedures and modeled to look like data on R-PAS administered protocols.

RELIABILITY AND VALIDITY

It is vital that a psychological assessment instrument be reliable and valid. Reliability, or consistency in scores, can take many forms, including making sure that scores do not change over time (test-retest reliability) and that two or more raters will score an item the same way (inter-rater reliability). Validity, in contrast, is whether the test measures what it intends to measure.

Reliability

There has been a great deal of emphasis on the reliability of the Rorschach. The majority of this attention has been focused on the inter-rater reliability of the various systems, as scoring any performance-based measure is going to be more difficult than using a self-report measure. Still, because of the guidelines offered by various sources (e.g., Exner, 2001, 2003; Meyer et al., 2011; Viglione, 2010), the subjectivity in coding a Rorschach should be minimized. Nonetheless, it is important to ascertain whether different raters are capable of scoring Rorschach responses the same way; if two raters score the same response in vastly different ways, this will result in different interpretations, and that can affect the quality of the results for the examinee. This is why inter-rater reliability is so important; it ensures that different raters score the same response the same way.

One of the most common criticisms regarding the inter-rater reliability of the CS is how that inter-rater reliability was calculated (e.g., Wood, Nezworski, & Stejskal, 1996). Exner (2003) used percent agreement to calculate inter-rater reliability, a statistic that does not take chance agreement into account. However, other researchers have completed various inter-rater reliability studies using more appropriate statistical procedures, and with promising results. In general, the results of recent inter-rater reliability studies have indicated that the majority of the Rorschach variables, both on the CS and R-PAS, can be coded reliably (Acklin, McDowell, Verschell, & Chan, 2000; Kivisalu, Lewey, Shaffer, & Canfield, 2016; Meyer et al., 2002; Sahly, Shaffer, Erdberg, & O'Toole, 2011; Viglione, Blume-Marcovici, Miller, Giromini, & Meyer, 2012). The most problematic variables are some Cognitive Special Scores (e.g., DV2). Not surprisingly, these are the variables that many students struggle to code correctly. Still, it seems that with appropriate examiner training, many Rorschach variables can be coded reliably. The strength and weaknesses of inter-rater reliability for the Rorschach are summarized in Rapid Reference 10.4.

≡Rapid Reference 10.4

Strength and Weaknesses of Rorschach Inter-Rater Reliability

Strength	Weaknesses
• Recent studies suggest inter-rater reliability for the vast majority of variables is at least adequate, and for many variables it is excellent.	• Exner's use of percentage of agreement may have overestimated inter-rater reliability in his sample. • Some studies have suggested that inter-rater reliability for a few specific variables may fall below the accepted minimum threshold.

Validity

Validity is whether the test is measuring what it claims to be measuring. In psychological testing, we are often most concerned with a specific type of validity, referred to as construct validity. A construct is a variable that is not tangible and is not directly observable. An excellent example of this is intelligence; we cannot "see" intelligence—what we can see are behaviors and characteristics that we assume are associated with intelligence, such as doing well in school. In order to assess construct validity, we generally compare scores on the target measure (i.e., the one we are trying to determine the validity of) to scores on another measure that is thought to assess for the same construct.

Validity has been one of the most contentious topics surrounding the Rorschach (e.g., Ganellen, 2001; Wood, Nezworksi, Stejskal, Garven, & West, 1999). Not surprisingly, there have been many studies assessing the validity of individual Rorschach variables (e.g., Baity & Hilsenroth, 2002; Bombel et al., 2009); however, not all Rorschach variables have been studied extensively (Mihura et al., 2013). This is likely due to some of the variables being very rare, such as the color projection Special Score on the CS. Scores for such responses as color projections are unlikely to appear with any frequency, or even at all, in research samples. This makes it exceedingly difficult to assess their validity, as there have to be data on a score before its validity can be assessed.

Some researchers have attempted to determine the validity of various aspects of the Rorschach by comparing this instrument to other personality measures, such as the MMPI-2. However, the research directly comparing the MMPI to the Rorschach has failed to show strong evidence of convergent validity (Archer &

Krishnamurthy, 1993a, 1993b; Krishnamurthy, Archer, & House, 1996). Some have taken this as an indication that the Rorschach is not valid; however, it is also possible that the reason the variables on the MMPI and the Rorschach did not show evidence of convergent validity was that the two tests were actually measuring different aspects of related constructs. In other words, the two tests may not be measuring the same constructs. This would not be unexpected, given the very different ways (self-report versus performance-based) that the two instruments attempt to assess personality.

Research has supported the notion that the MMPI and the Rorschach assess different aspects of related constructs. The results of a meta-analysis by Hiller and colleagues (1999) suggested that the validity of the Rorschach CS is similar to that of the MMPI, even though the two do not show evidence of convergent validity. Moreover, the recent meta-analysis by Mihura and colleagues (2013) has provided strong support for the validity of many, but not all, of the variables in the CS and R-PAS.

There are still concerns about certain aspects of the validity of both the CS and R-PAS; namely, there is little to no empirical support for the contemporary interpretation of some variables (e.g., AG or AGM, on the CS or R-PAS, respectively). Still, it is important to recognize that the validity of the majority of variables on both systems has at least some empirical support in the literature, with many showing evidence of strong support. I would advise the reader to review the Mihura and colleagues' meta-analysis (2013), along with Wood and colleagues' (2015) response and reanalysis of the data and Mihura, Meyer, Bombel, and Dumitrascu's reply (2015), in order to review the variables that are strongly supported, moderately supported, and so forth.

ADMINISTRATION

Accurate administration of the Rorschach, whether using the CS or R-PAS, is vital, as the data obtained from the administration is used for scoring and interpretation. If the quality of the administration is poor, then the data obtained from it, and the subsequent interpretation, will be limited in their usefulness.

Both CS and R-PAS administration have a number of strengths. First, the administration for both systems is standardized. There is more structure to R-PAS administration procedures, which is an additional strength of R-PAS. This high level of structure and the specificity of the instructions can make beginning examiners feel more at ease with learning the test and can make examinees feel less anxious about the test, as examinees are provided specific information about what to expect with the test. Other strengths for both systems are that the administration time is generally short (typically less than an hour), the administration procedures are the same with both adults and children, and that the examinee is not required to read. This makes that test useful for examinees who are illiterate or who read at levels below what is required to take the various self-report personality instruments.

However, the Rorschach has weaknesses as well. Administering a Rorschach, whether using the CS or R-PAS, can be difficult. There is a steep learning curve for both systems; the more an examiner practices and gets feedback on his or her administrations, the better subsequent administrations will be. The administration of a Rorschach, regardless of the system being used, is more challenging and time consuming for the examiner than the administration of a self-report measure, such as the PAI. Additionally, a proper administration requires an excellent knowledge of coding. Finally, examinees with language difficulties may find the test extremely challenging, as the test requires a relatively high level of verbal proficiency from the examinee. The strengths and weaknesses of Rorschach administration are summarized in Rapid Reference 10.5.

≡Rapid Reference 10.5

Strengths and Weaknesses of Rorschach Administration

Strengths	Weaknesses
• Administration is standardized.	• Administration can be challenging for the examiner.
• The same procedure is used for children and adults.	• Proper administration relies on knowledge of coding principles and categories.
• The use of the R-Opt procedures (in R-PAS) should reduce the risk of too short or excessively long protocols.	• CS administration may result in too short or excessively long protocols, making scoring and interpretation difficult.
• Administration is relatively short (typically less than an hour).	
• R-PAS administration is highly structured, which may reduce anxiety for the examiner and the examinee.	• Administration may be stressful for the examiner or examinee due to the nature of the task.
• The Rorschach can be used with individuals who cannot read or who read below the level required by self-report instruments.	• Examinees with language difficulties may find the test challenging or be unable to complete it.
	• The Rorschach is more time consuming for the examiner than some other measures of personality.

CODING (SCORING)

Coding is one of the most difficult aspects of the Rorschach to do correctly, because of the infinite number of objects an examinee can perceive on the blots. Consequently, it is impossible to provide specific coding rules for every possible percept. The CS has been criticized for not providing specific coding rules; other sources (e.g., Exner, 2001; Viglione, 2010) provide additional information and examples to assist with coding. However, the examples in Exner (2001) do not explain why responses were coded the way that they were. This lack of coding explanations can be frustrating for someone who is practicing coding and has a response that differs from what the answer key provides. The manual for R-PAS, in contrast, provides a significant amount of material regarding coding, including sample responses with explanations of why they were coded the way that they were. This is a significant benefit to using R-PAS; the presence of the detailed information on coding, coupled with the coding samples with explanations, should increase the coding accuracy of those who review the manual thoroughly. The strengths and weaknesses of Rorschach coding are summarized in Rapid Reference 10.6.

≋Rapid Reference 10.6

Strengths and Weaknesses of Rorschach Coding

Strengths	Weaknesses
• There are multiple resources to assist with coding. • The R-PAS manual provides examples with explanations that should help to improve coding on that system. • Inter-rater reliability for many variables is high, indicating that with training, individuals should be able to code either system accurately.	• Rorschach coding is time consuming, especially for the beginning examiner. • There are no explanations for the sample coding of responses in Exner's (2001) *Rorschach Workbook.* • There are many variables to code, increasing the likelihood of an error. • It is impossible to provide information for all possible responses, due to the infinite number of items examinees can perceive on the blots.

INTERPRETATION

Interpretation of both the CS and R-PAS is complex. Each system requires the examiner to have an excellent knowledge of not only the Rorschach but of personality theory and psychopathology as well. Still, both the CS and R-PAS provide a great deal of information to assist the examiner with interpretation, including research support for the variables used in the systems. Both systems have provided an interpretation framework to use when interpreting. However, the CS's reliance on raw scores rather than standardized ones may make interpretation more difficult for an examiner, as determining whether a score deviates from the norm requires directly comparing the score to the normative data tables. R-PAS, in contrast, uses standardized scores. This makes it easier to determine when a score deviates from the norm; it is not necessary to compare a score to normative data tables to determine whether it is in the average range or not, as the value for the standard score provides information on how much, if at all, that score differs from the mean.

The primary Rorschach texts provide a great deal of information regarding interpretation (Exner, 2003; Meyer et al., 2011). However, Exner's (2003) work is dense, and beginning examiners often report that interpretation is an arduous task as a result. The R-PAS manual, conversely, appears to be more streamlined and accessible. Another concern with Exner's text is that it can be seen as a "cookbook" for interpretation, as it provides "potential findings" for the variables, rather than a summary of what high and low scores mean. Each step has a limited number of potential findings, causing some practitioners to assume that if the value for a particular variable is not in a potential finding, then the variable should not be interpreted. I have found that beginning examiners, in particular, often focus on these potential findings rather than the overall picture of the client and what that variable means for that client. These issues seem less likely to occur with R-PAS, as the focus in the interpretive part of the manual is on what the variables mean rather than potential findings.

One of the biggest strengths of the CS is that Exner designed it to be atheoretical; this makes it accessible to examiners who ascribe to a variety of theoretical views, including psychodynamic and cognitive behavioral orientations. Still, there are some clearly psychodynamically related concepts in the system, such as the search for projected material. R-PAS also can be used by those with varied theoretical orientations; however, examiners who are not psychodynamically oriented may have more difficulty interpreting certain aspects of R-PAS, including the mutuality of autonomy and the oral dependency language variables. These variables are derived from psychoanalytic and psychodynamic theory. It is important to note that there is empirical support for both of these variables in the literature (Bombel et al., 2009; Bornstein, 1996). The strengths and weaknesses of Rorschach interpretation are summarized in Rapid Reference 10.7.

≡Rapid Reference 10.7

Strengths and Weaknesses of Rorschach Interpretation

Strengths	Weaknesses
• Both systems can be used by examiners with varied theoretical orientations.	• Examiners who are not psychodynamically oriented may have difficulty with some aspects of both systems (e.g., certain variables on R-PAS; the search for projected material).
• Many resources exist to assist with interpretation (e.g., Choca, 2013; Weiner, 2003).	• CS can present as a "cookbook," causing examiners to focus on findings rather than the overall picture of the examinee.
• R-PAS use of standardized scores streamlines interpretation.	• CS use of raw scores requires comparing an examinee's score to a normative data table for interpretation.
• Both systems provide a great deal of data regarding various facets of the examinee's functioning.	• Both systems have some variables that have not been empirically supported in the literature or that have minimal empirical support.

COMPARISON OF THE CS AND R-PAS

The CS and R-PAS are similar in many respects. This is not surprising, given that a goal of both systems was to identify and include variables that had empirical support (Exner, 2003; Meyer et al., 2011). Still, there are differences between the two systems. This section will compare the administration, coding, and interpretation processes of the two systems.

Administration

There are some similarities in the administration processes for the two systems. First, and foremost, both systems introduce the inkblots to examinees with the phrase "What might this be?" Additionally, both the CS and R-PAS have standardized administrations with two phases. In the first phase—the Response Phase in both systems—the task of examinees is to respond to the blot and to tell the examiner what it looks like to them. In the second phase—the Inquiry Phase on the CS and Clarification Phase on R-PAS—examiners need to ensure they have enough information to code the contents, location, and determinants (the *what, where,* and *why*). Both systems also require that the examiner record the examinee's verbalizations and relevant gestures verbatim, in order to facilitate coding.

However, there are also differences between the two systems when it comes to administration. Specifically, R-PAS tends to be more structured than the CS. The introduction to the CS is relatively vague, especially regarding the number of responses per card. However, R-PAS instructions are very specific and request the examinee to supply two or three responses per card. This increased structure can be seen throughout R-PAS administration, as even the queries tend to be more specific on R-PAS than on the CS.

There is also a difference in the amount of intervention the examiner can provide during the administration. R-PAS allows for more examiner intervention, especially during the Response Phase, than the CS does. The CS allows the examiner to prompt for an additional response only on Card I and Card IV and only under specific circumstances. However, during an R-PAS administration, examiners can prompt for additional responses on every card. Similarly, on the CS the examiner can stop the examinee from providing additional responses only under very specific circumstances; during an R-PAS administration, the examiner can "pull" every card. As a result, on R-PAS, the maximum number of responses an examinee can provide on each card is four (for a maximum total of forty responses); there is no maximum number of responses on the CS.

The CS and R-PAS also differ in the number of responses necessary for a valid administration. The CS requires fourteen responses while R-PAS requires sixteen responses. The systems also have different processes to use when the examinee has not provided sufficient responses by the end of the first phase. On the CS, the examiner essentially starts over from scratch, as the examiner cannot include responses from the initial administration unless the examinee provides them again during the readministration. However, on R-PAS, the examiner retains all of the responses from the initial administration and requests that the examinee add more responses; this step is not a readministration. The similarities and differences in CS administration and R-PAS administration are summarized in Rapid Reference 10.8.

Coding (Scoring)

There are significant differences between coding practices on the CS and on R-PAS, ranging from the variables used by each system to the ways the variables are coded. Still, there are also similarities between the two systems, as both use many of the same variables.

≋Rapid Reference 10.8

Similarities and Differences in CS and R-PAS Administration

Similarities	Differences
• Administration is standardized. • Examiner introduces each card by saying, "What might this be?" • Each system has two phases: Response and either Inquiry (CS) or Clarification (R-PAS).	• The number of responses required for valid administration differs (14 vs. 16). • The introductions to orient the examinees differ, with R-PAS being more directive. • The amount of examiner intervention allowed is less on the CS and more on R-PAS. • When examiners need to go through the cards again due to the examinee not providing sufficient responses, previous responses are retained on R-PAS but are not used again on the CS unless the examinee provides them anew.

Source: Based on information from Exner, 2003; Meyer et al., 2011.

The variables that are the same on both systems include the location codes, the location numbers, and many of the content codes, determinants, and Special Scores. Some variables have been renamed; for example, the CS's ALOG code is conceptually similar to R-PAS's PEC code. Similarly, the concept of DQ on the CS is roughly similar to the object qualities variable on R-PAS.

One significant difference between the systems is that they code space differently. For example, on R-PAS, the examiner needs to differentiate responses where the examinee integrated white space with the chromatic parts of the blot (SI) from responses where the examinee reversed the figure and the ground (SR) (Meyer et al., 2011). On the CS, this differentiation is not necessary (Exner, 2003).

FQ is also coded differently on the two systems. The biggest difference involves the use of the u code. On the CS, FQu indicates that the response followed the contours of the blot but was not a commonly seen response (Exner, 2003). However, on R-PAS, FQu can also indicate that the response moderately fits the contours of the blot (Meyer et al., 2011).

There are some significant differences in how determinants are coded on the two systems. First, there is one determinant (Cn) that is coded on the CS but not on R-PAS. Additionally, there are differences in how some variables are coded. For example, on the CS, the examiner is supposed to determine the relative importance of form when coding achromatic color (C') and the shading variables (T, V, Y); however, this differentiation is not necessary on R-PAS. All texture responses are coded as T; there is no need to differentiate whether the response was a T, TF, or FT on R-PAS. There are also nuanced differences in how specific responses should be coded on R-PAS and the CS; perhaps the best example of this is that an animal engaging in any animal movement, even if it is not specific to the species, is coded as an FM on R-PAS (Meyer et al., 2011). On the CS, however, if an animal is engaging in a movement that is not specific to the species but is still an animal movement, that response should be coded as M (Exner, 2000, 2003).

There are also some differences in how content is coded on the two systems. The primary difference is that many content codes coded on the CS are not given specific classifications on R-PAS (e.g., Cl) (Exner, 2001, 2003; Meyer at al., 2011). Instead, these contents are all coded as NC on R-PAS (Meyer et al., 2011).

The final difference in coding between the CS and R-PAS relates to the Special Scores. Although the Cognitive Special Scores are the same on both systems, there are differences in how some of these variables are coded. For example, the colloquial addition of a "-y" or "-ish" ending to a word would usually be coded as a DV on the CS; however, on R-PAS, these types of verbalizations typically do not warrant a special score (Exner, 2003; Meyer et al., 2011).

The thematic and content-based Special Scores differ between the systems. Specifically, CP and PSV are coded on the CS but not on R-PAS. Conversely, AGC, MAH/MAP, and ODL are coded on R-PAS but not traditionally on the CS (Exner, 2003; Meyer et al., 2011). Of course, any of these variables could be coded as part of the CS, but historically they have not been used in that system. The similarities and differences in CS coding and R-PAS coding are summarized in Rapid Reference 10.9.

Interpretation

As with administration and coding, there are some similarities in CS and R-PAS interpretation. First, both systems rely on the deviation principle for interpretation; scores that deviate from the norm are considered to be atypical. Additionally, many of the same variables are interpreted in both systems.

The primary differences in interpretation between the two systems are related to the process of interpretation. The two systems use different normative standards;

≡ Rapid Reference 10.9

Similarities and Differences in CS and R-PAS Coding

Similarities	Differences
• Location is coded the same way. • Most content codes are coded the same way. • Most determinants are coded the same way. • Most of the Cognitive Special Scores are scored the same way.	• Some content codes are present only on the CS. • Space is coded differently on the two systems. • The way some determinants are coded varies between systems. • Some Thematic Special Scores are coded in R-PAS but not the CS.

Source: Based on information from Exner, 2003; Meyer et al., 2011.

although it should be noted that the international norms can be used with the CS as well. Another main difference is that the scores on R-PAS are standardized and the scores on the CS remain as raw scores. Finally, CS interpretation proceeds by clusters, organized through a Key Variable search, whereas R-PAS has no Key Variable search. Instead, the domains on R-PAS are divided into Page 1 and Page 2 variables, with the Page 1 variables generally having higher levels of empirical support than the Page 2 ones. The similarity and differences in CS interpretation and R-PAS interpretation are summarized in Rapid Reference 10.10.

≡ Rapid Reference 10.10

Similarity and Differences in CS and R-PAS Interpretation

Similarity	Differences
• Interpretation in both systems relies on the deviation principle.	• The two systems use different normative standards • The CS uses raw scores and R-PAS uses standardized scores. • The CS interprets "clusters" of variables organized through a Key Variable search, and R-PAS interprets variables organized into "domains" and into Page 1 (more supported) and Page 2 (less supported) variables.

Source: Based on information from Exner, 2003; Meyer et al., 2011.

FINAL THOUGHTS ON THE CS AND R-PAS

The use of the Rorschach is certainly one of the more contentious, if not the most contentious, topic among psychologists, with a marked division between those who are pro-Rorschach and those who are anti-Rorschach. It is easy to get caught up in the rhetoric between the Rorschach proponents and the Rorschach opponents. I would suggest that readers not focus on the rhetoric and instead focus their attention on the research behind the Rorschach when deciding whether to use the instrument and when deciding which system to use.

Like all psychological tests, the Rorschach, both the CS and R-PAS, has strengths and weaknesses. For example, one of the significant strengths of the Rorschach, regardless of the system being used, is its ability to detect difficulties with cognition. This is where the Rorschach truly excels. Both systems have weaknesses as well, including that they are both time intensive to administer, code, and interpret.

Only time will tell what the future holds for the Rorschach. Nevertheless, the Rorschach has been shown to have staying power. The renewed focus on empiricism started by Exner (2003) and continued by Meyer and colleagues (2011) should increase the likelihood that the Rorschach will continue to be used by mental health practitioners for some time to come.

🐀 TEST YOURSELF 🐀

1. **Which of the following statements is true about the validity of the CS and R-PAS?**
   a. The majority of the variables on both the CS and R-PAS have at least some empirical support.
   b. Only 30% of the variables on R-PAS have empirical support.
   c. Only 30% of the variables on the CS have empirical support.
   d. Both b. and c. are true.
2. **True or False: Both CS administration and R-PAS administration are standardized.**
   a. True
   b. False
3. **Which R-PAS coding category is most similar to the CS DQ?**
   a. Location
   b. Determinant
   c. Space
   d. Object qualities

4. **Which variable is coded on R-PAS but not traditionally coded on the CS?**
   a. MAH/MAP
   b. Space
   c. CP
   d. Color

Answers: 1. a; 2. a; 3. d; 4. a.

Appendix

SAMPLE COMPUTERIZED SCORE REPORTS

This appendix includes computerized score reports from the Rorschach CS and R-PAS. The first half of this appendix includes all the scores from the Rorschach CS Sequence of Scores and Structural Summary that were used for the CS case study and cited in Chapters 4 and 5. This first half of the appendix is divided into three sections that accord with the three pages of the RIAP printout shown in Figures A.1, A.2, and A.3. After each figure, there are larger tables that contain the same data as in the figure in order to make it easier for the reader to see the data contained in each section. The first section (Tables A.1 through A.3) provides the data for the first page (Sequence of Scores and Summary of Approach). The next section (Tables A.4 through A.18) provides the information for the Structural Summary. The remaining section (Tables A.19 through A.24) provides the data for the constellations.

The second part of the appendix includes the Code Sequence, Protocol Level Counts and Calculations, and Summary Scores and Profiles that were used for the R-PAS case study and cited in Chapters 8 and 9. This second half of this appendix contains the Code Sequence (Table A.25), followed by the Protocol Level Counts and Calculations (Figure A.4), and the Summary Scores and Profiles Pages (Figures A.5 and A.6).

IMPORTANT!
. . . .

The data and images in this first half of the appendix are reproduced by special permission of the publisher, Psychological Assessment Resources, Inc., 16204 North Florida Avenue, Lutz, Florida 33549, from the Rorschach Interpretation Assistance Program: Version 5, Copyright 1999, 2001 by PAR Inc. Further reproduction is prohibited without permission of PAR, Inc.

CS: SEQUENCE OF SCORES AND SUMMARY OF APPROACH

This section displays the Sequence of Scores (coding) and the Summary of Approach. Figure A.1 is the first page of the Rorschach Interpretation Assistance Program (RIAP) printout for the coding of the case study presented in this book.

RIAP™ Sequence of Scores Report

Client Information

Client Name: Sarah Frazier	Gender: Female	Test Date: 01/15/2016
Client ID:	Date of Birth: 03/10/1990	Description:

Sequence of Scores

Card	Resp. No	Location and DQ	Loc. No.	Determinant(s) and Form Quality	(2)	Content(s)	Pop	Z Score	Special Scores
I	1	WSo	1	Fo		A		3.5	
	2	Wo	1	FMao		A	P	1.0	
II	3	Wo	1	CF.C'F.FMau		A		4.5	
	4	Do	3	FD-		An			
	5	DS+	5	Ma.FC'u		Cg, H		3.0	GHR
III	6	W+	1	Ma.C.mpo	2	H, Sx, Bl, Hh	P	5.5	AG, MOR, PHR
	7	Do	2	Fu		H, An			DV, GHR
IV	8	Wo	1	Ma.FYo		(H)		2.0	GHR
	9	W+	1	Ma.FDo		(H), Sc	P	4.0	GHR
V	10	Wo	1	FMao		A		1.0	
	11	Ddo	99	FMau		A			
VI	12	Wo	1	Fo		Ad, Hh, Sx	P	2.5	
	13	Do	4	Fo		Sc			
VII	14	Do	2	Mpo	2	Hd	P		GHR
	15	DSo	10	Fo		Hh			
VIII	16	W+	1	FMa.rFo		A, Na	P	4.5	
	17	Do	2	FCu		Cg			
IX	18	Dv/+	2	map.CFo		Na		2.5	
X	19	DdSo	99	FC'.FC-		H, Sx, Cg		6.0	PHR
	20	Do	9	Fo		A			PER

Summary of Approach

I :	WS.W	VI :	W.D
II :	W.D.DS	VII :	D.DS
III :	W.D	VIII :	W.D
IV :	W.W	IX :	D
V :	W.Dd	X :	DdS.D

Figure A.1 RIAP™ Sequence of Scores Report for Ms. Frazier (pseudonym)

Source: Rorschach Interpretation Assistance Program: Version 5, Copyright 1999, 2001 by PAR Inc.

Tables A.1 through A.3 contain the same information as Figure A.1, but present it in larger tables so the data can be more easily reviewed.

Table A.1 Client information

Client Information		
Client Name: Sarah Frazier (pseudonym) Client ID:	Gender: Female Date of Birth: 03/10/1990	Test Date: 01/15/2016 Description:

Source: Rorschach Interpretation Assistance Program: Version 5, Copyright 1999, 2001 by PAR Inc.

Table A.2 Sequence of Scores

			Sequence of Scores					
Card	Resp. No.	Location and DQ	Loc. No.	Determinant(s) and Form Quality	(2)	Content(s)	Pop	Z Score	Special Scores
I	1	WSo	1	Fo		A		3.5	
	2	Wo	1	FMao		A	P	1.0	
II	3	Wo	1	CF.C'F.FMau		A		4.5	
	4	Do	3	FD–		An			
	5	DS+	5	Ma.FC'u		Cg,H		3.0	GHR
III	6	W+	1	Ma.C.mpo	2	H, Sx, Bl, Hh	P	5.5	AG, MOR, PHR
	7	Do	2	Fu		H,An			DV, GHR
IV	8	Wo	1	Ma.FYo		(H)		2.0	GHR
	9	W+	1	Ma.FDo		(H),Sc	P	4.0	GHR
V	10	Wo	1	FMao		A		1.0	
	11	Ddo	99	FMau		A			
VI	12	Wo	1	Fo		Ad, Hh, Sx	P	2.5	
	13	Do	4	Fo		Sc			
VII	14	Do	2	Mpo	2	Hd	P		GHR
	15	DSo	10	Fo		Hh			
VIII	16	W+	1	FMa.rFo		A,Na	P	4.5	
	17	Do	2	FCu		Cg			
IX	18	Dv/+	2	map.CFo		Na		2.5	
X	19	DdSo	99	FC'.FC–		H, Sx, Cg		6.0	PHR
	20	Do	9	Fo		A			PER

Source: Rorschach Interpretation Assistance Program: Version 5, Copyright 1999, 2001 by PAR Inc.

Table A.3 Summary of Approach

I:	WS.W	VI:	W.D
II:	W.D.DS	VII:	D.DS
III:	W.D	VIII:	W.D
IV:	W.W	IX:	D
V:	W.Dd	X:	DdS.D

Source: Rorschach Interpretation Assistance Program: Version 5, Copyright 1999, 2001 by PAR Inc.

CS: STRUCTURAL SUMMARY

This section displays the Structural Summary. Figure A.2 is the second page of the RIAP printout. The top part of the Structural Summary contains the counts for each variable (e.g., how many times each variable occurs). The bottom half of the Structural Summary contains the ratios and variables, divided by cluster, that are to be interpreted using the Comprehensive System. Tables A.4 through A.18 contain the same information as Figure A.2 but in a larger format.

RIAP™ Structural Summary

Client Information

Client Name: Sarah Frazier	Gender: Female	Test Date: 01/15/2016
Client ID:	Date of Birth: 03/10/1990	Description:

Location Features

Zf	=	12
ZSum	=	40.0
ZEst	=	38.0
W	=	9
(Wv	=	0)
D	=	9
W+D	=	18
Dd	=	2
S	=	4

DQ

		(FQ-)
+	= 4	(0)
o	= 15	(2)
v/+	= 1	(0)
v	= 1	(0)

Form Quality

	FQx	MQual	W+D
+	= 0	0	0
o	= 13	4	13
u	= 5	1	4
-	= 2	0	1
none	= 0	0	0

Determinants

Blends	Single	
CF.C'F.FM	M	= 1
M.FC'	FM	= 3
M.C.m	m	= 0
M.FY	FC	= 1
M.FD	CF	= 0
FM.rF	C	= 0
m.CF	Cn	= 0
FC'.FC	FC'	= 0
	C'F	= 0
	C'	= 0
	FT	= 0
	TF	= 0
	T	= 0
	FV	= 0
	VF	= 0
	V	= 0
	FY	= 0
	YF	= 0
	Y	= 0
	Fr	= 0
	rF	= 0
	FD	= 1
	F	= 6
	(2)	= 2

Contents

H	=	4
(H)	=	2
Hd	=	1
(Hd)	=	0
Hx	=	0
A	=	7
(A)	=	0
Ad	=	1
(Ad)	=	0
An	=	2
Art	=	0
Ay	=	0
Bl	=	1
Bt	=	0
Cg	=	3
Cl	=	0
Ex	=	0
Fd	=	0
Fi	=	0
Ge	=	0
Hh	=	3
Ls	=	0
Na	=	0
Sc	=	2
Sx	=	3
Xy	=	0
Idio	=	0

S-Constellation

☐	FV+VF+V+FD > 2
☑	Col-Shd Blends > 0
☑	Ego < .31 or > .44
☐	MOR > 3
☐	Zd > ±3.5
☑	es > EA
☑	CF + C > FC
☑	X+% < .70
☑	S > 3
☐	P < 3 or > 8
☐	Pure H < 2
☐	R < 17
6	Total

Special Scores

		Lvl-1	Lvl-2
DV	=	1 x1	0 x2
INC	=	0 x2	0 x4
DR	=	0 x3	0 x6
FAB	=	0 x4	0 x7
ALOG	=	0 x5	
CON	=	0 x7	
Raw Sum6	=	**1**	
Wgtd Sum6	=	**1**	
AB	= 0	GHR	= 5
AG	= 1	PHR	= 2
COP	= 0	MOR	= 1
CP	= 0	PER	= 1
		PSV	= 0

RATIOS, PERCENTAGES, AND DERIVATIONS

CONTROLS

R = 20	L = 0.43

EB = 5 : 4.5	EA	= 9.5	EBPer	= N/A
eb = 7 : 4	es	= 11	D	= 0
	Adj es	= 10	Adj D	= 0

FM = 5	SumC' = 3	SumT = 0
m = 2	SumV = 0	SumY = 1

AFFECT

FC:CF+C	= 2 : 3
Pure C	= 1
SumC':WSumC	= 3 : 4.5
Afr	= 0.33
S	= 4
Blends:R	= 8 : 20
CP	= 0

INTERPERSONAL

COP = 0	AG = 1
GHR:PHR	= 5 : 2
a:p	= 10 : 3
Food	= 0
SumT	= 0
Human Content	= 7
Pure H	= 4
PER	= 1
Isolation Index	= 0.20

IDEATION

a:p	= 10 : 3	Sum6	= 1
Ma:Mp	= 4 : 1	Lvl-2	= 0
2AB+(Art+Ay)	= 0	WSum6	= 1
MOR	= 1	M-	= 0
		M none	= 0

MEDIATION

XA%	= 0.90
WDA%	= 0.94
X-%	= 0.10
S-	= 1
P	= 6
X+%	= 0.65
Xu%	= 0.25

PROCESSING

Zf	= 12
W:D:Dd	= 9:9:2
W : M	= 9 : 5
Zd	= +2.0
PSV	= 0
DQ+	= 4
DQv	= 0

SELF-PERCEPTION

3r+(2)/R	= 0.25
Fr+rF	= 1
SumV	= 0
FD	= 2
An+Xy	= 2
MOR	= 1
H:(H)+Hd+(Hd)	= 4 : 3

PTI = 0	☑ DEPI = 5	☐ CDI = 2	☐ S-CON = 6	☐ HVI = No	☐ OBS = No

Figure A.2 RIAP™ Structural Summary for Ms. Frazier (pseudonym)

Source: Rorschach Interpretation Assistance Program: Version 5, Copyright 1999, 2001 by PAR Inc.

Table A.4 Location Features

Location Feature	Value
Zf	12
ZSum	40.0
ZEst	38.0
W	9
(Wv)	0
W + D	18
Dd	2
S	4

Source: Rorschach Interpretation Assistance Program: Version 5, Copyright 1999, 2001 by PAR Inc.

Table A.5 Developmental Quality (DQ)

	Value	(FQ–)
+	4	(0)
o	15	(2)
v/+	1	(0)
v	0	(0)

Source: Rorschach Interpretation Assistance Program: Version 5, Copyright 1999, 2001 by PAR Inc.

Table A.6 Form Quality (FQ)

	FQx	MQual	W + D
+	0	0	0
o	13	4	13
u	5	1	4
–	2	0	1
none	0	0	0

Source: Rorschach Interpretation Assistance Program: Version 5, Copyright 1999, 2001 by PAR Inc.

Table A.7 Determinants

Blends	Single	
Determinant	Determinant	Value
CF.C'F.FM	M	1
M.FC'	FM	3
M.C.m	m	0
M.FY	FC	1
M.FD	CF	0
FM.rF	C	0
m.CF	Cn	0
FC'.FC	FC'	0
	C'F	0
	C'	0
	FT	0
	TF	0
	T	0
	FV	0
	VF	0
	V	0
	FY	0
	YF	0
	Y	0
	Fr	0
	rF	0
	FD	1
	F	6
	(2)	2

Source: Rorschach Interpretation Assistance Program:
Version 5, Copyright 1999, 2001 by PAR Inc.

Table A.8 Contents

Item	Value
H	4
(H)	2
Hd	1
(Hd)	0
Hx	0
A	7
(A)	0
Ad	1

(continued)

Table A.8 Continued

Item	Value
(Ad)	0
An	2
Art	0
Ay	0
Bl	1
Bt	0
Cg	3
Cl	0
Ex	0
Fd	0
Fi	0
Ge	0
Hh	3
Ls	0
Na	2
Sc	2
Sx	3
Xy	0
Idio	0

Source: Rorschach Interpretation
Assistance Program: Version 5,
Copyright 1999, 2001 by PAR Inc.

Table A.9 Suicide-Constellation (S-CON)

☐ FV + VF + V + FD > 2
☑ Col-Shd Blends > 0
☑ Ego < .31 or > .44
☑ MOR > 3
☑ Zd > ± 3.5
☑ es > EA
☑ CF + C > FC
☑ X+% < .70
☑ S > 3
☐ P < 3 or > 8
☐ Pure H < 2
☐ R < 17
  6 Total

Source: Rorschach Interpretation
Assistance Program: Version 5,
Copyright 1999, 2001 by PAR Inc.

Table A.10 Special Scores

Score	Lvl-1		Lvl-2	
DV	1	×1	0	×2
INC	0	×2	0	×4
DR	0	×3	0	×6
FAB	0	×4	0	×7
ALOG	0	×5		
CON	0	×7		

Raw Sum6 = 1
Wgtd Sum6 = 1

Score	Value	Score	Value
AB	0	GHR	5
AG	1	PHR	2
COP	0	MOR	1
CP	0	PER	1
		PSV	0

Source: Rorschach Interpretation Assistance Program: Version 5, Copyright 1999, 2001 by PAR Inc.

Table A.11 Controls

R = 20		L = 0.43
EB = 5:4.5	EA = 9.5	EBPer = N/A
eb = 7:4	es = 11	D = 0
	Adj es = 10	Adj D = 0
FM = 5	SumC' = 3	SumT = 0
m = 2	SumV = 0	SumY = 1

Source: Rorschach Interpretation Assistance Program: Version 5, Copyright 1999, 2001 by PAR Inc.

Table A.12 Affect

Affect	Ratio
FC:CF + C	2:3
Pure C	1
SumC':WSumC	3:4.5
Afr	0.33
S	4
Blends:R	8:20
CP	0

Source: Rorschach Interpretation Assistance Program: Version 5, Copyright 1999, 2001 by PAR Inc.

Table A.13 Interpersonal

Interpersonal	Value
COP	0
AG	1
GHR:PHR	5:2
a:p	10:3
Food	0
SumT	0
Human Content	7
Pure H	4
PER	1
Isolation Index	0.20

Source: Rorschach Interpretation Assistance Program: Version 5, Copyright 1999, 2001 by PAR Inc.

Table A.14 Ideation

Ideation	Value	Ideation	Value
a:p	10:3	Sum6	1
Ma:Mp	4:1	Lvl-2	0
2AB + (Art + Ay)	0	WSum6	1
MOR	1	M–	0
		M none	0

Source: Rorschach Interpretation Assistance Program: Version 5, Copyright 1999, 2001 by PAR Inc.

Table A.15 Mediation

Mediation	Value
XA%	0.90
WDA%	0.94
X–%	0.10
S–	1
P	6
X+%	0.65
Xu%	0.25

Source: Rorschach Interpretation Assistance Program: Version 5, Copyright 1999, 2001 by PAR Inc.

Table A.16 Processing

Processing	Value
Zf	12
W:D:Dd	9:9:2
W: M	9:5
Zd	+2.0
PSV	0
DQ+	4
DQv	0

Source: Rorschach Interpretation Assistance Program: Version 5, Copyright 1999, 2001 by PAR Inc.

Table A.17 Self-Perception

Self-Perception	Value
3r + (2) / R	0.25
Fr + rF	1
SumV	0
FD	2
An + Xy	2
MOR	1
H:(H) + Hd + (Hd)	4:3

Source: Rorschach Interpretation Assistance Program: Version 5, Copyright 1999, 2001 by PAR Inc.

Table A.18 Constellation Values

	PTI = 0	
☑	DEPI = 5	
☐	CDI = 2	
☐	S-CON = 6	
☐	HVI = No	
☐	OBS = No	

Source: Rorschach Interpretation Assistance Program: Version 5, Copyright 1999, 2001 by PAR Inc.

CS: CONSTELLATIONS

This section displays the information for the Constellations. Figure A.3 is the third page of the RIAP printout. Tables A.19 through A.24 contain the same information as Figure A.3 but in a larger format. The values for the Constellations are on bottom of Page 2 of the RIAP printout (see Figure A.2 and Table A.18).

RIAP™ Structural Summary Report
Client Name: Sarah Frazier
Client ID:

CONSTELLATIONS TABLE

S-Constellation (Suicide Potential)

☐ Positive if 8 or more conditions are true:
NOTE: Applicable only for subjects over 14 years old.

☐ FV+VF+V+FD [2] > 2
☑ Col-Shd Blends [2] > 0
☑ Ego [0.25] < .31 *or* > .44
☐ MOR [1] > 3
☐ Zd [2.0] > ±3.5
☑ es [11] > EA [9.5]
☑ CF + C [3] > FC [2]
☑ X+% [0.65] < .70
☑ S [4] > 3
☐ P [6] < 3 *or* > 8
☐ Pure H [4] < 2
☐ R [20] < 17
___
6   Total

PTI (Perceptual-Thinking Index)

☐ (XA% [0.90] < 0.70) *and* (WDA% [0.94] < 0.75)
☐ X-% [0.10] > 0.29
☐ (Sum Level 2 Special Scores [0] > 2)
  and (FAB2 [0] > 0)
☐ ((R [20] < 17) *and* (WSum6 [1] > 12)) *or*
  ((R [20] > 16) *and* (WSum6 [1] > 17))
☐ (M- [0] > 1) *or* (X-% [0.10] > 0.40)
___
0   Total

DEPI (Depression Index)

☑ Positive if 5 or more conditions are true:

☐ (FV + VF + V [0] > 0) *or* (FD [2] > 2)
☑ (Col-Shd Blends [2] > 0) *or* (S [4] > 2)
☑ (3r + (2)/R [0.25] > 0.44 *and* Fr + rF [1] = 0)
  or (3r + (2)/R [0.25] < 0.33)
☑ (Afr [0.33] < 0.46) *or* (Blends [8] < 4)
☑ (SumShading [4] > FM + m [7])
  or (SumC' [3] > 2)
☐ (MOR [1] > 2) *or* (2xAB + Art + Ay [0] > 3)
☑ (COP [0] < 2)
  or ([Bt+2xCl+Ge+Ls+2xNa]/R [0.20] > 0.24)
___
5   Total

CDI (Coping Deficit Index)

☐ Positive if 4 or more conditions are true:

☐ (EA [9.5] < 6) *or* (AdjD [0] < 0)
☑ (COP [0] < 2) *and* (AG [1] < 2)
☑ (Weighted Sum C [4.5] < 2.5)
  or (Afr [0.33] < 0.46)
☐ (Passive [3] > Active + 1 [11])
  or (Pure H [4] < 2)
☐ (Sum T [0] > 1)
  or (Isolate/R [0.20] > 0.24)
  or (Food [0] > 0)
___
2   Total

HVI (Hypervigilance Index)

☐ Positive if condition 1 is true and at least 4 of the others
are true:

☑ (1) FT + TF + T [0] = 0
- -
☐ (2) Zf [12] > 12
☐ (3) Zd [2.0] > +3.5
☑ (4) S [4] > 3
☑ (5) H + (H) + Hd + (Hd) [7] > 6
☐ (6) (H) + (A) + (Hd) + (Ad) [2] > 3
☐ (7) H + A : Hd + Ad [13:2] < 4 : 1
☐ (8) Cg [3] > 3

OBS (Obsessive Style Index)

☐ (1) Dd [2] > 3
☐ (2) Zf [12] > 12
☐ (3) Zd [2.0] > +3.0
☐ (4) Populars [6] > 7
☐ (5) FQ+ [0] > 1
- -
☐ Positive if one or more is true:

☐ Conditions 1 to 5 are all true
☐ Two or more of 1 to 4 are true *and* FQ+ [0] > 3
☐ 3 or more of 1 to 5 are true
  and X+% [0.65] > 0.89
☐ FQ+ [0] > 3 *and* X+% [0.65] > 0.89

NOTE: '*' *indicates a cutoff that has been adjusted for age norms.*

Figure A.3 RIAP™ Constellations for Ms. Frazier (pseudonym)

Source: Rorschach Interpretation Assistance Program: Version 5, Copyright 1999, 2001 by PAR Inc.

Table A.19 Suicide Constellation (Suicide Potential)

☐	Positive if 8 or more conditions are true:

☐	FV + VF + V + FD [2] > 2
☑	Col-Shd Blends [2] > 0
☑	Ego [0.25] < .31 *or* > .44
☐	MOR [1] > 3
☐	Zd [2.0] > ±3.5
☑	es [11] > EA [9.5]
☑	CF + C [3] > FC [2]
☑	X+% [0.65] < .70
☑	S [4] > 3
☐	P [6] < 3 or > 8
☐	Pure H [4] < 2
☐	R [20] < 17
	6 Total

Note: Positive if 8 or more conditions are true is applicable only for subjects over 14 years old.
Source: Rorschach Interpretation Assistance Program: Version 5, Copyright 1999, 2001 by PAR Inc.

Table A.20 Perceptual-Thinking Index (PTI)

☐	(XA% [0.90] < 0.70) *and* (WDA% [0.94] < 0.75)
☐	X–% [0.10] > 0.29
☐	(Sum Level 2 Special Scores [0] > 2) *and* (FAB2 [0] > 0)
☐	((R [20] < 17) *and* (WSum6 [1] > 12))
	or ((R [20] > 16) *and* (WSum6 [1] > 17))
☐	(M– [0] > 1) *or* (X–% [0.10] > 0.40)
	0 Total

Source: Rorschach Interpretation Assistance Program: Version 5, Copyright 1999, 2001 by PAR Inc.

Table A.21 Depression Index (DEPI)

☑	Positive if 5 or more conditions are true:

☐	(FV + VF + V [0] > 0) *or* (FD [2] > 2)
☑	(Col-Shd Blends [2] > 0) *or* (S [4] > 2)
☑	(3r + (2) / R [0.25] > 0.44 *and* Fr + rF [1] = 0)
	or (3r + (2) / R [0.25] < 0.33)
☑	(Afr [0.33] < 0.46) *or* (Blends [8] < 4)
☑	(SumShading [4] > FM + m [7]) *or* (SumC' [3] > 2)
☐	(MOR [1] > 2) *or* (2 × AB + Art + Ay [0] > 3)
☑	(COP [0] < 2) *or* ([Bt + 2 × Cl + Ge + Ls + 2 × Na] / R [0.20] > 0.24)
	5 Total

Source: Rorschach Interpretation Assistance Program: Version 5, Copyright 1999, 2001 by PAR Inc.

Table A.22 Coping Deficit Index (CDI)

☐	Positive if 4 or more conditions are true:

☐ (EA [9.5] < 6) *or* (AdjD [0] < 0)
☑ (COP [0] < 2) *and* (AG [1] < 2)
☑ (Weighted Sum C [4.5] < 2.5) *or* (Afr [0.33] < 0.46)
☐ (Passive [3] > Active + 1 [11]) *or* (Pure H [4] < 2)
☐ (Sum T [0] > 1) *or* (Isolate / R [0.20] > 0.24) *or* (Food [0] > 0)
2 Total

Source: Rorschach Interpretation Assistance Program: Version 5, Copyright 1999, 2001 by PAR Inc.

Table A.23 Hypervigilance Index (HVI)

☐	Positive if condition (1) is true and at least 4 of the others are true:

☑ (1) FT + TF + T [0] = 0
☐ (2) Zf [12] > 12
☐ (3) Zd [2.0] > +3.5
☑ (4) S [4] > 3
☑ (5) H + (H) + Hd + (Hd) [7] > 6
☐ (6) (H) + (A) + (Hd) + (Ad) [2] > 3
☐ (7) H + A: Hd + Ad [13:2] < 4:1
☐ (8) Cg [3] > 3

Source: Rorschach Interpretation Assistance Program: Version 5, Copyright 1999, 2001 by PAR Inc.

Table A.24 Obsessive Style Index (OBS)

☐ (1) Dd [2] > 3
☐ (2) Zf [12] > 12
☐ (3) Zd [2.0] > +3.0
☐ (4) Populars [6] > 7
☐ (5) FQ+ [0] > 1
☐ **Positive if one or more is true:**
    ☐ Conditions 1 to 5 are all true
    ☐ Two or more of 1 to 4 are true *and* FQ + [0] > 3
    ☐ 3 or more of 1 to 5 are true *and* X+% [0.65] > 0.89
    ☐ FQ+ [0] > 3 *and* X+% [0.65] > 0.89

Source: Rorschach Interpretation Assistance Program: Version 5, Copyright 1999, 2001 by PAR Inc.

R-PAS: CODE SEQUENCE

This section presents the Code Sequence for the R-PAS case study presented in Chapter 9.

Table A.25 R-PAS Code Sequence for Ms. Frazier (pseudonym)

C-ID: Sarah Frazier (pseudonym) P-ID: 7 Age: 25 Gender: Female Education: 16

Cd	#	Or	Loc	Loc #	SR	SI	Content	Sy	Vg	2	FQ	P	Determinants	Cognitive	Thematic	HR	ODL (RP)	R-Opt
I	1		W			SI	A				o		F					Pr
	2		W				A				o	P	FMa					
II	3		W				A				–		FMa, CF, C'					
	4	@	D	6, 3			An				–		FD					
	5		D	5	SR		H, Cg	Sy			u		Ma, C'			GH		
III	6		W				H, Bl, NC	Sy		2	o	P	Ma, mp, C		AGM, MOR, MAP	PH		
IV	7		D	2			H, An				o		F			GH	ODL	
	8	v	W				(H)				u		Ma, Y	DV1		GH		
	9	@	W				(H), NC	Sy			o	P	Ma, FD		AGC	GH		
V	10		W				A				o		FMa					
	11		Dd	99			A				o		FMa					
VI	12		W				Ad, NC				o	P	F					
	13	>	D	4			NC				o		F					
VII	14		D	2			Hd			2	o	P	Mp			GH		
	15		D	10	SR		NC				o		F					
VIII	16		W				A, NC	Sy			o	P	FMa, r		AGC			
	17		D	2			NC				u		FC					
IX	18		D	2			NC				u		ma-p, CF					Pr
X	19	@	Dd	99	SR	SI	H, Cg	Sy	Vg		u		FC, C'			PH		
	20		D	9			A				u		F		PER		ODL	

Source: ©2010–2016 R-PAS. Used by permission of Rorschach Performance Assessment System, LLC.

IMPORTANT
∙∙∙

Table A.25 and Figures A.4, A.5, and A.6 are reproduced from the Rorschach Performance Assessment System® (R-PAS®) Scoring Program (© 2010–2016) and excerpted from the *Rorschach Performance Assessment System: Administration, Coding, Interpretation, and Technical Manual* (©2011) with copyrights by Rorschach Performance Assessment System, LLC. All rights reserved. Used by permission of Rorschach Performance Assessment System, LLC.

R-PAS: PROTOCOL LEVEL COUNTS AND CALCULATIONS

This section presents the Protocol Level Counts and Calculations for the R-PAS case study presented in Chapter 9 (see Figure A.4). It is divided into sections that correspond to the sections on the Code Sequence page (e.g., Responses and Administration, Location, etc.). Each section has the counts, of the number of times each variable appears on the protocol, as well as any calculations that use the variables in that section.

R-PAS Protocol Level Counts & Calculations

C-ID: Book Sample   P-ID: 7   Age: 25   Gender: Female   Education: 16

Section	Counts		Counts		Calculations	
Responses & Administration	R	= 20	R8910	= 5	R8910%	= 25%
	Pr	= 2	Pu	= 0		
	CT	= 4				
Location	W	= 9	D	= 9	W%	= 45%
	Dd	= 2	WD	= 18	Dd%	= 10%
Space	SR	= 3	SI	= 2		
	AnyS	= 4				
Content	H	= 4	An	= 2	SumH	= 7
	(H)	= 2	Art	= 0	NPH	= 3
	Hd	= 1	Ay	= 0	NPH/SumH	= 43%
	(Hd)	= 0	Bl	= 1		
	A	= 7	Cg	= 2		
	(A)	= 0	Ex	= 0		
	Ad	= 1	Fi	= 0		
	(Ad)	= 0	Sx	= 0		
			NC	= 8		
Object Qualities	Sy	= 5			Sy%	= 25%
	Vg	= 1			Vg%	= 5%
	Pair	= 2				
Form Quality and Popular	FQo	= 12	WDo	= 11	FQo%	= 60%
	FQu	= 5	WDu	= 5	FQu%	= 25%
	FQ-	= 3	WD-	= 2	FQ-%	= 15%
	FQn	= 0	WDn	= 0	WD-%	= 11%
	M-	= 0	P	= 6		

Section	Counts		Counts		Calculations	
Determinants	M	= 5	FC	= 2	WSumC	= 4.5
Blends:	FM	= 5	CF	= 2	SumC	= 5
FMa,CF,C'	m	= 2	C	= 1	(CF+C)/SumC	= 60%
Ma,C	C'	= 3	Y	= 1	MC	= 9.5
Ma,mp,C	T	= 0	V	= 0	M/MC	= 53%
Ma,Y	r	= 1	FD	= 0	YTVC'	= 4
Ma,FD			F	= 6	mY	= 3
FMa,r					F%	= 30%
ma-p,CF					PPD	= 11
FC,C'					MC - PPD	= -1.5
	a	= 10	p	= 3	p/(a+p)	= 23%
	Ma	= 4	Mp	= 1	Mp/(Ma+Mp)	= 20%
	Blend	= 8	CBlend	= 2	Blend%	= 40%
Cognitive Codes	DV1 (1)	= 1	DV2 (2)	= 0	WSumCog	= 1
	INC1 (2)	= 0	INC2 (4)	= 0	SevCog	= 0
	DR1 (3)	= 0	DR2 (6)	= 0	Lev2Cog	= 0
	FAB1 (4)	= 0	FAB2 (7)	= 0		
	PEC (5)	= 0	CON (7)	= 0		
Thematic Codes	ABS	= 0	PER	= 1	MAHP	= 1
	COP	= 0	MAH	= 0	MAP/MAHP	= NA
	AGM	= 1	AGC	= 2	GPHR	= 7
	MOR	= 1	MAP	= 1	PHR/GPHR	= 29%
	ODL	= 2			ODL%	= 10%
	GHR	= 5	PHR	= 2		
Other Calculations	IntCont	= 0	TP-Comp	= 0.6	Complexity	= 75
	CritCont%	= 25%	V-Comp	= 3.7	LSO	= 29
	EII-3	= -0.4	SC-Comp	= 5.3	Cont	= 22
					Det	= 24

Counts and Calculations in Bold Font are on the Summary Scores and Profiles Pages

Figure A.4 Protocol Level Counts and Calculations for Ms. Frazier (pseudonym)

Source: Used by permission of Rorschach Performance Assessment System, LLC.

R-PAS: SUMMARY SCORES AND PROFILES

This section presents both Summary Scores and Profiles pages for the R-PAS case study presented in Chapter 9 (see Figures A.5 and A.6). The variables on the pages are divided into sections (e.g., Engagement in Cognitive Processing, Perception and Thinking Problems, etc.). For each variable the raw score and the percentile and standard score based on that raw score are presented. The standard scores are also graphed on the standard score profile section. For most variables, the Complexity Adjusted percentile and standard score are presented as well; however, these values are not graphed on the standard score profile section.

R-PAS Summary Scores and Profiles — Page 1

C-ID: Book Sample | P-ID: 7 | Age: 25 | Gender: Female | Education: 16

Domain/Variables	Raw Scores	Raw %ile	Raw SS	Cplx. Adj. %ile	Cplx. Adj. SS	Standard Score Profile R-Optimized	Abbr.
Admin. Behaviors and Obs.							
Pr	2	82	114				Pr
Pu	0	40	96				Pu
CT (Card Turning)	4	58	103				CT
Engagement and Cog. Processing							
Complexity	75	57	103				Cmplx
R (Responses)	20	21	88	14	84		R
F% [Lambda=0.43] (Simplicity)	30%	27	91	25	90		F%
Blend	8	88	118	85	116		Bln
Sy	5	37	95	37	95		Sy
MC	9.5	75	110	70	108		MC
MC - PPD	-1.5	56	102	58	103		MC-PPD
M	5	72	109	62	105		M
M/MC [5/9.5]	53%	51	100	52	101		M Prp
(CF+C)/SumC [3/5]	60%	61	104	61	104		CFC Prp
Perception and Thinking Problems							
EII-3	-0.4	42	97	46	98		EII
TP-Comp (Thought & Percept. Com...)	0.6	53	101	59	103		TP-C

Figure A.5 Summary Scores and Profiles (Page 1) for Ms. Frazier (pseudonym)

Source: Used by permission of Rorschach Performance Assessment System, LLC.

	1	18	86	17	85	
WSumCog						WCog
SevCog	0	35	94	35	94	Sev
FQ-%	15%	77	111	78	112	FQ-%
WD-%	11%	71	108	64	105	WD-%
FQo%	60%	55	102	47	99	FQo%
P	6	59	103	66	106	P
Stress and Distress						
YTVC'	4	49	100	45	98	YTVC'
m	2	66	106	53	101	m
Y	1	48	99	42	97	Y
MOR	1	51	100	48	99	MOR
SC-Comp (Suicide Concern Comp.)	5.3	71	108	69	108	SC-C
Self and Other Representation						
ODL%	10%	52	101	52	101	ODl%
SR (Space Reversal)	3	92	122	92	122	SR
MAP/MAHP [1/1]	NA					MAP Prp
PHR/GPHR [2/7]	29%	36	95	36	95	PHR Prp
M-	0	36	95	36	95	M-
AGC	2	34	94	31	93	AGC
H	4	81	113	75	110	H
COP	0	21	88	24	89	COP
MAH	0	26	90	26	90	MAH

Figure A.5 (Continued)

R-PAS Summary Scores and Profiles — Page 2

C-ID: Book Sample **P-ID:** 7 **Age:** 25 **Gender:** Female **Education:** 16

Domain/Variables	Raw Scores	Raw %ile	Raw SS	Cplx. Adj. %ile	Cplx. Adj. SS	Standard Score Profile R-Optimized	Abbr.
Engagement and Cog. Processing							
W%	45%	61	104	61	104		W%
Dd%	10%	37	95	39	96		Dd%
SI (Space Integration)	2	38	96	48	100		SI
IntCont	0	11	81	11	81		IntC
Vg%	5%	55	102	52	101		Vg%
V	0	29	92	29	92		V
FD	2	84	115	86	116		FD
R8910%	25%	11	81	10	81		R8910%
WSumC	4.5	71	108	68	107		WSC
C	1	82	114	82	114		C
Mp/(Ma+Mp) [1/5]	20%	17	85	17	85		Mp Prp
Perception and Thinking Problems							
FQu%	25%	32	93	36	95		FQu%
Stress and Distress							

Figure A.6 Summary Scores and Profiles (Page 2) for Ms. Frazier (pseudonym)

Source: Used by permission of Rorschach Performance Assessment System, LLC.

		Raw Score				
PPD	PPD	11	66	106	64	105
CBlend	CBlend	2	88	117	79	112
C'	C'	3	77	111	70	108
V	V	0	29	92	29	92
CritCont% (Critical Contents)	CrCt	25%	68	107	70	107
Self and Other Representation						
SumH	SumH	7	65	106	64	106
NPH/SumH [3/7]	NPH pRP	43%	21	88	20	87
V-Comp (Vigilance Composite)	V-C	3.7	66	106	65	106
r (Reflections)	r	1	81	113	81	113
p/(a+p) [3/13]	p Prp	23%	19	87	18	86
AGM	AGM	1	75	110	75	110
T	T	0	28	91	28	91
PER	PER	1	72	109	72	109
An	An	2	71	108	71	108

Figure A.6 (Continued)

References

Acklin, M. W., McDowell, C. J., Verschell, M. S., & Chan, D. (2000). Interobserver agreement, intraobserver reliability, and the Rorschach Comprehensive System. *Journal of Personality Assessment, 74*(1), 15–47. doi:10.1207/S15327752JPA740103

Allard, G., & Faust, D. (2000). Errors in scoring objective personality tests. *Assessment, 7*(2), 119–129

Archer, R. P., Buffington-Vollum, J. K., Stredny, R. V., & Handel, R. W. (2006). A survey of psychological test use patterns among forensic psychologists. *Journal of Personality Assessment, 87*(1), 84–94.

Archer, R. P., & Krishnamurthy, R. (1993a). Combining the Rorschach and the MMPI in the assessment of adolescents. *Journal of Personality Assessment, 60*, 132–140.

Archer, R. P., & Krishnamurthy, R. (1993b). A review of MMPI and Rorschach interrelationships in adult samples. *Journal of Personality Assessment, 61*, 277–293.

Baity, M. R., & Hilsenroth, M. J. (2002). Rorschach Aggressive Content (AgC) variable: A study of criterion validity. *Journal of Personality Assessment, 78*(2), 275–287. doi: 10.1207/S15327752JPA7802_04

Ball, J. D., Archer, R. P., & Imhof, E. A. (1994). Time requirements of psychological testing: A survey of practitioners. *Journal of Personality Assessment, 63*(2), 239–249.

Bandura, A. (1954a). The Rorschach white space response and "oppositional" behavior. *Journal of Consulting Psychology, 18*, 17–21.

Bandura, A. (1954b). The Rorschach white space response and perceptual reversal. *Journal of Experimental Psychology, 48*, 113–117.

Bellak, L., & Abrams, D. M. (1996). *The TAT, the CAT, and the SAT in clinical use* (6th ed.). New York, NY: Allyn & Bacon.

Bombel, G., Mihura, J. L., & Meyer, G. J. (2009). An examination of the construct validity of the Mutuality of Autonomy (MOA) Scale. *Journal of Personality Assessment, 91*(3), 227–237. doi:10.1080/00223890902794267

Bornstein, R. F. (1996). Construct validity of the Rorschach Oral Dependency Scale: 1967–1995. *Psychological Assessment, 8*, 200–205.

Bornstein, R. F., & O'Neill, R. M. (1997). Construct validity of the Rorschach Oral Dependency (ROD) scale: Relationship of ROD scores to WAIS-R scores in a psychiatric inpatient sample. *Journal of Clinical Psychology, 53*(2), 99–105.

Butcher, J. N., Graham, J. R., Ben-Porath, Y. S., Tellegen, A., & Dahlstrom, W. G. (2001). *Minnesota Multiphasic Personality Inventory-2 (MMPI-2): Manual for administration and scoring* (rev. ed.). Minneapolis, MN: University of Minnesota Press.

Choca, J. P. (2013). *The Rorschach Inkblot Test: An interpretive guide for clinicians.* Washington, DC: American Psychological Association.

Constantinou, M., Ashendorf, L., & McCaffrey, R. J. (2005). Effects of a third party observer during neuropsychological assessment: When the observer is a video camera. *Journal of Forensic Neuropsychology, 4*, 39–47.

Corsino, B. V. (1985). Color blindness and Rorschach color responsivity. *Journal of Personality Assessment, 49*(5), 533–534.

Corum, M. E., & Gurley, J. R. (2015). *Doctoral student training in personality assessment and internship director satisfaction.* Poster presented at the Annual Convention of the Society of Personality Assessment, Brooklyn, NY.

Dean, K. L., Viglione, D. J., Perry, W., & Meyer, G. J. (2007). A method to optimize the response range while maintaining Rorschach Comprehensive System validity. *Journal of Personality Assessment, 89*(2), 149–161.

Del Giudice, M. J. (2010). What might this be? Rediscovering the Rorschach as a tool for personnel selection in organizations. *Journal of Personality Assessment, 92*(1), 78–89. doi:10–1080/00223890903382385

Del Giudice, M. J., & Brabender, V. M. (2012). Rorschach assessment of leadership traits in college student leaders. *Comprehensive Psychology, 1*, 12.

Diener, M. J., Hilsenroth, M. J., Shaffer, S. A., & Sexton, J. E. (2011). A meta-analysis of the relationship between the Rorschach Ego Impairment Index (EII) and psychiatric severity. *Clinical Psychology & Psychotherapy, 18*(6), 464–485. doi:10.1002/cpp.725

Exner, J. E. (1974). *The Rorschach: A Comprehensive System: Vol. 1. Basic foundations.* New York, NY: Wiley.

Exner, J. E. (1997). The future of the Rorschach in personality assessment. *Journal of Personality Assessment, 68*(1), 37–46.

Exner, J. E. (2000). *A primer for Rorschach interpretation.* Asheville, NC: Rorschach Workshops, Incorporated.

Exner, J. E. (2001). *A Rorschach workbook for the Comprehensive System* (5th ed.). Asheville, NC: Rorschach Workshops, Incorporated.

Exner, J. E. (2003). *The Rorschach: A Comprehensive System: Vol. 1. Basic foundations and principles of interpretation* (4th ed.). Hoboken, NJ: Wiley.

Exner, J. E. (2007). A new U.S. adult nonpatient sample. *Journal of Personality Assessment, 89*(Suppl. 1), S154–S158.

Exner, J. E., & Erdberg, P. (2005). *The Rorschach: A Comprehensive System: Vol. 2. Advanced interpretation* (3rd ed.). Hoboken, NJ: Wiley.

Exner, J. E., & Weiner, I. B. (1994). *The Rorschach: A Comprehensive System: Vol. 3. Assessment of children and adolescents* (2nd ed.). Hoboken, NJ: Wiley.

Exner, J. E., Weiner, I. B., & PAR staff. (2001). *Rorschach Interpretation Assistance Program: Version 5 [Software].* Lutz, FL: Psychological Assessment Resources.

Fonda, P. (1951). The nature and meaning of the Rorschach white space responses. *The Journal of Abnormal and Social Psychology, 46*(3), 367–377.

Fowler, J. C., Brunnschweiler, B., Swales, S., & Brock, J. (2005). Assessment of Rorschach dependency measures in female inpatients diagnosed with borderline personality disorder. *Journal of Personality Assessment, 85*(2), 146–153.

Fowler, J. C., Piers, C., Hilsenroth, M. J., Holdwick, D. J., & Padawer, J. R. (2001). The Rorschach Suicide Constellation: Assessing various degrees of lethality. *Journal of Personality Assessment, 76*(2), 333–351.

Frank, G. (1993). On the validity of Rorschach's hypotheses: The relationship of space responses (S) to oppositionalism. *Psychological Reports, 72*, 1111–1114.

Ganellen, R. J. (1996). Comparing the diagnostic efficiency of the MMPI, MCMI-II, and Rorschach: A review. *Journal of Personality Assessment, 67*, 219–243.

Ganellen, R. J. (2001). Weighing evidence for the Rorschach's validity: A response to Wood et al. (1999). *Journal of Personality Assessment, 77*(1), 1–15. doi:10.1207/S15327752 JPA7701_01

Garb, H. N. (1999). A call for a moratorium on the use of the Rorschach Inkblot Test in clinical and forensic settings. *Assessment, 6*(4), 313–318.

Gavela, J., Gil, L., & Sciara, A. (2014). *Comparison of Rorschach CS web based administration, coding and interpretation vs. traditional. Psicologia.* Retrieved from http://www.psicologia .pt/artigos/textos/A0776.pdf

Graceffo, R. A., Mihura, J. L., & Meyer, G. J. (2014). A meta-analysis of an implicit measure of personality functioning: The Mutuality of Autonomy Scale. *Journal of Personality Assessment, 96*(6), 581–595. doi:10.1080/00223891.2014.919299

Grove, W. M., Barden, R. C., Garb, H. N., & Lilienfeld, S. O. (2002). Failure of Rorschach-Comprehensive-System-based testimony to be admissible under the Daubert-Joiner-Kumho standard. *Psychology, Public Policy, and Law, 8*(2), 216–234. doi: 10.1037 //1076–8971.8.2.216

Gurley, J. R., Hugonnet, M. H., Clemons, M., Friedman, J., MacAleney, B., & Sheehan, B. (2011). *The use of Rorschach in court: An examination of case law.* Poster presented at the Annual Convention of the American Psychology Association, Washington, DC.

Gurley, J. R., Sheehan, B. L., Piechowski, L. D., & Gray, J. (2014). Admissibility of the R-PAS in court. *Psychological Injury and Law, 7*(1), 9–17. doi:10.1007/s12207 –014–9182–2

Harrison, P., & Oakland, T. (2015). *Adaptive Behavior Assessment System, Third Edition (ABAS-3).* Torrance, CA: Western Psychological Services.

Hartmann, E. (2001). Rorschach administration: A comparison of the effect of two instructions. *Journal of Personality Assessment, 76*(3), 461–471.

Hartmann, E., & Vanem, P. (2003). Rorschach administration: A comparison of the effect of two instructions given to an inpatient sample of drug addicts. *Scandinavian Journal of Psychology, 44*, 133–139.

Hertz, M. R. (1986). Rorschachbound: A 50-year memoir. *Journal of Personality Assessment, 50*(3), 396–416.

Hiller, J. B., Rosenthal, R., Bornstein, R. F., Berry, D.T.R., & Brunell-Neuleib, S. (1999). A comparative meta-analysis of Rorschach and MMPI validity. *Psychological Assessment, 11*(3), 278–296. doi:10.1037/1040–3590.11.3.278

Hilsenroth, M., & Charnas, J. (2007). *Training manual for Rorschach interrater reliability* (2nd ed.). Unpublished manuscript, Derner Institute of Advanced Psychological Studies, Adelphi University, Garden City, NY. Retrieved from http://www.ror-scan.com /RorschachTrainingManual2ndEd.pdf

Holaday, M. (1997). Rorschach active-passive superscripts. *Journal of Personality Assessment, 69*(1), 39–52.

Hopwood, C. J., & Richard, D.C.S. (2005). Graduate student WAIS-III scoring accuracy is a function of Full Scale IQ and complexity of examiner tasks. *Assessment, 12*(4), 445–454. doi:10.1177/1073191105281072

Hunsely, J., Lee, C. M., Wood, J. M., & Taylor, W. (2014). Controversial and questionable assessment techniques. In S. O. Lilienfeld, S. J. Lynn, & J. M. Lohr (Eds.), *Science and pseudoscience in clinical psychology* (2nd ed., pp. 42–82). New York, NY: Guilford.

Huprich, S. K., & Ganellen, R. J. (2006). The advantages of assessing personality disorders with the Rorschach. In S. K. Huprich (Ed.), *Rorschach assessment of personality disorders* (pp. 27–53). New York, NY: Routledge.

Kernberg, O. (1967). Borderline personality organization. *Journal of the American Psychoanalytic Organization, 15*, 641–685. doi:10.1177/000306516701500309

Kivisalu, T. M., Lewey, J. H., Shaffer, T. W., & Canfield, M. L. (2016). An investigation of interrater reliability for the Rorschach Performance Assessment System (R-PAS) in a nonpatient U.S. sample.: *Journal of Personality Assessment.* Advance online publication. doi:10.1080/00223891.2015.1118380

Kivisto, A. J., Gacono, C., & Medoff, D. (2013). Does the R-PAS meet standards for forensic use? Considerations with introducing a new Rorschach coding system. *Journal of Forensic Psychology Practice, 13*(5), 389–410.

Krishnamurthy, R., Archer, R. P., & House, J. J. (1996). The MMPI-A and Rorschach: A failure to establish convergent validity. *Assessment, 3,* 179–191.

Lally, S. J. (2003). What tests are acceptable for use in forensic evaluations? A survey of experts. *Professional Psychology: Research and Practice, 34*(5), 491–498. doi:10.1037 /0735-7028.34.5.491

Lis, A., Parolin, L., Calvo, V., Zennaro, A., & Meyer, G. (2007). The impact of administration and inquiry on Rorschach Comprehensive System protocols in a national reference sample. *Journal of Personality Assessment, 89*(Suppl. 1), S193–S200. doi:10–1080/00223890701583614

Magnussen, M. G. (1960). Verbal and nonverbal reinforcers in the Rorschach situation. *Journal of Clinical Psychology, 16*(2), 167–169.

Masling, J. (1965). Differential indoctrination of examiners and Rorschach responses. *Journal of Consulting Psychology, 29,* 198–201.

Masling, J., Rabie, L., & Blondheim, S. H. (1967). Obesity, level of aspiration, and Rorschach and TAT measures of oral dependence. *Journal of Consulting Psychology, 31,* 233–239.

Meloy, J. R., Hansen, T. L., & Weiner, I. B. (1997). Authority of the Rorschach: Legal citations during the past 50 years. *Journal of Personality Assessment, 69*(1), 53–62.

Meyer, G., Erdberg, P., & Shaffer, T. (2007). Toward international normative reference data for the Comprehensive System. *Journal of Personality Assessment, 89*(Suppl. 1), S201–S216.

Meyer, G. J., Hilsenroth, M. J., Baxter, D., Exner, J. E., Fowler, J. C., Piers, C. C., & Resnick, J. (2002). An examination of interrater reliability for scoring the Rorschach Comprehensive System in eight data sets. *Journal of Personality Assessment, 78*(2), 219–274. doi:10.1207/S15327752JPA7802_03

Meyer, G. J., Hsiao, W. C., Viglione, D. J., Mihura, J. L., & Abraham, L. M. (2013). Rorschach scores in applied clinical practice: Perceived validity by experienced clinicians. *Journal of Personality Assessment, 95*(4), 351–365. doi:10.1080/00223891.2013.770399

Meyer, G. J., & Kurtz, J. E. (2006). Advancing personality assessment terminology: Time to retire "objective" and "projective" as personality test descriptors. *Journal of Personality Assessment, 87*(3), 223–225. doi:10.1207/s15327752jpa8703_01

Meyer, G. J., Viglione, D. J., & Giromini, L. (2016). *Current R-PAS transitional child and adolescent norms.* Retrieved from http://r-pas.org/CurrentChildNorms.aspx

Meyer, G. J., Viglione, D. J., Mihura, J. L., Erard, R. E., & Erdberg, P. (2011). *Rorschach Performance Assessment System®: Administration, coding, interpretation, and technical manual.* Toledo, OH: Rorschach Performance Assessment System, LLC.

Michel, A., & Mormont, C. (2002). Was Snow White a transsexual? *Encephale, 28*(1), 59–64.

Mihura, J. L., Meyer, G. J., Bombel, G., & Dumitrascu, N. (2015). Standards, accuracy, and questions of bias in Rorschach meta-analyses: Reply to Wood, Garb, Nezworski, Lilienfeld, and Duke (2015). *Psychological Bulletin, 141*(1), 250–260. doi:10.1037/a0038445

Mihura, J. L., Meyer, G. J., Dumitrascu, N., & Bombel, G. (2013). The validity of individual Rorschach variables: Systematic reviews and meta-analyses of the Comprehensive System. *Psychological Bulletin, 139*(3), 548–603. doi:10.137/a0029406

Millon, T., Grossman, S., & Millon, C. (2015). *Millon Clinical Multiaxial Inventory-IV (MCMI-IV).* Minneapolis, MN: Pearson.

Morey, L. C. (2007). *The Personality Assessment Inventory professional manual*. Lutz, FL: Psychological Assessment Resources.

Murray, H. A. (1943). *Thematic Apperception Test*. Cambridge, MA: Harvard University Press.

Musewica, J., Marczyk, G., Knauss, L., & York, D. (2009). Current assessment practice, personality measurements, and Rorschach usage by psychologists. *Journal of Personality Assessment, 91*(5), 453–461. doi:10–1080/00223890903087976

Paykel, E. S., & Weissman, M. M. (1973). Social adjustment and depression: A longitudinal study. *Archives of General Psychiatry, 28*(5), 659–663.

Reese, J. B., Viglione, D. J., & Giromini, L. (2014). A comparison between Comprehensive System and an early version of the Rorschach Performance Assessment System administration with outpatient children and adolescents. *Journal of Personality Assessment, 96*(5), 515–522. doi:10.1080/00223891.2014.889700

Ritzler, B., & Sciara, A (2009). *Rorschach Comprehensive System international norms: Cautionary notes*. Rorschach Training Programs. Retrieved from http://www.rorschach training.com/rorschach-comprehensive-system-international-norms-cautionary-notes

Rorschach, H. (1921). *Psychodiagnostik*. Bern, Switzerland: Hans Huber.

Rorschach, H. (1942). *Psychodiagnostics*. New York, NY: Grune & Stratton. (Original work published 1921)

Sahly, J., Shaffer, T. W., Erdberg, P., & O'Toole, S. (2011). Rorschach intercoder reliability for protocol-level Comprehensive System variables in an international sample. *Journal of Personality Assessment, 93*(6), 592–596. doi:10.1080/00223891.2011.608761

Sangro, F. M. (1997). Location tables, form quality, and popular responses in a Spanish sample of 470 subjects. In I. Weiner (Ed.), *Rorschachiana XXII: Yearbook of the International Rorschach Society* (pp. 38–66). Ashland, OH: Hogrefe & Huber.

Schwartz, N. S., Mebane, D. L., & Malony, H. N. (1990). Effects of alternate modes of administration on Rorschach performance of deaf adults. *Journal of Personality Assessment, 54*(3–4), 671–683.

Sciara, A. D., & Ritzler, B. (2009). *Rorschach Comprehensive System: Current issues*. Retrieved from http://www.rorschachtraining.com/rorschach-comprehensive-system-current -issues

Sciara, A. D., & Ritzler, B. (2015). *Frequently asked questions and answers. Rorschach Training Programs July/August Newsletter*. Retrieved from http://www.rorschachtraining.com /category/newsletters

Simons, R., Goddard, R., & Patton, W. (2002). Hand-scoring error rates in psychological testing. *Assessment, 9*(3), 292–300.

Skadeland, D. R. (1986). Bruno Klopfer: A Rorschach pioneer. *Journal of Personality Assessment, 50*(3), 358–361.

Smith, S. R., Gorske, T. T., Wiggins, C., & Little, J. A. (2010). Personality assessment use by clinical neuropsychologists. *International Journal of Testing, 10*, 6–20. doi:10.1080 /15305050903534787

Stricker, G. (1976). The right book at the wrong time. *Contemporary Psychology, 21*, 24–25.

Sultan, S., & Meyer, G. J. (2009). Does productivity impact the stability of Rorschach scores? *Journal of Personality Assessment, 91* (5), 480–493.

Urist, J. (1977). The Rorschach test and the assessment of object relations. *Journal of Personality Assessment, 41*, 3–9.

Viglione, D. J. (1999). Review of recent research addressing the utility of the Rorschach. *Psychological Assessment, 11*(3), 251–265.

Viglione, D. J. (2010). *Rorschach coding solutions* (2nd ed.). San Diego, CA: Author.

Viglione, D. J., Blume-Marcovici, A. C., Miller, H. L., Giromini, L., & Meyer, G. J. (2012). An inter-rater reliability study for the Rorschach Performance Assessment System. *Journal of Personality Assessment, 94*(6), 607–612. doi:10.1080/00223891.2012.684118

Viglione, D. J., Meyer, G., Jordan, R. J., Converse, G. L., Evans, J., MacDermott, D., & Moore, R. (2015). Developing an alternative Rorschach administration method to optimize the number of responses and enhance clinical inferences. *Clinical Psychology and Psychotherapy, 22*(6) 546–558. doi:10.1002/cpp.1913

Wechsler, D. (2008). *Wechsler Adult Intelligence Scale, Fourth Edition (WAIS-IV)*. San Antonio, TX: Pearson.

Weiner, I. B. (2003). *Principles of Rorschach interpretation* (2nd ed.). Mahwah, NJ: Erlbaum.

Weiner, I., Exner, J., & Sciara, A. (1966). Is the Rorschach welcome in the courtroom? *Journal of Personality Assessment, 67*, 422–424.

Weissman, M. M., Paykel, E. S., Siegel, R. & Klerman, G. L. (1971). The social role performance of depressed women: Comparisons with a normal group. *American Journal of Orthopsychiatry, 41*(3), 390–405.

Wood, J. M., Garb, H. N., Nezworski, M. T., Lilienfeld, S. O., & Duke, M. C. (2015). A second look at the validity of widely used Rorschach indices: Comment on Mihura, Meyer, Dumitrascu, and Bombel (2013). *Psychological Bulletin, 141*, 236–249. Retrieved from 10.1037/a0036005

Wood, J. M., Nezworski, M. T., Garb, H. N., & Lilienfeld, S. O. (2001). Problems with the norms of the Comprehensive System for the Rorschach: Methodological and conceptual considerations. *Clinical Psychology: Science and Practice, 8*, 397–402.

Wood, J. M., Nezworski, M. T., Garb, H. N., & Lilienfeld, S. O. (2006). The controversy over Exner's Comprehensive System for the Rorschach: The critics speak. *Independent Practitioner, 26*(2), 73–82.

Wood, J. M., Nezworski, M. T., & Stejskal, W. J. (1996). The Comprehensive System for the Rorschach: A critical examination. *Psychological Science, 7*, 3–10.

Wood, J. M., Nezworski, M. T., Stejskal, W. J., Garven, S., & West, S. G. (1999). Methodological issues in evaluating Rorschach validity: A comment on Burns and Viglione (1996), Weiner (1996), and Ganellen (1996). *Assessment, 6*, 115–129.

Index

A

Abraham, L. M., 158

Abrams, D. M., 2

ABS: Abstract Representation, 252

Achromatic color, 56–57; Achromatic Color-Form and Form-Achromatic Color (C'F and FC'), 56–57; as example of key word, 30 (Rapid Reference 2.4); light and dark, 58–59; as locator, 59; Pure Achromatic Color (C'), 56–57; and shading codes, 60 (Rapid Reference 3.6)

Acklin, M. W., 319

Adaptive Behavior Assessment System, Third Edition (ABAS-III; Harrison and Oakland), 6

Adj and D: magnitude of stress, 118

Adj and D: validity, 117

Adj D and CDI: stress tolerance and ability to control thoughts, emotions, and behaviors, 109–111, 109–111

Adj D and D: magnitude of stress, 118

Adj D and D: validity, 117

Adj es: daily demands and accuracy of Adj D, 112–113

Affect: Affective Ratio (AFR): interest in emotions and emotional situation, 129; blends: unusual complexity, 133; Color Projections (CP): positive emotions replacing negative ones, 130; color-shading blends: confused by emotion, 133; content analysis (Pure C responses), 131; coping style (EB and Lambda), 127; emotional expression (FC:CF + C), 130–131; example of interpretation of blends within affect cluster, 134–135 (Rapid Reference 4.14); expression of emotions (SumC': WSumC; Constriction Ratio), 128–129; intellectualization index: tendency to intellectualize emotions, 129–130; interpretation of affect: how variables are calculated and assessed, 124–126 (Rapid Reference 4.12); interpretation of color-shading blends, 123 (Rapid Reference 4.11); oppositionality (Space responses), 131–132; pervasive coping style (EBPer), 127–128; psychological complexity (blends), 132; recommended order of interpretation, 126–127; shading blends: presence of painful emotions, 133; situational stress blends: impact of stress on psychological complexity, 132; unusual levels of distress (right side of eb), 128; variables, 124

AFR: Affective Ratio, 129

AGC: Aggressive Content, 254–255, 282–283

AGM: Aggressive Movement, 254, 295

Allard, G., 98

ALOG: Inappropriate Logic, 91–92

American Psychological Association (APA), 5

An: Anatomy, 296

An + Sy: body focus, 162–163

a:p ratio: fixed attitudes and beliefs/active or passive role in relationships, 154

Archer, R. P., 5, 6, 7, 320–321

Ashendorf, L., 21

B

Baity, M. R., 282, 320

Ball, J. D., 6–7

Bandura, A., 132, 280

Barden, R. C., 5

Baxter, D., 319

Beck, S., 8, 9, 10

Beck system, 5

Bellak, L., 2

Ben-Porath, Y. S., 1

Berry, D.T.R., 315

Binet, A., 7

Blend, coding, 47

Blondheim, S. H., 166

Blume-Marcovici, A. C., 319

Bombel, G., 255, 320, 321, 324

Bornstein, R. F., 166, 280, 315, 324

Brabender, V. M., 283

Brock, J., 280

Brunell-Neuleib, S., 315

Brunnschweiler, B., 280

Buffington-Vollum, J. K., 5

Butcher, J. N., 1, 317

About the Author

Jessica R. Gurley, PhD, is an associate professor in the clinical psychology doctoral program at the American School of Professional Psychology at Argosy University, Washington, DC, where she teaches courses on psychological assessment and forensic psychology. She has presented her research on assessment and forensics at numerous national conferences and is the author of book chapters and articles on various aspects of psychological assessment. As part of her private practice work, she regularly consults with other professionals, including psychologists, attorneys, and officers of the court, on psychological assessment.